The Clinical Application
of Psychological Tests

THE CLINICAL APPLICATION OF PSYCHOLOGICAL TESTS

Diagnostic Summaries and Case Studies

BY ROY SCHAFER, M. A.

Staff Psychologist, The Austen Riggs Foundation

Formerly *Associate Psychologist,* The Menninger Foundation

FOREWORD BY
DAVID RAPAPORT, Ph. D.
The Menninger Foundation

INTERNATIONAL UNIVERSITIES PRESS, INC.

New York   New York.

First Paperback Printing, 1995

To Sarah

CONTENTS

ACKNOWLEDGMENTS

I am pleased to acknowledge my indebtedness to the excellent faculty of the Psychology Department of The College of the City of New York, especially to Drs. Gardner Murphy, Max Hertzman, Isidore Chein, and Martin Scheerer, for having introduced me to the absorbing problems of dynamic psychology in general and clinical psychology in particular. I must also express my appreciation to the officers of The Menninger Foundation for their encouraging attitude toward the practice of clinical psychological testing and for their material aid in preparing this manuscript. I am indebted to my colleagues in the Psychology Division, especially to Margaret Brenman, Walter Kass, Sarah Schafer, and George S. Klein, for their constant stimulation of my thinking about the problems of clinical testing. In this connection I must also express my debt to the psychiatric staff of The Menninger Foundation, not only for their interest and support, but for their unhesitating criticisms of vagueness and inaccuracy in our everyday work.

Drs. David Rapaport, Robert R. Holt, and Max Hertzman have been kind enough to review the original manuscript and have offered many helpful suggestions and criticisms. I am grateful to Dr. Margaret Brenman for reviewing the descriptions of clinical syndromes in Chapter 2, and to Dr. Merton Gill for reviewing the case history summaries in Chapter 3. My wife, Sarah, patiently prepared the scrawled test records for publication. Miss Roselle Yakle, Mrs. Hazel Bruce, and Miss Mary Taylor typed the manuscript in its different phases.

Most of all I am indebted to David Rapaport. His friendship and teaching have instructed me in more ways than I can know.

ROY SCHAFER

The Menninger Foundation
Topeka, Kansas
August, 1947.

9

FOREWORD

We are living in a time in which clinical psychology is developing into an accepted professional discipline. If it is to stand up as such, its scientific premises must be clarified. That, to my mind, necessitates that its procedures change from the "private procedures" of the artisan to the "public procedures" of the professional. To further this transition we need published records of our diagnostic and therapeutic procedures. One way to achieve this is to publish the raw material our procedures elicit from a wide variety of cases together with the investigator's interpretations and a clarification of his point of view. Once the investigator's point of view is stated, both the raw material in his records and its interpretation will become instructive to clinical psychologists. If, however, only studies of isolated cases are published, or only raw material, or only interpretation, or only statements of points of view, our publications will remain limited in their instructiveness and our procedures will, of necessity, remain "private" and fail to become the common property of the entire profession.

Mr. Schafer, in his present volume, gives us a case collection which includes verbatim test records, interpretations of these and sketches of the clinical picture of each case discussed. His point of view is clearly stated. It is roughly the one given in *Diagnostic Psychological Testing*[1]). Mr. Schafer has succeeded in avoiding the pitfalls into which so many test interpreters fall. Since his interpretations are, in my opinion, free of "test lingo", they will be understood by clinicians whether they are psychologists, psychiatrists, or social workers. For the same reason, this volume should be useful in bringing clinical problems and concepts successfully to the attention of academic psychologists. For the clinical psychologist, whether or not he finds himself in agreement with the techniques and point of view of Mr. Schafer, this will be a rich source and reference book. Mr. Schafer handles test data sensitively and with

---

1) Rapaport, D., Gill, M., Schafer, R., *Diagnostic Psychological Testing*, Chicago, Year Book Publishers, Volume I, 573 pp., 1945; Volume II, 516 pp., 1946.

11

great care; his interpretations reveal sound clinical understanding and intuition as well as a firm hold on data. Theories and intuition are backed by data and not used by him to take the place of data.

I feel that Mr. Schafer has made an important and unique contribution to clinical psychology with this volume. It richly complements the case collections in Rorschach's *Psychodiagnostics,* in Beck's *Rorschach's Test,* and in Murray's *Explorations in Personality.*

David Rapaport

Topeka, Kansas
September, 1947

INTRODUCTION

PURPOSE

This book is a sequel to the two volumes of *Diagnostic Psychological Testing*.[1]) Those volumes have been justifiably criticized for not including broad diagnostic summaries and concrete case studies. This book will attempt to fill that gap. The three of us who collaborated on *Diagnostic Psychological Testing* agreed beforehand that such summaries and studies would be prerequisite to the clinical application of the concepts and findings presented, but it has only now become possible to carry out our original plan.

The discussions to follow presuppose that the reader is familiar with the psychological rationale we have previously advanced concerning the various tests in the battery we use. Most of the present formulations will, however, be sufficiently developed in themselves that the reader who is generally familiar with the pertinent tests should not feel compelled to make frequent or detailed references to the previous volumes.

In this book I will not mechanically summarize and apply the previous findings, which pertained only to group trends. I will be as much concerned with individual variations and their implications as with group trends. The discussions will refer frequently to diagnostic indications that were not studied in the previous volumes, and will also include interpretations of content—an aspect of clinical testing only briefly touched on in *Diagnostic Psychological Testing*. Thus, this volume will be a clinical exposition, frequently referring to patterns and interpretations whose validity has been established only in clinical experience.

RELATION TO *DIAGNOSTIC PSYCHOLOGICAL TESTING*

Several important differences between this and the previous two volumes must be pointed out in advance.

---

1) Rapaport, D., Gill, M., and Schafer, R. *Diagnostic Psychological Testing*, Chicago: Year Book Publishers, 1945.

1. A few of the diagnostic indications previously emphasized have been found in subsequent experience to require qualification. Also, a number of additional diagnostic indications have been observed. This book will present all those diagnostic patterns that, *according to our present understanding,* appear to be valid.

2. Since the publication of *Diagnostic Psychological Testing,* the composition of the battery of tests used at The Menninger Foundation has changed. We no longer routinely administer the interesting Vigotsky or Hanfmann–Kasanin Test because it has proved to be time-consuming and too often diagnostically ambiguous. Except for the Immediate and Delayed Story Recalls, we have also eliminated all of the Babcock Test subtests because they overlap too much with the Bellevue Scale subtests. The Story Recall or Learning Efficiency tests are now administered in conjunction with the Sorting Test, immediate recall being tested before the sortings begin and delayed recall being tested approximately ten minutes later—ten minutes being the average time between the two recalls in the Babcock Test. The list of stimulus words in the Word Association test has been modified.[2]) Thus the present battery of tests includes the Wechsler-Bellevue Scale, the combined Sorting and Learning Efficiency Tests, and the Rorschach, modified Word Association and Thematic Apperception Tests. We have used this smaller battery for the past two years and have not found it to be any less useful than the original, larger battery. This book will discuss the different groups and individual cases in the light of results obtained by using this *revised* battery of tests. In this connection it should be noted that the title of the book is somewhat pretentious, since the book deals only with a selected battery of tests. It is felt, however, that once a clinical tester has steeped himself in the rationale, recurring patterns of scores, and qualities of content and verbalization in one such battery of tests, he will be better equipped to use and explore the meaning and potentialities of other tests and other batteries of tests.

3. This book includes discussions of narcissistic and psychopathic character disorders and addictions; these illnesses were not taken up in the previous volumes. The generalizations to be advanced about them are not based on formal statistical investigation; they are considered to be valid because we have had a high degree of success in applying them in our everyday work.

4. I have dropped two of the diagnostic terms introduced in the previous volumes—*coarctated preschizophrenia and over-ideational pre-*

---

2) See p. 126 for the old list and p. 105 for the new.

schizophrenia—and have replaced them by what I take to be more adequate terms: *schizoid character, incipient schizophrenia* and *schizophrenic character*. The clinical features of each of these groups will be
described in the text. The previous groups of preschizophrenics have
been found to be too heterogeneous in composition to warrant retention in the present work; they included patients who were literally
pre-schizophrenics or incipient schizophrenics as well as patients whose
difficulties were characterological and therefore fairly stable in nature
and who ranged from markedly schizoid but not disorganized (schizoid
characters) to extremely schizoid and disorganized (schizophrenic
characters or ambulatory schizophrenics). I am not certain that the diagnostic headings to be used here satisfactorily embrace all the cases previously included in the preschizophrenic groups. In a sense I have chosen
what I consider to be the lesser of two evils. An altogether satisfactory
nosology in this respect has yet to be developed. I have, however, described the clinical syndromes of each of the groups and have attempted
to relate the diagnostic indications in the test results to the various
features of the syndrome rather than to the diagnostic label itself; this
should preserve the significance of most of the indications discussed
even if the nosological divisions prove to be unsatisfactory.

PLAN OF THE VOLUME

This presentation has been conceived in three main parts: (1) a
brief introduction dealing with the sources and psychological implications of test responses, and with the nature of the process of diagnostic
reasoning from test results; (2) a review of the indications of the outstanding personality characteristics and pathological tendencies of various types of neurotic, character-disordered, depressive, schizophrenic
and normal persons; (3) presentations and discussions of concrete sets
of test results, which illustrate the patterns found in the various clinical
groups, supplemented by final test reports and case history summaries.[3])

---

3) Unfortunately the presentation of test records in Chapters 3 and 4 will probably not be quite as easy to survey as might be desirable; these results have been
crowded together in paragraph form in order to avoid the great increase in the price
of the book which would result from more spacious and difficult composition of pages.

Chapter One

GENERAL CONSIDERATIONS

Clinical psychological testing starts with the proposition that a person's distinctive style of thinking is indicative of ingrained features of his character make-up. Character is here understood as the person's enduring modes of bringing into harmony internal demands and the press of external events; in other words it refers to relatively constant adjustment-efforts in the face of problem situations. The modes of achieving this harmony are understood to consist essentially of reliance on particular mechanisms of defense and a selective responsiveness to stimulation associated with these defenses. The defenses emphasized may be repression, denial, projection, intellectualization, or any of the others described in the psychoanalytic literature. The selective responsiveness to stimulation is the attempt to guarantee that life situations will be so perceived or organized as to preclude the entrance into consciousness of especially disturbing material.

The second proposition is that the responses to the various test items of the battery we use are, almost entirely, verbalized end-products of thought processes initiated by these items. A test response is not a score; scores, where applicable, are abstractions designed to facilitate intra-individual and inter-individual comparisons, and as such they are extremely useful in clinical testing. However, to reason—or do research—only in terms of scores and score-patterns is to do violence to the nature of the raw material. The scores do not communicate the responses in full. For example, in response to the question *why should we keep away from bad company?* both of the following responses obtain a maximum score of 2: "They have a terrible influence on our character and lead us into evil ways!" and "I don't have much use for the concept bad company but we're supposed to believe that they will corrupt us!"

17

Scheerer[1]) has ably criticized the conception of a response as merely a plus-sign or minus-sign, and has stressed as the primary psychological data facts about the processes by which solutions are achieved. The subject communicates more than he wittingly intends; he also communicates more than can be scored. Test responses, because they represent the subject's style of thinking, allow for inferences concerning predominant features of character make-up.

The third proposition is that the subject must be made to think in a variety of problem situations to enable the examiner to distinguish the pervasive, fundamental or pathological aspects of his characteristic adjustment-efforts. In any one situation he may present a one-sided picture; in a variety of situations—in a *battery* of tests—a rounded and hierarchical picture can be expected.

The fourth proposition is that two general aspects of thinking must be studied intensively; first, thinking that primarily reflects past achievements and second, thinking that primarily reflects creative application of assets and liabilities to new problems. In other words, we must concern ourselves both with *what* the subject has characteristically achieved and failed in the past and with *how* he makes new achievements and suffers new failures at the present time. The former aspect indicates those efforts at adjustment that have been given extended try-outs during development; the latter aspect indicates those efforts at adjustment currently emphasized. As a rule, the test results indicate considerable continuity between past and present adjustment-efforts, but there are cases where a striking discrepancy is present. For example, it is not infrequent that women who have developed an obsessional neurosis demonstrate in their test results that premorbidly intense repressive efforts were characteristic and that the more basic obsessional trends were in the background. Another example is the frequent presence in the records of schizophrenics of indications of premorbidly emphasized obsessive, repressive, or other types of defense. Thus the mustering of past achievements as well as the application of present assets and liabilities to current problems must be investigated. This is most fruitfully done by comparing the results of tests of different intelligence functions (Bellevue Scale, Sorting Test, Learning Efficiency) with the results of the more "projective" tests (Rorschach, Word Association and Thematic Apperception Tests). Of course, any test response has both a past achievement aspect and a current creative aspect: the variety of content in most Ror-

---

[1]) Scheerer, M., Article in *Annals of the N. Y. Academy of Sciences*, 46, 1946.

schach and Thematic Apperception Test records refers primarily to past achievments; the verbalization of simple information or definitions has its creative aspect, as can be seen in the variety of ways in which different subjects formulate the same fact.[2]) Nevertheless, one of these aspects is usually more significant than the other in any one test response.

As has been indicated, we consult mainly the tests oriented to the subject's intelligence, particularly the Bellevue Scale, for our appraisal of varied developmental emphases, for the delineation of those areas of ego functioning in which the subject has most vigorously attempted to develop assets and those areas from which he has shied away. The Bellevue Scale, of all the tests in the battery under discussion, offers the most clearly structured problems: for the most part it requires as answers very specific facts, commonly accepted judgments or concepts, normally acquired facility in specific mental manipulations, or the reproduction of explicitly given material. From the results on the Bellevue Scale one can ask whether verbal (rational) or motor (action) assets have been cultivated, whether possession of information or reliance on convention or sharpness of social anticipations has been emphasized, and so forth. In contrast, the "projective" tests, notably the Rorschach Test, throw more light on the creative application of assets and liabilities to new problems, because the problems they offer are much less structured than those of the Bellevue Scale.

To make this argument more concrete, we can consider as an example the typical test patterns of hysterics. Among their past achievements we find that verbal abilities, particularly the fund of general information, are relatively underdeveloped compared to performance abilities; furthermore, passive reliance on conventional judgments as guides to behavior appears to have taken precedence over reliance on individual assets and insight. In the area of creative application to problems we find a type of responsiveness which selectively leans heavily on the emotional aspects of situations and greatly ignores the more rational or fanciful aspects. Impulsive, emotional response replaces reflectiveness. This generalized devaluation of independent, constructive, rational thought can be understood grossly as a consequence of excessive reliance on repression as a mechanism of defense and its curtailing effect on receptivity toward new, potentially threatening ideas or information. As

---

2) It might also be considered that the style of knowing and verbalizing a fact is part of the fact for the particular subject.

will be seen in Chapter 2, the reverse pattern is found in obsessive cases.[3])

The fifth proposition is that certain aspects of the test results indicate the effectiveness of the characteristic efforts at adjustment. Intensity and pervasiveness of anxiety, degree of emotional lability, rigidity and indiscriminateness of approach, inhibition of productivity, fluctuations of efficiency, and other features all pertain to ineffectiveness of these efforts. If the test results indicate excessive emphasis on certain defenses and selective principles at the same time as they indicate that these are ineffective in curtailing anxiety and emotional lability, then it is likely that an illness of the type implied by the major defenses is present. For example, excessive rationalizing and pedantry in a setting of intense anxiety and tension often indicates an obsessional neurosis, and excessive reliance on avoidance in a setting of low anxiety tolerance and unchecked passivity often indicates a narcissistic character disorder.

The sixth proposition is that often the formal test indications of the same characteristics vary in different cases and that often the same formal patterns have different implications in different contexts. For example, a cautious paranoid schizophrenic may achieve quite a respectable Comprehension score in the Bellevue Scale, only to give away his basically impaired judgment through some absurd form responses in the Rorschach Test, while a confused, intellectualizing schizophrenic may indicate his poor judgment directly in a low Comprehension score. Furthermore the Comprehension or judgment score may be relatively low among the subtest scores in the Bellevue Scale as a result either of egocentric impulsiveness or schizophrenic impairment of reality testing; or this score may be relatively high as an expression of either passive, naive reliance on conventional precepts or fundamentally sound judgment.

Thus the clinical psychological tester must work in terms of contexts of responses, checking the implications of any one response or pattern against the implications of all other responses and patterns. When enough patterns can be found that have one or two major implications in common, an interpretation becomes possible. The examiner must work parsimoniously, seeking as few general conclusions as will embrace

---

3) The diagnosis of schizophrenia, however, is not indicated by any one type of characterological picture but is based on an appraisal of the quality of reality-testing, the effectiveness of interpersonal communication, and the appropriateness and amount of affective output; similarly the diagnosis of depression is not based on a derived characterological picture, but on indications of decrease in the speed, efficiency, and variability of thought and action.

all the significant patterns of results. If, for example, long and detailed verbalizations characterize a record, either genuine obsessiveness or pretentiousness may lie behind them; if, however, the remaining test results clearly indicate a narcissistic character disorder, the excessive verbalization can usually be safely interpreted as pretentiousness and the implication of obsessive characteristics can be ignored or relegated to the background.

The primary role of context in test interpretation is perhaps the greatest single obstacle to the acceptance of clinical tests into the domain of approved "objective" techniques. It all sounds very much like pure intuition. One purpose of this volume, especially of the summaries of diagnostic contexts in Chapter 2, is to demonstrate that to a large extent the composition of these contexts can be explicitly stated and therefore subjected to tests of validity.

The seventh and last proposition to be advanced here is that interpretations and diagnostic conclusions are two relatively discrete parts of test analysis, although the latter are quite dependent on the former. An *interpretation* is a prediction that certain phenomena of behavior or thinking will be found by direct observation to characterize the subject. It may further predict that the behavior or thinking will be such as to directly express that characteristic or that the behavior or thinking will only imply that characteristic; in other words it may specify whether the characteristic is overt or latent. An interpretation, strictly defined, does not commit itself to any diagnostic scheme; it refers always to behavior or thinking which can be immediately and concretely apprehended. An interpretation may, for example, state that the thinking of the subject tends characteristically to be concerned with fine detail, that it lacks wealth of reference or that it bears traces of fluidity; it may state that the behavior of the subject is characterized by impulsive acts with little forethought, or by a rigid clinging to orderliness, or by restlessness. An interpretation should be subject to immediate validation by refined observation. One implication of this definition must be stressed: the prediction must deal with a *characteristic,* with a mode of behavior or thinking that is enduring and that sets the subject off from many or most other subjects. Predictions that are "free rides" too easily can pass as meaningful interpretations. I have in mind vague statements such as "adjustment problems in difficult situations", "primitive impulses are active", or "occasionally becomes evasive". The least such statements require is a specification in terms of "more than" or "less than" other people in general.

A *diagnostic conclusion,* in contrast to an interpretation, generally involves subscription to a nosological scheme. It is in this area that clinical psychologists will most often disagree among themselves or with psychiatrists by fault of employing different diagnostic criteria. For example, the definition of what constitutes the inappropriate affect of a schizophrenic or the egocentricity of a narcissistic character disorder or the rationalizing of an obsessional neurotic more or less varies among diagnosticians. This does not appear to constitute a serious obstacle to the practice of clinical testing because a test report need not commit itself beyond its interpretations. However, if the psychologist is intimately familiar with the mode of diagnostic reasoning used by the psychiatrist with whom he is working, he may then attempt to follow through his interpretations by elaborating their diagnostic implications. This is no longer reasoning from the raw test material, however; it is sheer *clinical* reasoning and must stand or fall with the criteria it accepts and uses. If diagnostic conclusions are incorrect, if they do not agree with the implications of the findings of clinical examination, the fault may lie in the diagnostic reasoning of the psychologist and not at all in his interpretations proper.[4]

---

[4] Unfortunately most research into the clinical usefulness of tests has attempted to correlate test "signs" with diagnoses, and not with characteristics of thinking or behavior. These studies, when they have obtained positive results, have then tried, by reasoning rather than by experiment, to establish which personality characteristics assumed to be widespread among the members of any diagnostic group were responsible for the significantly frequent occurrence of the established "sign" or "signs". This is a fault of the statistical investigations in *Diagnostic Psychological Testing*. It is a roundabout method and can never yield conclusive results.

Chapter Two

DIAGNOSTIC SUMMARIES

In this chapter the reader will find summaries of the diagnostic indications of a variety of pathological syndromes. Each syndrome will be discussed separately and the pertinent diagnostic indications will be reviewed test by test.[1]) Although I have built this chapter around diagnostic headings, I have attempted, as far as possible, to relate the various indications to specific identifying characteristics of each syndrome and not to the name of the syndrome. The specific relationships should obtain regardless of the final diagnosis. For example, under the heading *hysteria,* a number of indications of emotional lability, fearfulness, impulsiveness, and naivete are mentioned. None of these characteristics is the sole property of hysterics; each may be found in many different normal and ill persons. *Thus the indications should be understood to refer to characteristics first and to diagnoses only second.* Accordingly, atypical patterns will not often be discussed in any detail in this chapter; it is hoped that the reader will cut through the diagnostic boundaries whenever necessary and seek the meaning of these variations in discussions of other groups.

OBSESSIVE-COMPULSIVE NEUROSIS

This diagnostic term covers those persons who rigidly and pervasively resort to the defenses of isolation, rationalization, and intellectualization in their efforts to cope with their impulses and the demands of the world about them. The bulk of their thought processes, whether elicited

---

1) There will be no discussion of the test records of manics, mental defectives, patients with organic brain damage, and catatonic and hebephrenic schizophrenics. This is unfortunate since it casts a shadow of doubt on the differential diagnostic arguments to be presented. Cases of these types have been seen too infrequently at The Menninger Foundation to permit generalizations about their test results at this time.

by everyday situations or by test items, almost invariably reflects the excessive reliance on this defensive structure.

It is difficult on the basis of test results to distinguish obsessive-compulsive *character* neurotics without classical symptoms from obsessive-compulsive neurotics with symptoms (obsessions, compulsive rituals). It is also difficult to distinguish those cases whose symptoms tend more toward the obsessional side from those whose symptoms tend more toward the compulsive side. Finally, it is often difficult to draw the line between normal and pathological obsessive-compulsive characteristics. The best, though not infallible, rule to apply is the following: as the incidence or extremeness of the indicators to be described increases, the chances that a character or symptom neurosis is present also increase. There is little point in trying to predict the presence of clear-cut symptoms; delineation of character make-up is the crucial job.

The chief characteristics to be sought out are pedantic intellectualizing (perfectionism and ostentatious, circumlocutory, circumstantial display of erudition), rationalizing and doubting (rumination, excessive qualification, overcautiousness), and rigidity (inability to be casual when casualness is appropriate, inability to permit full-bodied emotional experiences to develop).

BELLEVUE SCALE

The Bellevue Scale scattergram usually shows conspicuously high Information and Vocabulary scores, frequently with a relatively (but rarely absolutely) low Comprehension score and a relatively (but rarely absolutely) low Performance level. It is unusual to find an I. Q. in an obsessive case that falls below 100: the Total I. Q. is generally 110 or more; the Verbal I. Q. is frequently in the superior or very superior range. The low Comprehension score takes on special diagnostic significance if it is the outcome of a doubt-laden casting-about among alternative reasons or courses of action and pedantic rejection of popular beliefs; the high Information and Vocabulary scores take on special diagnostic significance if they are achieved through, or in spite of, over-detailed, often ostentatious factual reference, qualification, or specification; the relatively low Performance level takes on special diagnostic significance if it is clear from the observation of the performance that tension and resulting inefficiency rather than depressive retardation are pulling down the scores on the visual-motor subtests. When the Digit Span score remains on the general Verbal level, despite indications elsewhere of acute anxiety, obsessiveness is suggested, especially if the score is achieved by active organization of the numbers into groups.[2]) Occasionally the Similarities score is slightly lowered by doubting and pedantry.

There are a fair number of cases whose Comprehension score remains on the Information and Vocabulary level; however, the qualitatively obsessive features usually persist. In these cases, impairment of judgment is still indicated but is not as extreme as when the score drops. There are a fair number of cases whose Performance level does not drop, although the rest of the record (and battery) is clearly obsessive-compulsive; in these cases it is usually safe to assume some degree of chronicity and "adjustment" to the neurosis, such that the patient is not in a state of incapacitating tension at the time of testing. The obsessive character neurotics frequently have this pattern.

The most reliable indicator of obsessive-compulsive features in the Bellevue Scale is the quality of verbalization: if verbalization is over-detailed and doubt-laden, obsessive-compulsive features are conspicuous in the character make-up, if not in the pathology itself. We have seen obsessive-compulsive neurotics whose Performance level exceeded their Verbal level and whose Comprehension score exceeded their Information score, but whose obsessive-compulsive characteristics were nevertheless identifiable in their verbalizations of their thought processes.[3])

Examples of qualitative features: "There is a good deal of dispute as to who invented the airplane but the Wright Brothers get credit for it." "If I were lost in the forest in the daytime I might follow the sun ... or go by the moss on the north side of the trees ... or maybe follow a stream. Do I have a compass? If I had one I'd ... (etc.) ." (Which would you do?) "It depends on the terrain: if ... (etc.)." "A cedar is a coniferous tree, yields fragrant wood, generally used to make chests." "A diamond is a carboniferous stone, formed deep in the earth under high pressure, mined and sold as a gem or for industrial purposes; also a baseball diamond." "A dog and lion are alike in that they are four-legged mammals, possessed of fur, tails ... meat-eating ... can be tamed." [4])

----

2) Schizoid features may also be suggested by a well-retained Digit Span score. See p. 91.

3) Sometimes the possibility of *mixed* neurotic features must be considered in these instances. See pp. 38-39.

4) Sometimes patients with narcissistic character disorders and a pretentious front may give superficially similar verbalizations. See p. 47.

LEARNING EFFICIENCY [5])

Learning efficiency is almost invariably well-retained. Quantitatively the recall will be adequate for the general intellectual level, as indicated by the Information-Vocabulary level in the Bellevue Scale; qualitatively there will be no serious disruptions of the story structure and no introduction of totally new material. Occasionally the original wording will be "dressed up", so that words like "inundated", "extricated", and "suffered abrasions" will appear. If learning efficiency is badly impaired in a context of indications of this neurosis, it is necessary to consider the possibility that the subject is an incipient or acute schizophrenic [6]) with persisting obsessive-compulsive features.

SORTING TEST

If intelligence is average or higher, the conceptual level is generally abstract, occasionally functional and rarely concrete.[7]) The sortings or *concept span* in Part I tend to be mildly narrow; for example, imitations may be excluded from the sortings of silverware and smoking utensils. Overconceptualized sortings of two types occur: (1) for example, the ball is often conceptualized as "red, round, and rubber", with the result

---

5) Retaining only the two story recall subtests of the Babcock Test has given rise to a technical complication: the estimation of learning efficiency must now be made using the Vocabulary subtest of the Bellevue Scale as the standard or baseline. The following estimated norms have been found to be satisfactory: a Vocabulary score of 8 requires an average recall score of 12; proceeding up the scale, the relationships should be 9-13, 10-14, 11-15, 12-16, 13-17, and 14 and higher—at least 18. Our experience with subjects whose Vocabulary score is below 8 is too limited to allow for generalizations. The interpretations in this volume will be geared to these estimated norms.

6) See pp. 67 and 89.

7) The conceptualization of sortings may be *abstract*—referring to a common attribute (red, round, rubber, smoking equipment), *functional*—referring to a common function or use (to eat with, to build with), *concrete*—referring to a real life situation in which the objects are commonly encountered together (a table setting, things in a child's room), *fabulated*—weaving a story in which the objects are linked, or reinterpreting the meaning of the objects (a man works for a while and then eats and smokes a cigar), *syncretistic*—referring to an attribute which is shared by so many objects that the concept loses its delimiting aspect (all have molecules, all things we use), *symbolic*—built on a symbolic interpretation of the object or objects (red stands for danger, the lock stands for protection and so does the knife). The sorting or concept span may be *loose* or *mildly loose*—including more objects than conventional concept formation ordinarily accepts, or *narrow* or *mildly narrow*—including less objects than are commonly accepted.

that the only object which can be added is the red, round, rubber sink-stopper; (2) the paper circle, for example, is often conceptualized as "red and round", with the result that all other objects which meet either of these qualifications are sorted with the circle. Actually, two separate groups are formed in this instance and the sorting is not basically loose. The former type of sorting is indicative of rigid emphasis on precision; the latter type is indicative of rigid emphasis on exhaustiveness. Some obsessive-compulsive neurotics, once they have noted several possible abstractions, find it difficult to decide on only one abstraction and, after some vacillation, solicit the assistance of the examiner in coming to a decision.

In Part II split-narrow conceptualizations are frequent. The following are typical verbalizations: "Real and imitation silverware." "Real and imitation smoking equipment." "All paper except for the tobacco in the cigarette." These qualifications are all justified but it is the obsessive-compulsive who bothers with them. A less meticulous person has greater conceptual freedom, can overlook these discrepancies, and, unlike the rigid obsessive, can therefore comply with the test instructions by offering one inclusive concept. The qualities of verbalization outlined in the paragraphs on the Bellevue Scale frequently appear in this test also.

RORSCHACH TEST [8])

The many possible diagnostic indicators in this test will first be listed and then qualified or amplified wherever necessary.

(1) R above 35. (2) Numerous Dr,[9]) De and S responses, amounting to more than 15% of R. (3) Do responses. (4) $F\%$ higher than 80%. (5) $F+\%$ [10]) higher than 80% and relatively many very sharply conceived forms. (6) Many M or greater emphasis on M than on color in the experience balance. (7) $A\%$ higher than 50%; $P\%$ higher than 30%. (8) Frequent combinations and a few fabulized combinations.[11])

---

8) See list of Rorschach symbols and description of the scoring system, pp. 337-340.

9) The score Dr as used here refers to tiny areas or to larger but unusually outlined areas. The score Dd is almost entirely equivalent to Klopfer's d. The $DR\%$ is the total of the $Dr\%$, $De\%$, and $S\%$.

10) Four form-level scores may be given: $F+$ for popular or superior forms, $F\pm$ for essentially accurate forms with minor flaws, $F\mp$ for essentially inaccurate or vague forms with a few saving features and $F-$ for inaccurate or totally vague forms. In computing the $F+\%$, $F\pm$ is combined with $F+$, and $F\mp$ is combined with $F-$.

11) For example, to the lower middle green on Card X: "Two worms crawling out of a rabbit's eyes."

(9) Criticism of the accuracy of responses, stressing minor discrepancies between blot and concept. (10) Detailed descriptions of inkblots as to symmetry and asymmetry, color, shading, configuration. (11) Anal content or allusion.

1. R, the number of responses, is often above 50, referring to the obsessive-compulsive neurotic's characteristic ideational productivity. In a fair number of cases R falls below 35, but rarely does it fall below 20. If other indicators demonstrate that the patient is predominantly obsessive-compulsive, the low R may refer to depressive features[12]) or to such extreme rigidity, pedantry and perfectionism that relatively few responses are acceptable enough to the subject to be offered to the examiner. In some of these cases there may be such a distraught reaction to the "amorphous" inkblots that relatively few possibilities ever develop into presentable interpretations, and overcautious descriptions replace genuine responses.

2. Rare detail (Dr), edge detail (De) and space (S) responses often constitute more than 25%, and sometimes as much as 40% or 50% of the record. Usually, many of the responses to these areas are forced or extravagant. For example, strings of faces may be seen along the edges of Card VII, or the tiny projections on the lower contour of Card I may be seen as people in various postures or activities. Thus the productivity (high R) is often a bogus productivity, amounting to little more than excessive rumination about trivia or indiscriminate, "driven" intellectualizing. A few highly extravagant interpretations of tiny details, even in the absence of high $DR\%$, often indicate the presence of ideational symptoms. If, in an obsessive record, the $DR\%$ is increased by relatively many space responses, acute doubting is indicated.

3. Do responses in a setting of high intelligence reflect the effects of perfectionism and doubting. They are generally based on a refusal to extend an initial interpretation of an obvious detail to a larger area, when the larger area is popularly considered to support such an extension. For example, only the head of the "popular" man may be seen on Card III, while the idea that the rest of the popular area might look like a body is rejected as absurd. A more frequent variant of this meticulous, doubt-laden fragmentation is the breaking down of a popular or near-popular response, once it has been given, into parts which cannot reasonably be integrated. For example, the patient may see the complete man on Card III, and then, ruminating over the response, may add:

---

12) See p. 59.

"The head looks more like a duck; the arm more like a wing; the neck doesn't look natural; the leg isn't attached." This tearing apart of responses is often quite dramatic, giving the examiner a direct feeling of the intellectual nihilism of the doubter.

4. The high percent of form responses $(F\%)$ is a less reliable indicator. The $F\%$ has two parts according to our method of summarizing the record[13]): the $F\%$ based on the number of pure form responses and the $F\%$ based on the number of responses which are either pure form or dominated by form $(F, M, FC, FC'\ F\ (C), FCh)$, the latter being designed to measure more broadly the exercise of intellectual constraint. It is not infrequent that both parts of the $F\%$ are high in obsessive records, but there are many exceptions. The percent of pure forms may be lowered by the presence of many M's alone; the percent of responses dominated by form may be lowered by indications of emotional lability, tension and anxiety (CF, ChF). If the two $F\%$'s are high in an average-sized or dilated record, they indicate the rigid intellectual constraint of the obsessive-compulsive; if they are low in a record which otherwise looks obsessive, they suggest that the intellectual constraint has been ineffective in warding off intense affects and anxieties. Frequently the percent of responses dominated by form is close to 100%, indicating that a minimum of free affective experience is allowed.

5. The high percent of accurate forms $(F+\%)$ is also one of the less reliable indicators. When it occurs in an average-sized or dilated record, it indicates obsessive-compulsive characteristics. The high $F+\%$ refers to rigid efforts at accuracy and exactness. However, many of these cases, despite their strenuous efforts at accuracy, turn out a sizable amount of shoddy productions. For example, many of the De or Dr faces, which smother some of their records, are of poor quality and lower the $F+\%$ to 60%-70% and occasionally to 50%-60%. Where the $F+\%$ is high, a more successful perfectionism is indicated.

6. The accumulation of responses involving human beings seen in motion (M), and the predominance of these over responses based on color (FC, CF, C), generally indicate the presence of ideational symptom-formation—*if it is clear from other indications that the subject is ill.* Although emphasis on M may also refer to the presence of phobias [14]) or delusions [15]), in the absence of other indications of anxiety hysteria

---

13) See pp. 337-340 in the Appendix, for description of the scoring system.
14) See p. 37.
15) See p. 78.

or psychosis, it may be taken as an indication of obsessive-compulsive characteristics. One related indication of obsessive-compulsive features is the absence or spoiling of the popular M on Card III in the presence of other M's, especially if one or more of these are unusual. Another useful indicator is the weakening of the movement-impressions by the kind of doubting and meticulousness referred to above in the paragraph on *Do*. We score these responses *FM* and count them only as .5 instead of 1 in the experience balance. The M's are almost always $M+$; although an occasional $M-$ may be given by some such patients, $M--$ should always be considered suggestive of psychosis until proved otherwise. Occasionally the *sum C* outweighs the number of M's. Rorschach reported that this tended to correlate with compulsive rather than obsessive symptoms. This has not been borne out in our experience. The number of M can be greatly reduced by the intellectual inhibitions and the number of color responses can be increased by extreme passivity and deference (many *FC*) or by failure of the neurosis to reduce emotional lability (many *CF*). It is our impression that the high *sum C,* especially if based primarily on *CF* responses, tends to correlate with a proneness to somatization. Where extreme inhibition is present, the *EB* is usually quite coarctated (1—to—.5 or even 0—to—0).

7. The high $A\%$ and $P\%$ are not independent diagnostic indicators, but, in a setting of other indications of obsessive-compulsive features, reflect the characteristically cautious and inhibited intellectual approach to situations. Animal responses are, in most instances, the least daring responses, and popular responses, of course, are just safe and easy. The $A\%$ and $P\%$ need not be high, however; sometimes an excess of *Hd* and *Ad* responses indicates the intellectual restraint, and sometimes great variability of content may be present as an indication of cultural interests or pretentiousness.

8. The combination responses are usually accompanied by several fabulized combinations.[16] The two together indicate that although strong integrative efforts are being made, the basic obsessional impairment of abstractive ability leads to over-literal interpretation of situations. This appears to be another aspect of the conceptual difficulty seen in the Similarities and Sorting Tests, in the *Do* variations, and in the criticism of responses soon to be discussed. A caution is necessary,

---

16) The fabulized combination is often encountered in the records of obsessive normal persons also. It does not, therefore, necessarily indicate neurotic symptoms but it does retain, in all records, its implication of more or less strained, pseudo-integrative efforts to structure experience.

however: if the fabulized combinations become too numerous, or if they take on gory qualities ("Bugs chewing on the neck of a person"), an incipient schizophrenia must be seriously considered. Care must also be taken to distinguish fabulized combinations from the more clearly schizophrenic confabulations.

9. Criticism of responses, either directly or implicitly (as in the *Do* variants), is rarely absent. In some instances critical review of each response may be so extensive and detailed that a total of 20 responses may require 10 pages to record. In these cases extreme doubting is likely to characterize the neurosis.

10. Descriptions of the inkblots are also frequent, but pathological obsessiveness is indicated only when the descriptions are long-winded and begin to replace responses.

11. Anal content or allusions include seeing rear views of animals or humans, anal openings, the large intestine or colon, and the like. These generally refer to corresponding preoccupations and are most frequently found in the records of severe obsessive-compulsives. When the anal content becomes vivid, as in "a person defecating", or "feces", schizophrenia is suggested.

WORD ASSOCIATION TEST

Reactions are generally prompt and in conventional conceptual relationship with the stimulus words. Recall of original reactions is usually quite accurate.[17] The more rigid cases often manifest a tendency to fall back on multiword definitions in the face of temporary blocking. The extreme intellectualizers tend to employ ostentatious reaction words; for example, *dance* — "Terpsichore",, *mouth* — "orifice", *drink* — "imbibe", *house* — "domicile". It takes a pedant to have a "fancy" word so readily available when he is under the time pressure and other demands of this test. Images as first pre-verbal reactions to stimulus words tend to occur frequently.[18] During the inquiry period articulated introspective reports of fleeting half-thoughts preceding the responses are almost always indicative of obsessive features. Obsessive subjects often explain delayed reactions as consequences of having to choose between several possibilities which came to mind almost simultaneously; not infrequently the alternatives are opposites. Idiosyncratic responses, referring to personal experiences, are also frequent.

----

17) Once the reading of the stimulus words is completed, the list is again read to the subject and he is asked to repeat exactly what he said the first time.

18) This is also true of schizoid subjects. See p. 91.

THEMATIC APPERCEPTION TEST

The indications of the obsessive-compulsive neurosis are generally found in the structure of the story and in the pedantic verbalizations. Sometimes,when the stories are clearly self-references, the identification figures are described as paralyzed by doubt, vacillating or "too thoughtful", but content-indications of this type are not frequent. The stories are often dominated by circumstantial description of the pictures, inability to decide on any one story because the details of the picture cannot be integrated, refusal to predict the outcome because there are no "objective" indications as to what the outcome *will* be. It matters little to these neurotics that they need only say what the outcome *might* be; their defensive pedantry is so rigidly established that they cannot permit themselves the liberty of a free fantasy.[19]) Often, these patients attempt to reduce all statements regarding emotions and motives to logical derivations from the implications of various details in the pictures. This rigidly rationalistic procedure effectively takes the "kick" out of each story. Some compulsive subjects dictate punctuation; if they are trying their hardest consciously or unconsciously to irritate the examiner, they frequently correct their punctuation or syntax.

HYSTERIA

This diagnostic term covers those persons who rigidly and pervasively resort to the defense of repression in their efforts to cope with their impulses and the demands of the world about them. Excessive reliance on this defense appears to hamper the development of broad intellectual, cultural interests, to impair the ability for independent and creative thinking, and to make for striking emotional lability and naivete. One or another of these characteristics will color a large part of the thought processes elicited by the test items.

It is difficult on the basis of test results to distinguish hysterical character neuroses from hysterical symptom neuroses, anxiety hysterias (phobic symptoms) from conversion hysterias, and persons with strong repressive tendencies in the normal range from persons whose repressive tendencies are extreme enough to warrant the description "neurotic" even in the absence of clear-cut symptom formation. The best, though not

---

19) This difficulty arises in other types of cases also, particularly in those characterized by low intelligence, extreme inhibition, or strong avoidance tendencies based on very low anxiety-tolerance. The verbalizations and the remaining tests must decide the diagnostic issue.

entirely reliable, rule to apply is the following: as the incidence or extremeness of the indicators to be discussed below increases, the chances that a character or symptom neurosis is present also increase. Again it is more crucial to describe the character than to predict symptoms.

The chief personality characteristics to be sought out are emotional lability, impulsiveness, childish naivete in general and conspicuous sexual naivete, a tendency toward histrionics, minimization of active and independent ideation as a means of coping with problems, a basic dependence on conventional precepts as guides to behavior, egocentricity and blocking of thought processes when confronted with "traumatic" (usually sexual but often aggressive) material in the tests.

BELLEVUE SCALE

The Bellevue Scale scattergram is usually characterized by the Performance level equalling or exceeding the Verbal level, and a relative inferiority of Information and a relative superiority of Comprehension among the Verbal subtests. Among the Performance subtests, the subtests of visual-motor coordination and speed tend to obtain the highest scores. The low Information score takes on special diagnostic significance if none of the very difficult items (21-25) is passed and if there is considerable spottiness and temporary forgetting on the easier items; the high Comprehension score takes on special diagnostic significance if the responses have a naive, utterly unreflective, and highly "moral" quality; the discrepancy between the Verbal and Performance levels increases in diagnostic significance the greater it is.[20] However, when the Verbal level, and especially Information, are around the weighted score 13 or higher, this pattern loses its diagnostic specificity. It has been our experience that the widespread and intensive effects of the generally repressive mode of adjustment characterizing the development of hysterical characters is such as to render very unlikely the achievement of an over-all excellent Verbal level. There have, however, been exceptions. As a rule the Verbal I. Q. rarely reaches the superior range and may be as low as the borderline-defective range. The score on Digit Span is usually greatly lowered below the general Verbal level, reflecting the intense anxiety experienced by most hysterics. The rare cases of hysteria with *belle indifférence* tend to have a Rigid Span score on the general Verbal level, but their Verbal level is usually very much lower than their Performance level. If, in an hysterical setting, the Verbal level tends

---

20) This pattern is also typical of the records of psychopathic characters and narcissistic character disorders. See pp. 47 and 54.

to be at or above the Performance level, and if the Digit Span score is not lowered, the presence of phobic symptoms (anxiety hysteria in contrast to conversion hysteria) is suggested.[21])

There are some hysterics whose Performance level is much below their Verbal level; these cases usually show strong depressive features clinically.[22]) However, the scatter of the Verbal subtest scores generally follows the repressive (hysterical) pattern described above. There are some hysterics whose scatter pattern is inconclusive or even misleading. For example, the Information score may be superior to the Comprehension score, and the Verbal level superior to the Performance level. Some of these cases will, nevertheless, indicate hysterical features by the naive, moralistic quality of their verbalizations; others will be identifiable as hysterics on the basis of other tests, especially on the basis of the Rorschach Test.[23])

Examples of qualitative features: "We should keep away from bad company because they have an *evil* influence; it's not proper!" "People who are born deaf are usually unable to talk because God wanted it that way." "A fly and a tree are not similar: a fly is a horrible little pest and a tree is a beautiful thing in nature!" Some hysterics, usually on a low intelligence level, try to make a good impression and guess, but wildly: "Tom Sawyer wrote Huckleberry Finn." "Ballast is some kind of dance." "Lindbergh discovered the North Pole."[24])

LEARNING EFFICIENCY

Learning efficiency is usually well-retained. The quantity of recall matches or comes close to the subject's general Verbal level in the Bellevue Scale, and the structure of the story is preserved. In some cases, emotional elaborations of content occur, reflecting extreme emotional lability and domination of the intake of material by these easily aroused, intense affects; for example: "People were homeless", "Houses were washed away", "People caught pneumonia", "6,000 died", "His hands were severely injured." Some hysterics, particularly bland ones on a low

---

21) In general a well-retained Digit Span score, in the absence of signs of a schizoid trend or schizophrenia, and in the presence of signs of neurosis, can be taken as an indication of ideational symptom formation. See pp. 24-25 regarding obsessive-compulsive neurotics.

22) See p. 57 regarding depression.

23) See the discussion of mixed neurosis, pp. 38-40, for further elaboration of these ambiguous records.

24) See pp. 54-55 on psychopathic characters for similar responses.

level of verbal intelligence, may be able to remember very little of the story. Ordinarily this would suggest either schizophrenia, a severe depression, or organic brain damage; but if it is a hysteric who performs so poorly, the remaining tests almost always make this clear. In such a case, the low score can be taken as an indication of the special intensity of repressive defense.

SORTING TEST

As a rule, the level of achievement in the Sorting Test depends on the general level of verbal intelligence. If the subject is of average or higher verbal intelligence, the conceptual level is usually mostly abstract and somewhat functional and concrete. The concept span in Part I of the test is, in general, adequate, but tends unsystematically and as a reflection of conceptual insecurity to be mildly loose and mildly narrow .at the same time. If the subject is of below average intelligence, the conceptual level is likely to be predominantly concrete. Some hysterics demonstrate exceptionally egocentric concept formation by basing their sortings or conceptualizations on personal references or preferences; for example: "My son playing *ball* and this *lock* is on his bicycle," or, "After dinner (eating utensils) we usually smoke (smoking equipment) and then wash the dishes (sink stopper)."[25]) If meticulousness is apparent in this test and the remaining test results are clearly indicative of hysteria, superficial compulsiveness as an attempted check on emotional lability is suggested.

RORSCHACH TEST

The experience balance *(EB)* is the principal indicator of the hysterical neurosis in the Rorschach Test. With very few exceptions, *sum C* exceeds *M* and *M* is 1 or 0. If *M* exceeds 2 in an otherwise hysterical setting, a mixed neurosis is indicated. This does not mean that a *sum C* prevalence in itself indicates a neurosis, nor does it mean that even if a neurosis is indicated elsewhere, one can safely conclude that it is an hysterical neurosis on the basis of the *EB*. Other indications, in the Rorschach Test and elsewhere, are necessary. The *sum C* prevalence becomes particularly significant in this connection if *CF* exceeds *FC*, if color responses are given first on the colored cards, and if *CF*'s make their first appearance on Cards II and III. Some hysterics give more *FC* than *CF*, indicating the infantile dependency frequently seen in these

---

25) See also the discussion of narcissistic character disorders, p. 48.

cases. It is rare, however, to find a hysteric who gives only *FC*. Occasional pure *C* responses occur, and these are almost always "blood" on Cards II and III, or vague flower, cloud, nature or "painting" responses on Cards VIII, IX and X.

The characteristic predominance of *CF* and *C* responses refers to the emotional lability of the hysteric. The absence of *M* is assumed to reflect the strong repressive emphasis, inasmuch as *M*, broadly defined, is an index of efforts at constructive ideation as a means of delaying impulses, regulating behavior and coping with problems. When inhibition and repression are especially intense, even the color responses tend to disappear, and an *EB* of 0—to—1 or even 0—to—0 may result.

Some hysterics fail to respond to one or more cards, even if they are urged to keep trying for 2 or 3 minutes. Their failures are most frequent on Cards VI, VII, and IX. A few hysterics, especially if their intellectual and cultural level is very low, fail as many as 5 or 6 cards and give as few as 4 or 5 responses.[26] Delayed reactions to any of the highly shaded or colored cards occur frequently. The blocking implied by these failures and delays appears to relate to the hysteric's readily stimulated anxiety-reactions, low anxiety-tolerance and dependence on repressive defense in difficult situations.

Indications of free-floating anxiety (*ChF* and *Ch*) are usually present; these tend to be of the "X-ray", "map", or "cloud" variety. Also frequently present are direct manifestations of easily evoked anxiety-reactions and lability. Hysterics often refer to the cards as "weird", "ugly", or "sickening". The labile reactions may greatly shape the content of responses: dragons, monsters, King Kong, spiders, slimy snakes, and the like, will be seen. The content will suggest the naive fears we tend to identify as those of children.

R rarely exceeds 30, and the *W*% and *DR*% are usually low. Combinations and originals are infrequent. The emphasis is usually put on easy, obvious details as areas of response, on simple content, and on minimal integrative efforts or creativity. If these features are replaced by greater productivity or imaginativeness in an otherwise hysterical setting, a mixed neurosis is indicated.[27]

If the record looks hysterical, frequent anatomical responses suggest preoccupation with conversion symptoms; a few of the more usual sex responses suggest preoccupation with sexual symptoms. If the record

26) See pp. 50 and 59-60 for differential diagnosis from addiction and depression.
27) See pp. 38-39.

looks hysterical, phobic symptoms are suggested by the presence of more than one M, by a single M if it is on a card other than III, by one or two small M (Ms) or by a few sharply conceived and possibly fabulated Dr's; for example, to the lower middle Dr on Card VII: "A sprout breaking through the earth." Other scores vary considerably, but almost always stay within acceptable limits. The $F\%$ may rise if inhibitory efforts are strenuous, but then R is likely to be quite low; the $F\%$ may fall if lability is allowed full play. The $F+\%$ may rise if superficial compulsive defenses are emphasized; it may fall to 60% or even 50% if anxiety and lability induce numerous vague responses. If the $A\%$ is high, typical poverty of associative content is suggested; if it is low, anatomy responses may be numerous, indicating corresponding preoccupation, or plant and nature responses may abound because of the CF emphasis, indicating lability and childish naivete.

WORD ASSOCIATION TEST

Words with sexual connotations tend to elicit conspicuous delays of reaction; in some instances no response may be forthcoming. To a lesser extent this is true of words with aggressive connotations. Also outstanding is the tendency to express naive, often infantile affective or evaluative reactions in the responses, for example: *spring*—"pretty", *snake*—"ugly" or "slimy", *cockroach*—"hate" or "nasty", *masturbation*—"bad" or "even the word makes me feel sick!" Self-references are not unusual in these records, but because they also occur frequently in the records of schizophrenics and patients with narcissistic character disorders,[28]) they are not diagnostically conclusive. This egocentric orientation is seen in such responses as *mother*—"mine", *bowel movement*—"don't like", and in the affective reactions described above. In general, however, the hysterics give appropriate and quick reactions and have adequate recall ability. If images occur as initial reactions to stimulus words, phobic symptoms are suggested.

THEMATIC APPERCEPTION TEST

As in the Word Association Test, the "sexual" and "aggressive" pictures tend to elicit blocking. As in the Rorschach Test, the stimulus material easily evokes affective display and frequently the affective reaction intrudes into the story itself. For example, in response to the picture of a man in the dark by an open window: "It's a burglar; I hate

---

28) See pp. 50-51 and 74-75.

to think about such things; it makes me blue and depressed; I just hope he gets caught"; in response to the picture of an old man in a dark cemetery: "He looks weird; it's a terrible picture; he must be an evil old man!" Extreme dependency and fearfulness are often conspicuous themes; sometimes rather transparent oedipal themes are also conspicuous. Platitudinous, naive verbalizations and moralistic reactions to the "aggressive" and "sexual" pictures are often present. Of all subjects, except certain agitated depressives, hysterics are the most likely to weep during this test—or during any test for that matter. The transiency of these reactions bespeaks their histrionic component.

MIXED NEUROSIS

This diagnostic term designates those patients whose test results reflect the excessive application of the defenses characterizing both hysteric and obsessive cases. In other words, personality characteristics that include both hysterical and obsessive-compulsive features are likely to be present. Clinically this neurosis is defined by the presence of obsessive-compulsive and phobic symptoms.[29]) It is difficult to distinguish many mixed neurotics from hysterics or from obsessive-compulsive neurotics. It is difficult to distinguish others from normal personalities with mild repressive and rationalizing tendencies. In some instances it is difficult to tell that one type of symptomatology is dominant in the clinical picture over the other.

The chief personality features to be sought out are the pedantry, doubting, and rigidity of the obsessive-compulsive, and the lability, repressive emphasis, and naivete of the hysteric. Since the hysteric and compulsive-obsessive features have already been reviewed separately, the following discussion will concern itself with the varieties of over-all test patterns.

Many mixed neurotics, especially women, have given Bellevue Scale results that closely parallel those reported above as typical for hysterics and have given Rorschach Test results that closely parallel those reported above as typical for obsessive-compulsives. Other mixed neurotics have given the opposite pattern of test results, that is, obsessive Bellevues and hysteric Rorschachs. Although it may seem the height of mechanical

---

29) It seems advisable to reserve the term *mixed neurosis* for cases with obsessive and phobic symptoms and not to apply it to "mixed-up" neuroses in which anxiety, depression, inhibition, some minor obsessive-compulsive or hysteric characteristics, and so forth, are all present. Otherwise the specificity of this diagnostic term will be lost and the term will become a catch-all.

procedure, equivocation, or indecisiveness to conclude from either of these two patterns that mixed features are present, empirically this has generally proved to be the case. In these instances usually the tests other than the Rorschach Test have tended to side with the Bellevue Scale. However, our general experience has been that in these mixed cases the Rorschach Test will indicate which side of the diagnostic picture is more conspicuous. One recent case we encountered gave test results pervasively colored by the effects of repressive inclination on the development of intelligence functions, but gave a clearly obsessive Rorschach Test record. Clinically, although the repressive emphasis was clear in her development and current status, and although mild conversion symptoms were noted, a classical obsessive-compulsive neurosis, including ritualistic behavior, was the outstanding finding.

One might expect, if the experience balance is dilated and ambiequal, and if the *sum C* is based mainly on *CF* responses, that mixed symptoms will be present. In our experience, however, most such cases have been obsessive-compulsive neurotics who were prone to develop somatic symptoms, such as vague pains, headaches, or fatigue and not clear-cut conversion symptoms.

It also happens that the mixed features are discernible within one and the same test. For example, the Rorschach Test may be characterized by many M, a high $F+\%$ and numerous Dr's, at the same time as it is characterized by hysteric-like expressions of affective lability in reponse to the inkblots proper, quite uncontrolled CF and C responses, and content with a naive, childish quality ("Two little fairy queens; they're so pretty!"). The "pure" pedantic obsessive will not react to inkblots as "weird", "scary", or "ugly". The "pure" naive and labile hysteric will not give five or six M's or a $DR\%$ of 40. If both sets of indications are present, a mixed neurosis is suggested.

In the Thematic Apperception Test the same contrast of labile and naive reactions and meticulousness, fragmentation and rationalization may occur. In the Bellevue Scale the scatter pattern may stand in contrast to the quality of verbalization: there may be a "repressive" scatter pattern with circumstantial verbalizations or an "intellectualizing" scatter pattern with labile responsiveness and naive verbalizations. Often, however, the entire set of test results is one-sided, that is, clearly obsessive-compulsive or clearly hysteric. In these instances it is likely that the uniformity of bias of the test results will correspond to the more basic and more conspicuous pathology. In these instances it is safer in the long run not to clutch at straws in order to build up the diagnostic picture of mixed neurosis; otherwise, more cases will be misdiagnosed as "mixed", who are clinically only on one side or the other, than will be successfully detected as "mixed".

NEURASTHENIA

This diagnostic term designates those conditions in which lack of zest, physically unfounded bodily complaints, easy fatiguability, withdrawal, and loss of interest are the most conspicuous symptoms. Inhibition and depressed mood are also frequently present.[30]

It is difficult to distinguish some neurasthenics from depressed, inhibited obsessive-compulsive neurotics, depressed hysterics, or inhibited normal subjects. There are, however, certain distinctive patterns that occur with rather high frequency in the records of these cases.

The main personality features to look for are inhibition, low mood, bodily preoccupation, a decrease in productivity and speed as gathered from indications of a previously higher level and greater productivity, pervasive inefficiency and, most of all, a general quality of "flatness" or lack of intensity or variety of responsiveness. A leaden quality pervades the records.

BELLEVUE SCALE

Temporary inefficiencies are usually most striking: relatively easy items of Information, Vocabulary, Digit Span, Arithmetic, Picture Completion, and Block Designs tend to failed, while more difficult items are passed. If the original level was average or higher, extremely easy items are rarely failed, and the quality of those failures that do occur is not bizarre: in both respects the neurasthenic is distinguished from the schizophrenic who shows superficially similar spottiness of achievement. The Verbal scatter may tend either to the obsessive or repressive side, but the Performance level is likely to be well below the Verbal level. Fatiguability and withdrawal reactions to this test, as to the others, are often conspicuous. Arithmetic is likely to be especially fatiguing. Many neurasthenics, however, perform relatively smoothly and effectively on this test.

LEARNING EFFICIENCY

The recall of the story is often poorly integrated: the amount recalled may be relatively small, parts of the story may be omitted from their place and inserted later as afterthoughts, the facts of the story

---

30) It is true that neurasthenia is an outmoded diagnostic term, but the syndrome referred to above is occasionally encountered in clinical work. It seemed advisable to retain the term for purposes of this presentation.

may become vague ("*some* people died and *others* drowned"). In a few instances, learning efficiency is completely devastated; the recall may be indistinguishable from that typically given by schizophrenics and psychotic depressives:[31]) new material may be introduced and the original material may be fragmented or forced into new integrations. In these cases, providing that the remainder of the test results are clearly nonpsychotic, the extremely impaired learning efficiency should be taken as a malignant indication. In other words, a psychotic break—depressive or paranoid—is not unlikely. A small minority of neurasthenics have adequate learning efficiency.

SORTING TEST

Frequent failures, split-narrow conceptualizations, narrow sortings, and a tendency toward concrete concepts out of keeping with the subject's level of intelligence characterize the Sorting Test results of many of these cases. In this respect, neurasthenics resemble depressives. In itself this pattern is ambiguous; in building up a diagnostic argument it can be used only as supporting evidence, inasmuch as it suggests the inertia and inefficiency of these cases. Some neurasthenics perform adequately on this test.

RORSCHACH TEST

The following pattern characterizes the majority of the Rorschach Test records: R less than 20, $F+\%$ low, possibly very low; experience balance constricted; colors, if present, weak or forced (F/C, C/F); frequent anatomical, anal, and sexual content. These results imply ideational inertia and inefficiency, inhibition or depressed mood, poverty of emotional experience and output, and generalized bodily preoccupation. The $F+\%$ may be exceptionally low ($10\%-50\%$) if vague anatomical content dominates the entire record; in this instance, the low $F+\%$ cannot be construed to suggest psychotic impairment of reality testing.[32]) Sometimes vague cloud, geography, or geology responses determined only by form also lower the $F+\%$.

Actually the Rorschach Test records of neurasthenics divide into two groups, the one resembling the records of obsessives, and the other resembling the records of hysterics. The first type yields an experience balance with one or two M's and no color responses, and anal and sexual content; the second type yields an experience balance with no or one

---

31) See pp. 58-59 and 67.

32) See, however, pp. 82 and 85 for differential diagnosis from some schizophrenics.

M and several color responses, usually *CF* and *C/F,* embedded in anatomical content (flesh, heart, lungs). The more obsessive records indicate excessive rumination and vague doubting in the neurasthenic's clinical syndrome, possibly with the bodily preoccupations bordering on obsessional thoughts. The more hysteric records indicate histrionically solicitous display of incapacity, possibly with bodily dysfunction bordering on transient conversion symptoms. The latter cases might perhaps more correctly be considered uncrystallized conversion hysterias.

The anatomical content is often naively organized. For example, all of Card X can be seen as an anatomical picture: the pink as the lungs, the side blue as the kidneys, the small middle orange areas as the heart, the lower green as the intestines, the middle blue as the ribs.

Neurasthenics rarely give quantitatively or qualitatively dilated records. In a dilated record numerous anatomical responses usually refer to bodily preoccupation, but are not sufficient in themselves to indicate the presence of a neurasthenic syndrome.

WORD ASSOCIATION TEST

In many instances the test responses resemble those of depressives,[33] in that they are often slow, multiword functional definitions, or both. Occasionally such stimulus words as *stomach, bowel movement,* and *intercourse* elicit direct expressions of bodily complaints or elicit responses indicative of the need for further inquiry, the inquiry eliciting the complaints. For example: *bowel movement*—"pain" or "unpleasant" or "enema"; *stomach*—"pain" or "indigestion". Many neurasthenics, however, perform adequately in this test.

THEMATIC APPERCEPTION TEST

Again the records often resemble those of depressives,[34] in that the stories are meager, emotionally flat, and quite incomplete. Occasionally the dominant themes are fatigue, loss of interest, inability to perform one's duties, and other expressions of inadequate ability to apply oneself.

ANXIETY STATE

This diagnostic term refers to those conditions in which the chief symptom is acute, free-floating anxiety, manifested in restlessness, apprehensiveness, tremulousness, and other bodily expressions of anxiety,

---

33) See p. 60.
34) See p. 60.

and impaired attention and concentration. Depressed mood and striking inhibition are often present.

Some of these cases yield records that do not adequately distinguish them from normal subjects. In general, however, the patterns to be described occur with strikingly high regularity. Because acute anxiety is outstanding in most neuroses and many psychoses, many other types of clinical cases may partake of the patterns to be described below.

BELLEVUE SCALE

The most conspicuous features are, usually, a markedly lowered Digit Span score (impaired attention), a less markedly but still noticeably lowered Arithmetic score (impaired concentration), and a lowered Performance level (tension and resulting inefficiency). Qualitative analysis generally reveals many temporary inefficiencies which may be quickly followed by corrections, easily mobilized tension, and anxiety disrupting both intellectual and fine motor manipulations. The motor awkwardness and fumbling, as well as the impaired ability to plan and later to check the Block Designs and Object Assemblies for accuracy, lower the Performance level but make it clear that tension and not depressive retardation is responsible for this lowering. Word-finding difficulty, impulsive blurting out of unfinished or unchecked responses, and fumbling for proper formulations are also typical.

Typical verbalizations: "There are four pints in a quart... No! Two! Wait a minute... That's right! Four!" "If I was the first to see a fire in a movie I'd... er... I'd... get out as fast as I could... that is, I'd tell the... what do you call them?... Oh!... ushers... first and then I'd... er... I'd get out."

Acute anxiety and depressed mood are frequently the presenting symptoms in cases where decompensation of compulsive defenses is under way. In these instances, the scatter usually reflects both the anxiety state and the compulsive character make-up. Qualitatively, obsessive-compulsive features are outstanding: the record is dominated by pervasive but ineffective attempts at precision, stilted verbalizations, and cumbersome pedantry. For example: "A microscope may be defined as a visual instrument designed to optically enlarge and thereby make visible to the naked eye minutiae." Although the symptomatic diagnosis may be anxiety state or anxiety and depression, the characterological diagnosis will be obsessive-compulsive character make-up.

LEARNING EFFICIENCY

Learning efficiency is often, but by no means always, reduced by the generalized impairment of concentration. The poor efficiency results in a relatively low score. Qualitatively, an out-of-place memory or a fragment of a meaningful unit of the story ("... something about a boy ...") may be present.

SORTING TEST

Often, the general impression yielded is one of spottiness or inconsistency. Sortings tend to be both mildly loose and mildly narrow; conceptualizations fluctuate from the abstract to the concrete level; sporadic, unexpected failures occur. Feeble syncretistic concepts which are one step short of failure are also frequent; for example, "I don't know ... all come from the earth," or, "Maybe because they can all be used." If the anxiety state is present in the setting of a decompensating compulsive character make-up, the meticulous narrowness of the obsessive-compulsive neurotic usually prevails.

RORSCHACH TEST

The typical record has a reduced number of responses (less than 20) and a preponderance of vague and poorly conceived responses. It is as if the concentration impairment interferes both with perceptual articulation of the inkblots and with the summoning up of even an average wealth of associative references. The record seems one step short of extensive blocking, since the responses chosen are often easy ways out rather than full-fledged intellectual achievements. Many of the vague responses embrace the entire inkblot; consequently the $W\%$ may be high without reflecting "quality ambition", good integrative ability, or low-grade intelligence. The vague responses are usually clouds, X-rays, maps, smoke, and the like, with shading as a frequent and powerful determinant. A massing of these vague, heavily shaded responses (ChF and Ch) indicates acute, free-floating anxiety. Because the responses are vague, the form-level may drop below the acceptable range of 65%-80%. However, basically impaired reality testing is not indicated in these cases. Bodily preoccupation is frequent and vague anatomical content may also intrude into the record. The experience balance is usually constricted, reflecting the characteristic inhibition. If CF's accumulate, impulsive, anxiety-ridden outbursts may be expected. Usually, however, one or two F/C or C/F are the only color responses. If several pure C, several failures and a predominance of sexual and anatomical content distinguish the record, an incipient schizophrenia underlying the anxiety state is suggested. Extreme tension tends to reduce the number of shading responses, probably by blocking the relatively subtle introspections usually needed to establish the role of shading as a determinant.

Some of these cases indicate their restlessness and distractibility by massing trivial Dr responses, thereby, in a sense, artificially boosting R. In the absence of other indicators of obsessive-compulsive features, the resulting high $DR\%$ can be taken as indicative of restlessness alone. Other cases fail one or two of the shaded cards and possibly Card IX. In these instances anxiety of paralyzing proportions is suggested: productivity is sharply curtailed, and blocking and tension are dominant.

Some of the cases with anxiety states are characterized by marked irritability, negativism, and demanding aggressiveness. Usually they resist taking the test and are especially ready to reject a card if no easy response is immediately forthcoming. Consequently they often end up with a low R and a constricted experience balance. However, a few violent CF responses of the blood, explosion, and volcano variety may be present. The content and color prevalence of these responses indicates the characteristic irritability and likelihood of aggressive outbursts. Space responses, referring to the negativism, may also accumulate. These subjects are frequently working-class men or farmers, with poor educational backgrounds, who come for examination because of an anxiety state usually accompanied by somatization reactions. Many of them have been seen in the army and in a veterans' hospital by the author. Their general attitude is one characterized by extreme rejection of any free fantasying or thinking for the pleasure of thinking. They cling rigidly to the concrete aspects of experience and become intensely anxious and often seem on the point of a violent, aggressive outburst when "forced" to give responses.

If the anxiety state is present in the setting of a decompensating compulsive mode of adjustment, poorly disguised blocking will be discernible in circumstantial, often exasperating descriptions of the cards.

WORD ASSOCIATION TEST

Occasionally anxious blocking occurs similar to that seen in the records of hysterics; occasionally multiword definitions, which are in effect one step short of blocking, accumulate. Reaction times may be generally slightly delayed. As a rule the formal aspects of the test responses are not diagnostically instructive. The decompensating compulsives sometimes give many responses that are self-references; if strong obsessive-compulsive features dominate the remaining tests, these responses, although very likely indistinguishable in themselves from those given by patients with narcissistic character disorders,[35]) can be considered indicative rather of exacerbated self-preoccupation than of pervasive and enduring egocentricity. The recall of these idiosyncratic responses is usually adequate.

THEMATIC APPERCEPTION TEST

No suggestive diagnostic features other than sporadic blocking, flurries of anxiety in the course of telling the stories, and frequent themes of apprehensiveness are to be expected; even these do not occur frequently. The content of the stories may be quite revealing of the person, but the anxiety state itself will generally have to be inferred from other tests.

NARCISSISTIC CHARACTER DISORDER

This diagnostic term covers those cases characterized by striking egocentricity, extremely low anxiety tolerance, a rigid tendency to avoid anxiety-arousing situations, and solicitation of the affection and assistance of others with minimal return of affection and assistance and a weak capacity for empathy. Emotional lability is a frequent feature and tends to be exploited in shallow histrionics; over-demonstrativeness is frequently superimposed on the basic coldness and distance. Aggressively demanding behavior may also be prominent.

The chief personality features to be sought out are the rigid tendency to forestall, minimize, negate, or otherwise avoid anxiety-arousing, emotional situations; superficially outgoing and spontaneous but basically anxious and solicitous relating to the examiner; fleeting histrionic reactions, changing from problem to problem, test to test, and appointment to appointment. The avoidant tendency will be particularly apparent in attempts to avoid responsible, introspective thinking. Some of these patients will have developed a good deal of charm and wit, and will try to show the examiner a good time; the aim of all this, however, is avoidance and denial of serious problems rather than the expression of genuine friendliness or good spirits.

---

35) See p. 51.

BELLEVUE SCALE

It is most usual to find the Performance level equal or superior to the Verbal level. This discrepancy takes on special diagnostic significance if Picture Arrangement is relatively high and if Arithmetic is relatively low. The discrepancy between the Verbal and Performance levels usually refers to the characteristic emphasis on action or "doing things" and the avoidance of serious, rational application to problems. The high Picture Arrangement indicates the characteristically facile social anticipations. The low Arithmetic indicates the attempts to avoid the anxiety which is so readily stimulated in most patients by these "mental" problems. Low Arithmetic is most frequent in narcissistic *women*. The typical woman in this group protests vigorously that she has always been unable to do such problems, that she has been out of school too long, and so forth. Further, she will by histrionics, charm, or sudden rigid negativism attempt to eliminate the necessity for doing the problems. If the examiner inquires how wrong answers have been arrived at, these patients are prone, after brief floundering around, to say that they guessed. The examiner is usually able to see that the answer is not a guess—for example, "48 men" on Problem 10—and is able to infer that the patient would rather "fake" inadequacy than apply herself or himself responsibly to a more or less introspective and anxiety-arousing problem. Usually this evasiveness is most clearly seen in the Arithmetic subtest, but it is often present throughout the Bellevue Scale and the remaining tests. Another frequent qualitative indicator is the attempt to flaunt a social sophistication, which may vary from the smart alecky or roguish quality to utter disdain, ennui, and even horror at the examiner's naivete. The response to *why should we keep away from bad company?* is particularly instructive in these cases: eyebrows are arched, the concept is disputed, chuckles precede the response, or self-references are made. In Picture Arrangement the *flirt* and *taxi* sequences tend to elicit either impish or hilarious laughter or a bored, supercilious look. The "front" varies but the underlying message is the same: "I refuse to respond to this situation with any sincerity of feeling!" In the Vocabulary subtest impulsive guesses, sometimes based on clang-associations, are often present.

Some of these patients, especially if they are re-tested during the course of psychotherapy, take the test with an air of utmost seriousness, diligent application, and carefulness. The resulting record may resemble that of an obsessive. Careful observation and detailed analysis of verbalization usually reveals, however, that the thoroughness is an attempt to "look good" and thereby to solicit the examiner's approval. In contrast, the true obsessive will be as thorough as *his own demands* on himself require. The narcissist, if encouraged to be brief, can change his style easily; the severe obsessive does not know what brevity means.

Because of their relatively high Performance level and because of the labile affectivity, these patients often resemble hysterics. Hysterics, however, are generally more passive and less actively solicitous or demanding, more naive and less "sophisticated" or crassly egotistical, and generally more restrained, although sporadic affective displays may be much more intense. This same differential diagnostic problem arises in nearly all the other tests so that the tester cannot pass the buck to the Rorschach Test, for example, but must try to solve the problem in each test by careful qualitative analysis. Many patients with character disorders create an atmosphere of being easy to test; unless they are continuously pinned down, however, the examiner will be left with records full of evasions and ambiguities.

LEARNING EFFICIENCY

No characteristic indicators occur in this test. In some cases, there is a half-feigned catastrophic response upon hearing that a story will have to be remembered; as a result the intake of the material may be hampered and the quantity of recall may be relatively low. Extreme drops or qualitative distortions are not usual.

SORTING TEST

Conceptualizations generally fluctuate between adequate abstractions and concrete, egocentric fabulations. In Part I, the fabulatory approach usually leads to a few sortings that are loose. For example, the smoking items and, later, the index card may be sorted with the pipe: "Well, I guess I'll have to play I'm in a cigar store. There! I bought all these things; I might have to pay the check (index card)." Verbalizations of this type imply that the subject is not trying to adapt to conventional conceptual rules and demands, but is content to abide by immediate, personal associations—a basically egocentric approach. In Part II, when difficulty is encountered, fabulations of the above type or else vague, evasive concepts such as "all found in the house" are likely to occur. The fabulations almost invariably refer to home, family, children and grown-ups, and personal preferences; restriction to this type of content assists in eliminating the possibility that schizophrenic impairment of concept formation is involved.[36])

----

36) See pp. 67—69.

RORSCHACH TEST

Almost invariably the outstanding feature of the Rorschach Test is a weakness of, and resistiveness toward introspective efforts and sustained intellectual application of any type. As a result, R is rarely above average, the $F+\%$ is borderline (60% - 65%), the subtle experiencing of shading as a determinant is not elicited in inquiry even where the response is most likely based in part at least on shading, and easy, grossly articulated, evasive responses (maps, butterflies, insects) are numerous. There is a quality of basic passivity implicit in these records: the subject does not do much to the inkblot in order to pull out a response; the responses are equivalent to the vague concepts in the Sorting Test and the shoddy Bellevue Scale responses. Often a very low $W\%$ indicates the characteristic weakness of integrative efforts.

Many narcissists have a pretentious front and emphasize W's, but as a rule these W's are vague and nearly arbitrary. Some of these cases, characterized by excessive emotional lability, amass CF responses and neglect the FC responses; for example, the color distribution might be $3\,FC$ and $8\,CF$. In such instances, the genuine lability is likely to be displayed in dramatic, but none the less artificial over-responsiveness and over-demonstrativeness. The colder, more rigidly narcissistic characters tend to give few colors, perhaps one CF or one vague C, and one or no M's; in these instances, the histrionic, demonstrative quality of behavior is usually so shallow and transient that the entire person seems like a caricature. One recent case, a frequently divorced "Petty" girl in her late thirties, had an experience balance of one M and one pure C. Her record will be discussed in Chapter 4.

A few narcissists give quantitatively dilated records with R exceeding 40 or 50. They usually amass CF responses. Differential diagnosis from hysteria can in most instances be safely made on the basis of this productivity alone, since an hysteric rarely gives more than 30 responses. Differential diagnosis from the obsessive, who is also productive, can be made by reference to the emphasis on color over movement, the absence of meticulousness, the prevalence of sweeping, reckless interpretations (W may go as high as 15 or 20 with little real integration) and the massing of "gay" and sensuous content. The content frequently includes jewelry, dresses or materials, ornate household decorations, Mardi Gras costumes or impressions, foods and ice cream and cotton candy, and the like. In these responses the colors frequently have textural qualities (the *sheen* of satin or *graininess* of ice cream), indicating a characteristic sensuous quality. In these records $F(C)$ responses may also be frequent, referring to the narcissist's acute but superficial sensitivity to nuances of interpersonal relationships.

As a rule, the more productive of the character disorders are more actively, responsively, cleverly, and charmingly solicitous than the less productive cases, who tend to be more inert, inhibited, parasitic, and demanding rather than ingratiating.

If several M's are present in a dilated, clearly narcissistic record, or if extravagant fabulations are foisted onto more or less ordinary responses, it is implied that the subject experiences his play-acting so vividly that he can no longer sustain the distinction between what is sincerely felt and what is only feigned.

Occasionally one of these patients gives very few responses. We have seen as little as four responses in the Rorschach Test records of some patients with character disorders. In these cases there was no suggestion that the blocking resulted from a schizophrenic, hysteric, organic, depressive, paranoid or mentally defective condition. It appears that this restricted productivity is a consequence of extremely low anxiety tolerance and the associated need to avoid any unfamiliar, unstructured situation. This is avoidance *in advance* of the crystallization of any threatening situation. The few responses obtained are generally popular animals or human details. Some of these patients indicate their escapist tendencies in a massing of peripheral *De* and *Dr* responses, particularly on the heavily shaded and colored cards, in a context of generally restricted productivity.

WORD ASSOCIATION TEST

The more overtly narcissistic of these cases usually indicate their basic weakness of object-attachments by frequent, more or less bland self-references: *woman* — "me"; *intercourse* — "wonderful"; husband — "my own"; *party*—"lots of fun"; *men*—"yes!"; *masturbate*—"never!" and so on. It is less significant that the patient enjoys parties, men, and intercourse than that she apperceives the testing situation in a purely egocentric fashion and, by not being bound by conventional conceptual relationships when they are so compelling to most other subjects, demonstrates that this egocentricity has an ingrained and pervasive quality. These responses are reminiscent of the egocentric concepts in the Sorting Test. Exaggerated labile reactions to words like *snake* and *dirt* ("horrible!") and *gun* ("bang!") are also frequent and again raise the problem of differential diagnosis from hysteria. The avoidant tendency is frequently evident in the attempt to offer as responses the names of objects in the room, words thought of before hearing the stimulus words, clang associations or impulsive phrase-completions (book-"ends").

THEMATIC APPERCEPTION TEST

Generally the stories are characterized by one or more of four superficially different, but basically similar qualities: the stories may be flat, superficial, deliberately unrevealing; they may be meagre and incomplete; they may be spitefully or tauntingly anti-social, perverse, "lewd", or otherwise (the patient hopes) shocking; or they may be facetious, gay, and characterized by trick endings.

In the first instance the stories can be so pat, conventional, restricted to the most obvious connotations of the pictures and yet neatly complete that inquiry is forcefully discouraged. At least the patient hopes so. Compliance with instructions has been perfect. The obvious absence of empathy with any of the situations portrayed reflects the basic coldness and distance of the narcissist.

In the second instance, as in the Rorschach Test, the patient resists even considering the picture carefully and does not allow himself the dangerous liberty of a fantasy about it. Pressure to make him give the outcome of the situation or the motives behind the actions of the characters is usually fruitless. At best an arbitrary, "spiteful" ending or motive will be verbalized: "Because he was a crazy patient at Menningesr's"; "After he finishes looking out at the beautiful sunset, his mother sneaks up on him and pushes him out the window." Here again the strong avoidant tendency and the characteristically low anxiety tolerance are clear.

In the third instance, the stories may become quite callous: "This gal is a farmer's daughter and was just knocked up in the barn by a traveling salesman"; "This gal is getting ready to jump off the bridge; she does; she makes a little splash and drowns." Or the stories may become more or less "lewd": "This is a whorehouse and the man is complaining to the madam about this girl"; "This guy is handing the girl a line and she's falling for it; after a hot night in a hotel room, he takes off and leaves her to pay the bill."

In the fourth instance the patient hopes to forestall the experiencing of anxiety or a valid emotion by frantically and relentlessly trying to be funny. He may go so far as to tell formal jokes.

A series of these evasive, erratic, or cold stories implies that stable identification-figures and object-attachments are lacking, that there is no one life-role that is the subject's own and that he can sense as being reflected in the stimulus pictures, that capacity for empathy is weak and that there are few, if any, general values that he will stand up for.

ALCOHOL ADDICTION

The cases in this group fall on a continuum between *essential* alcoholism and *reactive* alcoholism.[37] The essential alcoholics are unreliable, irresponsible, insincere persons, who begin drinking in their teens without significant precipitating factors in reality, never demonstrate sufficient perseverance and desire for mastery to accomplish anything worthwhile, seldom maintain friendships over long periods of time, are predominantly dependent and demanding in their interpersonal relationships, depend on multiform oral gratifications, and easily develop gastrointestinal disturbances. Orality is the keynote of these character disorders. Reactive alcoholics, in contrast, begin drinking relatively late in their careers following some special stress and have a history that demonstrates a responsible attitude toward themselves and others; in these cases, the alcoholism stems from a decompensation of compulsive defense and a relatively unchecked emergence of passive needs.

According to our experience the test results of patients who approximate the above description of the essential alcoholics include many or all of the indications pertaining to narcissistic character disorders. Low anxiety tolerance, generalized avoidant tendencies, egocentricity, weak introspectiveness, facetiousness, and demanding, dependent relationships are prominent in their test results. In addition, rather clear indications of the pervasive orality of these cases are usually present. The Rorschach Test frequently contains responses involving food, eating, or mouths. The Thematic Apperception Test stories may refer frequently to drinking and eating, intoxication and alcoholic bouts.

Strong conflict over oral-passive needs is almost invariably indicated in the Word Association Test: conspicuous disturbances in reaction to words with oral connotations (breast, drink, suck, mouth, bite, and so forth), are generally abundant. These disturbances include delayed reactions, affective expressions, false recall, and unusual or vivid responses. One recently tested woman addict, whose word associations were generally orderly and conventional, responded to *drink* with a vivid image of a Bourbon and soda which included ice-cubes, bubbles, and frost on a tall glass, and she responded to *suck* with a vivid image of herself sucking the juice out of an orange through a small hole cut

---

37) Knight, R. P. "The Dynamics and Treatment of Alcohol Addiction," *Bulletin of the Menninger Clinic*, 1937, Volume 1, No. 7:233-250.

in the shell. These overspecific, vivid responses, if they stand in contrast to the rest of the record, suggest an addictive trend. A word of caution: these "oral" stimulus words are more or less disturbing to most patients, presumably because oral-passive needs play such an important role in most illnesses; only if these are the *only* or the *most* conspicuously disturbing words is an addictive trend suggested. Of course, the low anxiety tolerance and the passivity should be evident throughout the tests before any specific statement can be made.

Severe addictions of very long duration present a special problem. The test results, particularly in the Bellevue Scale and Rorschach Test, are often characterized more than anything else by debilitation, sloppiness, fluidity, and unintegratedness. It is frequent to find the Verbal level consistently lower than the Vocabulary level by 2 or 3 points, and some of the Performance functions may be quite impaired relative to the Vocabulary level. Easy Information items may be inexcusably missed, word misusages may be frequent, the sequence of reasoning may be loose. Learning efficiency may be greatly lowered. In the Rorschach Test the form level is usually quite low, the use of colors may be arbitrary, and fluid or arbitrary responses suggestive of contaminations may occur. Perceptual distortions tend to occur frequently in the Thematic Apperception Test. Differential diagnosis from schizophrenia is often difficult; only the fact that clear-cut schizophrenic productions are absent makes it probable that the test results reflect the breakdown of integrative functions associated with chronic addiction. In some instances the emotional blunting and inappropriateness, and the looseness of thinking are so severe that a psychotic, non-schizophrenic condition is indicated.

The reactive alcoholics frequently present the test picture described in the section on anxiety states as typical for decompensating compulsive characters. In addition, it is usual to find a special emphasis on oral content in the projective tests. In many instances of reactive addiction the addictive trend is not evident in the test results.

PSYCHOPATHIC CHARACTER DISORDER

This diagnostic term as used here is not meant to apply indiscriminately to overtly aggressive persons, nor to those who commit crimes on the basis of particular neurotic conflicts. It is meant to be applied in a narrow sense to persons who are characterized by the following features: (1) a long history of coming into conflict with legal or social rules or both; (2) blandness with respect to anti-social acts and to the absence of an over-all life pattern, although in individual situations remorse or anxiety may be felt or feigned; (3) a general lack of time-perspective; (4) minimal capacity for delay of impulses; (5) a superficially ingratiating, over-polite, and deferent manner of relating to other persons.

The chief personality features to be sought out are weak integrative ability and underlying primitiveness of thinking, blandness, ostentatious overcompliance covering a basic callousness and inability to empathize with others, impulsiveness, fabulizing, and preoccupation with anti-social behavior. The patterns to be described have been seen mainly in the records of adolescent psychopaths, but appear to represent adequately the test results of many older psychopaths.

BELLEVUE SCALE

The characteristic pattern is a superiority of the Performance level over the Verbal, low scores on Comprehension and Similarities and high scores on the tests of visual-motor coordination and speed. Often the Digit Span score does not drop, reflecting the characteristic blandness. Frequently Picture Arrangement is conspicuously high; this is especially true for shrewd "schemers". If Picture Completion is high, over-alertness or watchfulness is probably characteristic. The over-all pattern will indicate that this is a bland, unreflective, action-oriented person whose judgment is poor, whose conceptual development is weak, but whose grasp of social situations may yet be quick and accurate.

Qualitatively the chief feature is usually blazing recklessness in guessing at answers. This is particularly apparent in Information and Vocabulary: "George Bernard Shaw wrote Faust." "Magellan discovered the North Pole." "Chattel means a place to live (chateau)." "Ballast is a dance (ballet)." "Proselyte means prostitute," and so forth. These smack very much of the naive guesses of some hysterics or narcissists with low intelligence levels, but the high Picture Arrangement, the low Comprehension score, the blandly high Digit Span, the consistently brazenly pretentious and ostentatiously complaint quality of the verbalizations, and the remaining test results will facilitate the differential diagnosis. It is rare to find a psychopath with a Verbal IQ above the average range; the Performance IQ in contrast may reach the superior or very superior range.[38]) If the Verbal IQ is high, but the other features persist, the clinical diagnosis is likely to be character disorder. The responses to

---

38) Although the Block Designs subtest clearly involves conceptual processes, psychopaths often do exceptionally well in this subtest despite exceptionally weak *verbal* concept formation.

why should we keep away from bad company? and *why are laws necessary?* are likely to be perfect.

LEARNING EFFICIENCY

No particular patterns have been observed. The amount of retention should be appropriate to the general Verbal level in the Bellevue Scale.

SORTING TEST

A few fabulations in a setting of generally concrete conceptualizations are usual. These tend to occur in Part II. The psychopath is inclined to be cautious in all the tests—even the reckless guesses in the Information and Vocabulary subtests are blandly considered to be "good tries" —so that as a rule only when he cannot form an adequately comprehensive concrete concept does he resort to a fabulation.

RORSCHACH TEST

Usually the Rorschach Test is flat and vague; however, the psychopath characteristically adds numerous embellishments to the gross, colorless responses in a clearly fabulatory manner. Thus the number of responses is usually 10 to 20, the $A\%$ is high, the $F+\%$ low ($50\%-65\%$), and sharp percepts are rarely developed. The popular bear skin on Cards IV or VI is often described in detail and inferences drawn: "When he was cutting this skin off, the trapper must have been using a dull knife because it's so ragged; he probably skinned it because it had this unusual stripe down the back." A few CF's may be present or only a few FC's. The former pattern suggests conspicuous aggressiveness and impulsiveness; the latter pattern suggests a special emphasis on an overcompliant "front". Shading—the chief indication of anxiety in this test—is likely to be absent. Some of these patients may give exceptionally primitive records with several DW or DW-tendencies, perseverative content (anatomy, crabs, or maps), and a pervasive absence of articulated percepts. In these instances the $W\%$ is usually high but, because it is based on vagueness, it refers to weak analytic and integrative abilities. As a rule, however, the weak integrative ability is seen in a low $W\%$, even in a small record. We have seen records given by psychopaths with as few as one or two W's. The contrast of the alert, pretentious "front" and the shallow, primitive, but embellished creative thinking in the Rorschach Test record is a reliable diagnostic pattern.

WORD ASSOCIATION TEST

Psychopaths are likely to give a few clang associations, particularly when they do not know the meaning of a stimulus word. *Masturbation* may elicit "operation" or "master" or "bait" purely on the basis of phonetic associations. They are also likely to give a few phrase-completions (*book*—"worm", *table*—"cloth", *mountain*—"top"). In a setting of low verbal intelligence, both types of response indicate an impulsive, unreflective mode of thinking.[39]) Occasionally a psychopath will, like the evasive narcissist, systematically name objects in the room, prepare answers in advance, or search for rhymes.

THEMATIC APPERCEPTION TEST

Three types of stories are most usual, and frequently occur in the same record: (1) detailed, vivid, and often instructive stories about burglaries, hold-ups, murders, prison sentences, and jail-breaks; (2) idyllic stories, in which love, honor, and "virtue is its own reward" are prevailing themes; (3) rambling, tediously overdetailed stories with no point to them at all.

The first type of story is a reflection of a dominant preoccupation, especially if it is frequent. Sometimes an entire record will be one big "cops and robbers" sequence, indicating an orientation to the world almost exclusively based on the conflict between makers and breakers of laws. Guilt feelings are conspicuous by their absence. Other values, identifications, or interests are quite weak. Empathy for persons in trouble is rarely evident, while a callous "save your own skin" attitude may be striking.

The second type of story usually is not to be taken seriously once the psychopathy is established; it may appear as if the subject has some depth, warmth, or hopes for himself in these stories—which is exactly the impression he intends to convey—but the isolation of these themes and their beatific quality give them away as unreliable.

The third type of story is usually an example of aggressive overcompliance. For example, a story will be told of a young man leaving home; he goes into the army; his army experiences are described; he comes back home; he opens a hardware store; his business troubles are described; he gets married; he has three children—two boys and a girl; and so forth, and so forth. There will come a time when the examiner

---

39) Some intelligent normals with superior verbal facility tend to give these also.

will almost desperately take the card away from the zealous subject, only to face a similar barrage of cold "compliance" on the next card.

NEUROTIC AND PSYCHOTIC DEPRESSION

In these cases, pervasive sadness and inertia, self-directed rage and feelings of worthlessness are outstanding. Psychotic depressives have delusions of guilt and may be withdrawn and extremely inert, or agitated; neurotic depressives have strong feelings of guilt and despair·but are not delusional and do not reach the extremes of agitation or inertia seen in psychotic depressives.

It is difficult to distinguish severe neurotic depressives from psychotic depressives, psychotic depressives from acute paranoid schizophrenics with depressive features[40]), neurotic depressives from other types of neurotics who are depressed at the time of testing or from tense and inhibited normals.

The chief features to be sought in the test results are retardation of perceptual, associative, and motor processes, emotional inhibition, frequent expressions of inadequacy and despair, and irritability or negativistic passivity.

BELLEVUE SCALE

The Performance subtest scores, particularly the scores on the visual-motor subtests, are usually clearly much lower (3 or more units) than the scores on Information and Vocabulary. The greater this discrepancy, the more profound the depression is likely to be. This pattern does not indicate that depression is the only symptom, however; it merely indicates that depression is a conspicuous symptom. Only if no other diagnostic indicators accumulate, is it safe to diagnose the case as a depression.

It is important that all the Performance scores drop: if only one or two are extremely low, or if the Block Designs score is high while the rest are extremely low, schizophrenia is suggested; if only the Block Designs or Object Assembly score or both are clearly but not extremely low, not depression but more or less incapacitating tension is suggested. The latter is particularly true if observation of test behavior reveals that the attack on the visual-motor items is rapid, fumbling, and planless rather than slow and dispirited. Occasionally an *agitated* psychotic depressive achieves adequate Performance scores. More often it is the neurotic depressives who have retained some drive who achieve this, rendering the Bellevue Scale diagnostically ambiguous.

----

40) See p. 84.

Depressives are often in the older age range, where the test norms allow a certain amount of decline of performance abilities. Nevertheless a comparison of the Verbal and Performance IQ's, which should be approximately equal at all age levels (within 5—10 points of each other), usually demonstrates that the drop of the Performance level cannot be accounted for on the basis of advanced age alone.

Inspection of the scatter of Verbal subtest scores frequently facilitates differential diagnosis between psychotic and neurotic depression. Psychotic depressives tend to have great Verbal scatter. Especially Comprehension, but also Similarities and Arithmetic are the scores most likely to show a great drop below the Information-Vocabulary level. The subtests requiring active reasoning or concentration are thus more vulnerable than those dealing with more static achievements. The Verbal scatter, if not extreme, is helpful in determining the character make-up on which the depression is superimposed; i. e., obsessive, hysteric, schizoid. Digit Span is almost invariably low, reflecting the acute anxiety experienced by these cases. If Digit Span is high, schizophrenia or a severely schizoid character make-up is suggested and the differential diagnosis must be made.

Qualitatively the verbal responses tend to be monosyllabic, uncertain and self-critical. Depressives are rarely talkative and rarely yield any appreciable amount of spontaneous elaboration or qualification of responses. If the subject is articulate or loquacious, the depression is not likely to be profound; and if such a subject yields a record with an extreme drop of the Performance level, schizophrenia is indicated.[41] Peculiarities of verbalization are rare, even in the records of psychotic depressives, and in this setting are indicative of schizophrenia. A few perceptual distortions in Picture Arrangement and Picture Completion are found in the records of some psychotic depressives, and are usually indicative of paranoid features in the depressive delusions.

LEARNING EFFICIENCY

Learning efficiency is almost invariably profoundly impaired in the records of psychotic depressives, and is frequently much impaired in the records of neurotic depressives. The impairment is often indistinguishable from that of schizophrenics:[42] quantitatively the recall is meager;

---

41) Cases with organic brain damage may also yield this pattern. They often tend to be self-critical, too, expressing the decline of self-esteem associated with their loss of abilities.

42) See p. 67; organics often show similar impairment.

qualitatively it is scattered in sequence, fragmented, and colored by the introduction of new material and elaboration of old material. Particularly the aggressive connotations of the story are enriched or repressed. If the impairment is extreme, a psychosis is suggested, but differential diagnosis must be made on the basis of other tests. Some psychotic depressives refuse to try to remember, claiming in advance that they are too inadequate to do so.

SORTING TEST

The test record as a whole is generally characterized by narrowness of the concept span. Failures and narrow sortings are frequent in Part I; failures and split-narrow conceptualizations are frequent in Part II. Many of the concepts are concrete or functional. In general, the more severe the depression, the more these characteristics will prevail. In the records of some neurotic depressives, only traces of narrowing are detectable; consequently the record has a compulsive rather than depressed quality. The records of other neurotic depressives may be totally unrevealing. Fabulations and loose sortings are not to be glossed over: they are often among the few signs in all the tests which correctly suggest that the diagnosis is rather schizophrenia with depressive features than psychotic depression.

RORSCHACH TEST

The most striking features of the Rorschach Test are meagerness of productivity and flatness of quality. The Verbal scores in the Bellevue Scale generally make it clear that mental deficiency is not involved. The more profound the depression, the duller the record is likely to be. Except in the records of mild neurotic depressives, the following features are typical: (1) R below 20 and often below 15; (2) $F\%$ above 80; (3) no more than one M; (4) sum C no more than 1.5 (one pure C, usually "blood" on II or III); (5) $A\%$ above 50%; (6) $P\%$ above 30%; (7) no more than 4 or 5 W; (8) one or more failures; (9) generally elongated reaction times; (10) frequent self-criticisms, which may be implicit in criticism of responses offered or explicit; (11) occasional subtly aggressive criticisms of the test or examiner. Thus the record primarily indicates retardation of perceptual and associative processes, emotional inhibition, feelings of inadequacy and worthlessness, and pent-up aggressiveness.

In the records of some psychotic depressives the $At\%$ is quite high and the $F+\%$ is, accordingly, low. Otherwise the $F+\%$ of depressives is usually high—above 80%. If vague anatomical content is absent, the record generally consists almost entirely of the most simple and popular responses.

If rare, strained, or colorful responses suddenly intrude into an otherwise dull, stereotyped, and blocked record, a schizophrenia or an obsessional neurosis with severe depressive features must be suspected. One recent case, a blocked acute paranoid schizophrenic, gave a record in all respects similar to a depressive record, except for the following response on Card VIII: "Two animals (side pink) climbing a mountain (upper gray-green)." The strained integrative effort (distorted perspective) implicit in this response was one of the few crucial features in the entire battery that assisted the differential diagnosis from depression. This rule holds only in most and not in all cases; we have seen a few psychotic depressives who gave confabulated responses.[43])

WORD ASSOCIATION TEST

The total record is usually characterized by absence of associative freedom or agility. Reaction times generally exceed 2 seconds and only on the "easiest" words (dog, chair, and the like) may they be shorter. The "traumatic" words, regardless of specific connotation, generally elicit the longest delays. Qualitatively the associations are characterized by conceptual "closeness" to the stimulus words: blocking and retardation preclude too much success in the search for "another word", and as a result multiword, often functional, definitions are frequent. A few purely personal and apparently "distant" associations may occur. Schizophrenics with depressive features may give similar records; most of these, however, give several bizarre definitions and thereby facilitate the differential diagnosis.

THEMATIC APPERCEPTION TEST

Several types of records may be obtained. In some profound depressions, nothing beyond monosyllabic descriptions of each picture may be offered spontaneously, and inquiry will be like "pulling teeth". In others, the pictures may elicit agitated, tearful reactions, the patient being over-responsive to their gloomy implications. A third type of record is that replete with symbolic interpretations centering around happiness and unhappiness: shadows symbolize dark despair and light areas symbolize hope, success, or joy. A fourth type of record deals in

---

43) See p. 478, *Diagnostic Psychological Testing*, Vol. II.

the main with crime and punishment, guilt and expiation through suffering or destruction. A fifth type, more often obtained from neurotic depressives, contains numerous themes indicative of despair: ventures are unsuccessful, escape from ruin is impossible, loss of love objects is inevitable, death is desirable, and so forth. The stories of some neurotic depressives, though revealing of preoccupations and conflicts, do not, however, indicate the depression. Long stories are not to be expected from any depressive; if present, they suggest that depression is not the central diagnostic feature. The stories should be short, incomplete, vague, and stereotyped.

SCHIZOPHRENIA

INTRODUCTION

Before beginning the discussion of the differential diagnosis of schizophrenia, it is necessary to take up several considerations which will be basic to the entire subsequent presentation.

Schizophrenic disorganization is indicated by four aspects of the intra-individual and inter-individual variations of efficiency and achievement. 1. *What varies?* In the Rorschach Test, for example, variations in the number of responses are generally less diagnostically significant with reference to schizophrenia than variations in the number of color responses. 2. *In which direction does it vary?* In the Bellevue Scale, for example, variations of Digit Span *upward* rather than downward are generally the diagnostically most significant. 3. *How much does it vary?* In the Word Association Test, for example, a few personal associations have little significance whereas a preponderance of personal associations is ominous. 4. *What is the quality or content of the variation?* In the Sorting Test, for example, a syncretistic concept such as "all come from the ground" has little significance when compared to "all piercing or stabbing instruments"; and in the Rorschach Test the pure C response "decayed flesh" is diagnostically significant while the pure C response "sunset" is diagnostically ambiguous.

It is not necessary that the indications of schizophrenia in any particular set of test results embrace all four aspects of variation. Usually only two or three aspects are clear and sometimes even one type of variation will suffice to indicate the correct diagnosis. Herein lies one of the main problems or pitfalls of research into, or expositions of, the test results of schizophrenics: for the most part no one type of variation can be shown to be present in a sufficiently large percentage of cases to be firmly established on statistical grounds as a valid diagnostic indication. It is partly for this reason that publications of the scatter patterns of schizophrenics in the Bellevue Scale so often disagree among themselves regarding what is "typical" or whether anything is "typical". The fact remains that test results, especially those obtained by a *battery* of tests, will in the great majority of individual cases indicate whether or not schizophrenia is the diagnosis. It is one purpose of the following discussion to demonstrate that this contradiction between the results of studies of groups and studies of individuals is not to be dismissed as merely illustrating the inevitable clash between science and intuition. To a large extent specification of the four aspects of diagnostic variation is possible.

This specification of diagnostic variations is, however, complicated by a second major problem. The test responses of almost all schizophrenic subjects are greatly shaped by enduring, non-schizoid aspects of premorbid character make-up. Thus a person who has relied heavily on obsessive defenses, and who has ultimately developed a schizophrenia, will most likely yield patterns throughout the tests that are clearly indicative of past achievements and present qualities referable to obsessiveness. Similarly for a person with a pronounced premorbid emphasis on repressive defense. Now, we have already seen that the diagnostic Bellevue Scale patterns of the intellectualizing obsessives and the repressive hysterics are, as a rule, markedly different from each other. Psychologically there is no reason to expect that the development of a schizophrenia represents a *complete* abandonment of premorbid adjustment efforts and a *complete* loss of associated achievements; and, on the basis of empirical test results, it is clear that there is no such complete break with the past. Consequently, if the scatter patterns of a premorbidly hysteric-like schizophrenic and a premorbidly obsessive-like schizophrenic are compared, it is likely that in one case the score on the Information subtest will be strikingly low and that in the other it will be strikingly high. In other words, *it cannot be assumed that all variations in test results are referable to the presence of the psychosis.* Nor can it be assumed that the non-psychotic variations are purely random. Extreme exaggerations of certain patterns will often indicate both the persistance of premorbid adjustment-efforts and achievements based on them, and the effects of the psychosis on these achievements and adjustment-efforts. Here, then, is another pitfall of research and exposition. The following discussion, in the very incomplete way our present understanding allows, will attempt to distinguish variations referable to non-schizophrenic factors and variations pertaining directly to the effects of the psychosis on intellectual and emotional processes and achievements.

A third pitfall of research and exposition is that different diagnostic indications in the test results pertain to different aspects of the schizophrenic syndrome. A pattern of test results does not indicate schizophrenia; it indicates an identifying characteristic of schizophrenia. Depending on whether the patient is a paranoid or unclassified or simple schizophrenic, whether he is in an acute or chronic or deteriorated stage, whether he is distinguished by confusion and blocking, or excitement, or blandness, the diagnostic patterns will vary. In most studies of schizophrenics there has been no subdivision of cases according to the various possible identifying characteristics; this has been particularly true in studies of patterns of scatter in the Bellevue Scale. Rapaport, Gill, and Schafer in *Diagnostic Psychological Testing* attempted this type of breakdown and demonstrated to some degree that diagnostic patterns do change with changes in the schizophrenic syndrome. We are, however, far from fully comprehending the specific significance of many of the patterns we use in diagnosing schizophrenia.

With these considerations in the mind, the reader may find the discussion of the test results in schizophrenia more meaningful. The following discussion will first present a general summary of diagnostic indications, and will then take up the distinctive patterns of the various schizophrenic sub-groups. As far as possible, the patterns will be linked to particular aspects of the schizophrenic syndrome.

BELLEVUE SCALE

1. *Extreme scatter of subtest scores.* If one or more of the scores deviates extremely from the Information-Vocabulary level, or if nearly all the scores show striking, though not necessarily extreme variability among themselves, schizophrenic disorganization of thinking is suggested. The following sets of subtest scores exemplify this rule:

	Case No. 1	Case No. 2	Case No. 3	Case No. 4	Case No. 5	Av.
Comprehension	12	5	11	7	10	9.0
Information	10	11	12	10	14	11.4
Digit Span	14	6	3	11	16	10.0
Arithmetic	6	7	14	13	8	9.6
Similarities	11	8	12	8	15	10.8
Vocabulary	11	13	12	10	15	12.2
Picture Arrangement	8	10	4	8	11	8.2
Picture Completion	6	8	10	13	6	8.6
Block Designs	12	6	10	10	16	10.8
Object Assembly	12	6	11	10	13	10.4
Digit Symbol	6	13	9	6	10	8.8

The averages are included to indicate how diagnostic patterns tend to cancel each other out when *groups* of schizophrenics are studied. The high Digit Span of Case No. 1 and the low Digit Span of Case No. 3 can both be diagnostic; the high Arithmetic and high Picture Completion of Case No. 4 and the low Arithmetic and low Picture Completion of Cases No. 1 and No. 5 can all be diagnostic.

There are, however, certain scores which tend to drop more often and more dramatically in the records of schizophrenics than in those of other types of cases, and these are the scores on Comprehension, Arithmetic and Picture Completion. Thus the characteristic impairments of judgment and concentration in schizophrenia are often immediately apparent in the scatter. Other scores—the scores on Digit Span, Picture Arrangement and Object Assembly—drop in many types of cases, including some normals; only if there is an extreme drop of these scores (8 or more points if the general level is superior, or 6 or more points if the level is average or below) does the scatter of these scores become diagnostically suggestive. As is generally true, the scatter analysis must be supported by qualitative analysis and by the results in other tests.

2. *Qualitative indications.* (a) *Information:* failing a number of very easy items and passing a number of difficult ones; incorrect answers or "can't remember" on items which should be passed on the basis of special interests or training, as when a musician fails the *Faust* item, a lawyer fails the *habeas corpus* item, or a history teacher fails the *Rome* or *Tokyo* items; wild guesses in a setting of high intelligence, such as that "Marco Polo discovered the North Pole," "Rickenbacker invented the airplane," "Tom Sawyer wrote Huckleberry Finn"; stilted, neologistic verbalizations, such as "A thermometer is an emercurated tube to measure the degrees of temperature in Fahrenheits"; impulsive, absurd answers even if corrected, such as "Washington's birthday is July 4". Most of these patterns reflect disorganized memory functioning and loss of previous achievements. (b) *Comprehension:* failing one or more easy items and passing the difficult ones; bringing in irrelevant preoccupations such as syphilis on the *born deaf* item; consistently egocentric responses *offered seriously,* such as neglecting the letter in the street because "it's not my business" or reading the letter because of "curiosity"; elaborating clearly inappropriate courses of action, such as singing the national anthem from the stage of the burning theater to prevent panic, or building a hut in the forest "until someone found me"; inappropriately intense moralistic reactions to the *bad company, laws,* and *marriage license* items; irrelevant intellectualizing, such as (on the *taxes* item), "It all began with the idea of no taxation without representation";

answering other questions than those put by the examiner, such as explaining why people should be "good" on the *bad company* item. In general, these types of errors reflect schizophrenic impairment of judgment. (c) *Digit Span*: clear-cut superiority of digits backward over digits forward, such as 7 backward and 4 forward; extreme superiority of digits forward over digits backward, such as 9 forward and 3 backward; arbitrary "systems" to facilitate remembering, such as "adding them up". The last is a clear instance of impaired judgment. (d) *Arithmetic*: failing most of the easy items and passing one or more of the last three difficult items; [44]) approximate answers such as "about 50" or "roughly 100"; inability to profit from even the most obvious assistance on easy items which have been failed; bizarre attempts at solution; adherence to the idea of 3-cent stamps on the stamp items; a literal approach to the problems which is sincere and not feigned for the sake of a laugh (as is often the case with character disorders), such as disputing that 7 pounds of sugar cost 25 cents. The unusual failures appear to reflect impairment of the ability to concentrate; the literality reflects the concreteness of thinking so often seen in schizophrenia; the bizarre attempts to approximate answers reflect impaired judgment. (e) *Similarities*: failing or contaminating good answers on easy items ("orange and banana are *citrus* fruits"), and passing difficult ones; extreme syncretistic, expansive concepts such as "composed of cells", or "inanimate objects", or "lacking human intelligence"; extreme concrete and fabulated concepts,[45]) such as, "Fly and tree are similar in that you may be fly-fishing and catch your line in the branches of a tree", or "Egg and seed are alike because you have to feed seed to the chicken and it will be healthy and can lay eggs"; consistent, negativistic denial of similarity, yielding a low score, when the intellectual level is above average; consistently offering differences in addition to or instead of similarities. (f) *Vocabulary*: failing easy items and passing difficult ones; blandly associating to vocabulary words, such as *fur*—"soft" and *diamond*—"pretty"; impulsive, extremely strained clang-associations as bases for defining words,[46]) such as, "Traduce means three deuces when you play cards", or "Belfry means a kind of bellboy". (g) *Picture Arrangement*: distorted percepts or confusion, such as seeing the Little King as two different persons in

---

44) Certain patients with character disorders may do the same, however.

45) Certain patients with character disorders may do the same, however.

46) Mildly strained instances of this are not unusual in the records of character disorders, psychopaths, and naive hysterics. The distinction is often difficult to draw. Sometimes subjects with a low intelligence level and weak cultural background also do the same.

the same story, or not being able to identify the elevator despite good intelligence; *extreme* discrepancies between the sequence offered and the story told; fragmentation or blocking of anticipations on easy items so that each picture is discussed in isolation and continuity is lost; strange and arbitrary anticipations which are based on peripheral details or even totally extraneous considerations. (h) *Picture Completion*: failing easy items and passing difficult ones; frequently referring to attributes or details obviously not intended to be present, such as colors, designs, the rest of the body in a picture of a head, the other eye in profile pictures, food in the pig's bucket, or the captain on the bridge of the steamer; inability to recognize certain objects, such as the playing card or light bulb, despite good intelligence (usually occurs where confusion is a symptom) . (i) *Block Designs*: using colors other than red and white, especially if red or white blocks are being used at the same time; persistent acceptance of grossly incorrect designs as correct, such as building diagonal rows of all-red and all-white blocks on item 6 and insisting on the correctness of the result after being asked to "make sure"; persistent rendering of the designs upside down; planless but relaxed rotation and "fitting" of blocks until some solution is reached (pattern coherence); readiness to ruin a correct design at the least suggestion from the examiner that it may be incorrect. For the most part these errors reflect defective reality testing or impairment of conceptual thinking. (j) *Object Assembly*: misrecognition or lack of recognition of the profile or the hand after the object has been assembled; planless but relaxed fitting of contours, frequently leading to correct solution, but often so unresponsive to cues as to indicate defective reality testing and blocking of anticipations, as by getting one-half of the ear correct on the profile after the face parts and occipital piece are correctly placed, and then trying to fit the other half-ear all around the periphery of the head; acceptance on any of the items of absurd placements, such as accepting or even seriously attempting the reversal of arms and legs on the mannikin.[47]) (k) *Digit Symbol*: frequent errors of copying other than changing the reversed N; frequent skipping of spaces and thereby entering what would have been the correct symbol in the wrong box; gross distortions of symbols; marked fluctuations of rate of work.

---

[47]) Organic cases may attempt this; impulsive subjects may also attempt it but are quick to reject it as soon as they check what they are doing.

LEARNING EFFICIENCY

Schizophrenia should be considered as a diagnostic possibility if the *quantity* of recall is markedly below what would be expected on the basis of the subject's achievements in the Information and Vocabulary subtests of the Bellevue Scale or if the *quality* of recall is distinguished by frequent recombinations of story elements, by frequent introduction of new material, or by striking fragmentation of the story. Schizophrenia is also suggested if the delayed recall is markedly poorer than the immediate recall. It should be remembered, however, that severe depression and organic brain damage frequently yield the same results; differential diagnosis must be made using other tests. One or two severe distortions, even if the quantity of recall is adequate, are often found in well-preserved cases: for example, "a 14-year-old boy . . ." or "the bridge was washed away."

Example [48]): (Subject's weighted scores on Vocabulary and Information are 15.) "March 6: There was a catastrophe in Albany and 600 people were killed. A boy, in saving 14 people, drowned." Example: (Subject's weighted scores on Vocabulary and Information are 12 and 13 respectively.) "On December 6, last week, a flood in a town . . . something about some people . . . the water went into the basements . . . a boy . . . on a bridge . . . that's all I remember."

SORTING TEST

Part I

The concept span. The concept span of many schizophrenics is "loose". Either many more objects than are embraced by the conventional conceptual process are included in any one sorting, or two or three objects which conventional concept formation almost never relates to each other are sorted together. An example of the former type is the subject's starting with the fork and adding all the silverware, tools, smoking equipment, sugar, corks and sink stopper; an example of the latter type is the subject's starting with the ball and adding the block of wood with the nail in it and the cigar. Mild loosening occurs in many

----

48) The original story reads as follows: December 6: last week a river overflowed in a small town 10 miles from Albany. Water covered the streets and entered the houses. 14 persons were drowned and 600 persons caught cold because of the dampness and cold weather. In saving a boy, who was caught under a bridge, a man cut his hands.

types of cases and cannot in itself be considered suggestive of schizophrenia: for example, including just the sugar or sink stopper with the silverware, or the block of wood with the tools, or the paper circle (as a placemat) with the toy silverware. Chain sortings are rare but are strongly diagnostic, and should not be confused with "radial chains";[49]) the latter refer more to compulsive exhaustiveness than to schizophrenic loosening.

The verbalized concept. The conceptualization of the sorting frequently indicates conceptual expansiveness by being either too inclusive in its abstractness (syncretistic) or by being too inclusive in its concrete fabulated content. As an example of the former type, "all have roundness" is offered and includes not only the strikingly round objects but the tools because their handles are round and the eraser because its printed trademark has an "o" on it. As examples of the latter type: "A man has to work (tools) to make money for food (eating equipment) and he might be smoking while he worked (smoking equipment) and could eat some sugar (sugar cubes) for energy to work," or, "Have to have a wall (wood block with nail) to throw the ball against (ball)." Symbolic interpretations should be watched for; for example, conceptualizing the sorting of the red circular piece of paper and the bell as "danger signals" or the sugar cubes and white card as "sugar rationing: the card could be your ration book." There are milder forms of this type of thinking which are diagnostically ambiguous, such as considering the paper circle and square as "coasters" in the context of a sorting of silverware. Where concretization of concepts is extreme, failures may be frequent: "Nothing goes with the ball because the only thing that could go with it is a bat," or "Nothing goes with the bell because it needs a bicycle or at least handlebars." [50])

Part II

The conceptualizations in Part II often have the same loose or overexpanded (fabulated or syncretistic) quality as those in Part I. The distinguishing feature of these concepts is that they could immediately or potentially include most or all of the remaining test objects, if not everything in the room. The examiner must be careful to distinguish schizophrenic expansiveness from the fabulations of egocentric subjects—usually narcissistic persons or naive hysterics. The latter sometimes make

---

49) Radial chains are of the following type: with the red rubber ball, the subject sorts all the red objects, rubber objects and round objects.

50) Subjects on a low intelligence level and organic cases may do the same, however.

loose sortings in Part I on the basis of fabulated connections between the objects, but the content of these fabulations is almost always of one type, namely, family activities (the son playing with his father, the parents smoking after a meal, the odds and ends in "my son's collection of toys," and so forth). Psychopaths also usually offer one or two fabulations. In these cases, the remaining tests almost always facilitate differential diagnosis. Consequently, superficially similar results in this test can usually be integrated into the character analysis as "conspicuous egocentricity" or "pathological tendency to fabulize" or "schizophrenic concretization and expansiveness of concepts", depending on the total set of test results.

RORSCHACH TEST

The principal indicators of schizophrenic disorganization are the following: (1) form-level or $F+\%$ below 60%, and especially below 50%; (2) relative massing of pure C, pure C exceeding CF and FC responses, especially if FC responses are absent or become arbitrary (pink bears) or if the pure C's take on gory qualities; (3) relative massing of sex responses, especially if these are frequently in unusual areas, of gory quality, of absurd form or if they pertain to the sex act rather than to individual sex organs; (4) sudden changes in the quality of the record, as in failing the last four cards after giving a dilated record up to that point, or giving perseverative pure C's on Cards VIII, IX, and X after an orderly record; (5) extremely irregular sequence of locations of responses, reflecting a "scattered" intellectual approach to situations; (6) deviant verbalizations: queer or absurd content, autistic reasoning leading to confabulated or contaminated concepts, breakdown of the patness of interpersonal communication leading to peculiar formulations and eventually to incoherence. Some of these require amplification.

1. *Low form level.* This indicator is most useful when it occurs outside of a coarctated setting; an anxiety state, neurasthenic condition, or severe depression can produce a low $F+\%$ but generally will do so in a coarctated setting. Thus, if R exceeds 20-25, if M or sum C is well above zero, if elaborate or highly original responses are present, this indicator is useful. The main caution is that some obsessives, by fault of padding their records with many strained Dr responses, may have a low $F+\%$ in a dilated record. The low $F+\%$ takes on added significance if a few absurd forms or $M-$ are present side by side with sharp and well organized responses. The low $F+\%$ of a schizophrenic is indicative of the extent of the breakdown of reality-testing and the suffusion of apperception with pathologically autistic thought content.

2. *Pure C responses.* If we exclude borderline C responses of the "painting" and "decoration" variety, and if we consider "blood" on Cards II and III doubtful, then the remaining C's can be used in building up a picture of schizophrenia. Such responses as "water", "sky", "egg", "urine", "oranges", and "blood" on Cards VIII, IX, or X are typical. Occasionally an hysteric, narcissistic character disorder, or a decompensated compulsive character gives two or three pure C's but the preponderant weight is usually on CF and FC. If not, then inspection of the content of the pure C's generally reveals that they deal with rainbows, sunsets, deep sea colors, and other colorful aspects of nature. But when the content turns to "blood mixed with dirt", "charred flesh", different foods, the different colors of easter eggs (Card X) or "two men having orgasms (pink and inner yellow, Card X)", schizophrenia is clearly implied. In a schizophrenic context, pure C's pertain to the breakdown of the control of impulses; the gory content or emphasis on pale colors usually pertains to blunting of affects. If FC's are absent, the elimination of adaptive controls is all the more striking. If M's are present in sufficient quantity to balance the pure C's,[51] sporadic breakdown and reinstitutions of controls rather than chronic feebleness of controls is implied.

3. *The sex responses* should be indiscriminate (given to many tiny projections, invaginations, or confluences), gory ("inflamed foreskin of a penis"), confabulated ("two women with their vaginas together"), or colored by blunted affect ("this one would be too loose"—speaking of a vagina). A single confabulated or otherwise strange or vivid sex response in a very constricted record may also be diagnostic; if several failures are present, and if the patient's presenting symptoms are not sexual in nature, schizophrenia must be suspected if even an ordinary sex response is offered; if the opening response to Card I is "a woman's sex organs (W)", schizophrenia is indicated. A few sex responses in the "usual" areas [52] can be given by any sexually preoccupied person and will be given by many schizoid persons even in the normal range. A sexually preoccupied obsessive may give many sex responses but the content of these should be in no way deviant. A person who has been in psychoanalysis may give not only many sex responses but vivid ones as well, and the examiner must make allowances for these. The disorganized or fantastic sex responses refer generally to the breakdown of defenses

---

51) This pattern is also found in manics.

52) Lower and upper middle, Card II; upper middle, Card IV; upper projection, Card VI; lower middle, Card VII; lower middle, Card IX.

against the emergence of normally unconscious material into consciousness. In an analysand, similar responses would therefore be expected; even in these cases, however, the *formal* aspects of the responses should be well-ordered, however dramatic the content. One recently tested chronic paranoid schizophrenic yielded a record of 27 responses, 22 of these dealing with sex: at the top of IV he saw "the vagina of a black horse"; at the top of VI he saw "a sperm, with wings so it can get up there"; at the bottom of III he saw "a vagina and anus (tiny midline) and this must be menstrual blood (middle red)". Another chronic schizophrenic woman saw two dozen incomplete or underdeveloped penises.

4. *Deviant verbalizations.* The manner in which the subject integrates, communicates, appraises and justifies his response is itself valid material for qualitative analysis. As a rule verbal stereotypy largely obscures the characteristic disorganization of thinking underlying responses. Therefore the examiner must be alert to odd verbalizations, using as his baseline the manner of verbalization characteristic of the general run of the normal population. Inquiry into the background of the odd verbalization often digs out a florid schizophrenic thought process. The deviant verbalizations to be discussed, in one way or another, reflect the distorted reasoning, defective reality testing or emotional inappropriateness of the schizophrenic.

One principal emphasis in the analysis of verbalization is to be put upon the subject's attitude toward the inkblot as indicated in his verbalization. The "objective" reality of the testing situation and the inkblot is taken neither too seriously nor too lightly by the normal subject. If it is taken too seriously, we can describe the subject's thinking as having *lost distance* from the card; if it is taken too lightly, the thinking shows an *increase of distance* from the card. In the former case, the subject reacts to the card as if it were immutable reality with which he must cope by reasoning and to which he must react with "appropriate" affect. In the latter case, the subject largely ignores the reality of the inkblot, and gives responses or embellishments of responses which have little or no support in the card itself. In many schizophrenic responses both loss and increase of distance can be seen in simultaneous operation.

The second principal emphasis is to be put upon the integrity of the verbal communication itself. Too often the schizophrenic speaks in a kind of verbal shorthand, condensing several thoughts into one phrase, and blithely assumes that the examiner is aware of exactly what he (the schizophrenic) is aware of. Too often, also, the examiner is deceived into thinking that the communication has been successful because he is automatically able to fill in the gaps from his awareness of the context of the response and the kinds of response usually given in that context. For this reason a sophisticated examiner as such is no competent judge of adequacy of communication; he must put himself in the place of a naive observer in order to test the adequacy of the verbalization as an interpersonal communication. In the following paragraphs a few examples of each of the various types of deviant verbalizations will be presented.[53]

a) *DW*: schizophrenic *DW*'s are generally distinguished by a tone of logical necessity. On Card X: "This all (*W*) *must* be a picture of Paris because here is the Eiffel Tower (upper gray)." On Card IV: "This (*W*) is a picture of the insides of a woman *because* here (upper middle *Dd*) it looks like her privates."

b) *Absurd form*: here the content of the response finds no support in the configuration of the inkblot; the percept is extremely arbitrary. Card IV, *W*: "A paramecium." Card I, *W*: "An ant." Card VIII, *W*: "Magnified fly eye."

c) *Confabulation* [54] : either several discrete contents are arbitrarily woven into a story or a story is implicitly or explicitly made up about a single content. Card X: "Two boxers (pink); referee is between them— his legs (lower green) and his eyeglasses (middle orange) ; the pole of the boxing ring (upper gray) ; and in the background the crowd is yelling them on (remainder of card)." Card VI, *W*: "Bacteriological smear with debris, or a vaginal smear of gonorrhea after sulfathiozol."

d) *Contaminations*: either two discrete contents for one area fuse into a single, final concept or the same area stands for two discrete concepts at the same time. Card VI, *W*, upside down: "Two children up a tree;" the tree and the children occupy the same area. Card X, lower middle (popular rabbit head): "A rabbit hand;" the area looks both like a rabbit head and like a hand with only the index and little fingers extended (rabbit ears) .

e) *Autistic logic*: autistic logic is involved in the *DW*, confabulation, and contamination responses, but sometimes makes an appearance in purer form. Either the premise, deduction, or both may be arbitrary. *Po* responses are included in this category, because in them the content

---

53) The reader is referred to pages 331-361 and 473-490 in Volume II of *Diagnostic Psychological Testing* for an extended discussion and collection of examples of deviant verbalizations.

54) Also occurs in the records of manics and some cases with organic brain pathology; mild forms may be seen in the records of psychopaths.

is decided "logically" on the basis of position and not at all on the basis of a normal determinant. Card V, *W*: "An abandoned road because it's not completed on each end." Card VIII: "The artist must have wanted to portray the theory of the similarity of nature, because these two animals (side pink) are the same; also that the world is only what it appears, because the animals look like they're moving but they aren't."

f) *Queer content*: Card VI, *W*: "A transverse cut of a sore." Card VIII, *W*: "An artistic design of a fly's foot." Card X, *W*: "Different genitals, on exhibition." Card X: "Two men (pink) having orgasms (inner yellow)." Card X, lower green: "Two worms sucking on a rabbit's eyeballs."

g) *Peculiar communications*: Card X, middle blue: "Looks like a bat, *personally*." Card I, *W*: "*Medically speaking*, it would be a pelvis." Card VII, *W*: "A *facing* map of Europe." Card VII, upper one-third: "Couple of jaws." Card IV, lower middle: "That isn't a bat! There are no wings on it." Card VI, *W*: "Some kind of insect; doesn't seem to have any bones." Card X, side blue: "A sea because the sea is blue in the Mediterranean or South America." Card I, *W*: "A bat because they have them in Carlsbad Caverns." Card VII, *W*: "Wolf hounds facing back to back." All these are instances of the breakdown of communicative facility in the schizophrenic; almost all are immediately understandable *if the gaps are filled in.* For example, in the Carlsbad Caverns verbalization the subject apparently meant to say: "I've seen bats in the Carlsbad Caverns and on the basis of that experience I am able to say that this looks like a bat."

h) *Relationship, reference and self-reference ideas*: when these are persistent and are given with an air of conviction and discovery, they indicate schizophrenia. Card II, *W*: "The butterfly of the previous picture (reference to Card I)." Card III: "These (popular figures) would have originated from here (lower middle *D*)." Card II, lower red: "Lips of the vagina: I look something like that myself."

i) *Confusion*: confusion may make an appearance in fluid percepts or fluid chains of ideas with sudden shifts of context. Feelings of unreality are suggested by these, as well as confusion proper. Card I: "Ghosts (middle *D*). . . now they seem to be on the side (side *D*)." Card IV, upper middle: "Looked like Moses a minute ago but now it looks like the devil." Card V: "A fur skin. (?) A tail, legs hanging down; it's hot—no! it's cold when you are wearing furs."

j) *Fabulized combinations*: an accidental spatial relationship between two discrete areas is taken to indicate a "real" connection and an *absurd* combination results. These responses are not singularly schizophrenic, tending to occur in the records of obsessive and schizoid characters also, and even in the records of some normals. If many of them are present in one record, however, schizophrenia, or at least the presence of pronounced schizoid characteristics, is indicated. Card VIII: "Prairie dogs (side pink) climbing on a butterfly (lower pink and orange)." Card III: "Two men (popular) holding kidneys (lower middle *D*)." Card X: "An octopus (side blue) waving a sheep (side green)."

k) *Fabulations*: these are emotional or factual elaborations of responses and are not at all distinctively schizophrenic; if, however, there is an abundance of these in a record *together with indications of withdrawal*, at least an incipient schizophrenia is suggested. Fabulations are often found in the records of psychopaths, some patients with character disorders, excessively fantasying schizoid subjects, obsessives, and imaginative normals. Card II: "Lake (space); dangerous rocks (black)." Card IV, *W*: "A cruel, evil monster." Card X, middle yellow: "A dog that has just won first prize in a dog show."

WORD ASSOCIATION TEST

The schizophrenic's disorganization of conceptual and associative processes is seen in: (1) sporadic blocking, manifested in marked variability of reaction time with little systematic relation between the delays and the connotations of the stimulus words; (2) a greatly lowered incidence of conventional (popular) relationships between stimulus words and reactions; (3) relatively frequent "distant" reactions; that is, reactions whose content is not clearly related to the stimulus words either conceptually or on the basis of conventional concrete contexts; it is especially diagnostic if reactions with aggressive or sexual content are given to usually neutral stimulus words; (4) clang associations and phrase-completions, the latter especially if they are frequent and strained (taxi-"dermist"); (5) an abundance of personal associations.

Examples of "distant" reactions: *bowel movement*—"eat (?) it's the elimination of food you've eaten;" *masturbation*—"loss (?) when you masturbate you have an orgasm and it's a loss of your semen;" *party*—"stand (?) people dance a lot at parties and I can't, so I stand around and watch;" *city*— "policeman (?) I was thinking of the other test (Bellevue Scale) and of the advantages of the city;" *dog*—"intercourse (?) had a mental picture of dogs having intercourse;" *hospital*—"funeral;" *trunk*—"torso (?) thought of a murder and cutting the body into little pieces and putting them in a trunk;" *movies*—"erection;" *dog*—"kill;"

horse—"had a picture of a horse defecating on the pile of feces I pictured when you said bowel movement (some 15 words before) ."

Depressives also have variable reaction times but are rarely fast, whereas schizophrenics are often very slow and very fast alternately. Psychotic depressives may also give a few distant associations but generally yield records dominated by definitions and blocking. Many self-references may be made by egocentric subjects or certain types of obsessives. If no strained logic is elicited in inquiry, if the choice of the personal reaction word is readily understandable, and if the remaining tests lack schizophrenic indications, the self-references can usually be understood as manifestations of extreme egocentricity or obsessive self-preoccupation.

THEMATIC APPERCEPTION TEST

The indications of schizophrenia may be found in bizarre story content, breakdown of the rational or emotional structure of the story, perceptual errors, or breakdown of interpersonal communication of ideas. The following are examples [55]) : (1) "unacceptable" content such as incest, homosexuality, matricide; (2) overelaborate symbolism dealing with life, death, God, and religion, virtue and sin, and so forth; (3) themes of withdrawal, explicitly dealing with complete withdrawal from the world, or frequent themes involving distance and lack of warmth for other people; (4) delusion-like content, such as ideas of influence, magical or "supernormal" powers, or world destruction; (5) disjointedness of meaning or affect, as when each explanation in inquiry requires further explanation, when sudden changes of mood occur, or when trivial, *irrelevant* details are considered in the midst of discussing a dramatic scene; (6) arbitrary story content which flouts the content of the picture; (7) frequent or extreme perceptual distortions, such as seeing the two women in F-11 as men or the sketches on the wall in Card 8 (Picasso) as live persons; (8) peculiar verbalizations, cryptic explanations, vague generalizations; for example, the opening statement to Card 8: "One sees mothers with babes, distracted wives and husbands, and other characters;" "completely slaughtered;" "a surprise of groceries;" or the understatement... "somebody might have forced her into rape when she wasn't interested;" (9) non-sequiturs or autistic logic, similar to that seen in the Rorschach Test; (10) the omission or only faint implication of ideas basic to the continuity of the story.

----

55) See pages 449-459 of *Diagnostic Psychological Testing*, Volume II, for an extended discussion of the following indicators.

UNCLASSIFIED SCHIZOPHRENIA

These are mixed or singular cases which do not fit neatly into any of the four classical categories—hebephrenic, paranoid, catatonic, or simple. Nevertheless, they clearly manifest several of the following features: inappropriate affect, withdrawal, breakdown of reality testing, generally disorganized thinking, blocking, confusion, delusions, hallucinations. "Acute" refers to cases whose symptoms are clear and of recent onset; "chronic" refers to cases who have been schizophrenic for some time. Any of the test features mentioned in the previous general section on schizophrenia may be present; the patterns to be discussed are mainly those that facilitate differential diagnosis.

BELLEVUE SCALE

In the acute cases, the Comprehension and Arithmetic scores tend to drop, indicating impairments of judgment and concentration. The Digit Span score often remains on or above the Information-Vocabulary level and high above the Arithmetic score, yielding the "out-of-pattern" relationship so characteristic of schizophrenic records.[56] Since these cases are not necessarily bland clinically, their well-retained Digit Span (attention) score cannot be taken as a sign of blandness, as it can in the records of certain hysterics, psychopaths, and chronic schizophrenics. This out-of-pattern attention-concentration relationship is the most reliable diagnostic feature of the scattergram but does not embrace more than half these cases, and is not a specific diagnostic indicator since schizoid subjects anywhere on the continuum of maladjustment may have it. If, however, the discrepancy becomes extreme, as it does in the Bellevue Scale record of the acute schizophrenic presented in Chapter 4, schizophrenia is specifically indicated. Sporadic, peculiar verbalizations and distorted perceptions are, however, generally present in the records of full schizophrenics and facilitate differential diagnosis. Picture Completion is frequently greatly impaired, reflecting the characteristic impairments of concentration, judgment and, possibly, visual organization. The acute anxiety of these cases is most likely to make a clear appearance in Object Assembly, where it will disrupt the development of planned attempts at solution.

As chronicity sets in, judgment is usually progressively impaired, and, accordingly, the Comprehension score usually drops much below

---

[56] Patients with narcissistic character disorders, particularly the women among them, often have a relatively low Arithmetic score; rarely, however, do they have a conspicuously high Digit Span score.

the Vocabulary-Information level. As a rule, the out-of-pattern relationship is no longer as striking as it is in acute cases, since with the characteristically increasing distractibility, attention also suffers. Consequently both Digit Span and Arithmetic are usually relatively quite low. If the Digit Span score stays up and there is evidence in the test battery for chronicity, this pattern indicates significant blandness. In many chronic cases all the Verbal subtest scores are two or more points below the Vocabulary level, indicating deterioration of intellectual abilities. With increasing chronicity the Object Assembly score tends to rise up to or above the Vocabulary level; Block Designs usually remains on a fair level, while Picture Arrangement, Picture Completion, and Digit Symbol are usually progressively lowered. The high Object Assembly score, and occasionally a very high Digit Symbol score can, in a setting of chronicity, be taken as indications of blandness. Peculiarities of reasoning and communication, and arbitrary percepts are usually abundant.

LEARNING EFFICIENCY

As a rule, learning efficiency is well-retained in acute cases; memory organization is in many respects well-preserved. It is not infrequent, however, that in the setting of a high score, two or three extreme distortions are present. As chronicity sets in, both the quantitative and qualitative aspects of the recall suffer: typically, the score is low, two or more points have to be subtracted for gross distortions, and the delayed recall is even more impaired than the immediate recall.

SORTING TEST

In the acute cases, the disorganization is most likely to show itself in Part I; as a rule, the responses in Part II are conceptually adequate. In Part I, two or three strikingly loose sortings are fairly frequent, though the conceptual level may remain generally abstract. Occasionally one or two striking syncretistic concepts are offered. The well-known extensive concretization of concepts is atypical in the records of acute cases.

As chronicity sets in, Part II becomes increasingly impaired. As a general rule, the more devastated Part II is, the more chronic the psychosis is likely to be. Part I, of course, is more impaired than ever. Fabulations, syncretistic concepts, and extensive concreteness out of keeping with the estimated premorbid intelligence level, are characteristic. Chain and symbolic concepts also make an appearance in some of these records.

RORSCHACH TEST

Except in blocked, depressed, or unintelligent patients, the record of an acute case is usually of average or greater length—at least 20-25 responses and frequently more than 30. The experience balance is generally dilated: there are usually several M's[57]) and several color responses, including some pure C's. FC's need not disappear; their early disappearance appears to be an unfavorable prognostic indication. Often FC's and arbitrary FC's ("blue bats") occur side by side and indicate that although adaptive efforts are continuing, they already have an arbitrary, "out of tune" quality. The form level is generally adequate but one or more absurd forms will probably be present. A few confabulations, contaminations, fabulized combinations, peculiar and queer verbalizations are usual. Sex responses, often confabulated, are also usual. In general then, the record indicates the absence of deterioration (adequate $F+\%$, M's, and FC balancing or exceeding pure C) at the same time as it indicates schizophrenic disorganization. Schizophrenics of low intelligence generally yield meagre records with fewer but no less dramatic diagnostic indications. If the patient is depressed or blocked, the record is likely to be coarctated and will often be diagnostically only suggestive at best. Blocked schizophrenics generally fail many cards or else give stereotyped, perseverative, and vague or fragmented responses, and utter at least a few peculiar verbalizations in so doing; these cases usually show conspicuous paranoid or catatonic features, or both.

As chronicity sets in, the M's and FC's tend to disappear and the pure C's accumulate; the $F+\%$ usually drops below 60% and frequently below 50%; the $P\%$ also tends to drop; the number of deviant verbalizations and absurd forms increases; neologisms, $Po,$ symbolic and "autistic" reasoning, and blunted deterioration-C responses (pus, gangrene, egg, wine, oranges) make an appearance. The picture now is one of blunted and inappropriate affect, devastated reality testing, extensive breakdown of communicative ability, and departure from conventional modes of perception and thought. As a rule, as the M's disappear, the capacity for systematized, intensely experienced delusions also disappears. Sex and anatomy responses tend to increase, usually reflecting corresponding preoccupations. Chronic cases given to expansive ideas tend to have a high $W{:}D$ ratio and a higher than average R. A schizophrenic record

---

57) It is not unusual that the sharpness or creativeness of the M's and of some excellent form responses will transcend the general premorbid, intellectual level of the acute schizophrenic patient as judged from the tests of intelligence and concept formation.

with many heavily shaded responses also indicates chronicity; the frequent use of shading in these records refers to the potentiality for panic attacks with bizarre features.

WORD ASSOCIATION TEST

It is not unusual that an acute case yields a set of responses that are diagnostically unrevealing. More often, however, a few distant associations occur. Sometimes inquiry reveals these to relate to delusional ideas, but more often they indicate only the loosened associative processes. A clearly disorganized record is to be expected mainly from chronic cases. Chronic schizophrenics usually give numerous distant associations, show marked variability of reaction time, and are sometimes strikingly inefficient in the recall part of the test. Inappropriate sexual or aggressive associations often accumulate in these records. Neologistic word usage and peculiar phrase-completions also occur frequently.

THEMATIC APPERCEPTION TEST

The stories are for the most part quite coherent and appropriate in the records of acute cases. One or two severe perceptual distortions, a handful of peculiar phrases, a sudden weird and disconnected fantasy, an occasional dramatic non sequitur, an occasional strange air about a story because significant implications have not been verbalized, are usually all the signs that are present. With chronicity, intellectual and emotional incoherence, perceptual distortions, bizarre themes, global impressions not subjected to reality-oriented articulation, and arbitrary verbalizations and reasoning all tend to increase. As in the Rorschach Test, chronic schizophrenics rarely escape detection.

PARANOID SCHIZOPHRENIA

This term designates those cases who are, as a rule, not generally bizarre but who have developed clear-cut, predominantly paranoid delusions of a grandiose or persecutory nature, and who are often confused, or apathetic and retarded.

On the basis of test results, it is difficult to distinguish some of the retarded acute paranoid schizophrenics from psychotic or severe neurotic depressives. As a rule, these cases can be detected only if a *battery* of tests is administered; the result, in any one test may be quite well organized. This quality of good preservation in the tests of acute paranoid cases appears to parallel the clinical observation that the delusional structure may barely touch the system of conventional logical relations. The chief features to be sought in the test results are sporadic appearances of basically disorganized thinking and arbitrary perceptual organization in a setting of inhibition and suspicious overcautiousness, or confusion and agitation. Again, however, any of the test features mentioned in the general section on schizophrenia may be present.

BELLEVUE SCALE

The most striking feature of the scatter in the records of acute cases is likely to be a more or less general drop of the Performance level; Block Designs, however, still tends to obtain the highest of the Performance scores. The Comprehension score is usually not strikingly lowered —a feature distinctively paranoid in its implications once the diagnosis of schizophrenia has been established elsewhere, since it reflects good preservation. Although some of these cases show extreme scatter of the general schizophrenic variety (great drops of the Comprehension, Arithmetic, and Picture Completion scores), in general it is the *paranoid* schizophrenics who yield little scatter. The greatly scattering paranoid cases are likely to be confused; the cases with little scatter other than a Performance drop are likely to be apathetic and retarded. A relatively high Arithmetic or Picture Completion score, or both, in a schizophrenic setting are indicative of paranoid over-alertness. A relatively high Similarities score also indicates prominent paranoid features.

Qualitatively, peculiar verbalizations, particularly in the Similarities subtest, and perceptual distortions in the Picture Arrangement and Picture Completion subtests, are especially likely to be present. In the *flirt* Picture Arrangement sequence, the woman may be seen as two different women—a Negress and a white woman—or the second chauffeur in the front seat may be seen as the woman inside the car; or the bust in the *taxi* sequence may be seen as a living person.[58] Because the chronic cases often have a "good front", the Comprehension score may remain on a high level even though there may be many peculiar verbalizations within that subtest. For example, in reply to *why are people who are born deaf usually unable to talk?* one patient said in a confidential tone: "Some people try to keep it a secret, but I happen to know that it's because they have the disease. (?) You know ... venereal disease ... and they pass it on to the children." With chronicity the Similarities or verbal concept formation score usually drops and the Block

---

[58] These distortions may also occur in the records of patients with paranoid conditions.

Designs and Object Assembly scores often rise. Peculiarities and distortions increase. The homoerotic features which are often evident in these cases may be indicated by misrecognitions of the sex of the mannikin and profile in the Object Assembly subtest. Negativistic, suspicious behavior is usually striking.

LEARNING EFFICIENCY

If the apathy or confusion are marked in the acute case, learning efficiency is likely to suffer in typical schizophrenic fashion; otherwise it may be, like most functions, well-retained. With chronicity, quantitative and qualitative impairments usually increase.

SORTING TEST

In acute cases, the concept span is usually more or less narrow; often, however, one or two striking loosenesses occur in this setting of constriction and caution. The conceptual level is generally abstract with one or two striking syncretistic or fabulated concepts. A typical loose sorting and fabulated concept is that in Part I where the rectangular piece of cardboard is placed with the ball because "it could be a baseball diamond". The acute paranoid schizophrenic, as a rule, tries desperately to be meticulous and cautious, but his basically impaired reality testing occasionally permits gross deviations from conventional conceptual paths. The same is true of the chronic cases, except that gross deviations tend to be numerous. Especially Part II of the test suffers in chronic cases: many fabulations, using all varieties of content, are common.

RORSCHACH TEST

In the records of acute cases, R is usually below 25 and often below 15; the experience balance is coarctated, containing perhaps 2 or 3 M's and practically no colors; the $F\%$ is high and the $F+\%$ adequate unless blocking and anatomical or other perseverations are present; the $A\%$ and $P\%$ are high; the $DR\%$ is high for a coarctated record—for example, 5 Dr's or several space responses with an R of 20. No more than two or three deviant verbalizations in the form of confabulations, contaminations, peculiar or queer verbalizations, absurd overabstracted[59]) responses or $M-$ are likely. The picture indicated is therefore one of blocking or inhibition and caution, defective reality testing behind a "good

---

59) For example, the entire upper contour of Card I may be called "the bottom of a shark's mouth", or all of Card VII may be called a "shoelace".

front", a tendency to seize on tiny or unusually abstracted details and over-elaborate their significance, and a tendency to force broad integrations in an arbitrary way. *Do* responses are not infrequent in these records, although a massing of *Do*'s usually refers to blocking. Seeing letters of the alphabet, geometric shapes or other symbols (music notes, dollar signs, and the like) is typically paranoid. Card I may be seen as an *A* or the middle red of Card III as an *H*; two tiny "diamonds" may be seen in the white spaces inside the lower middle *Dr* on Card II. Some of these patients emphasize "eyes", or things hidden behind other things. Relationship and reference ideas in the course of this test are typically paranoid.

Some of these cases retain *FC* responses, indicating the strong adaptive efforts often seen in paranoid patients; some of the confused cases indicate their confusion by the fluidity of their percepts and the tendency to give irrelevant responses to inquiry. It is not infrequent that an acute paranoid gets through the first nine cards with no more than one or two mildly peculiar verbalizations, only to "blow up" on Card X with a contamination or a confabulation embracing the entire card. It is also not infrequent that many failures occur; this, together with the general coarctation and orderliness, might suggest a severe depression. Differential diagnosis in this instance depends on the presence of several *M*'s, absurd or overabstracted forms, and schizophrenic verbalizations, as well as the findings in the other tests.

If pure *C*'s, much use of shading, a low $F+\%$ and many schizophrenic verbalizations are present, chronicity is indicated. As a rule the records of chronic paranoid cases are not very different from those of other types of chronic schizophrenics. However, a somewhat greater emphasis on logic and proof, and somewhat more frequent and more explicit psychotic theorizing are typical. Yet, a fair proportion of the records of chronic cases are flat, stereotyped, and deal in a perseverative way with anatomy and sex. A few peculiar verbalizations or one or two anatomical or sexual confabulations will indicate the diagnosis and the remaining tests will generally yield more than enough support. The implication will be that a flat, bland, more or less quiescent and stable chronic state has been reached. Another segment of the population of chronic paranoid schizophrenics tends to intellectualize expansively, yielding a more or less dilated record (high *R*) with a grandiose quality (high *W*) and clear evidence of disorganization (confabulation, queer content, and the like).

WORD ASSOCIATION TEST

The word associations of acute cases generally abide by conventional conceptual relationships. The records of the apathetic cases often have depressive features. The records of the confused cases are likely to have at least several distant associations. Stimulus words with aggressive connotations usually elicit long delays or unusual responses. Occasionally a paranoid schizophrenic will insist that an association not be recorded or that it be crossed out if it has already been recorded; or he may insist that he *cannot* tell the examiner what he has thought. This is most likely to occur where the stimulus word has clear sexual connotations and especially if the response is a "vulgar" word. Many well-preserved acute paranoid schizophrenics give diagnostically unrevealing word associations. This is much less true of the chronic cases but it does occur, and, if the remaining tests are clearly those of a chronic schizophrenic, the implication is that this case has strong *paranoid* features and is one which is fairly well-preserved that is, one capable of maintaining a fairly "good front".

THEMATIC APPERCEPTION TEST

Peculiar and frequent inferences, vague generalizations, cryptic statements, and striking perceptual distortions (especially glaring misrecognitions of sex) are often major diagnostic features. The peculiar inferences reflect both the overcautiousness and its ineffectiveness in the face of a breakdown of reality testing; they may appear in the context of deducing the artist's motive in drawing the picture or in the context of deducing all the major parts of the story from details in the picture and leaving nothing to free fantasy. Themes of attack from the rear, impending and mysterious danger, and unjust treatment are often elaborated. With chronicity the verbalizations, themes, and percepts become increasingly bizarre. Inappropriate moralistic reactions and generalized caginess are especially typical of paranoid cases.

SUMMARY AND DIFFERENTIAL DIAGNOSIS

The striking thing about the records of paranoid schizophrenics is the strenuous effort to maintain a "good front". This effort is often nearly successful so that as many as two or three of the tests remain diagnostically ambiguous and the patient appears to be merely compulsive. The overcautiousness is, however, betrayed by the defective reality testing in a few tests, and it is the resulting contrast of bizarre productions and coarctating caution that facilitates the differential diagnosis.

Specifically, the Comprehension score, the Sorting Test, and the Word Association Test are often well-retained and even most of the Bellevue Scale, Rorschach Test and TAT tend to be unrevealing. It is rare, however, that clear-cut signs of schizophrenia are entirely absent.

Differential diagnosis of acute paranoid schizophrenia from psychotic depression is sometimes difficult because both types of case may show retardation and coarctation. In both types of case, the Performance level may drop below the Verbal level in the Bellevue Scale, there may be relatively few responses in the Rorschach Test and these may be mainly stereotyped, there may be blocking in the Word Association Test, narrowness in the Sorting Test, and depressive themes in the TAT. Furthermore, because psychotic depressives are often paranoid, they may, like the paranoid schizophrenics, give evidence of distorted percepts. As a result, the examiner must capitalize on the least peculiarities of verbalization, on the most implicit evidences of fabulation, and, in the scattergram, on the single deviations from the typical depressive scatter in order to make the correct differential diagnosis of acute paranoid schizophrenia. Even if a diagnostic conclusion cannot be arrived at, it will still be clear that profound depression and paranoid ideas are clinically conspicuous. Chronic paranoid schizophrenics rarely present this problem of differential diagnosis.

SIMPLE SCHIZOPHRENIA

In these cases withdrawal, apathy, blandness, or absence of affective display, and peculiarities of behavior and thinking are the diagnostic clinical features. "Anti-social" acts may be conspicuous in this setting; in female simple schizophrenics this often takes the form of promiscuity. The experience to be summarized below ·has dealt in the main with simple schizophrenics twenty-five years of age or less; older cases have not been seen often at The Menninger Foundation. Occasionally there may be some difficulty in distinguishing simple schizophrenics from bland psychopaths or inhibited, schizoid, normal subjects of low intelligence or poor cultural background. The chief features to be sought in the test results are blocking and perseveration, "flatness", absence of indications of emotional responsiveness and efforts at rapport, peculiarities of thinking, and general loss of interest.

BELLEVUE SCALE

Typically the scores on the three tests of visual-motor coordination are high relative to the scores on the Verbal and Picture Arrangement and Picture Completion subtests. The Comprehension and Arithmetic scores are likely to be quite low, reflecting the basic impairments of judgment and ability to concentrate. The Digit Span score is often relatively high, indicating blandness, as do the well-retained Performance scores. Information and Vocabulary tend to be spotty at the low levels and the high levels are rarely reached, reflecting loss or lack of general interests. Often the Vocabulary score is strikingly low. Rarely will one of these cases obtain a Verbal IQ above the average range.

Some simple schizophrenics resemble psychopaths by guessing wildly but blandly on the difficult items. These are the simple schizophrenics who are likely to behave "antisocially". Misuse of words and borderline neologisms tend to occur. A few peculiar verbalizations in the Similarities and Comprehension subtests are usual. The peculiar formulations and misuse of words facilitate differential diagnosis from psychopathic character, and hysteria or character disorder on a low intelligence level. Perceptual vagueness and arbitrariness are often conspicuous: objects in the Picture Completion series may not be recognized, the bust in the *taxi* sequence of Picture Arrangement may be seen as a woman, and so forth.

The general intellectual picture will be one of pathological unreflectiveness, minimal general interests, vague reality testing and impaired judgment.

LEARNING EFFICIENCY

Learning efficiency is almost always poor in typical schizophrenic fashion.

SORTING TEST

Rarely are many abstract conceptual definitions present. The record is usually replete with failures and concrete concepts. In Part I, both extremely narrow and extremely loose sortings are likely to occur.

RORSCHACH TEST

The Rorschach Test record usually contains less than 15 responses, one or several DW's, one or no M's, no colors or perhaps one pure C, no shading responses, an $F+\%$ below 50%, several failures or perseverations, one or more absurd form responses, a high $A\%$ or $A\%$ plus $At\%$, minimal ability to introspect during inquiry, and one or two peculiar or queer verbalizations. The low R and M, the failures, perseverations, weak responses to inquiry, and restricted content indicate the blocking, extreme unreflectiveness, and ideational poverty of these cases; the

DW's, low $F+\%$, absurd form responses, and the few deviant verbalizations reflect the basically impaired reality testing; the absence of color and shading responses speaks for the withdrawn, bland, affectless aspects of the patient. The relative absence of bizarre verbalizations facilitates differential diagnosis from other, more florid forms of schizophrenia. If one or two M's or extravagant Dr's are present in this context, vague flickering delusions are indicated. Sometimes, when the stereotypy is manifest in a very high $A\%$, the $F+\%$ may be adequate; perseveration will, however, be evident.

WORD ASSOCIATION TEST

The typical record contains a few strikingly distant or even unrelated associations, a few clang associations, and frequent indications of blocking (delayed reactions, repetitions, perseverations, random naming of objects).

THEMATIC APPERCEPTION TEST

In general the stories are brief, incomplete, primarily descriptive, and lacking in emotional intensity. Blocking is usually evident. A few severe perceptual distortions and peculiar formulations may occur.

SCHIZOPHRENIC CHARACTERS

This diagnostic term is applied to those patients in whom a life-long, insidious, and extensive development of schizophrenic disorganization has taken place, and in whom this development appears to have reached an essentially stable state, the schizophrenic mechanisms seeming to be integrated into the character make-up. There has been no acute break and there is no reason to anticipate a rapid process of deterioration. The classical secondary symptoms (hallucinations, delusions) are absent, but the primary disorders of thinking and affect are evident upon clinical examination. Usually the major diagnostic features are bizarre, impulsive acts which are fantastically and blandly rationalized, and wild flights of fancy, the products of which often remain indistinguishable from fact in the patient's mind. Phobic, obsessive-compulsive, psychopathic, and histrionic features may all merge in these cases. As a rule, the orderly front they put up is adequate for most routine or simple social situations; for this reason these patients are often referred to as ambulatory schizophrenics.

TEST RESULTS

The test results invariably are colored from beginning to end by schizophrenic disorganization, such as could be accounted for only by a psychotic condition of long standing. Yet the characteristic patterns of a chronic paranoid, chronic unclassified, or simple schizophrenia are not consistently present. Thus there need not be a disappearance of M or FC and a dominance of pure C in the Rorschach Test, and there need not be distinctively chronic schizophrenic scatter in the Bellevue Scale. There are usually enough traces of preservation present to indicate that the patient is neither going downhill rapidly nor already "burned out". Much rather the examiner gets the impression from the pervasive, blithely expressed peculiar ideas that, so to speak, this is not a person overwhelmed by schizophrenic symptoms but that the schizophrenic style of thinking is comfortably established and is used blandly, indiscriminately, and with confidence.

In the Bellevue Scale the Performance subtest scores are frequently relatively high, suggesting that the difficulties are characterological in nature. The Rorschach Test record is usually dilated, sometimes extremely so: a pervasively schizophrenic record with more than 40 responses always suggests *schizophrenic character* as a diagnosis. The more usual chronic schizophrenics are rarely extremely productive. Pure C's and sex responses are usually abundant. Confabulated W's are also typical. The Thematic Apperception Test stories are often overelaborate, fantastic tales. Any and all of the signs discussed under the general heading of schizophrenia may be present. There is, however, great variability among these patients as to the place and form of appearance of the most patently schizophrenic thinking.

Schizophrenic characters often yield test results with a strong psychopathic coloring or a strong "intellectual" coloring. Mixtures of the two are not unusual, however. In the former cases fabulations, confabulations, aggressiveness, and impulsiveness tend to dominate the test results; in the latter cases grandiose and indiscriminate theorizing, bizarre pedantic formulations, extravagant interpretations and confabulations tend to predominate. Some of the intellectualizers, if they have come into contact with psychoanalytic literature, believe they have achieved deep insights and frankly (blandly and inappropriately, actually) report the occurrence of the most tabooed or "shocking" impulses and thoughts. In others, erotization of words and thoughts may be outstanding.

INCIPIENT SCHIZOPHRENIA

This term designates those cases characterized to a noteworthy degree by at least several features of the following syndrome: increasing seclusiveness, fantastic interpretations of one's own behavior and the behavior of others and even of inanimate objects, fantastic notions of the appraisal of oneself made by others, belief in mind reading and the possibility of control by others, hypochondriacal ideas involving estrangement of the body and beginning feelings of depersonalization, grandiose self-appraisal or depressive self-depreciation, peculiar obsessive thoughts, chronically low mood in which everything is seen as wrong, and fantastic remedies and explanations advanced, entanglement in contradictions, frequent illusions, a tendency to focus on insignificant aspects of events with subsequent disturbing analogies, panic attacks, distorted percepts and reasoning. The symptoms should be of relatively recent onset and frank, secondary symptoms such as delusions should be absent. This clinical syndrome implies that a psychotic break is imminent.

It is difficult to distinguish the test results of some of these cases from those of obsessional neurotics, severely schizoid personalities who are not in a process of disorganization, or full-blown acute schizophrenics. As a rule, the examiner should watch for dramatic but relatively few and isolated evidences of extremely loose concepts and associations, sudden and isolated or *pervasive* fantastic flights of imagination, and indications of withdrawal and slight inappropriateness of affect in a setting of otherwise generally well-ordered thinking. Caution and constriction should not be marked in the test results, since these features, together with those described above, indicate a paranoid schizophrenia.

The records of most, but not all of these cases yield the impression of sporadic, sharp breaks with reality but no pervasive disorganization. The line between "sporadic" and "pervasive" is difficult to draw (as it is also clinically) and often the test results resemble those of an acute schizophrenic. Some of these cases, however, present a different pattern of results: they appear to have withdrawn far into a vivid, pathologically autistic world of fantasy.[60])

It must be stressed that the prognostic diagnosis, *incipient* schizophrenia, is more or less presumptuous, since our knowledge in this area is still vague in many important respects. Nevertheless, we have seen a number of patients, so diagnosed from the test results, experience acute

---

60) One such case will be discussed in Chapter 3.

psychotic breaks relatively soon afterwards, and it therefore seems advisable to consider the patterns to be described as indications of a malignant process.

BELLEVUE SCALE

The responses in this test are generally quite orderly. The scatter and qualitative material may indicate that obsessive, repressive, schizoid, or depressive features are conspicuous. Occasionally there is an extreme drop of one subtest (particularly Digit Span, Arithmetic, or Picture Completion) to facilitate the diagnosis. Qualitatively, a few odd answers may occur in a setting of good intelligence. For example: "*Poem and statue* are both vertical." "*Moiety* means ... let's see, moi ... moi ... maybe something to do with a mortuary." No massing of peculiarities is to be expected; if present, it points to a fully developed psychosis.

LEARNING EFFICIENCY

Some of these cases have a profoundly impaired learning efficiency in a setting of otherwise generally intact intellectual functioning (Bellevue Scale). This discrepancy should never be underestimated. It is more frequent, however, that learning efficiency, like most other functions, is unimpaired.

SORTING TEST

As in the records of the acute schizophrenics, two or three loose sortings are usual in Part I without striking impairment of the conceptual level; and in Part II, the presence of one or two striking syncretistic concepts in a setting of abstract thinking is typical. Some cases give an entirely adequate set of responses.

RORSCHACH TEST

The Rorschach Test almost always indicates the early stage of the process of disorganization. Several of the following signs, but never many of them, can be expected: one or two $M-$; one or two arbitrary FC (yellow babies, green sheep) or a few pure C's bordering on the blunted deterioration-C's; one or two confabulations which are very likely to involve sexual or aggressive content; several fabulized combinations; one or two nearly contaminated responses; a few overabstracted W's (letters, geometric shapes); a few peculiar verbalizations which not infrequently are spontaneously labelled as such or corrected; an extremely unbalanced movement-color ratio (for example, 15-to-0 or 0-to-13.5 with 5 pure C's) especially if many fabulations are present or if the M's involve symbolic-like activities; an abundance of sexual and anal responses, one or two of which are fantastic in terms of the details on which they are based: "A person defecating" on Card II; "A diseased penis on the man" on Card IV; vivid physiognomic impressions with a symbolic flavor: Card VI, "A pictorial expression of some physical sensations: a feeling that the body . . . a straight channel through the center of the body (midline) which a feeling rushes through—sometimes a thrill starts very low, about abdominal, and fear seems about chest high, sometimes excitement in the throat (upper wings) . . . this center portion seems to be the strongest feeling and this lighter portion seems like a light feeling as it disseminates itself." Only two or three of these dramatic signs in a Rorschach Test record are sufficient to suggest the danger of an imminent break. The $M-$, arbitrary FC, sex responses, and confabulations are the most frequently encountered of these diagnostic indicators.

WORD ASSOCIATION TEST

The Word Association Test is often an exception to the rule that the indications of disorganization should be few and far between; frequently it is loaded with dramatic, deviant reactions. Inappropriate sexual or aggressive associations, extremely vivid imagery such that reports on the images replace one-word responses, and the expression of nearly bizarre feelings or ideas may dominate the record. The contrast of this test with an orderly Bellevue Scale often points to the correct diagnosis. A large proportion of these cases, however, give an orderly and diagnostically unrevealing set of associations.

THEMATIC APPERCEPTION TEST

The one or two confabulations in the Rorschach Test are often paralleled by one or two fantastic stories while the remaining stories are orderly and appropriate. Aggressive themes with explicit sadistic content, sexually perverse themes, and symbolic and magical fantasies are not unusual. A few peculiar formulations, word distortions, or condensations are likely. The fantasy-ridden, withdrawn incipient schizophrenics often lose distance from their stories and react to them with inappropriate empathy, as if they were external events.

SCHIZOID CHARACTERS

These are patients whose predominant personality characteristic is chronic withdrawal: inability to form or sustain object-attachments, feelings of loneliness, excessive dependence on fantasy-gratifications and a quality of *superficial* blandness in discussing apparently traumatic events are the usual manifestations of the withdrawal. A process of disorganization is not implied, however, and peculiarities of behavior or fantasy, though present, are not pervasive or dramatic.

TEST RESULTS

The test results usually contain a number of milder forms of the indications pertaining to schizophrenia. In the Bellevue Scale the Digit Span score is often strikingly high, and, to add to the significance of this pattern, the Arithmetic score may be relatively low. The digits are often visualized by these subjects in order to facilitate their reproduction. In the Sorting Test, one or two loose sortings and syncretistic concepts are usual. The Rorschach Test may contain an *EB* with at least several *M*'s but no colors or with a noteworthy but not extreme emphasis on pure *C*'s. In either instance withdrawal and the bland quality are indicated. If there are several *M*'s and no or very weak color responses, it is necessary to make a differential diagnosis between an emotionally inhibited obsessive and a schizoid character with a tendency toward excessive fantasying. Whereas the obsessive record is ordinarily distinguished by many *Dr*'s and pedantic verbalizations, the schizoid record is likely to be distinguished by fabulations and symbolic flavoring. Schizoid characters often yield one or two arbitrary *FC*'s, fabulized combinations, or peculiar verbalizations. They may see objects or figures upside down without reversing the card, draw incorrect distinctions between colors, or give unusual or numerous sex responses. The $W\%$, or in a dilated record the number of *W*'s, tends to be quite high. If inhibition or depressed mood is pronounced, as is often the case, R may be quite low and a few failures may occur. If, in addition, a long history of bodily and sexual complaints is present, the meagre record may be almost entirely restricted to sexual and anatomical content and the $F+\%$ will be low. The Word Association Test is likely to contain a few distant associations and many images. The Thematic Apperception Test usually elicits themes of loneliness, of being shut off from the world, and of the fragility of interpersonal bonds. Throughout the tests a few peculiar formulations usually occur. Differential diagnosis from incipient schizophrenia must be based on the absence of clear-cut, essentially *sufficient* diagnostic indicators such as extreme scatter, devastated concentration or learning efficiency, extreme syncretistic concepts, confabulations, an extraordinarily unbalanced movement-color ratio, extremely deviant or numerous sex responses, and so forth. Some of these cases, however, come for examination only after their withdrawal has been intensified by traumatic life experiences. Their test results will strongly resemble those of incipient schizophrenics and will thereby indicate the danger of further malignant developments.

PARANOID CONDITION

The patients to be discussed under this diagnostic heading are those who have developed single, enduring, encapsulated paranoid delusions and who do not, upon clinical examination, reveal either widespread disorganization or traces of a process of deterioration. They are generally able to function effectively and appropriately in most areas and may even be able to continue working while they are ill. These cases are among the most difficult to diagnose on the basis of test results. Many of them are indistinguishable from normals. Perhaps other tests than those included in .this battery might facilitate correct diagnosis of more of these cases.

BELLEVUE SCALE

In most instances, a conspicuously high Similarities score indicates a projective trend; the same inference can be made from conspicuously high Arithmetic and Picture Completion scores. Qualitative support for this inference should be, and usually is, present. One or two striking perceptual distortions in the Picture Arrangement and Completion subtests also indicate a projective trend.

LEARNING EFFICIENCY

No striking impairments are expected.

SORTING TEST

If psychopathic personality and character disorder can be ruled out on the basis of all the test results, fabulations in the Sorting Test are indicative of projective thinking. One or two fabulations may be present if a paranoid condition exists. Another possibility is that "difficult" items in either part of the test will be promptly and decisively failed as an expression of paranoid overcautiousness and divergence from the usual or popular view of things or events and their implications.

RORSCHACH TEST

Paranoid symptoms are suggested by: (1) a few strained, symbolic-like Dr responses in a coarctated record; for example, "A gun emplacement in a strategic position (lower middle Dr, VII);" (2) a sudden run of failures, usually on the last three or four cards; (3) many sharply or unusually articulated space responses, especially if these occur in a coarctated record; (4) an experience balance showing many *M*'s, no or practically no colors, with one or two of the *M*'s being *M*— or unusually articulated large *Dr*'s—ripped, as it were, out of the configuration of the inkblot; (5) a few *W*'s built up on the basis of several fabulized combinations; for example, on Card VIII: "A butterfly (lower pink and orange) ; this animal here (side pink) stepping on it with its hind feet; its front feet are being grasped by a human hand (side extensions of upper gray);" (6) exaggerated concern with relationships or resemblances between different areas of each inkblot or between different inkblots. In all these instances paranoid condition rather than paranoid schizophrenia is indicated only if no clear-cut schizophrenic reasoning and verbalizations are present in any of the test results.

WORD ASSOCIATION TEST

No diagnostic features are expected, except perhaps cautiousness in associating to the "sexual" words.

THEMATIC APPERCEPTION TEST

Themes of infidelity or of suspicious people are *not* reliable indicators of paranoid symptoms, unless they are unusually frequent or intense. The most frequent indicators are extreme perceptual distortions. For example, if the mother-figure holding the infant in Picasso's picture (Card 8) is seen as a man, or if the old woman looking into a room from the doorway (Card 2) is seen as a man, or—again in Picasso's picture—if the sketches in the background are perceived as real persons, paranoid symptoms are indicated. Again, schizophrenia must be ruled out before paranoid condition can be considered.

PARANOID CHARACTER

These cases are distinguished by pervasive suspiciousness and legalistic overcautiousness. Their life-pattern is built around proof and refutation, evidence and speculation, deduction and inference. In a sense, they are living examples of the syllogistic mind.

The test results are usually clearly diagnostic. Clear-cut schizophrenic responses are absent but the qualities of thinking mentioned above are all-pervasive. Obsessive-compulsive features are generally also striking, clinically and in the test results.

BELLEVUE SCALE

As in the paranoid conditions, the Similarities score tends to be conspicuously high. Verbalizations are overmeticulous to the point of caricature. The examiner's subjective reaction will usually be: "This is a person who, as far as he is able, will leave not the smallest loophole in any of his statements; he is responding as if he's being cross-examined in court." All possible meanings of the questions are explored if the least doubt arises. For example, when asked the *lost in a forest* Comprehension question, the patient may state: "If you say *lost*, you must be implying that I have no compass; otherwise it would be incorrect to say lost; therefore I will proceed on the assumption that I have no compass." When asked, also, to relate the last two Picture Arrangement stories, the patient may take into account the most minute details. The same applies to Picture Completion items where all gaps in lines as well as the correct responses tend to be pointed out. As a rule, the Picture Completion and Arithmetic scores are relatively high, indicating overalertness. These records can usually be distinguished from those of obsessives by the frequent legalistic formulations of responses.

LEARNING EFFICIENCY

No significant impairments are expected. Precision of recall is emphasized.

SORTING TEST

The emphasis tends to be on precision and exhaustiveness, but again the quality of the verbalizations facilitates differential diagnosis from obsessive-compulsive neurosis. Sortings are generally narrow or radial chains[61]) in Part I; in Part II, split-narrow amendments to abstract conceptualizations are frequent.

RORSCHACH TEST

Circumstantial descriptions, relationship verbalizations pointing out resemblances and differences among the cards, overconcern with symmetry and asymmetry, and many Dr's and S's are characteristic. The cautiousness and inhibition usually keep the $F\%$ and $F+\%$ quite high and the experience balance coarctated (one or two M's and no colors). The $A\%$ and $P\%$ also tend to be high as a consequence of overcautiousness. The record may be essentially a series of fabulized combinations,

---

61) For example, grouping all the red objects and all the rubber objects with the red rubber ball.

the configurations being taken too literally and all contents linked together. Frequent sharp or unusual space responses are more characteristic of these cases than of the paranoid conditions.

WORD ASSOCIATION TEST

No diagnostic patterns are expected. The stimulus word *frame* is occasionally understood in its colloquial legal sense.

THEMATIC APPERCEPTION TEST

This test generally elicits clear samples of legalistic thinking. The patient "builds up a case" for various possible interpretations of each picture, explicitly stating the details on which each inference is based. For example: "Since he has his hat in his hands, he has probably just arrived and is not leaving; if he were leaving he'd say goodbye before he got his hat." "I presume that it is an unpleasant situation, even though it looks like they are embracing, because her fingers seem to be pressing into his shoulder in an anguished way." Free, flexible fantasy, based on a general emotional orientation to the cards, is impossible. These cases usually do not grossly distort any of the pictures but numerous minor distortions are likely to be present; for example, the man in the graveyard may be seen as having handcuffs on or a broken string may be "seen" on the boy's violin.

THE NORMAL PERSONALITY

In clinical psychological testing the important questions are these: *how can we characterize the subject's typical efforts at adjustment?* and *how effective are these efforts?* The first question pertains to characteristic reliance on particular defenses and an associated selective organization of events; the second question pertains to the presence and degree of anxiety, emotional lability, and control and modulation of impulses. These questions can be asked for the ill and the healthy alike. *Normal* and *neutral* are not synonymous; each so-called normal person has his distinctive pattern of adjustment efforts and handicaps, and psychological testing of normal people therefore requires the same clinical orientation as the testing of any other type of case. Characteristic emphasis on obsessive or repressive defenses, inhibition or avoidance, and so forth, is to be sought out. While it is true that many subjects who are, clinically, apparently normal yield test results that are indistinguishable from those of neurotic subjects with the same general type of character make-up,[62]) it is also true that many others can be distinguished from their neurotic counterparts.

The test results should indicate the major character traits but should also indicate that these characteristics are not so rigid as to stifle spontaneity and be applied indiscriminately to all problem situations, nor so ineffective that unmodulated feelings, impulses, and anxieties dominate behavior. When rigidity in any one or several respects becomes pronounced or when controls appear ineffective, a neurosis is suggested. The reader is referred to the previous sections on neuroses and character problems for the indications of various character traits. Special attention has been paid to obsessive-compulsive, repressive, labile and impulsive, narcissistic, passive, schizoid, projective, depressive, anxious, tense, and inhibitory features. As a rule, the fewer and less dramatic the pertinent indications are, the less likely it is that these traits are crippling in their effects and the more likely it is that they are within the normal range. As a rule, indications of any of these traits, even when they are in the normal range, are discernible in the results of a battery of tests. It must be remembered, however, that the decision as to where a "normal" characteristic ends and where a "neurotic" one begins is most difficult in the tests and clinically. Diagnosing a case as falling within the normal range on the basis of test results is largely a matter of exclusion of the various pathological possibilities. It therefore seems advisable to carry on individual psychological testing only in a setting that includes independent clinical investigations as well.

---

62) Research in this area of testing—the differentiation of normal from neurotic character make-up—is urgently needed. Allied to this problem is the problem of assessing from test results the adjustment resources or "toughness" of normal personalities.

Chapter Three

CASE STUDIES

The cases selected for analysis in this chapter do not offer unusual or difficult diagnostic problems. For the most part, they have been chosen because they represent types of cases frequently seen in clinics, and because their test records contain an abundance of clear indications of character make-up and pathology. In the long run, few cases as clear as these will be encountered, but with these as diagnostic prototypes, the examiner can be better prepared to identify similar but less obvious cases. Thus the following analyses are not offered to illustrate all the subtleties of interpretation of test results. To the experienced clinical psychologist, much of what is to follow may seem gross and obvious. The aim has been to highlight the indications of major characteristics and pathological trends.

The following system of notation has been used in presenting the test records. 1. *Bellevue Scale.* In the Digit Span, Arithmetic and Picture Completion subtests all correct responses are simply scored + unless the verbalization of the response is interesting, in which case the verbalization is quoted and then scored +; all incorrect answers are simply quoted. In the remaining subtests, the verbalization of each response or, in the case of certain Performance subtests, the time of each response is followed by a numerical score in parentheses. Thus in the case of each subtest the raw score is the sum of all the + signs or numerical item-scores. 2. *Learning Efficiency.* Each correct memory unit is enclosed within parentheses; the final score is the number of these units, except that, following Babcock's instructions, four additional points are added to the raw score on immediate recall and one point is subtracted for each extreme distortion of the original story in either recall. 3. *Sorting Test.* In Part I, the starting item is named, the sorted objects are listed, the conceptualization of the sorting is quoted, and the sorting and conceptualization are then classified; in Part II, the subject's conceptualization of each of the examiner's twelve sortings is quoted and then classi-fied. 4. *Rorschach Test*. Each response is quoted, and, except for *W* responses, its location is given in parentheses immediately afterward. If inquiry was necessary, the response to inquiry is quoted in brackets immediately following the spontaneous verbalization and the location of the response. For example, on Card II, the following might be recorded: This looks like a butterfly (lower red). [(?) Because it had wings and a body. (?) It was red.])[1] The responses to each card are scored following the presentation of the responses, locations, and inquiries. The scoring symbols are listed at the end of this volume, on page 337. In the summary of scores following the record, additionals are noted in parentheses. 5. *Word Association Test*. Each stimulus word is listed and followed by the reaction time and the response. If the response was inquired into, the subject's comments, enclosed in brackets, follow the original response. False or delayed recalls are recorded in parentheses following the original response or the inquiry into it. For example, LOVE—8″—devotion [(?) I thought of my father first. (?) The way I feel toward him.] (6″—hate) .[2] The reader will note that two different forms of this test have been used. The old form begins with the word *world*; the new and preferred form begins with the word *hat*. 6. *Thematic Apperception Test*. The verbatim record of the spontaneous story and responses to inquiry is presented. Inquiry is made following the completion of the spontaneous story, if the story is incomplete in any essential respect; it is actually a form of prodding, except when the meaning of peculiar verbalizations is explored.

OBSESSIVE-COMPULSIVE CHARACTER NEUROSIS:

TEST RESULTS

Dr. C. Age: 32. Education: M.D. Occupation: Surgeon. Marital: 7 years, no children. Father: Merchant. Early Environment: Small town, Arkansas. Family Position: Older of 2. Religion: Methodist.

BELLEVUE SCALE

Comprehension

ENVELOPE: Put it in the mail box (2). THEATRE: Probably notify one of the management (2). BAD COMPANY: I don't know if that necessarily holds true. To prevent picking up their habits, I guess

---

[1] According to our method of administering the test, inquiry is not actually carried out after each response but after the subject has finished with each card.

[2] According to our method of administering this test, inquiry is actually pursued only after the entire test, including the recall section, has been administered.

(2). TAXES: In order to ... gain the environment which taxes are a necessary basis for. (?) Law and order, streets, sidewalks, government (1). SHOES: Tough and durable and pliable and at same time maintain a shine, look passable (1). LAND: Because of conveniences which are afforded. (?) It goes back to the taxes question: fire equipment, streets, walks, law, protection (1). FOREST: If possible ... moss on north side of trees, and if possible, find a river, determine the direction of flow and follow it. You could reach a peak or high point and sometimes you find a point that's familiar (1). LAW: Govern the behavior of people. (?) There has to be some maintenance of order by which government policies are carried out as well as personal behavior of individuals (1). LICENSE: In order to have records as to the legitimacy of the move. To provide some semblance of order. (?) Holdings, property, estate, children and their part in the family, to provide a legitimate name (1). DEAF: Because speech is more or less a reproduction or mirror of sound (2). RAW SCORE: 14.

Information

PRESIDENT: +. LONDON: +. PINTS: +. RUBBER: +. THERMOMETER: +. WEEKS: +. ITALY: +. WASHINGTON: +. HEIGHT: +. PLANE: Difficult to answer. Fouquet made an ascent in 1792 in a balloon. PARIS: 1500–1750. BRAZIL: East coast of South America; +. HAMLET: +. POLE: dk. VATICAN: +. JAPAN: +. HEART: +. POPULATION: +. H. FINN: +. EGYPT: +. KORAN: +. FAUST: Verdi. HABEAS CORPUS: Claiming the body. (?) Have to have writ by which to keep anyone in jail—or getting one out. (?) Get them out. ETHNOLOGY: Study of culture. APOCRYPHA: The top of. (?) More or less the last degree in whatever you want to apply it to. RAW SCORE: 18.

Digit Span

FORWARD: 3 and 4 on first try; fails both series of 5 by mixing in numbers of preceding series. BACKWARDS: 3 on first try; fails first series of 4 by reversal; fails first series of 5 by mixing in digits of preceding series; fails both series of 6. RAW SCORE: 9.

Arithmetic

ITEMS 1–8: +. ITEM 9: 10 yards (3"). No, 3 yards (12"). (Reread.) 9 feet (33"); +. ITEM 10: 12 times 8; 72 (15"). (?) 96 (35"). RAW SCORE: 9.

Similarities

ORANGE: Both fruit (2). COAT: Dress, arraignment (2). DOG: Animals, carnivorous (2). WAGON: Means of conveyance (2). PAPER: Means of deploying news (1). AIR: Means of conveyance also (1). WOOD: Fuel (1). EYE: Senses (2). EGG: Both seeds. (?) Say both ova (1). POEM: Arts (2). PRAISE: Means of criticism (1). FLY: Nature. (?) Both occur in nature (1). RAW SCORE: 18.

Picture Arrangement

HOUSE: + 3″ (2). HOLD UP: + 5″ (2). ELEVATOR: + 10″ (2). FLIRT: AJNET 21″ (2). FISH: EGFHIJ 20″ (1). TAXI: SALMUE 30″. (?) He was probably mussed up by lipstick. He was carrying a model. Afterwards getting in the cab and drawing the figure close. Then he turns around and it showed his cheeks smudged (1). RAW SCORE: 10.

Picture Completion

NOSE: +. MUSTACHE: Pupils and mustache; +. EAR: +. DIAMOND: +. LEG: +. TAIL: +. STACKS: Mast and rest of windows. DOORKNOB: +. SECOND HAND: +. WATER: +. REFLECTION: +. TIE: +. THREADS: Socket or the rings; +. EYEBROW: Part of the art. It should be showing the curls. SHADOW: +. RAW SCORE: 13.

Block Designs

ITEM 1: 16″ (3). ITEM 2: 10″ (5). ITEM 3: 10″ (5). ITEM 4: 25″ (4). ITEM 5: 31″ (5). ITEM 6: 150″. Good start, but breaks up first try, and starts elsewhere; some rotation. Places all-white block in center. No progress. ITEM 7: 65″. Rapid and no errors. "It's simpler when you keep looking at the design; at first I glanced at it and tried to remember it." (6). RAW SCORE: 28.

Object Assembly

ITEM 1: 10″ (6). ITEM 2: 35″ (8). ITEM 3: 115″. Places fingertips in grooves; tries all fingers, even thumb, in grooves and persists in this attempt for 80″ before gaining insight (6). RAW SCORE: 20.

Digit Symbol

60 correct. No errors. RAW SCORE: 60.

Vocabulary

APPLE: Fruit (1). DONKEY: Animal (1). JOIN: Hitch (1). DIAMOND: Stone. (?) Precious stone (1). NUISANCE: Something which grates upon someone else's life or behavior (1). FUR: Pelt (1). CUSHION: Seat (1). SHILLING: Coin. (?) Monetary unit in England (1). GAMBLE: Wager, I guess (1). BACON: Food. (?) Pork (1). NAIL: Holding device (1). CEDAR: Tree (1). TINT: A diluted color, with white (1). ARMORY: Place which houses armaments (1). FABLE: Story (1). BRIM: Edge (1). GUILLOTINE: A means of capital punishment by beheading (1). PLURAL: Many, more than one (1). SECLUDE: Isolate (1). NITROGLYCERINE: Chemical (1). STANZA: Means of division of poetry (1). MICROSCOPE: Instrument for enlarging (1). VESPER: Evening service (1). BELFRY: Housing for a bell (1). RECEDE: Withdraw (1). AFFLICTION: Disease (½). PEWTER: An alloy (1). BALLAST: Weight (½). CATACOMB: Maze. (?) Series of cells (½). SPANGLE: Something that glitters (1). ESPIONAGE: Spy system (1). IMMINENT: Almost certain to happen

(½). MANTIS: Insect (1). HARA KIRI: Form of suicide practiced by the Japanese (1). CHATTEL: Something which is put up as a forfeit. (?) In the case of a mortgage, piece of real estate. DILATORY: Adverse. (?) Dilatory effect, unwanted. AMANUENSIS: dk. PROSELYTE: To win over one's affections. It's applied to religion . . . win from one to another (1). MOIETY: A part (1). ASEPTIC: Without sepsis (1). FLOUT: To display in an ostentatious manner. TRADUCE: dk. RAW SCORE: 35.

Weighted Scores and IQ's

Comprehension 12	Picture Arrangement 9	Vocabulary 15
Information 13	Picture Completion 13	Verbal IQ: 123
Digit Span 6	Block Designs 13	Performance IQ: 120
Arithmetic 12	Object Assembly 12	Total IQ: 123
Similarities 14	**Digit Symbol 14**	

LEARNING EFFICIENCY

IMMEDIATE RECALL: (December 6) (last week) (10 miles) west of (Albany) (a river) (overflowed) (entering houses). (600 people) (caught cold). In attempting (to save) someone (a man) cut himself . . . in attempting to save someone (under a bridge). I forgot to say 600 caught cold (from the dampness) (and cold), which I doubt. (?) I have my own theory about colds. SCORE: 18.

DELAYED RECALL: (December 6) (last week) (in a small town) west of (Albany), (a river) (overflowed), (filling the streets) and (entering the houses). 10 . . .. 12 people, I guess, were killed. (600) (caught cold) as a result of (the dampness) and (cold). One (man) attempting (to save) (a boy) near a bridge . . . save the life of a boy (under a bridge), cut himself. SCORE: 16.

SORTING TEST

Part I

BALL: Adds eraser and sink stopper. (Considers corks but rejects them: "That would be another category, stoppers. (?) Without the ball.") "Rubber objects." Mildly narrow sorting, abstract concept. LARGE FORK: Adds all silverware and sugar. "Means of eating and sugar cubes as food. It could be carried on to cigarette, pipe and cigar— after dinner if you'd like." He does not extend the sorting. Mildly loose sorting, functional concept with an aborted fabulation introduced at the end. PIPE: Adds all smoking equipment. "All smoking implements, necessities." Adequate sorting, abstract concept. BELL: Adds lock and all tools except hatchet. "Bicycle bell, bicycle lock and tools for repair." Mildly loose sorting, concrete concept. CIRCLE: Adds rectangular and square paper. "Pieces of paper." Mildly narrow sorting, abstract concept. TOY PLIERS: Adds all tools, nails and block of wood with nail. "You can call these all tools, and if you want all metal, you can do that." (Adds all objects with some metal, including sink stopper and pipe.)

First sorting is mildly loose, abstract concept; the second is a loose sorting, abstract concept. BALL: Omitted; see first sorting.

Part II

RED: "Red." Abstract concept. METAL: "All metal." Abstract concept. ROUND: "Materials for production: paper for cigarettes, rubber, metal and cork." Syncretistic concept. TOOLS: "Tools." Abstract concept. PAPER: "Paper." (Adds imitation cigarette and real cigar.) "And this if it's a cigarette and the paper band on the cigar." Abstract concept, but because of pedantic thoroughness he flouts the implicit test instructions and adds objects on his own. PAIRS: "I see no reason why they should. (?) I could make a story out of it to include all of it. Other than just pairs I can't see why they should be put together." Starts with aborted fabulation but comes to an abstract concept. WHITE: "White." Abstract concept. RUBBER: "Rubber." Abstract concept. SMOKING MATERIALS: "Smoking implements." Abstract concept. SILVERWARE: "Because they're implements for eating." Abstract concept. TOYS: "Playthings." Abstract concept. RECTANGLES: "Material, I suppose, to get back to that again." Syncretistic concept.

RORSCHACH TEST

CARD I. Reaction time: 3″. Total time: 210″.

1. Butterfly, bat. 2. It could possibly be a ... two (sigh) dancers, whirling about a standard in the middle. [(?) They are turned outward, no definite face or legs.] I thought I got a contrast of dark and light ... 3. Oh ... face of a lynx or cat. 4. It could possibly be a very abused specimen of panhysterectomy: cervix, uterus, broader ligaments, connective tissue. [(?) Broad shadows.]

SCORES: 1: W F+A P. 2: W M+H Combination. 3: Ws F±Ad. 4: W FCh±Ats−Sex, Aggression.

CARD II. Reaction time: 15″. Total time: 270″.

1. First it appears ... two bears (black) with their front paws in apposition, hind legs ... two Russian dancers (same area). [(?) The face would be on the top (of the black) − it's not clear.] 2. It looks somewhat like the profile of a serving dish or casserole (upper middle *Dd* is handle of lid, edge of lid is ears of popular bear head. All black and center space.) [(?) With the white to exaggerate the light.] 3. It also looks like a Victorian piece of furniture, couch (black). [(?) It has the contour of the back of a couch.] 4. Two rather ridiculous looking people playing some children's game, perhaps claphands ... hands touching, knees almost ... wearing some type of costume, Halloween. [(?) Long noses and the type of headdress in red.]

SCORES. 1: D F+A−H. 2: DS FC′∓ Obj Orig. 3: D F±Obj Orig. 4: W MC+H P.

CARD III. Reaction time: 12″. Total time: 120″.

1. Looks like two waiters trying to lift something. [(?) Mess jackets in contrast to jacket and midriff, light shirt showing.] 2. It could in-

clude the cervical portion of a man wearing a red tie and the upper portion of the vest (middle red and center space). 3. Two flying fishes (legs of *P*).

SCORES.   1:   W MC′+H P.   2:   DS FCC′±Hd   Combination. 3: D F±A.

CARD IV. Reaction time: 30″. Total time: 210″.

1. Looks like some design, utilizing the head of a crane—long neck—coming out on each side. 2. A portion of it appears very much like an X-ray picture—the contrast—X-ray of spinal column (center section). 3. A door knocker (lower middle *D*). I pictured it in brass. [(?) Texture, and the rest (*W*) was a decorative design around it.] 4. Again, portions of it look like two shoes hanging with toes pointing outward (lower side *D*).

SCORES.   1: W F∓Design.   2: D ChF X-ray.   3: W FCh∓Obj Orig. 4: D F+Obj.

CARD V. Reaction time: 10″. Total time: 135″.

1. Again I think I'd have to say a bat. 2. Ballet dancer with wings attached. [(?) Arms above head, standing facing me, on tip toe.] 3. A poor imitation of a lip-stain. 4. With some imagination the "Flying Wing", new version of aeronautical design. 5. A stingaree, a type of jelly fish. [(?) Outline of it, general contour, the two tentacles.]

SCORES.   1: W F+A P.   2: W M+H.   3: W F–Lip-stain Orig. 4: W F±Obj.   5: W F∓A.

CARD VI. Reaction time: 8″. Total time: 180″.

1. Looks like a Navajo Indian rug design. [(?) Texture, pattern, lines radiating.] 2. Or a pelt rug (large *D*). [(?) Texture somewhat, displayed by shadow.]. 3. A type of toy which I have once seen. [(?) The handle: when you pulled the top, it would whirl around.] 4. Light house on a rock pinnacle (upper *D*). 5. A hand grinder tool, router drill. 6. Looks like a hand bell sitting on a base or on top of a table (upper *D*).

SCORES.   1: W FCh+Design.   2: D FCh+Ad P.   3: W F∓Obj. 4. D F+Arch. (W tend). 5: W F+Obj Orig. 6: D F+Obj (W tend).

CARD VII. Reaction time: 5″. Total time: 120″.

1. Looks like two girls with their hair in a top knot, facing; or one girl looking in a mirror (upper two-thirds). [(?) Head, shoulders, and bust.] 2. Two tropical fish (upper one-third, tail is uppermost projection). 3. Looks like an upside-down silhouette of George Washington (center space). 4. Looks somewhat like a type of vase of the early American period (center space).

SCORES.   1: D F+Hd P.   2: D F∓A.   3: S F+Hd.   4: S F+Obj.

CARD VIII. Reaction time: 10″. Total time: 225″.

1. First it looks like a, some ancient type of galley boat, coming toward me or going away; just the silhouette, end view. [(?) The two colored designs there are somewhat like flags; ropes, extending from the

mast.] 2. Two animals that are climbing at a rather dangerous angle up a stone cliff (side pink). 3. Chinese bowl or vase (all except side pink). [(?) The way the top of it lidded over. (?) Color perhaps impressed me.] 4. Two peasant girls sitting in the shade of a tree, sitting back to back at a small tree trunk (upper gray-green). [(?) The color, the overbranching, and eaves-like appearance.]

SCORES. 1: W FC+Galley boat Orig. 2: D F+A P (W tend). 3: D FC+Obj. 4: D Ms+H Orig.; Dr FC+Pl Combination.

CARD IX. Reaction time: 20″. Total time: 120″.

1. Looks like a candle burning, which had some foreign matter burned into it with differing colored smoke, maybe unwanted (center D). 2. The light portion somewhat like a profile of a woman's... not the side view... woman's head (center space). 3. Looks like two girls in green dresses in a very extravagant mood, dancing about on a pink raised block. [(?) Head unclear, billowing skirt.]

SCORES. 1: D FC+Obj. 2: S F±Hd. 3: D MC+H.

CARD X. Reaction time: 5″. Total time: 210″.

1. An orchid (pink). [(?) The long petals and the color.] 2. Two sandcrabs (side blue). 3. Two... what do you call these half-horse, half-fish affairs (pink). 4. Looks like two faces. It gives away the sex—boys' faces (upper inner pink). 5. I once saw a mural of sea figures like this (upper middle gray). 6. I can see several flowers. The yellow ones look like gladiolas (side yellow). 7. These two yellow look like very impressionistic flowers, I must say (inner yellow). [(?) It has a darker center bordering on brown.] 8. This very small part looks like a rabbit's head.

SCORES. 1: D FC+Pl. 2: D F+A P. 3: D F∓A. 4: D F+Hd. 5: D F+A. 6: D FC+Pl. 7: D CF Pl. 8: D F+Ad P.

Summary of Responses

R:46   EB:6—5.5

W 17 (3)	F+15	A 10	W% 37
D 25	F−1	Ad 3	D% 54
Dr 1	F±5	H 6 (1)	DR% 9
S 3 (3)	F∓5	Hd 5	
	M 1+, 1±	At 2	F% 57-96
	MC 2+	Obj 11	F+% 77-84
Qualitative	MC′ 1+	Pl 4	
Criticism	Ms 1+	Design 2	A% 28
Exactness	FC 6+	Arch 1	H% 24
Ostentation	FCC′ 1+	Galley boat 1	At% 4
	CF 1	Lip-stain 1	Obj% 24
	FC′ 1∓	Sex (1)	
	FCh 2±, 2+		P 9
	ChF 1		P% 20
			Orig 7±
			Orig % 15
			Combination 2

WORD ASSOCIATION TEST

HAT—1.5"—coat. LAMP—1.5"—light. LOVE—1"—hate. BOOK—1"
—review (2"—reading). FATHER—.5"—mother. PAPER—3.5"—writing.
BREAST—4.5"—mammary gland. [(?) I thought of the anatomical
term, thought more of a synonym for it.] CURTAINS—2"—window.
TRUNK (heard DRUNK)—1"—sober. DRINK—1.5"—thirst. PARTY—
2.5"—alone. [(?) I thought of a crowd enjoying themselves; common type
of occasion; and the opposite would be alone.] (3"—frivolity). SPRING
—1.5"—fall. BOWEL MOVEMENT—2"—defecation. RUG—1"—floor.
BOY FRIEND—1"—girl friend. CHAIR—1"—table. SCREEN—1"—window. PENIS—1.5"—vagina. RADIATOR—1"—heat. FRAME—1.5"—picture. SUICIDE—2.5"—murder; that was peculiar. [(?) At first it didn't
bring anything; then I was stymied. I wondered why.] MOUNTAIN—
1.5"—plain. SNAKE—1"—grass. HOUSE—2"—home. VAGINA—1.5"—
penis. TOBACCO—1"—smoke. MOUTH—1.5"—oral. HORSE—1.5"—
dog. MASTURBATION—2"—boy. WIFE—1.5"—husband. TABLE—1"—
chair. FIGHT—2.5"—pugilist. BEEF—1.5"—meat. STOMACH—2.5"—
ulcer. FARM—1.5"—land. MAN—5"—woman. TAXES—1"—government.
NIPPLE—1"—breast. DOCTOR—1"—nurse. DIRT—2"—earth (2"—land).
CUT—2.5"—trauma. MOVIES—1"—pictures (7"). COCKROACH—1.5"—
insect. BITE—1"—cut (7"). DOG—1.5"—cat. DANCE (heard VANS) —
3.5"—busses (2"—taxies). GUN—1.5"—hunting. WATER—1.5"—fish
(2"—fire). HUSBAND—1"—wife. MUD—1"—dirt. DANCE—4"—frivolity.
WOMAN—1"—man. FIRE—1"—water. SUCK—2.5"—sip. MONEY (heard
MUD)--2"—dirt (3"—wealth). MOTHER—.5"—father. HOSPITAL—2"—
doctor. GIRL FRIEND—.5"—boy friend. TAXI—2.5"—bus (6"). INTER-
COURSE—7"—woman. [(?) It left me cold at first.] (3.5"). HUNGER—
1"—thirst.

THEMATIC APPERCEPTION TEST

CARD 1. (Boy with violin.) This boy has for many years had a
great desire to possess a violin. The feeling perhaps that by its possession
he will be able to emulate the greatest masters. And now one has come
to him and the possibilities of this instrument more or less overwhelm
him. He sees in the violin the means by which his dreams can be fulfilled. (How get violin?) Perhaps he has probably expressed the desire
that at the next occasion on which presents are passed around that he
would like a violin. The paper is lacking the usual Christmas design
so that it is probably a birthday—just by deduction. (Outcome?) He
has had one of his greatest desires fulfilled and as we see him here now he
is looking at it with love and tenderness, more or less dreaming what it
will lead to, which I suppose ... (Lead to?) His becoming one of the
great masters of accomplishment in playing the violin. Perhaps he sees
himself in front of a great audience, swaying them with his music.

CARD 2. (Old woman in doorway.) This is a grandmother peeping
through the door into the parlor—looks old-fashioned—they used to call
it parlor. This action of hers is initiated by the quietness, stillness which
has replaced one of conversational tones she could hear ... in the room

where her granddaughter was entertaining a date. She, feeling in the role of a chaperone, felt she should look in upon the scene. She has an expression of joy mingled somewhat with a surprise at seeing her granddaughter perhaps in tender embrace and kissing her friend. (More about relationship?) Oh, perhaps she had been a confidante of the granddaughter who had expressed to her grandmother her hope that her friend would declare his love. The grandmother, knowing that the granddaughter desired this, was pleased.

CARD 3. (Old man in graveyard.) This is somewhat on the lines of a Salvador Dali painting—not quite that extreme—to represent loneliness, the loneliness being represented by this one animated body completely surrounded by the dead. This individual perhaps walked the territory looking for comradeship with one in his own form. Having failed to find it, he stands alone with the idea that he remains alone but alive among the dead. (Led up?) He had looked for another who also was alive or animated in the cemetery or city of the dead—failing to find that. (End?) He was there. (Final outcome?) The whole thing is a figurative drawing. (?) Explaining that would destroy the whole illusion created!

CARD 4. (Silhouette of man at window.) With a stretch of the imagination, although it is not shown in the picture, we could imagine the bars in the window—we can imagine a patient at Menninger's Clinic in East Lodge. However, taking the facts at hand, I'd say this was a man away from home, perhaps awakened in the middle of the night—or had gone to the window of the hotel and was viewing the panorama below him, and then looking at the rather bright full moon and thinking the moon was also shining over those beloved ones at home. He'd love greatly to be there, but he is accepting it somewhat stoically; the absence from home was necessary because of business or health or whatever it might be—could be a boy away at school.

CARD 5. (Heads of embracing couple.) This man is being parted from his wife for reasons which they both seem to realize are inevitable. The feelings are being manifested in the least outward demonstrative manner. They feel very deeply, however, but are making an attempt to prevent the other from realizing just how upset each is. On separation perhaps they will give way to their feelings and, quotation marks, break down and cry. (Why leaving?) Something, as I said, both feel to be inevitable. Might be he's leaving for the army, hospitalization, for some penal institution. (Outcome?) I told you! Upon separation both break down.

CARD 6. (Prehistoric animal, rocky road, bridge.) As a whole, it looks like some representation of a prehistoric period following a catastrophic upheaval. Perhaps two inhabitants of the earth at that period which had survived—one of them is an ancestor of the present goose or duck, at least it has a webbed foot and a long slender neck which is protruding from a niche or cavern in the cliffs. It is peering down upon a smaller animal which probably is an insect of some type, resembling somewhat a rather large grasshopper, with the intent of seizing it for food. The outcome is unknown: whether this lugubrious bird will get the grasshopper before the grasshopper gets away is questionable.

CARD 7. (Shadowy photograph of thumb.) This resembles a photomicrograph of one of the digits—fingers or thumb. Portions of the skin markings are seen in the second phalanx and terminal phalanx, the latter representing a portion of a fingerprint. Upon this fingerprint is a dark splotch which could be a representative of a drop of blood. The owner of this finger could be looking upon it with the realization that he was wounded or that this small globule represents a clue which might be the means of pointing him out as a guilty one in a murder. That's all.

CARD 8. (Nude couple; older woman with infant.) We have here three figures posing in an artist's studio who's made previous attempts to depict sorrow, pathos, but felt his endeavors had failed. He now has this grouping of a man and a woman representing the father and mother of a child held by a very stern-faced, rugged woman—rugged because of the artist's representation of her feet. This woman who now clasps the child of the man—the father and mother—and it is known that she is to separate the child from them. The child which is much wanted by the parents . . . the mother, in her grief at being separated, has turned to the father for sympathy and support—perhaps moral as well as physical support—and he in turn is attempting to dissuade this separation from the child. The grief and eagerness to have the child, displayed upon their faces, mingled with a rather awe, according to his face—in other words somewhat awe-stricken—he's helpless in his attempts to prevent the child from being taken away. The stern-faced woman could represent Death, I suppose, as a means of taking the child from them.

CARD 9. (Two chairs, table set for tea.) This is a conversational group. Period furniture. Remains of an afternoon cup of tea taken by a host and guest, both of whom have now departed, probably upon completion of a topic in which they are chatting upon mutual interests. The topic of conversation is probably one of culture rather than the more serious one of business because of the tête-à-tête appearance—which has undoubtedly taken place at home, and from the setting and the lack of cigarettes, ash trays, it's very likely that the host and guest were elderly and more interested in cultural subjects than more worldly things.

CARD 10. (Old man on shoulders of another old man.) Offhand it strikes me first as a surrealistic picture of two governmental forces which might be national or international, carrying out the old saying, "I'll scratch your back if you scratch mine," but each in turn fearing to turn his back to have it scratched because of mistrust of the other. The more naive has succumbed, however, to the possibilities and pleasure of the back-scratch and has submitted to the treatment. In his eyes, or in his expression is a great deal of wonderment as to what will take place with his back turned. In the scratcher's expression, one sees deviltry and the thought of "here's my chance at last". (Outcome?) He's going to take advantage of him. (?) It depends upon what the situation is (?) Without the original premise, it would be rather hard to tell the outcome. As I say, it could be two nations or two government departments. Upon relaxation of his guard, the other one is taking advantage of him.

CARD M 11. (Old woman facing away from young man.) The boy has come home to his mother with a tale of having . . . tale of confession of having wronged. A great love exists between mother and son, she feeling that he can never have wronged and the boy, realizing this feeling of his mother, is greatly hurt because of the . . . greatly grief-stricken because of the hurt he's given his mother. The mother upon hearing the confession is practically stunned. The greatest display of emotion which is demonstrated by a sagging of her body, facial musculature . . . In fact, she finds it hard to believe that her son could have committed any such act which he has now confessed. (Outcome?) The son is going to leave. Because of his intention of leaving which he thinks is perhaps best, he has appeared before his mother to explain why.

CARD M 12. (Man held by hands from behind.) This man is asleep on a bench in a railroad station. He's dreaming that unseen forces are clutching him, dragging him to torture or an act which he does not want to commit and he greatly resents. He's fighting in a passive sort of way really, although there are some signs of physical antagonism to the forces shown by the neck muscles—more really pain. He has a very determined expression—his chin especially—and he cannot be torn from his present place. There's a good deal of suffering, however, which by the position of the neck . . . the mental part seems to be greater than the physical. (?) Physical suffering is usually manifest more by somatic changes; this seems to be a furrowing of the brow—more mental anguish than physical. (What being dragged to?) Rather than torture to himself, he would be . . . he's being forced to look upon the torture of someone he loves. (Outcome?) Let's hope that the outcome will be that he'll wake up.

CARD M 13. (Figure on floor by couch.) Is it fair to ask what the object is in the corner? This is a boy—teen age—young teen age because he has knickerbockers on. He's suffered a great deal through worry about one he loves, which must be a relative: mother, father, sister, or grandparent. He's lying on the couch, probably quite ill, and in his childish enthusiasm he had hoped to spend a night at the bedside caring for them, but after rather long hours of the night he is no longer able to stay awake and has fallen asleep with his head upon the foot of the bed, on the side of the bed, toward the foot. The toy or wood-carving in which he's attempted to interest himself during the long hours to maintain alertness has fallen to the floor. (Outcome?) He will waken somewhat abashed but will receive a great deal of praise for the help he's given although it's been little and the praise will be enough so that although he felt somewhat abashed he'll think perhaps he did do a great deal of good.

CARD M 14. ("Hypnosis" scene.) This looks as if it were an experiment in the stages of hypnosis. The hypnotist, using his hand as an object for concentration, has failed although the subject was very co-operative and had probably hoped that he would be found a fit subject. His failure probably had been a result of overtrying because the impression is that his eyes are being held closed with a great deal of self-control but not relaxation. His knee or leg is flexed and the relaxation is not complete. From the expression on the subject's face, the experiment will probably continue because he seems to be quite determined. (Succeed?) Probably not.

CARD M 15. (Old man looking at younger man.) This young man here appears to be almost dazed. He's probably spent many many hours of sleeplessness, worry, awaiting the outcome of the delivery of his wife and their first child. He's now being told by the doctor . . . they don't seem to fit together, the doctor has a rather sly expression. The man looks as if the report wasn't so favorable. I suppose he must have had quadruplets to stun him and amuse the doctor—that's rather facetious—perhaps the doctor has an expression of pity rather than slyness. The young man is being told that though all was done that was possible, the wife and child died.

CARD M 16. (Man on rope.) We have here a rather brutal-looking, greatly developed from a muscular, physical point of view, man, who's making an escape from a high point—could be a window or over a wall—by letting himself down on a lowered rope; when he's suddenly seen or heard something which has frozen him in his attitude before making another movement of any sort. He is being very cautious, attempting to interpret this noise which he's heard by careful intensive concentration and listening. He feels that his next movement will be quite rapid in descending the rope and his escape, that far at least, will be successful. (Escape from what?) Some structure, high wall . . . could be a penal institute . . . from someone who's attempted to maintain him physically within bonds, from something which is physical and man-made rather than any act of God such as a fire or storm.

CARD M 17. (Figure by table; bats and owls.) This picture could be termed or named "Bats in the Belfry". This artist is probably a writer of mystery, fantastic stories dealing with more or less unnatural subjects —vampires, bats and all. It is very late. He's fallen asleep over his work and is now dreaming of some of the subjects or objects on which he's written. He will awaken, probably greatly pleased that all such subjects are merely a figment of his imagination.

CARD M 18. (Man on bed, face in pillow.) Frustration! . . . This man apparently has almost everything offered him but has failed to find sufficient interest in any of them and he has now, in his rather disquieted mind, thrown himself upon the bed exhausted with his efforts to find the "Bluebird", put quotes on Bluebird. Buried his head on the pillow, probably moving restlessly from side to side, wondering just what is the cause for this feeling he has. (Cause?) Goodness knows! (Outcome?) That remains to be seen. I can't say.

CARD M 19. (Shadowed figure with arms up.) We have here a plank-board wall, probably a barn or barn-like building, animal shelter, with a windowshade which is shattered and torn and partially shutting out the bright sunlight. The shadow of the remaining part of the blinds is projected on the wall. Only the night before, to the accompaniment of a mountain music band, a great deal of frivolity and festivity was taking place in the form of square dances, Virginia reels, and such, at which time the shattered torn blind, or rather plank-board wall, the plainness of the wall was never noticed. But with the end of the party, the sun rising, shining upon the plainness of this room, only a part of it—the sunlight filtered out due to a remnant of the blind—all the faults and irregularities were blatant. (Shown picture to check percept.) I can make out the silhouettes of many things: one of a Halloween ghost I noticed; perhaps that can be tied up with the story—ghost, peaked cap, humped back, face, arms.

CARD M 20. (Unkempt man and well-groomed man.) This is a representation of failure and success in not only business endeavor, but breeding. The man in the foreground represents success from the standpoint of business or profession, his vocation. He's well-groomed and has a very shrewd, brilliant expression and appears to be capable of meeting any obstacles which might arise in his march to ambitious goals. In the background, we see the opposite. The man is more or less dirty, no grooming whatever, shaggy appearance. His features are coarse with no refinement or culture although he has a rather moderate expression of perseverance. One feels that minor obstacles prevent his reaching his goals, if he had goals. It's probably more the lack of goals which has allowed him to fall into his present state of dilapidation. The finer features of the foremost man represent those which we ordinarily look upon as representing higher types of breeding. The coarse features, wide nose, rather narrow-set as well as deep-set eyes: all together make a picture of a poor type of breeding—Jukes family type. (Relationship?) Only for contrast—the fact that they were both human beings.

ANALYSIS OF RESULTS

BELLEVUE SCALE

The Verbal level suggests developmental emphasis on intellectual pursuits. However, the fact that Information is 2 points below Vocabulary suggests some weakness of application in this respect—perhaps superficiality of interests and poor integration of achievements. On this high level the lower Information score cannot safely be taken as indicative of the dominance of a repressive emphasis during development. The great drop in Digit Span indicates intense anxiety, and, since it is as much as 9 points below Vocabulary, it suggests the imminence of a process of disorganization; if, however, no other evidence accumulates for this latter inference, it can be dismissed. The lesser drop of Arithmetic indicates some impairment of ability to concentrate. The relatively well-retained Performance level suggests a character problem rather than an acute neurosis with more or less incapacitating symptoms. As a rule, more acute conditions either lower the entire Performance level or give rise to striking scatter; Object Assembly is especially likely to drop. The drop of Picture Arrangement suggests a weakness of anticipations, but this pattern is so frequent that its diagnostic import is not clear.

In Information, the response to the *airplane* item ("Difficult to answer that; goes back very far... Fouquet made an ascent in 1792 in a balloon") is clearly that of an obsessive, in that the need for historical precision is dominant over adherence to widely accepted stereotypes. The types of incorrect answers to the *Faust, habeas corpus* and *ethnology* items, all indicate loosely integrated cultural interests, and the strained response to *apocrypha* (apotheosis?) has a pretentious quality. At this point, then, an intellectualizing and somewhat pretentious mode of thinking is apparent.

In Comprehension, a characteristic "sophisticated intellectual" response is given to *bad company* ("I don't know if that necessarily holds true ...") in that he again disclaims conventional ideas because of their inaccuracy. The use of the words *environment, afforded, determine, legitimacy, semblance* within this subtest has a distinctively intellectualizing quality, and the strained formulations ("In order to gain the environment which taxes are a necessary basis for ...") point to the rigidity and pretentious character of the "intellectual" approach. It is now even clearer that intellectualizing is probably a major defense in the character structure and that, diagnostically, this is likely to be an obsessive-compulsive character problem or neurosis.

The Arithmetic score is evidently lowered by temporary inefficiencies: he follows the general procedure for solving the last two problems but makes computational and other minor errors. No profound concentration impairment is, however, indicated. In Similarities he trips over the *coat-dress* item confusing *raiment* with *arraignment*. Again the pretentious straining and poor integration of intellectual achievements are evident. "Deploying news" is also a nice specimen of pretentiousness. Verbal concept formation remains on a high level, however.

In Picture Arrangement, his performance is somewhat better than the score would suggest since he gets the point of the *fish* story and gets it quickly (20"), but a minor error in sequence pulls his score down from a potential 6 to 1. Failing to get the point of the *taxi* sequence is extremely frequent. The perception of the blush-lines as lipstick smudges is unusual. In Picture Completion, "part of the art" is an awkward formulation. Detecting the absence of pupils on the *mustache* item suggests unusually alert attention to detail—a likely feature in an obsessive subject.

In Block Designs, the note, "Rapid," and his excellent score on the last item reflect his high intelligence level; the failure on item 6 indicates tension. In Object Assembly the impaired performance on the *hand* item also indicates tension, and the persistent efforts to fit the fingertips into the grooves between the finger bases suggest that rigidity characteristically accompanies increase of tension—another likely feature in an obsessive subject.

In Vocabulary, aside from occasional ostentatiousness, the definition of *nuisance* is noteworthy. Most subjects speak of a bother or a pest, but his definition has an unusual intensity to it: one's *life* is disrupted by a nuisance. This suggests a high degree of irritability and intolerance once he is irritated.

In general, the Bellevue Scale results describe an intelligent, obsessive-compulsive man who is rigidly, somewhat ostentatiously, and often ineffectually, an "intellectual". Other minor indications mentioned require more direct support.

LEARNING EFFICIENCY

The average score of 17, and particularly the delayed recall score of 16, are somewhat low compared to a Vocabulary score of 15. A mild concentration impairment, rather than any basic impairment of learning ability, is indicated. The persistence of "west of Albany" in the delayed recall suggests the rigidity already noted. The statement, "...which I doubt...", in the immediate recall is another indication of this obsessive's nearly inappropriate pedantry.

SORTING TEST

In Parts I and II the conceptual level is essentially abstract. The concept span in Part I fluctuates from mildly loose to mildly narrow, a pattern more indicative of anxious uncertainty than of any special character trait. A tendency toward clear-cut looseness is evident on the *toy pliers* item but is offered only as a second possibility. In Part II, a tendency toward syncretistic concepts is evident in two instances, but is not extreme. A mild schizoid trend may lie behind these responses. This would be supported by the loose sorting of metal objects on the *toy pliers* item of Part I, where even the pipe and sinkstopper are included because of small metal attachments.

RORSCHACH TEST

In the record of an obsessive person, we expect a relatively high R, high $DR\%$ and either many M or an emphasis on M in the experience balance. We also expect frequent critical, pedantic verbalizations.

The actual R of 47 is high relative to the average of the general population, and the EB of 6-to-5.5 does include significantly more M than the average record. The 7 original responses are noteworthy in this respect. It is clear therefore that this is an ideationally active person and one likely to have obsessive characteristics. We do not find, however, a high $DR\%$ but instead an absolutely high number of W. This is atypical in obsessive records but not inexplicable: we have already seen clear indications of strained perfectionism and the high W in this case probably refers to this characteristic—an intellectually pretentious man trying to outdo himself in his integrative efforts. The 6 space responses, in this context of obsessiveness, indicate that doubting is likely to be conspicuous.

The $F\%$ and $F+\%$ are within normal limits and do not contribute directly to the diagnostic picture. The color distribution is noteworthy: there are 9 FC's and 1 CF. The overwhelming emphasis on FC indicates that he is characteristically overcompliant in his interpersonal relationships, and further suggests that passive needs are likely to be quite strong. Ideally a few more CF's should be present, since these would indicate that his adaptiveness was warm and spontaneous rather than forced and rigidly compliant.

His spontaneous approach to Card I is rigidly abstract: he gives 4 W's and then leaves off. His approach is at the same time very cautious: "Could possibly be a . . ." and ". . . a very abused specimen of a. . .". The latter quotation has a double implication: on the one hand he is perfectionistically indicating how imperfect the idea is and on the other hand the *form of expression* of his dissatisfaction has a distinctively aggressive quality. He could have said merely, "Not a very good resemblance." Seeing things as *whirling* appears to be frequent in the records of persons disturbed by their homoerotic impulses. Sexual preoccupation with an aggressive tinge is suggested by the *hysterectomy* response. On Card II the integrative drive, as well as ruminativeness, is apparent in his returning in the fifth response to his first response, but this time getting a head on the figure. Criticism persists in the "ridiculous looking people"; the need to disown this response as a childish display suggests that humor is not one of his assets.

On Card III, ". . . *trying* to lift something" has an overtone of feelings of inadequacy; most subjects who give this response merely say "lifting something".

On Card IV the delayed reaction, the vaguely integrated design, the vague X-ray, and the somewhat forced door-knocker precede the only unequivocally good response, the shoes. Efficiency is impaired by intense anxiety but this only seems to drive him on to greater productivity. Obsessives characteristically keep punching in these situations, however feeble their punches become. In this case, the first response is empty.

Most striking on Card V is the "lip-stain" response, which is reminiscent of the perceptual error (lipstick) in the *taxi* sequence in Picture Arrangement and of the whirling figures on Card I. In other words, men who see lipstick marks or lips in the Rorschach Test are usually characterized both by sexual preoccupations and a pronounced homoerotic trend. This indication ties in with the passivity implied in the color-distribution. On Card VI the sequence *W-D-W-D-W-D* indicates rigid, compulsive efforts to remain on an abstract, all-inclusive level of thinking even though the configuration of the card keeps beating him down. On Card VII, he sees one response upside down: inverted percepts characteristically occur in the records of schizoid subjects, and this response therefore lends some support to the mild schizoid implications of the Sorting Test responses.

Card VIII rarely elicits *W*'s which are predominantly determined by form, but here again this subject quickly (rigidly) comes through with a *W* determined only by form. On Card IX, the gay musical comedy response, because he disowns it as "extravagant", offers another suggestion of sexual preoccupation at the same time as it indicates how alien such "frivolity" is to his self-conception. On Card X, his concern with the sex of the faces again suggests the homoerotic trend and its manifestation in doubts about sexual identity. It is not implied that he is an overt homosexual, but merely that a solid acceptance of the masculine role has not been achieved.

Throughout the test, the cultural overspecificity of responses (Victorian, Navajo, early American, ancient galley boat, Chinese bowl, peasant girls, a mural) has the somewhat ostentatious quality which has been seen already in the other tests and other aspects of this test. It is also noteworthy how on Cards VIII, IX, and X he begins with an *FC* and how on VIII and IX the *M* comes last. This sequence indicates how automatically he will restrict himself to passive, compliant responses in emotionally disturbing situations; self-expressive responses are inhibited and pushed into the background.

WORD ASSOCIATION TEST

Intellectualizing is evident in *book*—review, *breast*—mammary gland, *mouth*—oral, *fight*—pugilist, *cut*—trauma, *dance*—frivolity. The last response has an ascetic flavor as well. *Party*—alone suggests strong feelings of loneliness and is reminiscent of the few mild indications of a schizoid trend. The erroneous recall *party*—frivolity expresses a rejecting attitude, probably associated with his expressed discomfort. Mishearing *money* as *mud* and responding with "dirt", especially in the context of an obsessive-compulsive character make-up, suggests special concern with cleanliness and dirt. Mishearing *trunk* as *drunk* and responding with "sober" seems to relate to the already indicated presence of acute conflict over oral-passive needs. Delay in reaction to *breast* and delayed recall on *bite* reinforce this inference. The passivity evident in the Rorschach Test and this accumulation of disturbances in reaction to stimulus words with oral connotations suggest that an addictive trend may be present. The disturbed response to *suicide* is noteworthy for its depressive overtones. Finally the blocking in reaction to *intercourse* and his striking description of the experience of blocking—"left me cold at first"—suggest powerful sexual inhibitions.

THEMATIC APPERCEPTION TEST

Ostentatious word usage and attention to detail run throughout this test and will not be commented upon except in unusual or instructive instances.

Card 1. (Boy with violin.) The theme is dreams of success, success being equated with greatness and fame. This is a conventional theme but is expressed with intensity ("greatest desires"; "love and tenderness"; "overwhelm him") and indicates great dreams of himself. In the midst of all this, however, and in traditional obsessive style, he takes time out for a tiny detail and deduces the occasion of the gift. Only the boy's fantasy is emphasized and there is no statement of ensuing action. This, together with the fact that the violin is a "present", suggests the passivity already noted. Card 2. (Old woman in doorway.) The theme is an affectionate relationship between mother-figure and daughter-figure. There is somewhat too much talk about the girl and none about the boy: when this partiality becomes frequent or striking, it is indicative of a latent feminine identification. A strong dependent attachment to a kindly mother-figure is suggested, especially by the unusual apperception of the woman as "pleased" rather than apprehensive. Card 3. (Old man in graveyard.) The theme is loneliness. The elaboration of the theme is singular and highly personal. The word association *party*-"alone" takes on greater significance now. He is describing himself as a person who has been unable to form strong attachments and is locked within himself. The reference to Dali is unfortunate.

Card 4. (Silhouette of man at window.) The theme is stoic acceptance of loneliness. The reference to loved ones at home is in apparent contradiction with the strong statement on Card 3 and probably reflects a wish. The theme of loneliness during a separation occurs frequently on this card, but accepting it "stoically" is personal and negates the expression of emotional ties. The reference to the Menninger Sanitarium sets the stage for a story built around self-reference. Card 5. (Heads of embracing couple.) The theme is suppression of feeling at separation from a presumed love-object. The reference to hospitalization at the end indicates a self-reference. He expresses genuine sadness and tenderness here but rejects these feelings by putting their expression "in quotes". This "least outward demonstrative manner" refers to the emotional inhibition so frequently observed in obsessives. This is the exact opposite of the free expression of affect characterizing the Thematic Apperception Test record of the hysteric in this chapter. Card 6. (Prehistoric animal, rocky road, bridge.) The theme is struggle for survival in a catastrophic world, a theme which speaks for itself. The cautious attitude toward stating the outcome is pathologically pedantic.

Card 7. (Shadowy photograph of thumb.) The theme is betrayal of aggressive impulses by small signs, another theme which speaks for itself. Card 8. (Nude couple; older woman with infant.) The theme is the male-figure's ineffectiveness and "weakness" as a husband. When he should be assertive, he is "awe-stricken" and disappoints the dependent wife. Events are inevitable (note the idea of inevitability in the previous stories of separation) and beyond his control—a rationalization of a passive attitude. That this is a personal reference is indicated by the relatively rare interpretation of the man's attitude; he is usually seen as protesting, explaining, or commanding. A subsidiary theme is implied in the opening sentence: inability to express affect freely. Again he ruptures the emotional continuity of the experience by attention to detail (feet) —a classically obsessive device and one which appears to fall into the category of defense by isolation. Card 9. (Two chairs and table set for tea.) The theme is the maturity implicit in cultural interests. From his generalized strenuous efforts to prove himself a man of culture, the statement of this ideal is not surprising. Careful attention to detail is striking but too many *inferences* from tiny details are beginning to accumulate. Any such accumulation suggests a projective trend.

Card 10. (Old man on shoulders of another old man.) The theme is the danger of letting one's defenses down, however pleasurable it may be to relax and take a completely passive role. The final statement makes this clear. A somewhat paranoid resistance to assuming a vulnerable, passive role is implied. The aggressive connotations of the picture are intellectualized in terms of nations and are not coped with directly: he avoids dealing with concrete, individual hostility. Card M 11. (Old woman looking away from young man.) The theme is guilt because of failure to meet a mother's expectations: this is the popular theme but is stated more strongly than is usual. The expression of "great love between them" is intense and seems personally valid (see also Card 2) even though the expression "he has appeared before his mother" has a hostile quality. Passive dependence on the mother-figure's approval is also implied. The man is an unworthy figure who hurts rather than brings pleasure to his love-objects. Note again the switch to detail and inference in the midst of this intense story. Card M 12. (Man held by hands from behind.) The theme is passivity and imminent failure in controlling one's impulses. The statement, ". . . fighting in a passive sort of way" and the emphasis on intellectual struggle as opposed to vigorous action appear to be excellent self-descriptions. When he is finally forced to add more content to the *torture* idea he expresses a sadistic attitude toward love-objects, but from behind a rationalized passivity (". . . forced to look") . Detail again breaks up the story.

Card M 13. (Figure on floor by couch.) The theme is personal weakness and unworthiness and inability to accept love from others. He apparently feels with some guilt that he is really neglectful of others, but that they are taken in by his outward show of affection and compliance —another typically obsessive concern. He implicitly criticizes his efforts at self-deception also. Card M 14. ("Hypnosis" scene.) The theme is inability to slip into a relaxed passive role, and is reminiscent of the story to Card 10 in which the danger of complete passivity without watchfulness were stressed. The present story probably relates to his minimal response to a test of hypnotizability which was a part of his current psychiatric examination. He seems aware of his tendency toward vigorous overcompliance. Card M 15. (Older man looking at younger man.) The theme is death of love-objects. Again a thinly rationalized expression of aggression is evident: the wife and child could have at least pulled through. The patient apparently tried to forestall this fantasy by becoming facetious, but, being his own severest critic, he drove himself back to compliance and expressed the alien fantasy. The older man is rarely seen with a *sly* expression and it is difficult to decide the basic import of this singular and highly projective percept: perhaps it represents an attempt to cover the subsequently expressed death-wish against the wife. Obsessives frequently are so attentive to fragmented detail that they elaborate contradictory affective connotations and, getting bogged down in doubt, bring the story to an abrupt end.

Card M 16. (Man on rope.) The theme is escape from restraint. *Escape* is a frequent theme but almost always the escape is from a prison or from some other specific restraint. Here there is just restraint. He is probably expressing a wish to be free of his inhibitions. Card M 17. (Figure by table; bats and owls.) The theme is bad dreams and is developed so conventionally that its personal reference is unclear. Card M 18. (Man on bed; face in pillow.) The theme, clearly formulated, is "frustration". Here is direct expression of what has already been indirectly inferred: the despair of a man who has not formed intense, gratifying object-attachments despite "the best of opportunities". In inquiry, his conscious recognition of the self-reference becomes apparent. "Put quotes on Bluebird" is pathetic, occurring as it does in the midst of a powerful expression of despair. Card M 19. (Shadowed figure with arms up.) The theme is the inevitable coming to the fore of faults and inadequacies and the futility of a "frivolous" front. This touching description is abstract on the surface, but from what we have already seen, the structure of the description expresses his self-conception. The two perceptual distortions reinforce the impression that a projective trend is present. Card M 20. (Unkempt man and well-groomed man.) The theme is lack of goals and its disastrous effects. He aspires to the role of the well-bred, brilliant, and cultured gentleman, but he feels that passivity with respect to obstacles and vagueness of goals are more characteristic and that he is therefore a rather worthless, dilapidated character. In general, his self-conception is depressively-toned and relentlessly critical.

No clear-cut signs of impending disorganization have been found, and the great drop of the Digit Span score in the Bellevue Scale may be interpreted as a reflection of intense anxiety.

Test Report

Intelligence and Thought Organization: Intelligence functioning bears the stamp of an obsessive-compulsive character development. Extreme compulsive attention to detail and rigid rationalistic and intellectualistic efforts at overall integration of experience pervade his thinking. This drive for integration and abstraction often leads to arbitrary results, with respect both to strained inferences from details and to final sweeping generalizations. This arbitrariness has a definite projective quality. However, gross misinterpretations are not likely to occur since the general accuracy of percepts and the general orderliness of thinking are essentially well-retained. He is much involved in being "correct". The intellectualizing aspect is conspicuous in his ostentatious, often stilted, and sometimes incorrect use of words and in his pedantic and circumstantial mode of discussing emotional material (as in the Thematic Apperception Test). Although cultural interests definitely appear to be present, they appear to be relatively poorly integrated; he flaunts rather pathetically the cultural odds and ends he has picked up. A mild schizoid trend is also evident. At present, his level of efficiency appears greatly lowered: a profound attention impairment is present and quickly mobilized anxieties often disrupt performance. Much doubting appears to be going on. His present I.Q. is 123.

Emotional Factors: The patient appears to be striving toward good rapport and object attachments and does have the capacities for these; however, obsessional doubting and caution probably stand in the way of lasting, intense gratifications. He is aware of this inability to experience real enjoyment and feels lonely and depressed. A further hindrance appears to be the presence of strong, pent-up aggressions which he has inadequate means of expressing, and which he characteristically tends to rationalize, project, or deny through passive compliance. They are likely to be expressed mainly in aggressive fantasies and irritability. Rationalizing and isolation appear to be his chief defenses against all strong feelings. Anxiety is intense and the tolerance threshold is only fair. He appears to feel that he is too passive and there are indications of intense passive needs: the general impression is that by way of intellectual self-sufficiency he rigorously attempts to combat any admission of passivity that he can recognize, but, at the same time, he is very alert to nuances of interpersonal relationships and automatically assumes a passive, compliant role. In this setting of acute conflict over passive needs and intense anxiety, an addictive trend is likely to be present. Sexual adjustment appears to be poor and it is suggested that a strong latent feminine identification is present. Some sexual preoccupation is likely.

Figures and Attitudes: As he says in one Thematic Apperception Test story, he can have "everything" and yet finds himself "uninterested". He feels himself to be a "lonely" and "frustrated" man, aspiring to culture and brilliance and, above all, to "ability to meet obstacles"; yet he feels that he cannot meet obstacles and that he is a failure because of "lack of goals". This self-conception appears to derive from his basically obsessional make-up. A strong attachment to the mother-figure is indicated; the wife-figure appears to be rejected and aggressive impulses toward her appear close to, if not already in, consciousness. He feels, too, that he must be constantly on guard since complete passivity, though pleasurable, leaves one open to "attack". He tends to belittle expression of affect, especially sadness; yet his own sadness appears to preoccupy him. He tends to overreact to aggressiveness as "brutal", yet it is likely that his fantasies and probably, indirectly, his behavior are often aggressive.

Diagnostic impression: Severe obsessive-compulsive character neurosis.

CLINICAL SUMMARY

Dr. C., a thirty-two year old surgeon, was referred for study and treatment because of excessive use of drugs and numerous somatic difficulties. His father is a rigidly honest, scrupulous businessman, who has always been affectionate toward the patient. He assigned relatively mature personal responsibilities to the patient at an early age. The patient appears to have incorporated his father's high and rigid ethical standards. The mother is described as being very tense and appears to have been overprotective.

The patient was very obedient as a child. Throughout his school years he was a star student, an excellent athlete, and a social leader. He was always ambitious to achieve the best in whatever he attempted and was disappointed when he did not do as well as he thought he could. He had a number of more or less casual sexual affairs before he met his wife-to-be. He tended to keep women at a distance and lost interest in them when they became too involved in the relationship. While in medical school, about eleven years ago, symptoms of a duodenal ulcer appeared. From that time to the present he has had several stomach operations and many whole blood transfusions, several attacks of pneumonia, frequent and severe headaches and recently he has lost 40 pounds of weight. After the third year of college he married a young woman wl ɔ was a student of engineering. From the beginning their sexual adjustmant was poor and it has become increasingly so, until at the present time they have intercourse infrequently. After marriage the patient became asocial, in contrast to his previously highly social ways. Because of headaches and fatigue he preferred to spend evenings quietly at home. His wife "nagged and screamed" at him to be more sociable but he characteristically said nothing. He became generally fatigued and tense and his headaches were severe. About a year ago he began to depend on seconal for sleep. A few months ago he began using codeine for relief of his headaches. He also began to feel depressed. The patient was greatly relieved when his wife and colleagues independently arranged for his hospitalization.

He complains chiefly about his tension and fatigue. These have been so bad that he has had to drive himself to fulfill his duties and has had to discontinue active hobbies. During his interviews he tended to avoid reference to anything unpleasant about his family or close acquaintances. He states that he has always "held things in", even though he is frequently angry, because this seems easier than arguing. His attitudes toward his illness and toward his very poor marital adjustment are very passive. He feels that he has lost interest in his work and in himself. His appearance has an apathetic quality. Nevertheless, during interviews, he struggled to give "perfectly correct" answers. The clinical diagnosis was anxiety state with psychosomatic symptoms and symptomatic addiction in a compulsive personality.

HYSTERIA: TEST RESULTS

Mrs. K. Age: 34. Education: 1 year college. Occupation: Housewife. Marital: 12 years, 2 sons. Husband: Clerk. Father: Business Manager. Early Environment: Small town. Family Position: Oldest of 9. Religion: Protestant.

BELLEVUE SCALE

Comprehension

ENVELOPE: Take it to the nearest mailbox or post office (2). THEATRE: Yell fire and get out as fast as I could. BAD COMPANY: Your friends will talk about you; if we want to live in a good environment we must choose good company (1). TAXES: Means of keeping the Treasury Department reimbursed; money to pay debts the government owes (2). SHOES: They are soft, long-wearing, pliable, comfortable (?). LAND: City people have more facilities, advantages (1). FOREST: Look for the sun; comes up in the east (2). LAWS: To have a law-abiding group of people; otherwise they would corrupt the city. LICENSE: To prevent bigamy. DEAF: Without ever having heard the human voice, they wouldn't learn how to use their voice (2). RAW SCORE: 12.

Information

PRESIDENT: +. LONDON: +. PINTS: +. RUBBER: +. THERMOMETER: +. WEEKS: No idea...48. ITALY: Is it Sicily? WASHINGTON: +. HEIGHT: I don't know... 5—2? PLANE: +. PARIS: No idea...3000? +. BRAZIL: +. HAMLET: + NORTH POLE: Magellan. VATICAN: +. JAPAN: +. HEART: +. POPULATION: 30 to 50 million? I'm just guessing. H. FINN: ...I can't think of it now. EGYPT: I was reading about it only the other day ... can't recall ... Europe? KORAN: dk. FAUST: dk. HABEAS CORPUS: Something to do with a body. ETHNOLOGY: dk. APOCRYPHA: dk. RAW SCORE: 13.

Digit Span

FORWARD: 3, 4, and 5 on first try; fails both series of 6 by dropping numbers. BACKWARDS: 3 on first try; fails both series of 4 by reversals. RAW SCORE: 8.

Arithmetic

ITEMS: 1–4: +. ITEM 5: 7 (8″) (?) Oh! ... 8 (20″). ITEMS 6–8: +. ITEM 9: 12 feet. (?) I can't make my mind work ... (?) I don't know how I got it! ITEM 10: 112 men. (?) I can't concentrate, I get confused. Isn't it 8 times 12? 112. RAW SCORE: 7.

Similarities

ORANGE: Fruit (2). COAT: Clothes (2). DOG: Animals (2). WAGON: Vehicles (2). DAILY PAPER: News, information (2). AIR: We need both to live (2). WOOD: Something to burn (1). EYE: Two of our five senses (2). EGG: Reproduction. (?) Oak comes from a seed and egg is the means of a chick (1). POEM: Both dedicated to something (1). PRAISE: As a child we get both praise and punishment. FLY: A fly flies in the air and a tree waves its branches. What trivial questions! I'd say they weren't alike! RAW SCORE: 17.

Picture Arrangement

HOUSE: + 5″ (2). HOLDUP: + 9″ (2). ELEVATOR: + 17″ (2). FLIRT: JNAET 24″ (3). FISH: EFGHIJ 93″ (?) He threw the fish back into the water (3). TAXI: SAMUEL 50″ (?) He got embarrassed (3). RAW SCORE: 15.

Picture Completion

NOSE: +. MUSTACHE: +. EAR: +. DIAMOND: dk. LEG: Marks on back. TAIL: +. STACKS: Sail. KNOB: +. SECOND HAND: +. WATER: +. REFLECTION: Her other arm. TIE: +. THREADS: +. EYEBROW: dk. SHADOW: dk. RAW SCORE: 9.

Block Designs

ITEM 1: 12″ (4). ITEM 2: 9″ (5). ITEM 3: 15″ (4). ITEM 4: 27″ (3). ITEM 5: 52″ (3). ITEM 6: 112″; much trial and error rotation of blocks (3). ITEM 7: 205″; trial and error rotation; 2 blocks not placed at time limit. RAW SCORE: 22.

Object Assembly

ITEM 1: 11″; one arm up (5). ITEM 2: 27″; ear reversal (4). ITEM 3: 49″; index and middle finger reversed (4). RAW SCORE: 13.

Digit Symbol

35 correct; 6 reversals of 2-symbol. RAW SCORE: 38.

Vocabulary

APPLE: Fruit (1). DONKEY: Animal (1). JOIN: Put together (1). DIAMOND: Gem (1). NUISANCE: A bother (1). FUR: Pelt of an animal (1). CUSHION: A soft pillow (1). SHILLING: Piece of money. (?) English (1). GAMBLE: To throw your money away. BACON: Meat, pork (1). NAIL: A piece of steel that, to put boards together (1). CEDAR: A tree (1). TINT: To dye, color (1). ARMORY: Large gathering place for soldiers: a building (1). FABLE: Myth (1). BRIM: Ledge, part of a hat. (?) Edge (1). GUILLOTINE: Gallows, it means putting your head down and being beheaded (1). PLURAL: More than one (1). SECLUDE: Hide away (1). NITROGLYCERINE: Explosive (1). STANZA: More than 4 lines; stanzas of national anthem ($\frac{1}{2}$). MICROSCOPE: Instrument to magnify small objects (1). VESPER: Church services, song service (1). BELFRY: Tower in which bell is hung (1). RECEDE: Go back (1). AFFLICTION: I have an affliction. Means to be maimed or have something happen to you that you can't help; like losing some part of your body ($\frac{1}{2}$). PEWTER: Rare metal. (?) I have a pewter vase at home ($\frac{1}{2}$). BALLAST: Ship has to have ballast. (?) Sail ... I have to have ballast; somebody you depend on, keep you going. CATACOMB: Underground burial place in Rome (1). SPANGLE: Something that glitters, like sequins, only larger (1). ESPIONAGE: That's like the FBI catching spies. IMMINENT: dk. MANTIS: dk. HARA KIRI: Japan's leader. CHATTEL: Something belonging to someone ... in the South, his slaves ($\frac{1}{2}$). DILATORY, AMANUENSIS, PROSELYTE, MOIETY, ASEPTIC, TRADUCE: dk. FLOUT: To flaunt, show off. RAW SCORE: 27.

Weighted Scores and IQ's

Comprehension 11	Picture Arrangement 13	Vocabulary 12
Information 10	Picture Completion 8	Verbal IQ: 111
Digit Span 4	Block Designs 10	Performance IQ: 101
Arithmetic 9	Object Assembly 6	Total IQ: 107
Similarities 14	Digit Symbol 9	

LEARNING EFFICIENCY

IMMEDIATE RECALL: Last Sunday (December 6) (in a small town) (near Albany) (a river) (overflowed) (and covered the streets). (14 persons) (drowned), (600) (caught cold). (A man) got injured (in rescuing) (a small boy) ... something about a bridge. SCORE: 16, after subtracting 1 for "last Sunday".

DELAYED RECALL: Last Sunday (December 6) (in a small town) (10 miles) west (of Albany) (a river) (overflowed) (covering the streets) (and entering houses) ... basements ... 16 persons (drowned) and (600) (caught cold) (from the dampness). (In rescuing) (a small boy) (from under a bridge) (a man) hurt his finger. Exposure: there was dampness and exposure up there where they caught cold. SCORE: 14, after subtracting 1 for "last Sunday" and 1 for "basements".

SORTING TEST

Part I

LARGE SCREWDRIVER: Adds the nails, block with nail, lock, all tools. "All tools of manual labor. Something to build with and fix." Mildly loose sorting, mixed abstract-functional concept. LARGE FORK: Adds all silverware. "Tableware, silverware, eating implements." Adequate sorting; abstract concept. PIPE: Adds all smoking equipment. "Smoking equipment." Adequate sorting; abstract concept. BELL: Adds ball. "Playthings." Narrow sorting; abstract concept. CIRCLE: Adds index card. "Both pieces of paper, cardboard." Narrow sorting; abstract concept. TOY PLIERS: Adds large pliers. "Both pliers, wrenches." Narrow sorting; concrete concept. BALL: Adds sinkstopper, eraser, rubber cigarette. "All rubber articles." Mildly narrow sorting; abstract concept.

Part II

RED: "These two are rubber, these two are paper; they don't all belong together." Split-narrow failure. METAL: "All made out of metal." Abstract concept. ROUND: "Because they are all round." Abstract concept. TOOLS: "Tools." Abstract concept. PAPER: "All paper." Abstract concept. PAIRS: "All pairs." Abstract concept. WHITE: "These two are sugar; this (cigarette) has paper covering and this (index card) is cardboard—but they don't all belong together." Split-narrow failure. RUBBER: "Rubber." Abstract concept. SMOKING MATERIALS: "Smoking equipment." Abstract concept. SILVERWARE: "Silverware." Abstract concept. TOYS: "All made of metal and rubber; they don't go together at all though." Split-narrow failure. RECTANGLES: "They don't. I can't see that any of them have any association to each other. I beg your pardon: the shapes." Abstract concept.

RORSCHACH TEST

CARD I. Reaction time: 5". Total time: 120".

1. That looks like a bat to me: is that correct? Or a butterfly. I guess it's more like a butterfly. These look like wings, this the body, and these the little feelers of the butterfly. I can't think of anything else it resembles to me.

SCORE: W F+A P.

CARD II. Reaction time: 28". Total time: 90".

You mean what it suggests to my imagination? 1. Looks like two Scottie dogs to me... like the nose and ears (black). 2. ∨ This way it could resemble a butterfly again, upside down. [(?) The shape, the feelers. (?) No.] That's all I can see in this.

SCORES. 1: D F+A P. 2: W F+A.

CARD III. Reaction time: 80". Total time: 120".

∨ ∧ ...I can't, don't... it doesn't make sense to me... maybe I am doing it wrong... 1. ∨ ... these look like skulls to me (lower middle). That's how my mind runs all the time! I want to get away from it! 2. That looks like blood (outer red) and that's all I can... see ...

SCORES. 1: D F+Skull. 2: D C Blood.

CARD IV. Reaction time: 65″. Total time: 120″.

Such weird shapes! ... 1. This down here looks like a pelt of something (lower middle). [(?) Little lines going through it like a pelt has; like in cabins; faded down... stripes... the formation.] 2. And this looks like a bat... these (lower sides) the bat's wings. That's all I can see in this.

SCORES. 1: D ChF Ad. 2: W F±A.

CARD V. Reaction time: 13″. Total time: 90″.

1. Everything suggests bats to me... ∨ more like a butterfly... They are all so confusing! ... Just glancing: a butterfly. And when those wings are spread out, it looks like a black bat.

SCORE: W FC'+A P.

CARD VI. Reaction time: 23″. Total time: 240″.

1. The top part of it, without the lower part, looks like a miller. You know those millers that fly at the screen... and the bottom part of it doesn't look like much of anything to me... (Anything else?) 2. I see these two pieces coming up: looks like two birds to me, like they were on a tree (figures at base of upper projection). 3. This might seem funny, but you know what it suggests to me? A watermelon (center section) cut in two and here are the seeds. 4. This up here: two high cliffs... high cliffs here, and here it is lower where you come down (upper outer corner of large D plus lower side projection). Little feet of the owls (central light gray spots; reference to second response).

SCORES. 1: D F + A. 2: Dr F±A. 3: D ChF Food. 4: Dr F∓Cliff.

CARD VII. Reaction time: 50″. Total time: 120″.

1. At first glance, a piece of dough. When I bake a doughnut, when you put it in hot grease: forming different formations. [(?) I could just see the dough bubbling in the pan. (?) Darker and lighter.] 2. Two weird faces... just a weird face (apprehensive tone) ... facing each other (upper 1/3). 3. This looks like an X-ray picture down here with a spot in the middle (lower 1/3). [(?) Light gray... and the center gets darker; likeness of the two sides.]

SCORES. 1: W Ch Food. 2: D F + Hd P. 3. D ChF At.

CARD VIII. Reaction time: 10″. Total time: 150″.

1. At first it just reminds me of animals (side pink). Do you see what I see? Fur sticking up. A rat. I see another one (other side). 2. This reminds me of a butterfly (lower pink and orange). [(?) The pretty, light colors... yellow and pink... the shape of it too.] 3. These two remind me of the shape of our flag... You see what I mean? ... Of our

American flag (middle blue). 4. This reminds me of what we got from the Cave of the Winds: pointed, shaped like this, colored like this, and jagged edges; stalagmite (upper gray-green). [(?) Gray.] Our crossed flags! (reference to third response).

SCORES. 1: D F (C) +A P. 2: D FC+A. 3: D F+Obj. 4: D FC′∓ Geol.

CARD IX. Reaction time: 20″. Total time: 180″.

This looks like, everything looks so weird to me! 1. Two men with tall caps and swords, bottles to their mouth: no! blowing a horn (orange). Do you see what I see? 2. This here, just one side, looks like snapdragons I have in my flower garden (lower pink) ... the shade and shape of it ... Then again it doesn't. [(?) Color and the round cover.] 3. You might think I am silly: when I vomited bile—that (green) looked like a little pool, green, and how it rounds out.

SCORES. 1: D M+H. 2: D CF Plant. 3: D CF Vomit.

CARD X. Reaction time: 15″. Total time: 150″.

That's more cheerful! 1. Pretty pastel shades like flowers. 2. ∨ This looks like a green tomato worm (lower green). 3. ∨ This blue reminds me of ink, like when you spill blue ink and it goes over the paper (side blue). 4. This looks like a dog's head (lower side orange). It all seems so confusing to me! So many little spots here and there! It just seems confusing! That's all.

SCORES. 1: W C Plant. 2: D FC+A. 3: D CF Ink. 4: D F+Ad.

Summary of Responses

R:26   EB:1–7

W 6	F+10	A 10	W% 23
D 18	F±2	Ad 2	D% 69
Dr 2	F∓1	H 1	Dr% 8
	M 1+	Hd 1	
	FC 2+	Food 2	F% 50-73
	CF 3	Plant 2	F+% 92-89
Qualitative	C 2	Blood 1	
Affect	F (C) 1+	Skull 1	A% 46
Naivete	FC′ 1+, 1−	At 1	H% 8
Oral	ChF 3	Obj 1	P 5
	Ch 1	Geol 1	P% 19
		Vomit 1	
		Ink 1	
		Cliff 1	

WORD ASSOCIATION TEST

WORLD—1″—I didn't get it. LOVE—7″—caresses. FATHER—1″— mother (8″—male). HAT—2″—pretty and gay. BREAST—2″—bosom. CURTAINS—2″—windows. TRUNK – 2″ – trees. DRINK – 7″ – water. PARTY—2″—gay time (13″—having a good time). BOWEL MOVE-

MENT—13″—well, B.M., that's what came into my mind. BOOK—1″—read. LAMP—1″—light. RUG—2″—covering. CHAIR—1″—care (1″—furniture). BOY FRIEND—3″—beau. PENIS—14″—penis... Oh that's a man's... I don't know how to explain it to you... testicles? Would that be right? This makes me nervous (2″—a child's testicles). DARK—2″—night. DEPRESSED—1″—blue. SPRING—4″—sunshine. BOWL—10″—dish. SUICIDE — 3″ — Mm! death. MOUNTAIN — 8″ — high place. HOUSE—3″—home. PAPER—5″—read. HOMOSEXUAL—3″—I'll have to skip it; I don't know what it means. RADIATOR—2″—heat. GIRL FRIEND—3″—sweetheart. SCREEN—2″—door. MASTURBATE—4″—skip it. FRAME—9″—window. MAN—5″—male. ORGASM (understood as ORGANS)—3″—heart (27″). MOVIES—1″—show, theatre. CUT—2″—hurt. LAUGH—2″—gay. BITE—9″—eat. WOMEN—2″—female. DANCE—2″—pleasure. DOG—2″—animal. DAUGHTER—6″—girl (2″—little girl). TAXI—2″—car. MOTHER—15″—when you say mother, I always think of my mom. TABLE—3″—furniture. BEEF—2″—meat. NIPPLE (heard NIBBLE)—2″—bite (6″—something for a baby to eat out of). RACE—13″—I don't know how to say that... American people (6″—American). WATER—2″—river (2″—drink). SUCK—2″—(laughs) baby. HORSE—7″—that's an animal. FIRE—3″—burn. VAGINA—4″—that's the mouth of the womb... how could you say vagina in one word? FARM—2″—acres. SOCIAL—2″—friendly. SON—5″—when you say son, I think of my little boys. TAXES—11″—we all pay them... money we have to pay the government... money. TOBACCO—3″—cigarettes. CITY—2″—town (2″—large town). INTERCOURSE—12″—it means... Oh, I don't know how to say it in one word... sexual satisfaction between a man and woman (8″). HOSPITAL—2″—sickness. DOCTOR—5″—somebody to make me well.

THEMATIC APPERCEPTION TEST

Card 1. (Boy with violin.) That's a little boy sitting by his violin. It looks to me like he's kind of drowsy. He's been practicing or playing. It looks to me like he has kind of dozed off to sleep. It looks like the exercises have been kind of hard.

Card 2. (Old woman in doorway.) It looks like an elderly woman entering the door of her home. She has probably been sitting out on the porch and she has come in for the evening before she retires for bed. She has the table lamp burning and there is a bouquet of flowers on the table. It all looks very quiet and peaceful. (Thoughts and feelings?) She looks like she is worried about something: her face isn't so very peaceful—but I wouldn't know what it would be about. As if she dreads to come inside. (Why?) I don't know. I can't think of anything in here. Everything looks peaceful, only she has a worried look on her face.

Card 3. (Old man in graveyard.) This is nice and cheerful (protesting tone)! This looks like a man grieving in a graveyard. He has such a weird looking face and the tombstones are kind of weird looking. It pictures Death. His head looks kind of like a skull and his hands are long and bony, and his long frock coat depicts a character from Charles

Dickens' novels. (More about the man?) It just brings to my mind old Scrooge in the Christmas Carol. Maybe he is in the graveyard repenting for some wrong that he has done.

Card 4. (Silhouette of man at window.) This looks like a man entering a window. It looks like he was breaking in or entering some home or store. And that's all because there's nothing further inside. It just looks like a picture of a man entering some place where he shouldn't! (End?) I can't tell you that. (?) I don't like to make up that kind of stories. I just hope he gets caught, that's all! When I think of things like that I get blue and depressed!

Card 5. (Heads of embracing couple.) First I thought that was a little boy but it isn't. That looks like a man and his wife. It looks like he is giving her a tender caress. She has her head snuggled down in his arm, on his shoulder. He is giving her a tender glance of affection. They both look very happy. That's about all! It's just a picture of a man and woman embracing each other.

Card 6. (Prehistoric animal, rocky road, bridge.) This looks like a picture of medieval times—on the high cliffs of rock. The little winding bridge that goes across, spans the river or something. It looks like some men trying to push something off up there—over the cliff. It looks kind of like a gloomy picture to me. Nothing cheerful. It doesn't even look pretty. (Happening?) I can't see anything: it's indistinct. The rocks are shaded. I would have to have a very vivid imagination. I like more cheerful things to make a story out of. (What being pushed?) A big stone, log or stone.

Card 7. (Shadowy photograph of thumb.) (Turns card.) This looks like a picture of a bug on a hand or wrist. It looks like something seen through a microscope maybe. It would take a better person than me to make a story out of that.

Card 8. (Nude couple; older woman with infant.) Well, that's . . . um . . . that looks like a picture of nudes. It don't look like any work of art. There's a woman dressed with some shawls and there's a little baby. She has a mean expression on her face. There's some pictures of nudes in the background. None of them are very pretty! (Story!) I can't see much of a story there. In fact it don't make much sense to me. The only pretty thing about it is that little babe up there in the woman's arms. It looks like it's sleeping. (Happening?) Nothing—unless this woman had taken this baby away from the couple, and the father could be pleading for the child and the mother has her head on his shoulder. (Led up?) Well, that's not in the picture. My imagination don't tell me anything there to the events that would lead up to it or what will come after. It just looks silly, or am I supposed to tell you that—that it looks silly? (Story!) It just looks silly to me, that's all. It just seems like I have no desire to tell any story about it.

Card 9. (Two chairs and table set for tea.) Umm—that's better! That looks like a little corner in the living room of some home—cozy little corner—and the large chair looks like it's for the man of the house, the husband, and the little chair looks like it's for the lady of the house, the wife. It looks like they're about to have tea, afternoon tea by candle-light. Looks like the chairs and the table are waiting for them to come in and sit down and have a pleasant evening.

Card 10. (Old man on shoulders of another old man.) Ooh! Such things! You just don't like to look at such things! It just looks like a picture of two horrid old men. This one looks like Mahatma Ghandi. When you don't like to look at unpleasant pictures and things, you should just look at them and conquer them! Lately, I have just wanted to think pretty thoughts, nothing morbid or blue. I'm not crazy; I'm just nervous. It's awful to be like that, but it's a good thing we have places like this to go to, don't you think? (Story!) I don't see any story. I think someone just drew these lines in to confuse me. Maybe I don't want to tell a story. If they were women, it could be witches like in Halloween. (Happening?) Well, one has got his hand on his hair like he's pulling it. You can just see their heads and their bodies, but you can't tell what's going on.

Card F 11. (Hag behind young woman.) You give me such weird pictures! It's hard to make . . . I see here a young woman, dark complect-ed, and behind her to the side, standing, a haggard and wrinkled woman. She looks like an old witch. She must be this woman's mother —their eyes look alike—dark eyes. It looks to me like this elderly woman has been telling this younger woman a bit of advice or something, that displeased the younger woman but the elderly woman looks like she is getting pleasure out of it. She has a smirk on her lips and an evil ex-pression on her face . . . But as to the outcome, I don't know—just two characters in the picture. I don't know what led up to it, or what the outcome would be. That's just my thoughts as I look at the picture.

Card F 12. (Men unloading boat, girl on bridge.) This looks like it might be a place in Holland or Venice where they have canals. What looks funny to me is that it's dark and still the sun appears to be shin-ing. I see a large mill and a girl bending over the bridge. And I see a boat drawn up and anchored to the platform down below the bridge. Several men getting off with large sacks thrown over their shoulders, going into the mill. There is a fellow there standing with his hands on his hips, and a striped sweater. He acts, to me, like he is bossing those fellows off the boat, and directing them to where they should go. Also this girl is watching—a lookout for them. They may be a band of smug-glers or just a bunch of hard working men coming in from work.

Card F 13. (Boy with book, two girls in background.) This looks to me like a picture of a home dining room. I can't see the mother but evidently she has been talking to her three children. There is a son and two daughters. They all look like bright studious youngsters, clean, cleancut. And it seems to me that they have been studying, and they are . . . the mother has the floor, speaking. They all have their eyes upon her and are listening raptly . . . to what she is telling them. (Telling what?) Something about their school studies.

Card F 14. (Woman turning away from man.) This looks like a nice little domestic quarrel, scenes such as you see in the movies. It seems that the wife is just about to leave the apartment, the home, and her husband is trying to plead with her and to beg her to come back home—to not leave. She seems to be a very frivolous type of person, and his appearance suggests a kind, hard working man ... The scene is evidently taking place in the doorway. He is trying to embrace her and beg her not to leave but she has her head thrown back and her mind made up to leave. (Quarrel about?) I don't know. Some disagreement; could be any number of reasons, but none seems to come to my mind.

Card F 15. (Girl leaning against wall, arm outstretched.) This looks like the picture of a young girl who is heartbroken over something. She has her hands up over her face. Looks like she is weeping; in despair over something that has happened. That's about all I can see. (Happened?) Either something could have happened to her sweetheart or husband or maybe she is married and something happened to her children.

Card F 16. (Man at window.) It looks like the picture of an elderly man looking through a window. He seems to have a sad expression on his face as if the scene he is looking at is not pleasant, or his thoughts might be away from that on something else. (Scene?) Oh, it could be that he is watching his son go down the walk, going away to war. It looks like he is pondering deeply and thinking.

Card F 17. (Two women struggling on stairway.) Well, that is a very unpleasant scene. It's a picture of two young women engaged in a bitter quarrel. The picture shows one of the young women strangling the other or trying to, and the picture of the one that is trying to—that has her arms around the throat of the victim—looks like she has suddenly gone mad for a moment. It's taking place at the foot of the staircase. (Led up?) Well, it could be any number of things. Women are a catty lot when they get together: it might be over a love affair. (Outcome?) Well, I hope not too tragic. I hope she comes to her senses in time not to harm her victim too badly. I like stories with happy endings.

Card F 18. (Maid in hallway.) This looks like a picture of a coy little housemaid, parlor maid. I judge her to be a real flirtatious type, one that likes to flirt. She is real pert looking and trim and neat, with a pretty little face. From the picture here, it looks like she is trying to flirt either with a gentleman who has come to call on the lady of the house or the doorman or the butler. (Outcome?) Probably she will get a date, or maybe she is just flirting to pass the time.

Card F 19. (Woman on bed; dishevelled man standing.) Well, this looks like to me a picture of a drunken brawl. It looks like it takes place in some cheap rooming house or tavern such as you see in the movies once in a while. There's a bottle and glass on the table and the young man's face looked very weak like he lacked character. His hair is awry—it's all over his face—and his clothing is disarrayed. He is very ill-bred looking and the companion, it seems to be a woman companion asleep on the bed. (Led up?) Too much drinking, I imagine. It looks like he is standing there now in deep concentration as if he suddenly realizes the wrongs that he has done. (Wrong?) Well, drinking and carousing. (Companion?) Evidently it isn't his wife because a man would have more respect for his wife than that. Evidently some cheap companion that he picked up someplace. (Outcome?) Oh, he will probably leave. She is still asleep in the bed. Probably not a happy ending. (?) Judging by the type of picture and type of character—those stories never do have a happy ending.

Card F 20. (Bearded old man.) This looks like a picture of a real elderly man in the eighties and possibly up to the nineties. He has a real snow-white beard. He has his hands over his eyes and his face, as if he is in deep despair. Possibly he has lost his companion, his wife of a good many years and he wonders how he will carry on without her. He possibly thinks that life isn't worth while any more so long as she is gone and he is so old. (Outcome?) It will probably end by his living his time out, probably grieving over her or making the best of things.

ANALYSIS OF RESULTS

BELLEVUE SCALE

The scatter is most indicative of depressive features: the visual-motor subtest scores average only 8.3 while the essentially Verbal subtest[3]) scores average 11.8. Intense anxiety is indicated by the profound impairment of attention: Digit Span drops 8 points below the Vocabulary level. This drop is so great as to suggest a condition prodromal to a psychotic break and from this point on we must be on the lookout for every indication that might imply a process of disorganization. With respect to character make-up, the Verbal scatter and Verbal level suggest a primary repressive emphasis: Information is only 10 although this patient spent a year at college; Information is two points below Vocabulary and is also exceeded by Comprehension. The fact that there is only a one-point difference between Comprehension and Information is misleading, since it is usual to find in the scatter of non-repressive patients a greater or lesser drop of Comprehension below Information; consequently we can set the baseline for the Comprehension score at 8 or 9, with the result that its actual position at 11 becomes all the more striking. The repressive pattern of the Verbal scatter suggests that hysterical pathology is likely to be present; a drop of the Performance level, however, is not ordinarily expected in the record of an hysteric, since the Performance abilities usually clearly exceed the Verbal. Two diagnostic hypotheses are possible: either this is an hysterical neurosis with depression as a conspicuous secondary symptom or this is a neurotic

----

[3]) Comprehension, Information, Similarities, and Vocabulary.

depression in a woman of hysterical character make-up. Neurotic depression rather than psychotic depression is suggested by the not too great Verbal-Performance discrepancy (Verbal IQ is 111, Performance IQ is 101), the retention of a high Similarities score, and the absence of striking scatter among the essentially Verbal subtests.

Qualitative analysis bears out the repressive-hysteric hypothesis. In Information, in addition to failing all of the last five "cultural" items, she does not know the capital of Italy, the location of Egypt, and not even the number of weeks in a year or the population of the U. S. Her inability to capitalize on exposure to higher education implies a selective neglect or shying away from intellectual pursuits, which in turn implies a repressive-hysterical character make-up. Naivete—a frequent feature of strongly repressive subjects—is apparent in the Comprehension subtest: on *bad company* she speaks of corrupting the city and refers to the problem of reputation so concretely that the verbalization could well have come from a child. (Note also the naive definition of *gamble* in Vocabulary: to throw your money away. This type of verbalization is characteristic in subjects with a strongly moralistic background.) In Arithmetic a ready retreat into passivity, usually associated with low anxiety tolerance, is apparent: "I can't make my mind work" implies a definite passive attitude toward her subjective experiences and getting "confused" reflects how little she is able to withstand the onslaughts of intense anxiety (see Digit Span score). Therefore, voluntary and effortful concentration, as well as passive attention, is impaired. The Picture Completion and Object Assembly scores also reflect the impairment of efficiency associated with intense anxiety. Her responses to *affliction, pewter* and *ballast* in the Vocabulary subtest indicate striking egocentricity.

LEARNING EFFICIENCY

The average score of 15 is relatively low for a person with a Vocabulary score of 12: a score of 15 is appropriate for a Vocabulary level of about 11 and her score should have been 16 or 17. However, no disorganization of the story can be detected and the drop is not very great. The score is therefore consistent with other indications of impaired concentration. One qualitative note: the content with aggressive connotations is poorly handled. In the immediate recall she thinks of *drowned* but rejects it, thereby eliminating deaths from the story; however, *caught cold* is changed to "injured"; *cut his hands* is also changed. In the delayed recall the boy is "hurt" under the bridge—an elaboration. It is implied that there is especial difficulty in coping with aggressively-toned situations. This general type of recall performance, though not diagnostic in itself, is quite frequent among hysterics because of their emotional lability.

SORTING TEST

A tendency toward narrowness of concepts is reflected in this test, especially in Part I. Narrowness usually implies depressive or compulsive features. There have been no striking indications of compulsiveness so far, but depression has been rather clearly indicated in the Bellevue Scale results. That the Sorting Test concepts are *depressively* narrowed is borne out by analysis of the sortings in Part I. Here we find no systematic cautiousness of the split-narrow variety but rather small groupings, the conceptualizations of which would encourage broader sortings in even the most compulsive record. The implication is that a quality of inertia, of minimal capacity for sustained application, is present. Notice, however, that the conceptual level is nicely sustained and that there are few failures. This is atypical in severe depressions, and suggests, in view of all the results thus far, that the essential pathology may be hysterical, with depression as a secondary feature.

RORSCHACH TEST

If the prediction is correct that this is a case of hysteria, we should find an experience balance in which colors clearly outweigh movements and in which $CF+C$ outweighs FC, with the chief emphasis on CF. If depression is the major symptom, we should find a constricted experience balance with perhaps a trace of special emphasis on color (because of the hysterical personality background), a high $F\%$, high $A\%$ and $P\%$, and a low R.

Actually the test record satisfies the prediction of hysteria, containing an EB of 1–7, with 2 FC, 3 CF, and 2 C. With the $F\%$ only 50-73, R at 26, $A\%$ 46 and $P\%$ 19 the depression is not likely to be profound. Much rather, on the basis of the CF and C emphasis, the striking characteristic is likely to be emotional lability, which may, however, be manifest at least partly in depressive mood swings. Emotional lability, as used here, implies the potentiality for mood swings as well as excitability, fearfulness, and other manifestations of the domination of thinking and behavior by easily stimulated affects. The manner of approach is nicely balanced. The 6 W's are, however, all either simple, more or less popular forms or unarticulated; of the 26 responses, only one—the M on IX— reveals clear-cut integrative efforts. The implication is that integrative zeal and ability are weak and that this is not likely to be an active and independent thinker. The form-level is unusually high for an hysteric (92-89) but the $F\%$ is low (50-73). The latter implies that critical controls are underemphasized or ineffectual in the present picture; the former indicates strong attempts to be correct and accurate. The two percentages considered together indicate that there is no basic impairment of reality testing but that critical restraint is not applied extensively enough. As already indicated, the *EB* is typically hysteric. The devaluation of independent, creative thinking is reflected in the solitary *M*; the characteristic emotional lability is seen in the emphasis on *CF* and *C*. The presence of 2 *FC*'s indicates that adaptive efforts are being made and that some successful rapport may be achieved, but the emphasis on *CF* and *C* implies that these successful adaptations are likely to be short-lived. The presence of 3 *ChF*'s and 1 *Ch* indicates the great intensity and free-floating quality of anxiety in the clinical picture. This is consistent with the inference from the great drop of Digit Span and other aspects of the Bellevue Scale results.

Turning to the actual verbalizations we find clear evidences of the naivete and lability already mentioned. Regarding naivete, note the following: Card I—"Is that correct?" Card III—"Maybe I am doing it wrong..." Card VI—"This might seem funny..." Card VII—Self-reference. Card VIII—"Do you see what I see?" and "Our American flag... our crossed flags!" Card IX—"Do you see what I see?" Self-reference and "You might think I am silly..." Egocentricity is also apparent in some of the foregoing. Regarding lability and fearfulness, note the following: Card III—"That's how my mind runs all the time! (etc.)" Card IV—"Such weird shapes!" Card V—"All so confusing!" Card VII—"Two weird forms." Card IX—"So weird to me!" Card X—"That's more cheerful!" and "So confusing!" Card X is an excellent study in the manifestations of extreme lability: the same objective situation changes from cheerfulness to confusion in almost no time at all. The low anxiety tolerance is evident in her hasty retreat from Card III after the *blood* response, and in "I want to get away from it!" after the *skull* response. The striking oral content (watermelon, dough, vomit, bottles to their mouth) indicates intense oral conflicts and suggests that conversion symptoms may have invaded oral functions. This inference would stand even without her spontaneous reference to vomiting. The fearfulness evident in her reactions to the cards and the out-of-place single *M* indicate that phobic features are also likely to be conspicuous.

WORD ASSOCIATION TEST

Noteworthy blocking occurs in reaction to these stimulus words: love, drink, bowel movement, penis, bowl, mountain, bite, daughter, mother, race, horse, taxes, intercourse. With the exception of *race, horse, mountain,* and *taxes,* these words have more or less clear relationships with oral, anal, sexual, familial, and aggressive material and it is therefore suggested that unresolved and acute conflicts exist in all these areas. The errors in recall, particularly on *father, party, penis,* and *nipple* reinforce this conclusion. Naivete is apparent in the responses to *penis* and *race* and in her fairly systematic attempt to give synonyms—the reactions to *vagina* and *intercourse* are good examples. Her generally repressive mode of adjustment is reflected in her ignorance of the words *masturbate, homosexual, orgasm,* and uncertainty about the word *penis,* especially when we bear in mind that her education included a year at college. The egocentricity of her thinking and her characteristic lability are clear in the responses to *hat, mother, son, doctor.* The response to *doctor* is also an open statement of her generally passive outlook. The delay in reaction to *mountain* is reminiscent of the *cliff* response in the Rorschach Test (a *Dr* on Card VI) and hints at phobic symptoms in this area.

THEMATIC APPERCEPTION TEST

Card 1. (Boy with violin.) The theme of the story is passive withdrawal from difficulty. *Difficulty* is a popular theme but the solution she offers is not a usual one and appears to express her characteristic passivity and low anxiety tolerance. Card 2. (Old woman in doorway.) The theme is unwarranted apprehensiveness. *Apprehensiveness* is a popular theme, but so clear a verbalization of nameless dread appears to be directly self-expressive. Sensitivity to the atmosphere of different settings is frequent in characteristically labile subjects and also in depressed subjects. The spontaneous ending of the story before the apprehensiveness is mentioned appears to be another indication of low anxiety tolerance: this time she attempts to avoid dealing with an emotionally disturbing theme. Card 3. (Old man in graveyard.) She avoids the disturbing theme, offers no spontaneous story and verbalizes only the global, affective response, "Death". The examiner's pressure elicits the popular and essentially ambiguous theme of remorse for past sins. Most striking is her sensitivity to the "weird" atmosphere of the situation.

Card 4. (Silhouette of man at window.) The theme here is violation of the moral code. Her drastic reaction to this idea is classically hysterical both in its naivete and its moralistic tone: she completely loses distance from the picture and participates in it actively as if it were a real situation. The crime depresses her and she hopes the criminal gets caught. The severity of the moral reaction in this setting indicates extreme repression; thinking about an ordinarily peripheral event (a crime) can be this disturbing only if lability is so pervasive as to appear indiscriminate. It is also implied that she is quick to experience feelings of guilt. Avoidance of disturbing material is again clear in the response to inquiry. Card 5. (Heads of embracing couple.) The theme is marital tenderness, affection, and bliss. Having described the affective import of the picture, she stops, feeling that she is through. This manner of approach also characterizes the stories to Cards 2 and 3, and indicates her overresponsiveness to affective implications of events to the almost complete exclusion of rational and creative efforts. This too is classically hysterical. The theme itself is not too frequent among patients; leave-taking or reunion are the popular themes. In terms of the generally depressive tone of the stories, the present theme can be considered a statement of a wish: the wife-figure is happy in a passive role (and position) and is being fed affection. The incipient misrecognition of sex at the beginning indicates an underlying masculine identification and, in terms of the stories which follow, a strong positive attachment to the father-figure.

Card 6. (Prehistoric animal, rocky road, bridge.) No spontaneous theme is offered; she states only her emotional reaction. Inquiry is ineffective. She vigorously refuses to cope with the aggressive connotations of the picture. Her verbalizations make clear how she divides events and situations into the two categories—gloomy and cheerful. Card 7. (Shadowy photograph of thumb.) No story is elicited. This is frequent and, in itself, unrevealing. Card 8. (Nude couple; older woman with infant.) There is really no story elicited, even under pressure. In typically hysterical fashion she is essentially blocked in reaction to this "sexual" picture, and characteristically takes a passive role with respect to her emotional reaction: "It just seems like I have no desire to tell any story about it." There is some attempt at an aggressive rationalization—"It's silly"—but she is amazingly correct when she finally relates her difficulty to a blocking of motivation or *desire*. Nevertheless the verbalization at the end retains its negativistically passive quality. Note also the characteristic statement, "The only pretty thing about it is...". The mother-figure is portrayed as a "mean" and depriving person, but this is a popular portrayal and its special meaning for this patient does not become clear until Card F-11. Card 9. (Two chairs and table set for tea.) No story is developed; she is again restricted to an essentially affective description.

Card 10. (Old man on shoulders of another old man.) This story reveals striking blocking in the face of aggressive material; the blocking, like that on Card 6, appears to be referable to the general repressive emphasis. The labile and naive aspects of her verbalizations speak for themselves. The statement, "You should just look at them and conquer them!" has the parrot-like quality of a little girl reciting her lessons; it is as if to say, "I must try to act like a grown-up." Card F-11. (Old hag behind young woman.) The theme is a mother's aggressiveness toward her daughter. The conception of the old woman in this picture as a malevolent figure is not unusual but the explicit statement of *sadistic pleasure* on the part of a *mother* is singular and would suggest that this was a genuine conception of her own mother. This interpretation is reinforced by the sequence of verbalization: "She looks like an old witch: she must be this woman's mother." Only afterwards, in the comparison of eyes, is a covering rationalization introduced. The daughter does nothing in the story, implying unusual passivity in this disturbing situation. Putting together the implications of the stories to Cards 5, 8, and F-11, it is apparent that she rejects the mother-figure as hostile and longs for the benevolence and affection of the father-figure. Card F-12. (Men unloading boat; girl on bridge.) A conventional theme of smuggling, denied as soon as it is stated. The denial probably stems from the rigid moral code already indicated.

Card F-13. (Boy with book; two girls in background.) A conventional theme of studying. The benevolent mother-figure is probably the patient herself. This is the first theme where she is at all active, but even here, where most subjects would say the parent is *helping* the children, she remains indefinite. Card F-14. (Woman turning away from man.) The theme is the unworthiness of "frivolous" women who leave good "hardworking" husbands. This is an unusual theme: the man is generally the culprit and it is likely that this possibility does not come to her mind because she has to repress rigidly hostility to the husband-figure. He is "hard-working" or, in terms more appropriate to this context, a good provider for a passive woman. The prudish term "frivolous" and her generally moralistic outlook imply that essentially she disowns the woman in the picture; yet, because of the unusual characterization of the woman, it is likely that she is describing what she considers to be an essential aspect of her own personality and one which gives rise to guilt feelings. She immediately attempts to negate any personal reference (responsibility) by making it a movie (unreal) story; this evasive aspect is made clear by her inability, even under pressure at the end, to allow herself to think of a hostile motive. Again the verbalization is distinctively passive: "None seems to come to my mind."

Card F-15. (Girl leaning against wall; arm outstretched.) The theme is "heartbreak". She characteristically avoids mention of motives or precipitating causes. Inquiry elicits a list of possible causes—a frequent type of non-committal evasion—but it is noteworthy that the husband or children have been hurt in some way. This is not an infrequent idea on this card, but her inability to follow through on the story suggests that the aggressive idea does have personal reference, is anxiety-arousing and is therefore repressed. Card F-16. (Man at window.) The theme, elicited by inquiry, is sadness at loss of a child. Her spontaneous, naked evasion—". . . or his thoughts might be away from that . . ."—is noteworthy. Card F-17. (Two women struggling on stairway.) The theme is hostility toward women. This is the popular, appropriate interpretation. The omission of the motive and outcome is characteristic of this patient as is her abortive attempt to make the incident trivial: "Women are a catty lot." This is the first instance where direct aggressions are verbalized and, as on Card 4, she loses distance from her story and ends it with "I hope . . .". The expression of aggression is implicitly rejected.

Card F-18. (Maid in hallway.) The theme is casual flirtation. The categorization of the maid as a "flirtatious type" with the aim of "passing time" implicitly disowns such characteristics within herself, but she does not seem exceptionally upset or rejecting. Card F-19. (Woman in bed; dishevelled man standing.) The theme is the "cheapness" and weakness of character involved in carousing. Again the attitude is moralistic and rejecting: the behavior is "wrong" and the characters "ill-bred". Guilt feelings about sexual activity are likely to be conspicuous. She disclaims responsibility for the idea by referring it to the movies. Card F-20. (Bearded, old man looking down.) The theme is despair at loss of a love object. The content is popular and does not allow for an interpretation of a *characteristic* attitude.

Since there was no evidence for the presence of a process of disorganization other than the great drop in Digit Span, this drop can be referred to the presence of intense anxiety alone.

TEST REPORT

Intelligence and Thought Organization: Although intelligence functioning is on an average level—her I.Q. is 107—its quality is definitely naive. Passive acceptance of precept and conventional concept, and a striking inertia of creative, independent thinking are outstanding. Her thought processes also appear to be generally disrupted by extreme emotional lability: for example, at the time of testing, her thinking was just about paralyzed whenever she had to deal with emotional material other than that pertaining to warmth, love, or gaiety. She is aware of this tendency; in fact she deliberately uses it extensively and often negativistically. However, when she does try to apply herself, she gets "confused"—a term which expresses blocking mixed with acute anxiety rather than confusion proper. The basic passivity and naivete of her thinking are seen in her uncertainty about the correctness of any of her responses; it is as if to say that they can be correct only if the examiner explicitly accepts them as correct. Often she will begin a trend of thought easily and will continue until she encounters the first point of difficulty; then the emotional atmosphere surrounding the thought process changes from calm to agitation and she gets "confused". Nearly all percepts and concepts appear to have a conscious and strong emotional tone; this implies that conflict-free ego functioning is reduced to a minimum and that a general quality of egocentricity colors all her thinking. The most ordered thinking she achieves is merely a circumstantial account of details but this seems to be just another defense against recognizing and coping with disturbing situations. In general this is the intelligence make-up of an hysterical character: informational and cultural interests are weak (her education left little mark on her), attention span is extremely limited by free-floating anxiety, efficiency is spotty, persistence restricted, active and creative application minimal, integrative ability feeble.

Emotional Factors: Overwhelming emotional lability and free-floating anxiety, and powerful passive needs are most conspicuous. Her capacity for rapport is barely adequate, and is of the passive, submissive variety. The passivity has, however, a decidedly negativistic, demanding, and aggressive quality. With respect to both her lability and passivity she appears to feel guilty that she cannot do the "right" thing and face situations squarely. It also appears that she has been making some "rational" attempts, of a circumstantial variety, to curb too direct expression of her lability and passivity; these attempts do not, however, stem from any genuine compulsiveness but rather from efforts to "be good" and "grown-up". A strict, naive moral code is indicated and guilt feelings appear to be easily stimulated. She appears quite depressed at present, which seems in line with the potentiality for mood swings as one aspect of her lability, and she overreacts to the somber implications of ideas or situations. The world at present is one of "gay, pleasant, and warm" situations and "weird, gloomy, distasteful, and confusing" situations. She seeks the former rigidly and cannot tolerate the latter. The complexion of situations can rapidly change from one of cheerfulness to one of distress. Aggressive, sexual, familial, oral, and anal connotations of experience seem disturbing. Phobias and conversion symptoms are likely to be present.

Figures and Attitudes: The easy liberation of intense affects is such as would actually correspond to a world-picture in which there is only a minimum of neutral events and objects: to her it is a threatening, labile world and the way out is to think only of the bright things in life. This attitude cannot be successfully maintained, however, and she is constantly confronted by acutely distressing situations. The ego-centricity of approach is so pervasive in the test data that little information concerning her conception of, and attitude toward, other figures is present. It can be inferred from this negative finding that her conceptions of others are unstable, and that her subjective images change with her own mood and the mood of others. It can be seen, however, that she characteristically assumes a passive, demanding child-like role, easily experiences guilt over the expression of aggressive and sexual impulses, longs especially for the affections of a benevolent father-figure and rejects the hostile mother-figure. Hostility to the husband- and children-figures appears to be strongly repressed.

Diagnostic Impression: Hysteria with depressive features.

CLINICAL SUMMARY

Mrs. K's parents are described as cheerful and sociable. The mother was an immaculate housekeeper and emphasized cleanliness. The patient is the eldest of nine children. At the age of seven she had poliomyelitis involving one side of the body. Although most of the symptoms disappeared, there was some atrophy of one arm. She claims to have had "sick headaches" since the attack of polio. She has been afraid of the dark since she was a child, fearing that someone might grab her. Occasional attacks of photophobia also occurred, but these are infrequent now. She received good grades in school and was popular but felt inferior because of her arm. At the age of twenty she had a sexual affair which resulted in pregnancy. At her father's insistence she did not marry the man—because he drank—and went to another city to have her child. Her parents made her feel ashamed of herself. She married three years later and has always maintained the impression that the child is the result of a previous marriage. Her husband is of lower middle class status, a status lower than her father's. After marriage the patient devoted herself to the house and children.

The patient's illness began about two years ago. After several operations, including an hysterectomy, she began to vomit and ate poorly, but nevertheless gained much weight. She became easily fatiguable, irritable, depressed, and fearful. Fear of death developed and was reinforced by an incorrect diagnosis of cancer; her own death is a frequent theme in her dreams. Clinical examination revealed her to be a naive, "simple", outgoing, and emotionally labile person. At present she complains especially of frequent and burning passages of urine and pain in the lower abdomen. Additional symptoms which were noted during her illness included vomiting, fear of falling, gross trembling of one hand, acute dysmennorrhea, and intense premenstrual pains accompanied by morbid preoccupations. Intercourse, which was previously pleasurable, has become painful and infrequent. Acute anxiety, diffuse worrying, and tremulousness are also striking.

NARCISSISTIC CHARACTER DISORDER: TEST RESULTS

Mr. N. Age: 30. Education: high school. Occupation: Salesman, draftsman. Marital: 8 months; getting divorced. Father: Manufacturer. Early Environment: Big city. Family Position: 5th of 6. Religion: Episcopalian.

BELLEVUE SCALE

Comprehension

ENVELOPE: I'd mail it (2). THEATRE: I believe that I'd just get up and leave and inform the management. Of course, that's what I believe sitting here when there's no fire. (?) Damned if I know. I don't know if I'd get panicky or not. I wouldn't think so. I've never been panicked yet (2). BAD COMPANY: (laughs) I'm a good example of that, Mr. Kass.[4]) (?) Don't tell me you wrote that down. Well, I believe it gets you in too much trouble—drink and lots of crime. I miss the crime element, I guess (1). TAXES: For the support of the government. In the state of Oklahoma, for the gratification of the politician (2). SHOES: Flexibility, I would imagine, and durability (1). LAND: Because of its commercial value ... You're talking about Kansas Avenue, not this part of town? (?) ... Higher rent it could command, and because of shopping and business districts (1). FOREST: Which direction did I come in? (?) Well, you could always find directions by the sun providing it's not obscured by a cloud. (?) You could tell east and west (2). LAW: I'd say to help maintain conventions, protect society against itself. (?) Well, it wouldn't be any good if I could run around and bash you in the head; well, it wouldn't be any good, would it? I mean without cause (1). LICENSE: That I don't know. (?) I don't believe in it. (?) What is the state's reason? To prevent polygamy. (?) I doubt if it would

---

4) At The Menninger Foundation the administration of the battery of tests is usually divided up among several psychologists; hence only some of the records presented in Chapters 3 and 4 have been obtained by the author.

help because they probably never check the records anyway, but they could... if they were honest (1). DEAF: Because they have never heard any conversation. The only way we learn to talk is through association. (?) By association with other people in conversations. A child that is born not deaf can't talk till it can make enough connections and know what words are. I speak like a father, don't I? (1). RAW SCORE: 14.

Information

PRESIDENT: +. LONDON: +. PINTS: +. RUBBER: +. THERMOMETER: +. WEEKS: +. ITALY: +. WASHINGTON: Some time in February. (?) I would guess the 22nd, but I wouldn't swear to anything; +. HEIGHT: +. PLANE: +. PARIS: Strictly a guess; +. BRAZIL: +. HAMLET: +. POLE: I don't have any idea. VATICAN: +. JAPAN: +. HEART: Beats. (?) It is the pump... most people call it circulation; +. POPULATION: 132 million and some odd thousands, according to the 1940 census. I wouldn't know; +. H. FINN: +. EGYPT: North Africa; +. KORAN: dk. FAUST: Isn't that a character in one of Shakespeare's plays? HABEAS CORPUS: A writ permitting one who is locked up to get out. I wouldn't know for sure. ETHNOLOGY: dk. APOCRYPHA: dk. RAW SCORE: 19.

Digit Span

FORWARD: Passes 3, 4, 5, 6, 7 on first try; fails first series of 8 by reversing 2 digits but passes second series of 8 and first series of 9; uses method of grouping numbers all along. BACKWARDS: Passes 3, 4 on first try, fails first series of 5 by misplacing one digit but passes on second try; passes first series of 6 and fails both series of 7. RAW SCORE: 15.

Arithmetic

Items 1-8: +; very fast. ITEM 9: + + (6″). ITEM 10: + + (3″). RAW SCORE: 12.

Similarities

ORANGE: Fruit (2). COAT: Clothes (2). DOG: Animals (2). WAGON: Transportation (2). DAILY PAPER: News (1). AIR: Uh... I can't think of the word I'm looking for... part of the atmosphere, though water's not atmospheric. Both part of the earth. WOOD: Alcohol comes from wood. EYE: Organs (1). EGG: They're both seeds. (?) An egg is a seed from which a chick comes. Both planted. (?) Doesn't a rooster plant what it takes to make an egg—that's a fertile egg I'm thinking of. POEM: Both art (2). PRAISE: Rewards for an act, deed or something, conduct. FLY: I fail to see any similarity. RAW SCORE: 12.

Picture Arrangement

HOUSE: + 2″ (2). HOLD UP: + 4″ (2). ELEVATOR: + 8″ (2). FLIRT: AJNET 8″ (2). FISH: EFGHIJ 40″; "He had a boy down at the bottom putting the fish on the hook for him." (4) . TAXI: SAEMUL 25"; "The gentleman had his mannikin or whatever you call that and after catching the cab, he was thinking how it looked from the rear view (A little slower, please!) I can't think slow; so he moved her ... it," RAW SCORE: 12.

Picture Completion

NOSE: +. MUSTACHE: +. EAR: +. DIAMOND: +. LEG: +. TAIL: +. STACKS: bridge; top deck. KNOB: +; looks like a door in a jail. SECOND HAND: +. WATER: +. REFLECTION: Leg of table. (?) +. TIE: +; lots of people don't wear them. THREADS: +. EYEBROW: +; but lots of people's don't show. SUN: Where is the old man's shadow? +. RAW SCORE: 14.

Block Designs

Subject comments, "You'll guarantee that everything you show me can be made?" ITEM 1: 8" (5). ITEM 2: 7" (5). ITEM 3: 6" (5). ITEM 4: 16" (4). ITEM 5: 23" (6). ITEM 6: 34" (6). ITEM 7: 64"; "4 by 4, 4 in each direction, that makes it more interesting." Makes outside frame first; systematic, accurate (6). RAW SCORE: 37.

Object Assembly

ITEM 1: 15" (6) ; "Can he be knockkneed? The feet are not looking in the same direction." ITEM 2: 15" (10). ITEM 3: 25" (9). RAW SCORE: 25.

Digit Symbol

38 correct; 9 reversals of the 2-symbol. RAW SCORE: 42.5.

Vocabulary

APPLE: Fruit (1). DONKEY: Animal (1). JOIN: Meet (1). DIAMOND: Gem (1). NUISANCE: Pest (1). FUR: Animal; that's a reference, that's not what I mean; pelt (1). CUSHION: Pillow (1). SHILLING: English coin (1). GAMBLE: Wager (1). BACON: Pork (1). NAIL: A building material. (?) Also a growth on the end of your fingers and toes; long cylindrical object with a head on the top of it (1). CEDAR: Tree, wood (1). TINT: Color (1). ARMORY: Storage place for arms is the actual definition I think, or a meeting place for the National Guard (1). FABLE: Story (1). BRIM: In the case of you and me, it's the projection on a hat. (?) I've seen women's hat brims that didn't project, if you can call those *hats*. GUILLOTINE: A knife with which the French use for decapitation, *which* the French used for decapitation (1). PLURAL: More than one (1). SECLUDE: I guess private, semi-private seclusion (½). NITROGLYCERINE: Explosive (1). STANZA: A verse (1). MICROSCOPE: An enlarger on a gigantic scale, magnifier (1). VESPER: A service, where I came from (laughs). I'll have to leave out these ad libs (1). RECEDE: To go out. (?) Such as the tide (½). AFFLICTION: Ailment or illness (½). PEWTER: A metal, an alloy (1). BALLAST: Weight. (?) On ships or aircraft ...

to get proper distribution of the weight they're carrying (1). CATA-COMB: A formation. (?) In the caves down in New Mexico; I don't know. SPANGLE: Ornament. (Can you tell me more about it?) Nothing. (?) Star-spangled banner, ornamented with stars; correct? Correct enough, next question! (½). ESPIONAGE: Intelligence service (1). IMMINENT: Near (1). MANTIS: dk. HARA KIRI: Japanese form of suicide (1). CHATTEL: A legal term, a form of security probably; dk. DILATORY: As having to do with the dilute; is that the word? AMANUENSIS: dk. PROSELYTE: dk. MOIETY: dk. ASEPTIC: dk; sounds like it has to do with a septic tank, but I don't know if it did or not or vice versa. FLOUT: Flaunt. TRADUCE: dk. RAW SCORE: 28.

Patient comments during testing, "When you write down what I say, do you write exactly the words I use?" At the end of the test, patient wants to go over it item by item and take notes in a little book.

Weighted Scores and IQ's

Comprehension 12	Picture Arrangement 11	Vocabulary 12
Information 13	Picture Completion 14	Verbal IQ: 122
Digit Span 14	Block Designs 16	Performance IQ: 127
Arithmetic 17	Object Assembly 16	Total IQ: 127
Similarities 11	Digit Symbol 10	

LEARNING EFFICIENCY

IMMEDIATE RECALL: On December 6 (last week) (a river) (overflowed) in a small (village) (10 miles) (from Albany). (14 people) were (drowned) and (600) (caught cold). In (saving) (a boy), (a man) (cut his hands) (under a bridge). SCORE: 19.

DELAYED RECALL: On December 6 (last week) (a river) (overflowed) in a (small town) (10 miles) (from Albany). High (waters flooded the streets) and (entered the houses). (14 people) were (drowned) and (600) (caught cold) (due to the dampness) and (cold air). In (rescuing) (a small boy) (under a bridge) (a man) (cut his hands). SCORE: 19.

SORTING TEST

Part I

Patient remarks after hearing the instructions, "That isn't clear to me. Actually, if we were to imagine this to be a dime store, they could all go." LARGE PLIERS: Adds all tools. "They're all tools." Adequate sorting, abstract concept. LARGE FORK: Adds all silverware. "They're eating utensils." Adequate sorting, abstract concept. PIPE: Adds all smoking utensils. "All the necessary items for smoking, except pipe tobacco. I imagine you got it in your pocket." Adequate sorting, functional concept. BELL: Patient comments, "Now I'll fool you on this, maybe;" adds all toy objects. "They're all toys." Adequate sorting, abstract concept. CIRCLE: Adds cardboard square and matches. "They're all paper. (Asked at end of test, "How about the other paper objects?")

"I just wasn't watching close, I guess.") Narrow sorting, abstract concept. TOY PLIERS: Adds all tools and nails. "They're tools again." Mildly loose sorting, abstract concept. BALL: Adds all toys. "They're all toys." Adequate sorting, abstract concept.

Part II

RED: "Well, they're all manufactured objects. That's all I can see. Of course, that can go for everything on the table." Syncretistic concept. METAL: "They're all metal." Abstract concept. ROUND: (long delay) "I can think of no conceivable reason except that they're manufactured." Syncretistic concept. TOOLS: "Tools." Abstract concept. PAPER: "Except for the tobacco, they're all paper." Split-narrow, abstract concept. PAIRS: "They're in pairs." Abstract concept. WHITE: "They're all white." Abstract concept. RUBBER: "Except for the metal ring, they're all rubber." Split-narrow, abstract concept. SMOKING MATERIALS: "Smoking equipment." Abstract concept. SILVERWARE: "All table hardware." Abstract concept. TOYS: "Toys." Abstract concept. RECTANGLES: "They're rectangular in shape, square or rectangular." Abstract concept.

RORSCHACH TEST

CARD I. Reaction time: 13″. Total time: 70″.

What it could look like or might be ... Well, it's an inkblot. 1. The only thing I could see in it would be a butterfly. As a whole, I don't see anything else. 2. Part of a lobster (top middle) there possibly. (Covers sides.) [(?) The gadgets look like they could possibly represent lobsters' front claws.] (?) Mm ... I don't have much imagination.

SCORES. 1: W F+A P. 2: Dd F±Ad.

CARD II. Reaction time: 12″. Total time: 70″.

The red's confusing. 1. Looks like a couple of dancing bears or elephants (nose is middle of upper edge of popular animal head). [(Point to nose.) I can't see what difference it makes.] Let me ask one more question. Shall I take it all as a whole or just in parts? 2. The place where the black meets the top looks like two spearheads bound together, arrowheads ... That's all. That's what you call visual imagination.

SCORES. 1: D F+A (P). 2: Dd F+Obj.

CARD III. Reaction time: 6″. Total time: 80″.

1. I can see two women but I don't know what they're doing. [(?) It looked like it remotely could be a human being and it looked like it had breasts so it couldn't be a man very easily.] < > ∧ I can't associate this red with any thing or theme. 2. One of these reds looks like it possibly could be a monkey hanging by its tail; if you want to get far-fetched on this thing. 3. If you were really going to let your imagination go, I could see the upper part of a human skeleton, from the neck down (bottom center). That's all, Mr. Schafer.

SCORES. 1: D M+H P Homoerotic. 2: D FMs+A. 3: Dr F−At.

CARD IV. Reaction time: 40''. Total time: 130''.

You're like cash: you get harder as you go along, don't you? > ∨ There's only one thing I can see. These are two eyes (in center of lower *D*) but I don't know what they belong to. They look like cow eyes, nice and forlorn (dramatic).That's all I can see. (?) I still can't see anything. I don't see a darn thing ... < ∨.

SCORE: Do F±Ad (Eyes) Fabulation Aggression.

CARD V. Reaction time: 8''. Total time: 70''.

1. ∧ ∨ Here again could be a butterfly. 2. I see something like a drumstick (side leg) , all fried, ready to eat on this thing. Which is right side up on this thing again? ... ∧ ... I think that's all, Schafer. If that's an inkblot, it's an awful poor photograph.

SCORES. 1: W F+A P. 2: D F+Food Fabulation.

CARD VI. Reaction time: 8''. Total time: 60''.

1. The top part of it looks it might be representative of a totem pole. > ∧ 2. Without it, it could be a pelt rug without the head. [(?) The way it was spread out, it looked like it had four legs on it, laying out flat ... couldn't see much fur.] That's all, Doctor, *Mister* Schafer. I call you Doctor to build up your morale.

SCORES. 1: D F+Obj. 2: D F+Ad P.

CARD VII. Reaction time: 78''. Total time: 105''.

Anybody who can see anything in that is crazy ... ∨ (Covers part of card.) ... (Covers parts.) ... *They* had pretty girls give their tests (refers to tests taken elsewhere recently) ... ∧ 1. A chimpanzee, I can see his profile after much looking (upper ⅓). He has a dirty face. [(?) Beetling brow. (Dirty?) The black. I don't think they have black around the face particularly; maybe they do.]

SCORE: D FC'+Ad (P) Fabulation.

CARD VIII. Reaction time: 7''. Total time: 100''.

1. > I can see an animal, but I don't know what it is. It's got a nose like a Koala bear and a body like I don't know what, no tail, like a Schipperke dog. [Goes into elaborate detail about the characteristics of this kind of dog.] ... ∨ > ∧ ... ∨ (Covers parts of card.) 2. That could be a butterfly again, without its antennae, if that's what they call the gadgets on a butterfly (lower section) . [(?) Wingspread on it. (?) Nothing. (?) Might be the coloring, that's all I saw. I'm not a student of zoology. Is that what's the study of butterflies?] That's all; the only thing I notice on here is if they are inkblots, they're doctored up. (How so?) The irregularity (points out asymmetries).

SCORES. 1: D F+A P Fabulation. 2: D FC+A (weak color) .

CARD IX. Reaction time: 70''. Total time: 170''.

Doctor, you show me some of the ghastliest looking things! I don't know what you got ... < ... ∨ ... > ... ∧ ... Nothing, just a bunch of screwy marks! (Rejects card.) (?) 1. Well, on either side there are two objects which could be eyes (in green-to-orange shading); one of them winking, but I don't know what they could be eyes of; just sitting out in the green. 2. > If one were imaginative, one could find a little woman sitting up in the red, (uppermost orange projection to center) man or woman, complete with belly-button by golly, and outside of the fact that this isn't a good blot again, I can't see anything else in it. I like you, Doctor, and I'm sorry I'm not doing so well. (How do you know?) You can about almost always tell.

SCORES. 1: Dr F—Eyes Fabulation. 2: Dd Ms + H Fabulation.

CARD X. Reaction time: 5″. Total time: 180″.

1. I see a rabbit's head. I beat the clock on that one. (Examiner started stopwatch late.) 2. I see something that makes me think of a frog but I can't see it (lower middle green). Maybe it's because the rabbit's eyes are sitting in the green. [(?) The green with those eyes in it, bulging. I'm just guessing. I don't know what made me think of a frog.] < ...∧... < ...∨... > ...∨... > ... Another bad blot, isn't it, Doctor? 3. There's something in there that could be a gentleman's profile, has a beard and an awfully hooked nose. It's only on one side (middle blue); takes an awful lot of imagination. That's all I can see, my friend.

SCORES. 1: D F + Ad P. 2: D C Ad. 3: D F(C)∓Hd.

Summary of Responses

R: 20   EB:2.5—2.

W 2	F + 8	A 5	W% 10
D 12	F— 2	Ad 7	D% 60
Do 1	F± 3	H 2	DR% 30
Dr 2	M1+	Hd 1	
Dd 3	Ms 1+	Obj 2	F% 65-95
	FMs 1 +	At 1	F+% 85-85
Qualitative	FC 1+ weak	Food 1	
Fabulation 5	C 1	Eyes 1 (1)	A% 60
Homoerotic	F (C) 1∓		H% 15
Verbal Aggr	FC′ 1+		At% 5
Facetious			Obj% 10
			P 6 (2)
			P% 30 (40)

WORD ASSOCIATION TEST

HAT—1″—coat. LAMP—1″—light. LOVE—1″—hate. BOOK—1.5″—read. FATHER—1″—mother. PAPER—1″—paper, that's what I thought (2″—write). BREAST—2″—titty; (laugh) I like this. CURTAINS—1.5″—windows. TRUNK—1.5″—pack. DRINK—3″—(sigh) lots. PARTY—2″—drink. SPRING—1.5″—fall. BOWEL MOVEMENT—1.5″—taking a crap; that's not a word. RUG—1.5″—floor. BOY FRIEND—1″—girl friend. CHAIR—1.5″—seat. SCREEN—1.5″—window. PENIS—1.5″—

peter. RADIATOR—1.5"—heat. Let's keep this conversation clean (referring to PENIS). FRAME—1.5"—window. SUICIDE—2"—death. MOUNTAIN—2"—hill. SNAKE—1.5"—grass. HOUSE—1.5"—home. VAGINA—3.5"—cunt. [(?) I really didn't completely understand you. I was taken aback.] TOBACCO—2.5"—smoke. MOUTH—2"—talk (1.5"—chew; I don't know what I said.) HORSE—2"—ride. MASTURBATION —2"—self-abuse. WIFE—2"—husband. TABLE—1"—chair. FIGHT—2" —win. BEEF—1.5"—gripe. STOMACH—2"—ache (6.5"). FARM—2.5"—ranch. MAN — 1" — woman. TAXES — 3" — pay. NIPPLE — 1.5" — tit. DOCTOR—2"—lawyer. DIRT—1.5"—earth. CUT—2"—wound. MOVIES —1"—show. COCKROACH—2"—insect. BITE—7.5"—chew. [(?) I was trying to think of another way to say bite.] (2"—wound, chew). DOG— 1.5"—cat. DANCE—3"—dance. [(?) I don't know, visual pictures is all. (?) Of a dance. I don't dance: that's probably why. (Other images?) I don't think so.] (3"). GUN—1"—shoot. WATER—1.5"—fall. HUSBAND —1"—wife. MUD—1"—dirt. WOMAN—1"—man. FIRE—2"—fight. [(?) Fire-fighting.] SUCK—5"—feed. [(?) I was thinking of a child nursing. (Image?) If it was, it was awful faint.] MONEY—5"—money? cash. MOTHER—1"—father. HOSPITAL—3"—illness. GIRL FRIEND—2"—boy friend. TAXI—1.5"—ride. INTERCOURSE—1.5"—fuck. What a nasty conversation! HUNGER—1.5"—thirst.

THEMATIC APPERCEPTION TEST

CARD 1. (Boy with violin.) I would say that the boy is taking violin lessons and he's probably told to practice and he's sitting there trying to talk himself into it or out of it and dreading, and will no doubt end up by practicing. Is that enough of a story? (?) I think that's human nature in small children. (Outcome?) He does the practicing. (?) Years hence? He's probably forgotten all he knew about the violin. I speak with authority on that because I took clarinet once.

CARD 2. (Old woman in doorway.) Well, it looks to me just like an elderly lady walking into a room, Doctor. Where she came from, I don't know. I imagine she's just on the way to sit down and die of peaceful old age.

CARD 3. (Old man in graveyard.) (Shakes head.) Well, there's the old gentleman has just come into a cemetery and is standing at somebody's grave, apparently in sorrow and he's probably ending up by just going back home, most people do. It seems like the Menninger Foundation should be able to get some better pictures than they've got. (Who died?) No doubt, the one that is buried there; probably the wife, or a child. (Thinking?) That's a damn good question, isn't it? I don't know what people think when they go to a cemetery. (?) Maybe he's wishing he could join them, 'cause he'd certainly be wrong if he was wishing he could be back here. (Explain?) Well, from what we're all taught, it's supposed to be pretty nice on the other side, isn't it? Weren't you taught that when you was a little boy, that death was nothing to fear and we could all go up and play harps and fly wings.

CARD 4. (Silhouette of man at window.) This looks like a bad case of insomnia. The man has been to bed. I'm assuming it's a man—from the silhouette it's hard to tell—and apparently couldn't sleep. So he's up and looking out the window, stargazing, probably daydreaming, and he'll go back to bed and go to sleep. (?) Oh, he might have been reliving an experience he'd had that evening or that day. (Specific?) I don't know the man. Maybe he had trouble with his job or his wife or his girl friend.

CARD 5. (Heads of embracing couple.) This looks like it might be a meeting after a separation for some duration. The woman looks rather pensive, like she's wondering if everything is as it should be. The man looks as though he were thinking that this is just what he wanted to get back to. He knows everything's all right. (Woman thinking?) Oh, she might be thinking that possibly the man has changed after a separation, if there was a separation, and how much. (Why away?) I don't know where he's been. Hell, if he's been to war, everybody changes. He seems awful happy to be there, though. (Outcome?) If they're in the right two-thirds of the population, they'll go on and live happily ever after. Isn't the divorce rate one-third or something like that?

CARD 6. (Prehistoric animal, rocky road, bridge.) Am I looking at that right side up? I'd say that was a very disjointed picture. I can't say anything. You've got a landslide someplace. The Gothic arch on the right suggests that it might have been a church or something, or part of a church. What's in the center of the picture, I don't know. I can't make it out. Looks like it is prehistoric due to the webfooted gadget coming out of the wall from the hole on the left. (Story?) I don't see a story, Mr. Kass. I don't see enough of the picture to see a story. (Try.) What! In fantasy? (?) I'm not that kind of a dreamer.

CARD 7. (Shadowy photograph of thumb.) It looks like somebody's cut their finger. I suppose you want to know how (laugh). Well, they were probably peeling potatoes or something and I'd say that the finger is being held for scrutiny, to look at that little drop of blood, and they'll probably end up by washing the blood off and go back to peeling the rest of the spuds.

CARD 8. (Nude couple; older woman with infant.) Looks like the older woman is kind of reprimanding the couple for running around without clothes on. The daughter doesn't have a very pleased look on her face. The man is apparently trying to explain something to her about what they're doing or something. I wonder if they're married. They ought to be, shouldn't they (slyly)? If they aren't they probably will be—maybe. That's all. (?) What's happening? I just told you! (?) Well, they're running around here without any clothes on. It looks like it's a nudist colony or something and I can't see any connection between the characters standing on the floor and the pictures on the wall. (?) I wouldn't have any idea. It looks like the old woman could be the girl's mother. That might be the reason for that glum look on her face. (?) I told you they're going to get married. They'd almost have to after that.

CARD 9. (Two chairs and table set for tea.) Two people, one of whom has excellent taste in wall paper—it is pretty paper, I like that sort of stuff—have just been sitting down to have a cup of tea, probably doing all the neighborhood gossiping while they were sitting there. By now they're probably at the front door saying good-bye to each other. After the visitor has gone, the lady who has been sitting in that wing-back chair will come in and clean up the table.

CARD 10. (Old man on shoulders of another old man.) Somebody, probably one of our guests (patients), is having a nightmare. God damn, there couldn't be any other association to this one. Like all other dreams, there's no rhyme or reason to this thing. When you start seeing transparent people and objects it's time to quit drinking or something. But he'll probably wake up and just find out it was a test. (Dream about?) Don't you know you can't remember dreams? Well, there's two old men, one of . . . both of which, no, one of which is superimposed over the other. You can't tell which one is front and which is back. There's a little fire and lightning and hell and brimstone— that's a good expression, I think—and some place in it there's a little mood of moonlight on water. That's all. (?) Well, it looks like one of these old gentlemen is clawing at the other one and the other one has got a rod or a weapon of some sort. He doesn't seem to be making any effort to defend himself and that seems all there is, there ain't no more. (Outcome?) You make it up, Doc. (?) It will just disappear 'cause it isn't. (?) I think that'd be a good ending; just flash back to natural and Ray Milland (reference to the movie, *The Lost Weekend*) throws the bottle instead of going to Menninger's. You better leave the last off, Doctor.

CARD M 11. (Old woman looking away from young man.) I'd say that the young man has done something that has rather hurt his mother and he's sorry for it and standing there trying to figure out what and how to say it; what to say and how to say it. She looks like a very understanding woman and she'll probably forgive him for whatever he's done and everything'll be all right again. (Done?) Maybe he came home drunk last night. That sometimes hurts one's mother.

CARD M 12. (Man held by hands from behind.) He's got one too many hands. Somebody is apparently apprehending the man in the picture, maybe the police. I don't know what he's done; maybe he's an arsonist and he's probably on his way I'd say, just the way these fingers have got a hold of him by the shoulder and arm. (Outcome?) He probably gets thrown in jail and sets for a while; then he gets tried and sentenced.

CARD M 13. (Figure on floor by couch.) Well, if you have a good imagination, that's a gun sitting there—lying there . . . lying there. You correct my English there, will you? And it looks like that boy has probably used that gun and he's very, very sorry he did it—whatever he did. I know you're going to ask me what he did. You want to know what's going to happen to him and I don't even know what he's done. He shot somebody and he's probably just waiting to be questioned by the police. He's either too afraid or too filled with remorse to run away. Maybe it was in self-defense and he has a good defense. (?) He gets tried and acquitted. He looks like a nice young man in knee pants. (?) Breaking and entering, attempted assault and battery, armed robbery or any of a number of things... I wasn't here when this picture was taken.

CARD M 14. ("Hypnosis" scene.) The gentleman sitting in the chair has just finished a correspondence course on hypnosis, so he's practicing on his friend. He's showing his friend how much he's learned, that hypnotism is a fact instead of a fancy, and the guest was somewhat skeptical and is feigning to be in a state of hypnosis just to make the old gentleman feel good. He'll get up in just a minute and laugh at it.

CARD M 15. (Older man looking at younger man.) There's just been a big street brawl and it looks like the older man might have been somewhat jeopardized and the younger man took his part in it and apparently the fight's about over and the young man is looking... he's taken a pretty good beating it looks like, and he's just looking and waiting to see if anybody else was going to fight some more. The old man seems to be very grateful and he'll probably go and get on a street car and go home and read his paper. That guy looks too mean. (?) The young one—a hard-looking character.

CARD M 16. (Man on rope.) It looks like this guy has been in prison and by some means he's gotten a rope and he's on his way out; I have jail on my mind, being locked up, haven't I? (Story?) That's a story in itself, isn't it?... Jailbreak. (?) He makes it. (?) He'll get caught again and then serve his time. Crime does not pay, Doctor. (?) Manslaughter, voluntary. He killed his mistress. Boy! If you want a story I'll give you a story from now on. I'll unwind on you.

CARD M 17. (Figure by table; bats and owls). This is the second dream sequence of our hangover, isn't it? Looks like the boy's been possibly reading or studying, and fell asleep. The wise old owls and the bats are about to get him—does my sarcasm have to go into this too?—and he'll awake in a little bit and finish what he was doing (pauses and looks slyly at examiner) ... which was reading.

CARD M 18. (Man on bed, face in pillow.) Well, this boy has had a hard day. He's interested in horses apparently, so I'll say he had a hard day riding horses and he came home, sat down in his room, lit his pipe and started to read a book, but he found that he was in an uncomfortable chair, very hard and he was a little touchy where he'd been riding the horses, so he lay face down on the bed to rest a while and fell off to sleep; and his wife'll call him for dinner after a while and he'll go down to eat dinner uncomfortably due to that tender spot and probably end up coming back up to bed.

CARD M 19. (Shadowed figure with arms up.) (Turns card.) Back in 1939, a war started and during this war there were lots of people killed by being shot or hung or gassed, and lots by starvation. This looks like just one of the examples of that starvation... and the Western Powers with Russia won the war and lost the peace. That's the end of that story.

CARD M 20. (Unkempt man and well-groomed man.) (Sigh.) The gentleman in the derby was walking down the street and the other fellow whom we will refer to as a bum approached him for some money. So the derby told the guy that he would take him over and buy him a drink. The bum refused and then the gentleman in the derby offered the bum a cigar and the bum refused. Then the gentleman in the derby offered to take the bum up to a house of ill-fame where they could play with the girls and the bum refused. He refused to go up to the cat-house. Now the gentleman in the derby is taking the bum home to dinner to show his wife what happens to men who neither drink, smoke, or run around with women.

ANALYSIS OF RESULTS

BELLEVUE SCALE

The scatter, with the relatively even Verbal level and the several excellent Performance scores, and with the superiority of the Performance IQ over the Verbal IQ, suggests a character disorder. The IQ difference is not great, but in most other types of illnesses the Performance level generally falls *below* the Verbal level, rendering the present pattern all the more diagnostic. This pattern is also frequent in the records of hysterics, but that diagnosis is not likely for two reasons: hysterical neuroses or character make-ups appear to be relatively rare in men, and the Information Score is not below the Vocabulary or Comprehension score as it would most likely be in the record of an hysteric. This pattern is also frequent in the records of psychopaths, but the absolute Verbal level is too high to support this diagnosis. The Arithmetic score is frequently very low in narcissistic cases, because of their low anxiety tolerance and its devastating effect on concentration. However, this is much more true among women than men. Therefore the high Arithmetic score in this record does not necessarily contraindicate the diagnostic impression. In fact it has a different implication when considered in conjunction with the Picture Completion score: both scores are nearly perfect and Arithmetic stands out above the rest of the Verbal level; where this is so, it is safe to assume the presence of noteworthy over-alertness with a paranoid background.

In Information the diagnostic impression gains good support. On the *Washington* item he says, "I wouldn't swear to anything" in a joking manner. Jokers in testing situations are usually patients with character disorders; too much wit implies strong avoidance tendencies and an intent to negate the seriousness of personal difficulties. This interpretation presupposes that the examiner has maintained a serious manner and has not stimulated or encouraged the patient to have a jolly time. The choice of content for his sally has a second implication: joke or no joke, it is an overcautious reaction and points up a paranoid trend. The emphasis on detail on the *population* item must be seen in the light of the previously reviewed indications, and, therefore, for the time being at least, should be considered pretentious rather than genuinely compulsive. On *Faust* he is clearly pretentious. The answer to *heart* is impulsive and implies no weakness of information: his IQ is 127.

The *theatre* item of Comprehension, with its "damned if I know" and "I've never been panicked yet" has an excessively self-assertive and breezy quality. Bringing in politicians on the *taxes* item has little to do with righteousness, and is more a declaration of personal intimacy with corruption and distrust of the integrity of others. On *laws* his breeziness takes on a clearly aggressive quality: he speculates about bashing in the examiner's head and how much good that would do. The self-reference itself is noteworthy: he identifies himself with the people whose impulses must be controlled by law; not only that, but he projects his picture of himself onto all of society. It is perhaps true that a sober, psychologically-minded person might say, "To protect society against itself," but we already have evidence that this verbalization has issued from an altogether different source. On *marriage* he is again intimate with the frailties of mankind and again injects an unnecessary self-reference.

In this setting, the good Digit Span score may be referred to his success so far at forestalling anxious reactions in the testing situation. In other words, he successfully maintains his superficial blandness, introduces an active concentration factor by grouping the digits, and performs on a level appropriate to his general level. His excellence in Arithmetic probably also reflects this unflustered approach, but suggests in addition an unusual but characteristic alertness. At the end of Similarities, he expresses concern with the verbatim nature of the recording, a concern which usually shows up more in the Rorschach and Thematic Apperception Tests, and which is typically expressed by more or less paranoid subjects. They indicate an anticipation that everything they say will be used *against* them, and not *for* them.

In Picture Arrangement, a "boy" on the *fish* sequence and a "gentleman" on the *taxi* sequence are too casual. He is pretentious, arrogant, and negativistic when he rejects the examiner's request to talk slower, saying, "I can't think slow". This is probably an accurate statement and is a warning at the same time that he is a "quick thinker". In Picture Completion he *had* to say "a door in a jail", "lots of people don't wear 'em" and "where is this *old* man's shadow?"

Before beginning Block Designs he asks a clearly paranoid question, though again his tone is casual; the question he asks implies a steady anticipation of being tricked and a distrust of the examiner's motives. In Object Assembly he is quick to seize on the hint of knock-knees on the mannikin for a laugh, and in Vocabulary his responses to *brim, vesper, spangle,* and *aseptic* are facetious. Yet, as his comment on the *vesper* item indicates, considerable self-awareness accompanies his facetiousness. Thus far it seems that the paranoid, watchful qualities are mostly kept in the background and covered by his hail-fellow-well-met attitude.

LEARNING EFFICIENCY

Learning efficiency is excellent. The average score of 19 is higher than would be required by a Vocabulary score of 12. There are a few minor distortions but these have no diagnostic significance. As in the Arithmetic subtest, concentration is excellent and again overalertness is suggested.

SORTING TEST

His conceptual level is excellent and his concept span is neither too loose nor too narrow. A hint of a fabulation is present in his opening verbalization about the dime store. He wisecracks on the *pipe* and *bell* items in Part I. In Part II he is again overalert and quibbles about what he considers to be minor inconsistencies in the examiner's sortings. The two syncretistic concepts are of a common variety and he recognizes their inadequacy; they are therefore not convincing indications of conceptual expansiveness. At the beginning of each part of this test he experiences difficulty in anticipating the conceptual norms to which he must adhere, although subsequently he does well. This pattern is often found in the records of patients with paranoid features.

RORSCHACH TEST

The summary of responses contains the following striking features: only 2 *W*'s, no shading responses, 6 fabulations, one weak *FC* and one pure *C*. In this setting the low *W* indicates basically weak integrative ability; the absence of shading indicates the low anxiety tolerance and its devastating effect on reflectiveness; the 6 fabulations are insincere, whimsical elaborations of more or less commonplace ideas; and the color distribution indicates a weak front of adaptiveness and a noteworthy potentiality for impulsive behavior. There is only 1 *C*, however, the $F+\%$ is high and 3 movement responses are present—the three together indicating that in the main he is likely to be able to delay the expression of impulses cautiously and that truly impulsive acts are likely to occur only sporadically. We have seen milder manifestations of apparently careless or impulsive behavior pervading a good deal of his responses so far, but if these were genuinely impulsive acts we should expect more color responses in the record—especially more CF and C. Pitting his verbalizations against the actual color and movement distribution and the high $F + \%$, we can conclude that much of his gaiety is feigned, put on for effect and used as cunningly as possible to gain an advantage in social situations. Together with the evidences of paranoid alertness and caution, these indications also imply that his impishness is deceptive and essentially amounts to putting out "feelers" and forestalling anxiety-arousing situations.

Turning to the actual verbalizations we find many facetious remarks; these need not be pointed out singly by now. They are basically aggressive throughout. He is also, however, overcautious about his responses, frequently at the same time as he is being facetious. The long delays on Cards IV, VII and IX indicate directly how difficult it is for him to cope with anxiety-arousing and affect-arousing situations. On Card IV, under the impact of anxiety, his integrative ability is so impaired that he is restricted to the eyes of what is frequently seen as a full animal head (lower middle D), and misses the popular W (animal skin) altogether. On Card IX, another frequently disturbing card, precisely the same thing happens: after a long delay he makes out a pair of eyes, one of which is frequently integrated into a full animal head. The choice of content "eyes" can be considered a further indication of his paranoid trend; because these responses occurred on difficult cards, it is likely that paranoid thinking will make its clearest appearance only when he is "on the spot", although traces of it will generally be evident. The prevalence of small M's among his movement impressions is a further indication of his projective trend. He recovers on Card IX after finding the eye and begins to fabulate: "One of them winking"— not merely *closed* but "winking". This response conveys in one stroke his entire outward manner of impishness and the more covert watchfulness. He picks up speed on the second response to Card IX, having a gay time with the "belly button". The verbalization at the end of this card is ingratiatingly frank, but more ingratiating than frank; narcissistic characters often include frankness among their weapons. He may have liked the examiner at the moment, but his intent in saying so was most likely not merely to declare his feelings but mainly a plea to the examiner to ease up.

The vivid food response on V is indicative of strong oral needs, and is a type of response frequently found in the records of parasitic personalities. On Card X the pure *C* (*frog*) response is so impulsively given that during inquiry he has to stop in the middle of a rationalization, recognizing its futility. Thus when impulsiveness does make an appearance, he is quick to defend himself but also careful not to get in deeper. Seeing the two men on Card III as women and puzzling about the sexual identity of the little figure on Card IX indicates that his conception of his own sexual role is blurred, and suggests that a feminine identification may underlie the parasitic, demanding qualities already noted.

WORD ASSOCIATION TEST

There has been no indication of disorganization thus far and the conceptual orderliness of his word associations is consistent with this trend. He blocks on *paper*, but presumably was distressed by the preceding word, *father*, even though no disturbance was apparent when *father* was called out. He also blocks on *dance*, but here a particular conflict is hinted at in inquiry. The wisecracks attached to his responses to the "sexual" words are consistent with his general defensive breeziness. The greatest massing of associative disturbances occurs in connection with the words with oral connotations: drink (reaction time and self-reference), *mouth* (recall), *stomach* (recall), *bite* (reaction time and recall), *suck* (reaction time). *Beef* being understood in the sense of "gripe" is no surprise. Intense oral conflicts are indicated by these disturbances and addiction is likely to be present. This is especially likely because of the low anxiety tolerance and avoidance tendencies which color the majority of his responses. The response to *drink* is, of course, an admission of alcoholism. His claim that there were "a lot of repetitions" is a claim often made by watchful, suspicious subjects. Impulsiveness is evident in the several phrase-completions: *water*—"fall", *fire*—"fight", *stomach*—"ache".

THEMATIC APPERCEPTION TEST

Facetiousness, as an effort to deny the emotional meaning of nearly every story, is the most striking feature of this test. This debunking attitude is maintained so rigidly that it takes on an air of desperation. (It is known that persons with this type of illness are basically terrified by a world they conceive to be cold and hostile.)

On Card 1 he pooh-poohs serious aspirations. On Card 2 he becomes downright callous. On Card 3 he sneers at the picture, negates the sadness of the scene with "most people do", "no doubt the one that's buried there" and his scorn for the idea of heaven. His comment about the error of wanting to return to the world appears to express sincerely how ungratifying life in this world seems to him. But when he is asked about the man's thoughts and feelings, he characteristically strenuously resists searching his heart for more specific sad content. On Card 4 the sexual identity of the figure is blurred—a relatively infrequent occurrence—suggesting that his own sexual role is not clearly conceived and that a feminine identification is present. On Card 5 he expresses apprehension about retaining his acceptance by the female-figure. However, when he approaches the question of his responsibility in this situation, he veers away with "Hell! Everybody changes!" — a characteristic attempt to reject the idea of personal responsibility. The unstructured situation of Card 6 is apparently too threatening to him and he cautiously refuses to have a fantasy about it. On Card 7, he implicitly brings in KP in the army, which is always good for a laugh.

On Card 8 he teases the examiner with his "shouldn't they?" and keeps the story on a superficial level; his hedging comments—"ought to be", "probably will be", "maybe"—are attempts to disclaim responsibility. He completely evades the aggressive implications of Card 10 with his spontaneous comments, resorting instead to a series of quips. The examiner's pressure forces him to admit the aggressive implications of the picture, and it is noteworthy that the victim in the situation is passive; however, the patient quickly flits away from this idea and takes up the theme of the movie, *The Lost Weekend*. His last comment implies that at the moment he feels it would be less painful to stop drinking than to tolerate the probing examinations he is undergoing. Altogether he appears unable to face his aggressiveness directly; this inability is usually evident in the records of passive, parasitic personalities such as essential alcoholics; admission of strong hostility would threaten their dependent status and they therefore defensively resort to denial, avoidance, and projection.

On Card 11 he banks on the mother-figure's indulgence, and expresses a little warmth at the same time as he scoffs at it. It is noteworthy that the identification-figure never does explain, apologize, or atone for his act. A dependent attachment to the mother-figure and expectations that she will remain nurturent to her "bad boy" are indicated. In the light of this finding, the story on Card 5 appears to express the same kind of dependency: "just what he wanted." Card 12 elicits a popular and essentially unrevealing story. On Card 13 as soon as the aggressive implications of the picture become clear, he digresses into problems of grammar; he returns briefly to the theme of aggression and then makes a bid to avoid going into details. He again returns to the theme and now acquits the identification-figure: it is self-defense and *there was no aggressive motive.* Inquiry still tries to track down the motive but fails, eliciting a buckshot barrage of possibilities. It is clear by now how desperate he is in his efforts to avoid facing his own aggressiveness. He feels free to discuss only the aggressiveness of the world about him (see Comprehension items of Bellevue Scale). The story on Card 14—insincere "cooperation"—speaks for itself.

On Card 15 the "beating" taken by the "hard-looking" young man sounds like a view of his own life and personality. He appears to be trying to say that people are not grateful for sincere efforts on their behalf: they go home and read the paper. The murder of the mistress on Card 16, though he afterwards aggressively claims to be trying to shock the examiner, is indicative of strong hostility to women. On Card 17 he is teasing again. On Card 18 he brings in the time-tested joke about sensitive spots after horseback riding. On Card 19 he expresses a feeling of futility at fighting battles for self-improvement. The choice of *starvation* suggests the orality already noted. On Card 20 he tells a formal joke, but one which is highly expressive: the idea is that virtue does not pay, a rationalization of a basically passive attitude toward his illness. He sneers at all conventional values, implying that they are synonymous with moral hypocrisy and mediocrity.

In this entire test it is noteworthy how little empathy is expressed for the characters and situations: a lack of stable identification-figures or crystallized sense of his own identity and values is implied.

Test Report

Intelligence and Thought Organization: This is a man with superior intelligence (IQ of 127) and well-maintained intellectual efficiency. He is inclined to be overalert, cautious, and defensive in a paranoid manner. He covers this watchfulness with a rigidly maintained front of facetiousness. His orientation to the world is largely egocentric, and his integrative ability is unusually weak, suggesting that his reasoning and behavior are likely to be limited in time-perspective and full of inconsistencies. He is inclined to fabulize freely and it is probable that he has difficulty in extricating objective facts from his insincere embellishments, and, therefore, in knowing when he is sincere and when he is acting.

Emotional Factors: His outward manner is impish, merry, and convention-defying; he plays the rogue, hoping desperately to forestall the crystallization of anxiety-arousing and affect-arousing situations. Anxiety tolerance appears to be very low. He is primarily narcissistic in his relations with the world about him: emotional output and capacity for object-attachments and empathy are minimal; a passive, demanding attitude, expressed ingratiatingly, runs through the greater part of his behavior. His facetiousness, however, is continuously aggressive, although when he is confronted with a demand to reflect on his aggressive motives or behavior he becomes frantically evasive. This reliance on the defense of avoidance is extreme, pertaining not only to aggressive content but to any personal content. Denial, avoidance, and projection appear to be the chief defenses used to protect his dependent status.

Figures and Attitudes: He continuously debunks conventional values —the only ones which exist for him—and has no serious values of his own to offer. It appears that he has not developed any stable concept of his own identity and has only a superficial view of himself as a "dirty", irresponsible, fun-loving "bad boy". His acceptance of a mature male heterosexual role does not appear to be well-established. He seems to be play-acting much of the time, rapidly changing to suit the fine changes of emotional atmosphere picked up by his covert watchfulness; each role he plays has the quality of a "feeler" seeking out the most immediately available gratifications and none is valid in its own right. There is a hint of strong hostile feelings toward women, although a dependent, parasitic attachment to the mother-figure is indicated. He takes a passive attitude toward his own illness and even attempts to rationalize it: virtue brings no rewards (pleasures) at all, efforts at self-improvement are in vain, and efforts on behalf of others are repaid with ingratitude.

Diagnostic Impression: Narcissistic character disorder. Addiction was openly admitted during the testing and seems consistent with his very low anxiety tolerance, avoidance tendencies and intense passive needs.

Clinical Summary

Mr. N. was referred because of alcoholism for the past ten years, which became especially severe during the last year. His father was a "self-made", successful, pompous manufacturer who tyrannized his entire family. He was unaffectionate, inconsistent, and never trusted the abilities of his children. He frequently spanked the patient. The patient still feels hostile toward him. The mother was overindulgent and overprotective; the patient states that she is the only woman he has ever loved. His ideal is his brother who was killed in an accident when the patient was twelve. The brother was "wild" and fun-loving, and was generally liked by people. The patient has never recovered from the intense grief and bitterness to the world he felt when his brother died. He vowed never to let anyone's death affect him again like this one had, and, in later years, while in the army, he took the death of two "buddies" casually.

The patient was active, energetic, and socially popular during his school years; he was a bright but not very industrious student. At the age of sixteen, he had a sexual affair with a girl for a period of one year which ended in her becoming pregnant and marrying another man. The patient feels no responsibility for the child. He worked for his father for several years, was underpaid relative to other employees because he was supposed to be "working his way up". He left at the age of twenty-one, either because, as he claims, he felt his talents were too great for his position, or, as his father claims, because he was fired for being insulting and unreliable. There followed a two-year period of rapid success as a salesman because of his ability to learn a business and make friends quickly. He left this job, as he says, for a better job, or, as his father says, because he was fired for excessive drinking. At twenty-three, he went to New York where he worked at odd jobs for two years, "bumming around", making enough money to drink, eat and sleep.

Then followed a five-year period in the army, distinguished by frequent courts martial for alcoholism, insubordination, and AWOL's. He was frequently "busted". He was overseas for about three years, had the DT's once, and did some gambling and stealing. He wrote checks his father had to make good. He was discharged on points and rapidly went through several thousand dollars by drinking and reckless spending. He proposed to a woman he did not love while drunk and was accepted. The marriage worked out poorly from the beginning. His drinking, which heretofore had made him feel like a "big shot" and had relieved his tension, now only made him more depressed. A vicious circle of drinking and depression ensued. When psychiatric treatment was suggested by his parents he felt that they were trying to "railroad" him. Suicidal preoccupation developed and he made an abortive suicidal attempt the day before he was to leave for Topeka. He came at his own request, telling his father that he could no longer leave alcohol alone.

While in the sanitarium, he received a wire from a recent girl friend stating that, as a result of their sexual relations, she was pregnant and needed money for an abortion. He "let it ride", putting the responsibility on her for not having protected herself adequately. Of his history of promiscuous sexual behavior, he stated that he enjoyed the feeling of companionship and a *quick* sexual conquest but that he never loved any of the women. He was aware that he characteristically tended to seek out female companions. His behavior in the sanitarium was boisterous and demanding; he chafed at all restrictions and quickly threatened to leave unless given more freedom. His manner was flippant and jovial, but restless. During interviews he concerned himself little with his illness and mainly with privileges and restrictions. Frustration-tolerance was conspicuously low. He left the grounds once to do some drinking and, upon his return, banged furniture around; thereafter he was generally hostile to the hospital regime.

PSYCHOPATHIC CHARACTER DISORDER: TEST RESULTS

Mr. F. Age: 28. Education: 3 years high school. "I was pushed through—really only 8 grades." Occupation: Odd jobs. Marital: Single. Father: Truck driver. Early Environment: Eastern cities. Family Position: Only child. Religion: Catholic.

BELLEVUE SCALE

Comprehension

ENVELOPE: I would take it and stick it in the nearest mail box (2). THEATRE: I wouldn't do nothing. It's not my business. (Heard *fight* instead of *fire*. Question repeated.) If I was the first one in there? No one else in there? (Question repeated.) Let everyone know, send in the alarm, or on second thought instead of starting a panic and getting children killed, I'd tell the manager (2). BAD COMPANY: Keep them in trouble all the time, have them in jail all the time (1). TAXES: For the up-keep of the country, the standing army and navy, and to protect the country and for the advancement of children to go to schools and colleges (1). SHOES: More durable (1). LAND: There is usually a demand for more business: jewelry stores, grocery stores; not much of a demand in the country (1). FOREST: If the sun was out, I would look for the directions (belches silently and excuses himself) if I didn't have a compass; also I'd try best to find the way I came in or pick a landmark. (?) The sun rises in east and sets in west (2). LAW: To protect mankind. (?) In other words, in order for people to live together and get along, to work together, go about everyday things (2). LICENSE: It's a law of the church. DEAF: I should think it affects the vocal cords some way. RAW SCORE: 12.

Information

PRESIDENT: +. LONDON: +. PINTS: +. RUBBER: +. THERMOMETER: Regulate heat and temperature, also takes temperature. (?) Tells how hot and cold it is. (?) It doesn't control the heat; +. WEEKS: +. ITALY: +. WASHINGTON: +. HEIGHT: 5'7". PLANE: Wright brothers were supposed to; another man, Dumont, a Frenchman —lot of argument about it; +. PARIS: +. BRAZIL: +. HAMLET: +. POLE: Byrd. VATICAN: dk. JAPAN: +. HEART: Works the blood system and regulates the blood pressure; pumps the blood through the body; +. POPULATION: Between 60 and 100 million. H. FINN: +. EGYPT: Oriental country, North African continent; +. KORAN: dk. FAUST: George Bernard Shaw? HABEAS CORPUS: Writ for court. (?) You have to present your body to court if a technicality comes up when your constitutional rights are jeopardized in some form. (?) Maybe like a case of incompetent counsel; can demand a retrial if found guilty. ETHNOLOGY: dk. APOCRYPHA: dk. RAW SCORE: 16.

Digit Span

FORWARD: 3, 4, 5, 6 on first try; fails both series of 7 by reversing numbers and adding extra numbers. BACKWARDS: 3 on first try; fails first series of 4 by changing last number; fails both series of 5 by mixing up the end of the series. RAW SCORE: 10.

Arithmetic

ITEM 1: +. ITEM 2: repeats question; +. ITEM 3: 16¢ (4"). (?) 17¢ (16"). ITEM 4: 8 (5"). (?) 9 (15"). ITEM 5: +. ITEM 6: +. ITEM 7: 4, no 28 (9"); +. ITEM 8: 1200 (8"). (?) A guess. (Figure it out!) I'd have to have paper and pencil. $\frac{1}{3}$ is 400. (Question repeated.) 200 equals... oh, I don't know, I'll guess 1200. (1/3?) 200 is 1/3. (3/3?) 1200. (1/3) 200. (2/3?) 400. (3/3?) 600, no 1200. (How many thirds in whole?) 4/3, no 3/3.(1/3 is 200: 3/3?) 1000 or 1200. ITEM 9: about 50 feet (12"). (?) I don't know—a guess. (Feet in 1 yard?) 10. ITEM 10: No insight. RAW SCORE: 5.

Similarities

ORANGE: Fruit (2). COAT: Clothes, wear them (2). DOG: Animals (2). WAGON: Vehicles (2). DAILY PAPER: Communicate the news to people (1). AIR: Air observes water. (Observes?) Absorbs water. WOOD: Alcohol comes out of wood, wood alcohol. EYE: Part of the body (1). EGG: You mean seed in an egg? (Question repeated). Egg is seed of life and seed is seed to produce tree. (?) Both produce some form of life. POEM: In the case where a poem is written about a statue or statue is about a famous man like Shakespeare and probably have a poem written about him. PRAISE: I wouldn't say they're alike. (?) Both do a person good: praise and punishment do him good—make a better man or woman out of him, either way (1). FLY: Fly is a form of life and so is a tree (2). RAW SCORE: 13.

Picture Arrangement

HOUSE: + 3" (2). HOLD UP: + 6". No way I can get that wrong! (2). ELEVATOR: + 6" (2). FLIRT: AJNTE 24". (?) He helps the woman into the car. FISH: IJEFGH 30". (Changes originally correct arrangement and accepts.) (?) He calls and the diver comes up with fish in his hand and lays it in the basket; then he fishes. (?) He goes down again or he comes out and lays fish in the basket and stays out. TAXI: SAMUEL 25". A timid man. (Insight.) (4). RAW SCORE: 10.

Picture Completion

(Subject names each picture before giving answers.) NOSE: +.
MUSTACHE: +. EAR: +. DIAMOND: +. LEG: +. TAIL: +.
STACKS: +. KNOB: +. SECOND HAND: +. WATER: +. REFLEC-
TION: +. TIE: +. THREADS: +. EYEBROW: Ear. SHADOW: Foot-
prints; this is supposed to be a desert? Shadow. (Which one?) Shadow;
22". RAW SCORE: 13.

Block Designs

ITEM 1: 9" (5). ITEM 2: 11" (4). ITEM 3: 8" (5). ITEM 4:
38" (3). ITEM 5: 58"; slow beginning, methodical but not quick (3).
ITEM 6: 115"; poor analysis, two errors, corrects and spoils; final design
correct but rotated 180°; accepts at 115". (Turned correctly?) Corrects
error. (Notice rotation?) No. ITEM 7: 300"; uses red-white block rotated 45° for center, then all-white block rotated 45° and builds around it;
after time limit he was shown top row: center correct but difficulty
with wedges and side column. RAW SCORE: 20.

Object Assembly

ITEM 1: 13" (6). ITEM 2: 32" (8). ITEM 3: 34" (8). RAW
SCORE: 22.

Digit Symbol

38 correct; no errors. RAW SCORE: 38.

Vocabulary

APPLE: A fruit (1). DONKEY: An animal (1). JOIN: Join something together. (?) Join a society, church (1). DIAMOND: A piece of
jewelry (1). NUISANCE: Something that makes a nuisance of itself,
disturbs people (1). FUR: Refers to animals; did you say fur or refer?
(?) Fur is on an animal. (?) Part of the animal, skin (1). CUSHION:
Something that you sit on (1). SHILLING: English money (1).
GAMBLE: In cards or ... in stock markets (1). BACON: A meat. (?)
Usually eaten at breakfast and comes from fat, beef (½). NAIL: Refers.
to the fingernail or nail that you drive in wood (1). CEDAR: Tree (1).
TINT: Something that has a tint to it, maybe a color (1). ARMORY:
Something like the National Guard armory, something that protects
them. (?) Build them in some towns; sort of a fort. FABLE: Something
that's fantastic (½). BRIM: Brim of a glass or cup. (?) Brim of a hat.
GUILLOTINE: Refers to *gilyintine*: French machine for executing
people. (?) Chop their head off (1). PLURAL: Refers to English grammar. (?) Like a plural noun. SECLUDE: You seclude someone by their
self (½). NITROGLYCERINE: (quickly) Explosive (1). STANZA:
Refers to music. (?) Like first stanza of a song (½). MICROSCOPE:
Something to magnify things that can't be seen by the naked eye, like
bacteria (1). VESPER: Something they wear in church. BELFRY:
Where they keep the bell in church (1). RECEDE: Like you'd say, "He
recedes into himself all the time," keeps his thoughts to himself all the
time. AFFLICTION: Getting sick, some kind of disease (½). PEWTER:
A mug, like. (?) With a top, like English pewter. (Made of?) Stainless

steel, or silver, or aluminum or copper. BALLAST: I guess that's some kind of stone or something. (?) Used for building. (?) Roads or prisons (½). CATACOMB: Like a cave, underground. (?) Like natural or man-made (½). SPANGLE: Could refer to something bright. (?) Like star-spangled banner; bright stars on it (½). ESPIONAGE: French word like ... spying (1). IMMINENT: (spelled) Like Tom Clark, the attorney-general, is a very imminent attorney. MANTIS: Could refer to an insect, like the praying mantis (1). HARA KIRI: Japanese word for committing suicide (1). CHATTEL: House of prostitution. DILATORY: dk. AMANUENSIS: dk. PROSELYTE: Either a doctor's word or referring to something belonging to *Buduists'* religion. MOIETY: dk. ASEPTIC: Like antiseptic; referring to some kind of medicine. FLOUT: Refers to flout something over the head. TRADUCE: dk. RAW SCORE: 23.

Weighted Scores and IQ's

Comprehension 11	Picture Arrangement 9	Vocabulary 10
Information 11	Picture Completion 13	Verbal IQ: 102
Digit Span 7	Block Designs 10	Performance IQ: 108
Arithmetic 6	Object Assembly 13	Total IQ: 105
Similarities 11	Digit Symbol 9	

LEARNING EFFICIENCY

IMMEDIATE RECALL: Last December ... there was a (flood) in Albany, New York, and ... (water covered a lot of the streets) went into the cellars of the homes ... and (600 people) were hurt, 400 (drowned), and I think 100 (caught cold) and in (saving) (a boy), (a man) (cut his hands). SCORE: 11, after subtracting 1 for "went into cellars of homes" and 1 for third group of casualties.

DELAYED RECALL: Dec. 6 ... 16. There was a flood in Albany ... (A river) (ran over), (flooded streets) and went into the cellars. (600 people) were hurt, 400 (drowned), 100 (caught cold). (A man) (under the bridge) (saved) (a boy) and (cut both his hands). SCORE: 9, after subtracting 1 for "went into the cellars" and 1 for third group of casualties.

SORTING TEST

Part I

LARGE KNIFE: Adds rest of large silver. "Eating utensils." Mildly narrow sorting, abstract concept. LARGE FORK: Omitted, see above. PIPE: Adds cigar, cigarette, matches. "Pipe you smoke, cigar has tobacco, cigarette has tobacco, matches you use to light them with. (?) Used for same thing." Mildly narrow sorting, concrete concept. BELL: Adds small screwdriver. "It's easier to fix this with a small screwdriver." Inadequate sorting, concrete concept. CIRCLE: Adds index card. "This is made of paper and so is this." Narrow sorting, abstract concept.[5])

---

[5]) After completion of the test, subject was asked about other paper and rubber objects (last item): "I overlooked them."

TOY PLIERS: Adds large pliers. "Something just like it . . . also a wire cutter and it's got teeth on it." Narrow sorting, concrete concept. BALL: Adds eraser. "Rubber." Narrow sorting, abstract concept.

Part II

RED: "They don't go . . . (?) . . . No." Failure. METAL: "Made out of metal." Abstract concept. ROUND: "Round." Abstract concept. TOOLS: "Tools." Abstract concept. PAPER: "Made of paper." Abstract concept. PAIRS: "*All* of them? I don't know . . . some are long but these aren't. I can't see why they all go together. (?) Maybe . . . no. (?) Household utensils." Syncretistic concept. WHITE: "Don't all belong together either. (?) These are cubes of sugar, aren't they? Maybe they could go in coffee, these could be doilies (index card and cardboard square) or big plate and little plate, and smoking after you eat." Fabulized concept. RUBBER: "Rubber." Abstract concept. SMOKING MATERIALS: "Used for smoking, except this is rubber and this is chalk (imitations)." Functional concept with split-narrow quality. SILVERWARE: "Eating utensils." Abstract concept. TOYS: "Things a child plays with." Functional concept. RECTANGLES: "All aren't together. (?) Wait! They do. They're square." Abstract concept.

RORSCHACH TEST

CARD I. Reaction time: 2″. Total time: 50″.

1. I think it's a pelvis. [(?) I've seen pictures of the pelvis before in books. (?) Spinal column and bones that come out here (demonstrates on self).] 2. Well, like a bat. 3. Like a spider. [(?) Front part of it had the stickers (demonstrates), and two little parts look like eyes (upper middle bumps). (?) No.] That's about all.

SCORES. 1: W F− At. 2: W F+A P. 3: DW F− A.

CARD II. Reaction time: 11″. Total time: 60″.

1. This looks like a butterfly. [(?) Mostly the front, the feelers that come out (lower red projections), and it had a piece sticking out from each wing (upper red). (?) No. (?) The wings.] 2. Or a pelvis. [(?) A little bit like the other picture in a way and that's what made me think of a pelvis. (?) No . . . (?) No, sort of looked like the spinal column in there but it doesn't show.] . . . or ∨ . . . or < ∨ ∧ 3. Maybe a crab. [(?) I couldn't see the legs; feelers in front (lower red projections). (Else?) No. (Just feelers?) Yes.] That's about all I can make on that.

SCORES. 1: W F±A. 2: W F−At. 3: DW F−A.

CARD III. Reaction time: 10″. Total time: 90″.

1. Well, I'll say pelvis again too, first thing . . . ∨ . . . ∧ . . . 2. This part, front part, looks sort of like a head of a big spider (lower middle D). Two eyes, stickers in front, and that would be about all.

SCORES. 1: W F−At. 2: D F−Ad.

CARD IV. Reaction time: 12″. Total time: 80″.

1. I'm going to have to say pelvis again (smile). 2. It could also be a . . . a crab. [(?) Those feelers coming out (projections on lower middle D). (?) The eyes. (?) I said also a spider. (Sure?) I think I did.] 3. A butterfly. 4. And maybe some sort of a fish, some tropical fish (head at bottom). [(?) I've seen a number of different types—can't think of the name but I remember one. (?) Like a small imitation of a stingray, but it didn't have a stinger on it.]

SCORES. 1: W F—At. 2: DW F—A. 3: W F∓A. 4: W F—A.

CARD V. Reaction time: 2″. Total time: 105″.

1. Butterfly, but . . . it looks like a bat except for these two feelers here at the bottom. [(But it looks like?) I meant and it looks like a bat too.] Looks sort of like a stingbug, blisterbug I should say; wings spread out. 2. Without these bumps here (on side D) I'd call it a . . . no, I'd not. (?) I was going to say "Flying Wing" if it didn't have so many bumps.

SCORES. 1: W F+A P. 2: W F±Obj.

CARD VI. Reaction time: 8″. Total time: 60″.

1. Well, this looks like a king crab. [(?) The long sword-like thing comes out in back (upper), and at the end it has feelers (lower middle hooks); the front has feelers like that.] 2. Also a scorpion? [(?) It has sort of a stinger running out like that in the back; it comes up over them when they're walking. (?) Hasn't any legs, but they could be on it. (?) I think they can bring their legs under like a turtle. (See legs?) No.] Maybe a centipede. [(?) The stinger, same thing. (Centipede with stinger?) I think like that; yeah.] That would be all.

SCORES. 1: W F±A. 2: DW F—A.

CARD VII. Reaction time: 12″. Total time: 70″.

1. Pelvis. [(?) The bottom part looked more like a pelvis. (?) The way the bones come out. (?) The opening in here (lower middle Dr).] 2. And would also look like a burner, sort of a small burner, like you use at a campfire (W and middle space). [(?) After it's out of the case. (?) Flame at the bottom; at top you set something on.] . . . Also . . ., that would be about all. (Else?) No. [(?) I was going to say a teapewter. (?) Where you cook tea. One of those knobs on the side could be where you lift it out and other where you pour (side projections). Could also be coffee too; put coffee in the top and it drips down (into the space).]

SCORES. 1: D F—At. 2: WS F—Obj.

CARD VIII. Reaction time: 15″. Total time: 120″.

1. Maybe a king crab on this too, although it has no feelers on bottom, but the top goes out. It could look like a sword on it (upper midline). [(?) Sort of the outline, shape. (?) No. It has a part where it looks like feelers should be.] 2. Pelvis too, bottom part. 3. Top part, extreme upper part, looks like the back of the neck where the spinal goes up into the head—the spinal *column*. Are these really meant to be something? That would be about all I could think of.

SCORES. 1 W F—A. 2: D F∓At. 3: D F+At.

CARD IX. Reaction time: 27″. Total time: 90″.

Well, this could be a ... one of those fancy vases, you know ... or fancy lamp, oil lamp, kerosene lamp with glass funnel (space) in it. The orange side could be a shade that reflects the light up. [(?) It had the two knobs with holes in the side (outer green). Bottom looked like vase and sort of looked like glass side would fit down and the two sides looked like a shade to reflect up. (?) The shape. (?) A wick in the middle.] That's all. (?) Yeah.

SCORE: WS F∓Obj.

CARD X. Reaction time: 15″. Total time: 90″.

1. This looks like a pelvis (vague at first, points to lower green and changes to upper half of pink plus middle blue). 2. And at the top, top looks more like a ... like the beginning of the column that starts in the neck (upper gray). 3. And on the side, these two look like crabs (side blue). That would be all. (?) No ... (?) ... 4. An orchid, and maybe some other kind of tropical flowers. [(?) All the brilliant colors, some parts look like they might be leaves, and different colors inside.]

SCORES. 1: D F−At. 2: D F−At. 3: D F+A P. 4: W CF Pl.

Summary of Responses

R:26   EB:0−1

W 15	F+ 4	A 13	W% 58
DW 4	F± 3	Ad 1	DW% 15
D 7	F∓ 2	Obj 3	D% 27
S (3)	F− 17	At 9	F% 96-96
	CF 1	Plant 1	F+% 28-28
Qualitative			A% 54
Perseveration			H% 0
Vagueness			At% 35
			P 3
			P% 12

WORD ASSOCIATION TEST

HAT−2″−cap. LAMP−2″−shade. LOVE−2″−hate. BOOK−4″−book, cover. FATHER−2″−mother. PAPER−2″−pencil. BREAST−2″−breast, bosom. CURTAINS−3″−curtains, curtain rods. TRUNK−2.5″−suitcase. DRINK−3″−drink, swallow. PARTY−3″−party, entertainment. SPRING−2″−water. BOWEL MOVEMENT−16″−bowel movement, (laughs) physic. [(?) No. (?) Nothing. (?) Nothing.] (4″−constipation, physic). RUG−3″−rug, carpet. BOY FRIEND−2″−girl friend. CHAIR −2″−table. SCREEN−3″−screen, window. PENIS−5″−penis, sexual gland. RADIATOR−4.5″−radiator, heat. FRAME−4″−frame, window. SUICIDE−5″−suicide, self-murder. [(?) I was going to say kill. (?) I don't know why I didn't.] (8″). MOUNTAIN−3″−mountain, hill. SNAKE−4″−snake, snake, lizard. HOUSE−4″−house, bungalow. VAGI-NA−2″−vagina, womb. TOBACCO−3″−tobacco, cigarette. MOUTH−

3"—mouth, talk (3.5"). HORSE—6"—horse, donkey. [(?) I was going to say pony. (?) I figured that's a baby horse, smaller. (?) Pony is not as good an answer.] MASTURBATION—2.5"—masturbation, self-abuse. WIFE—2"—wife, husband. TABLE (heard CABLE) —3"—electricity. FIGHT—3"—fight, trouble. BEEF—7"—you mean animal? cow. [(?) I was going to say ... wondering whether you meant beef, like someone beefs.] STOMACH—3"—stomach, ulcer. FARM—2"—farm, tractor. TABLE — 1" — table, chair. MAN — 1.5" — woman. TAXES — 3" — taxes, money. NIPPLE — 4" — nipple, milk bottle, baby's bottle (3.5"). DOCTOR—2"—nurse. DIRT—2"—dirt, mud. CUT—3"—cut? blood. MOVIES — 2.5" — movies, entertainment. COCKROACH — 4" — insect. BITE—3"—bite? pain. DOG—3"—dog, animal. DANCE—3.5"—dance, exercise (2"—recreation.) GUN—2"—gun, shoot. WATER—2"—water, drink. HUSBAND—1.5"—wife. MUD—3"—mud, dirt. WOMAN—2"— woman, man. FIRE—2.5"—fire, burn. SUCK—6"—suck, baby. [(?) I thought of baby bottle; I said that before; that's why I said baby now.] MONEY—3"—spend (7"—pleasure). MOTHER—2"—father. HOSPITAL —2"—doctor. GIRL FRIEND—2"—boy friend. TAXI—7.5"—taxi? taxi? transportation. INTERCOURSE—6"—intercourse, mating. [(?) I was going to say pleasure. (?) It's a little more important than the pleasure to it.] HUNGER—13"—hunger, food. [(?) I was going to say starvation. (?) I was feeling for a word to say, the closest to it.]

THEMATIC APPERCEPTION TEST

CARD 1. (Boy with violin.) Well, this boy looks like he's been learning to play a violin and he ... he looks like he's disgusted, he's just about on the verge of giving it up, giving this business up. That's all. (Led up?) He probably figured he just couldn't learn to play the violin, just got disgusted and quit. (Tried?) Looks like he might have tried.

CARD 2. (Old woman in doorway.) I can't think of any on this ... (After 40".) Maybe this lady's getting ready to go to bed, and she's coming in to turn the light off. That's all. (Thoughts and feelings?) She looks like she was worrying. (About what?) I wouldn't know. Maybe worrying about wasting electricity.

CARD 3. (Old man in graveyard.) This looks to me like either a ghoul or ... a man mourning at a person's grave or maybe it's supposed to be a ghost coming out of the grave. That's all. (Story?) Maybe he loves—someone he loves died and he's standing over the grave mourning and wishing they were living. He probably doesn't know it's nighttime; he will stay there till morning, probably had nothing to eat for hours, probably intends to stay for a few more hours and leave. (Whose grave?) Might be his son's or his wife's. (Which?) More like his son. (Why so?) Well, because he's a pretty old man, and maybe his son might have been killed in action.

CARD 4. (Silhouette of man at window.) This might be a convict in the window of his cell, looking out and wondering if ... or ... *when* he's going to get out and how it is out there—wondering maybe how he can get out before his time, or maybe he's ... in the habit of sitting in the window like that every day or every night. I think his feelings would be—he can't get outside. Might be thinking about someone he loves, wishing he was out in the street with them—something like that. (Outcome?) After he does all that thinking, he's still in jail.

CARD 5. (Heads of embracing couple.) This woman is probably grieved about something. The man is more than likely her husband, and she, she hopes to, she hopes to have her husband comfort her ... and he's probably wondering what she's worried about, why she is crying, and he's doing his best to comfort her. (Why crying?) Maybe she lost her son in the army or navy. (Outcome?) That her husband is comforting her.

CARD 6. (Prehistoric animal, rocky road, bridge.) This looks like it might be in the mountains of Peru and it looks like, it looks like an Indian having a lot of trouble with his llamas, and he probably feels that he's up pretty high, and if those llamas start getting stubborn he's liable to be killed and lose his own life and his goods or they'll probably be killed and he doesn't have money to get more, so he's probably trying to keep those llamas from getting killed until he gets out of those mountains; also he might be more afraid of losing those llamas than he is afraid of this dragon that lives in the rocks; maybe he figures if he didn't have the llamas in his cargo, he could get away faster from this dragon. (Outcome?) He ... he's just ... going to try his best. (?) Outcome is ... I don't see any outcome going to happen. (?) He'll lose his cargo and get away.

CARD 7. (Shadowy photograph of thumb.) This is a person's thumb and ... it seems there's a cut on the thumb and the person is holding it out for the doctor to fix or the nurse and ... the outcome would be he'll get a lot ... he's suffering pain now but they'll cleanse his wound and he'll be allright. He won't have no more pain and the cut will get better.

CARD 8. (Nude couple; older woman with infant.) I don't know what to think about this. (After 35".) This looks like maybe this woman —this baby belongs to this woman that hasn't any clothes on and this woman is committing adultery; and this person holding the baby, either a man or a woman, and they're probably taking this baby away from this woman because she's not able to take care of it. It's hard to make up a story about this ... and this man is probably comforting this woman, or plead with this other woman, maybe the mother-in-law, to give this woman a chance, that she probably won't do it any more. That's as far as I can see. (Relationship of man?) He was probably, wasn't her husband, just her lover. (Outcome?) This woman's mother-in-law will probably give in and give her another chance, let her keep the baby. (See more on card?) Pin-up pictures on wall. (Why hard to make up story?) The woman didn't have any clothes, the man had shorts, and the woman is holding a baby—hard to figure out. (After completion of test, asked about sex of clothed figure.) I think it's a woman. (On what basis?) On account of the bob on back of head. (Why doubt?) Back in the olden days some men used to wear their hair like that.

CARD 9. (Two chairs, and table set for tea.) This looks as if two people, table set for two people to have tea; probably one of them is sick maybe. The other one didn't show up. Because the other one didn't show up, the one that had the table set got mad and went up to her or his room and they'll probably have an argument over the phone and say they won't see each other no more. (Why didn't one come?) Maybe he was sick or maybe they had other business; maybe he didn't want to show up, or a misunderstanding or something.

CARD 10. (Old man on shoulders of another old man.) This looks like maybe it might be a dream—or nightmare . . . and the sort that would make him awful scared, and they probably . . . jump up and maybe holler or maybe the dream might pass away. (Story about picture!) I can't see any story in it. (?) I don't know. (?) It looks like this top man might be trying to kill this other man. (Led up?) Maybe some kind of argument or something. (About what?) About . . . any ordinary day occurrence. (Why kill?) Maybe he did something awful bad to him. (What?) Took something from him. (Outcome?) This man will wind up killing this other man.

CARD M 11. (Old woman facing away from young man.) This is probably a woman that loves her son an awful lot and she probably thinks he's still a baby and he should be home . . . and he . . . is trying to convince her that it's time for him to leave, and go out and make a life of his own, and it's awful hard for her to understand him because she loves him so much. The outcome will be that she'll give in and agree with him that he should go away and make his own life the way he ought to. (Son feel?) He probably feels sad: he loves his mother. He'll keep in touch with her and come and see her.

CARD M 12. (Man grasped by hands from behind.) This man is in the police station getting the third degree. More than likely, he might be an innocent man—ex-convict not getting into any trouble. Probably they picked him up because there was a crime in his neighborhood. He probably didn't commit the crime. They probably don't have the right person, so they're giving him the third degree because they got to have somebody to clear the records. He's bucking them as much as he can. He's probably taking a beating for it.

CARD M 13. (Figure on floor, against couch.) This looks like a woman. She's either in her room or in the state hospital or in jail. Looks like she's got a gun smuggled into her and is about to commit suicide. Looks like she's scared, crying, trying to get her nerve up. In the long run she'll probably go through with it. (Led up?) She probably might be a drug addict or has done something awful bad—might be a prostitute, just desolate; probably figures this will be an easy way out.

CARD M 14. ("Hypnosis" scene.) This man is either dying or dead . . . and if he's dying, he probably called for a priest to perform the last rites on him. He probably figured that'll be the best way out, having the priest perform the last rites on him. He's probably giving the priest some last message to give his people, probably tell what his life has been—faults have been. He might be a convict, criminal, and he's repenting and trying to make life as easy as possible these last few minutes. He'll probably die in peace.

CARD M 15. (Older man facing younger man.) These look like a couple of criminals waiting for the line-up. They're probably telling stories to each other, or they might be in on the same charge. Possibly one is innocent and the other guilty. They might be on the same charge and trying to figure out some story to tell, alibi to get, remembering someone who, that can give an alibi. They'll probably get the story straight and get an alibi and get out, get released. (Really guilty?) They might be, yes. (Feelings?) Probably that they're not guilty, framed, and if they're guilty, feel they got caught doing it and will suffer the consequences.

CARD M 16. (Man on rope.) This man is either an athlete or escaping from prison and it looks like he's pretty frantic and going as fast as he can to get up to the top of the wall. As he goes up, things go through his mind. He's wondering if the tower man is seeing him, watching him, or he's wondering if the spotlight will hit him . . . after he gets over the wall, if the guard will see him, and he's hoping he gets over the top, switch that rope and get down the side and get away safely. (Outcome?) He'll probably be able to get over that wall, or he's spotted and they cut the siren on. He'll have to make the best he can. They put crossfire on him. He might get away or might get shot.

CARD M 17. (Figure at table, bats and owls.) This woman is sleeping. She's having a nightmare, sees lots of owls and bats coming after her—looks like vampire bats—they're awful big. She's probably wondering when they'll jump on her. She's waiting, too scared to move. Probably when they jump on her, she'll start howling and run and get away. Outcome will be she'll wake up and find it's only been a nightmare.

CARD M 18. (Man on bed, face in pillow.) This man is probably drunk and he's sleeping it off, might be a drug addict. He probably is trying to . . . he probably committed some crime and he's wondering whether the police are coming after him or whether he should give himself up. If he does, the outcome will be—he's probably having visions of high gray walls, cells with big bars, putting stripes on and swinging a sledge hammer, which they don't do any more. The outcome will be he'll give himself up to the police and hope for the best.

CARD M 19. (Shadowed figure with arms raised.) This man looks like he might be in a concentration camp; they probably got him up before a firing squad. He's living his life over now, thinking of all the things he's done and all the people he loved and he's probably praying to God to stop the war, hoping that the Germans will have their day sometime, when they'll suffer for all the things they're doing to his kind of people.

CARD M 20. (Unkempt man and well-groomed man.) This looks like a man getting out of prison, without the hat—the other man might be a marshall or detective taking this man on a detainer to some other prison. The man feels that he's done a lot of time, probably feels it's an injustice to take his time and then give him some more time, and he's probably hoping that the outcome will be pretty good when he gets back to this place where the marshall is taking him.

ANALYSIS OF RESULTS

BELLEVUE SCALE

The scatter is distinguished by the superiority of the average Performance level (10.8) over the average Verbal level[6]) (9.8). This difference is also reflected by the Verbal IQ (102) being 6 points lower than the Performance IQ (108). The difference is not great but the baseline for comparison is not equality of the two levels but a slight inferiority of Performance abilities. A relatively high Performance level may suggest any of the following diagnoses: hysteria, narcissistic character disorder, psychopathic character or simple schizophrenia, because in these four conditions verbal achievements are more or less hampered or neglected by the persisting pathological character make-up. However, Information is above Vocabulary and equal to Comprehension and this is not the typical repressive (hysterical) pattern. In a more clear-cut psychopathic record there would be a relatively high Picture Arrangement score, because that indicates the psychopath's distinctive sharpness of social anticipations. Perhaps the relatively high Picture Completion score, ordinarily indicative of overalertness, has the same implication. The low Arithmetic score, implying low anxiety tolerance and poor concentration ability, is consistent with psychopathic, narcissistic, or simple schizophrenic features.

If this is a narcissistic disorder, facetiousness, evasiveness, and pretentiousness should be expected to distinguish the qualitative aspects of the record; if this is a psychopath, a deferent, ingratiating, and conscientious manner mixed with loosely integrated knowledge and pretentious guessing should be expected; and if this is a simple schizophrenic, peculiar verbalizations should be expected. Mainly psychopathic qualities are present in this record.

In Information the initial response to *thermometer* is just sloppy, as inquiry brings out. The references to Dumont on *airplane,* to Shaw on *Faust* and to the Orient on *Egypt* are clear fabulations. All kinds of odds and ends are tossed in for effect. The *habeas corpus* item is failed but he seems to be quite familiar with legal jargon ("jeopardized", "incompetent counsel") much beyond his level. A criminal background is not unlikely.

---

6) Excluding the Digit Span score.

In Comprehension the humanitarian and responsible flavor of his responses is typically psychopathic; psychopaths usually present a front of utmost respect for convention and the needs of others. On the *theatre* and *tax* items he is solicitous of the welfare of children and the nation; he offers correct responses to the *bad company* and *laws* items without batting an eyelash; the church is dragged in on the *marriage license* item. It is noteworthy that jewelry stores and grocery stores seem to be the focal business enterprises in cities: this is almost a caricature of what we would expect to be a thief's functional organization of city space. The general patness of his answers and the relatively high final score suggest a capacity for maintaining a bland front of social compliance.

On items 8 and 9 of Arithmetic, he offers incorrect answers quickly, indicating a characteristic bland unconcern. When asked how he got these answers he says that he does not know, that he guessed. It is clear from the common nature of the errors ($1200 and 50 feet) that he did not guess. When a subject falsely claims to have guessed in order to avoid further application to the problem, it is indicated that he is characterized by a noteworthy resistiveness to reflection or introspection, which has its origin in low anxiety tolerance. He would rather appear to be a fool than earnestly explore his own thinking. This occurs frequently in the records of narcissistic character disorders and psychopaths. The relatively low score and the inability to profit from the examiner's cues would, however, support the hypothesis that this is a simple schizophrenic.

In Similarities, the response to the *praise--punishment* item is in the same class as the responses to *laws* and *bad company* in the Comprehension subtest. If the diagnosis *psychopath* is correct, it is most likely that he is offering these responses sincerely; in the testing situation he probably does not relate these general moral ideas to himself at all. Note also the fabulation, with Shakespeare thrown in, on the *poem—statue* item. In Picture Arrangement, when he spontaneously and blandly comments on the *hold-up* item that there's no way he could get that wrong, a psychopathic history is established. "Footprints" on the last Picture Completion item is by now no surprise. In Vocabulary, fabulizing is evident on *plural, chattel* (brothel), *recede, proselyte*. Primitive syncretic thinking in the sense of Piaget and Werner is evident in his efforts on the *pewter* item: he probably has heard of *pewter mugs* and has concluded that pewter means mug. The examples he chooses to illustrate *imminent* (eminent) and *gamble* and the definition of *join* are also no accidents. The extensive use of the word *refer* is pretentious, especially when seen in the company of "gilyintine". A peculiar fluidity is evident on *fur* where he uses the word *refer* and then confuses it with the original word; simple schizophrenia with psychopathic features is still a possible diagnosis.

The scatter, the fabulations, the bland innocence, and the primitive thinking combine to indicate definitely the psychopathic features.

LEARNING EFFICIENCY

Learning efficiency is very poor: he averages 10 when, on the basis of a Vocabulary score of 10, he should average about 14. This low efficiency is frequent where schizophrenic disorganization or depressive retardation is present; since no depressive features have been evident thus far, the low score can be used to support the possibility of simple schizophrenia. There are, however, occasional cases in which poor concentration without a schizophrenic background impairs learning efficiency to this extent. It is significant that in both recalls he increases the amount of casualties.

SORTING TEST

In Part I, his sortings are narrow, but inquiry reveals this to be due to concreteness and carelessness rather than to cautious exclusiveness. The conceptual level fluctuates between abstractness and concreteness. In Part II, the conceptual level is surprisingly good: there are 7 abstract and 2 functional concepts. In the setting of psychopathic indications, this, like the Comprehension score in the Bellevue Scale, indicates a "good front". He does, however, fabulate in one instance after encountering difficulty. Many psychopaths do fabulate several times in this test, but do not do so spontaneously. Typically they first say that they see no reason why the objects go together, and only when they are asked the permissive question, "Can you think of any reason why they might?" do they weave their tale. The carelessness in Part I and this fabulation lend mild support to the diagnosis of a psychopathic character; the absence of any peculiar verbalization, absurd concept, or loose sorting weakens the argument for simple schizophrenia.

RORSCHACH TEST

The test record is distinguished by the primitive quality of his percepts and the stereotypy and perseveration of content. This is a frequent type of psychopathic record. Also consistent with this pattern is the constricted experience balance with an emphasis on *CF*, implying weakness of adaptive efforts (no *FC*), the potentiality for sporadic impulsive acts (only 1 *CF*) and weak capacity for thoughtful delay of impulses (no *M* or sharp forms). The absence of shading probably refers to blandness. The low *P* and *P*% suggest that basically he is not responsive to common, conventional ideas; this, combined with the low color-sum, suggests a generalized withdrawal. The typical flatness and poverty of the entire record demonstrate all the more strikingly the basic emptiness and pretentiousness of the psychopath.

The *DW*'s illustrate the characteristic *pars pro toto* reasoning of a primitively organized mind. Usually, however, psychopaths do not achieve so high a *W*%; because of their feeble integrative efforts, they are able to deal almost entirely with *D*'s only. The overspecificity of the anatomical responses and traces of superficial compulsiveness (the *flying wing* verbalization on Card V) reflect the superficial intellectual pretentiousness; the high *W*% probably has the same implication.

In this setting, the extremely low $F+$% cannot be taken to indicate directly that reality testing is devastated. The previous tests have indicated that this is not so. Note particularly the excellent Picture Completion score and the abstract concepts in Part II of the Sorting Test. A more reasonable interpretation would argue in terms of the extreme dependence of the concretely oriented mind on very familiar material. The Rorschach Test records of pre-school children and of mental defectives often have the same global syncretic quality. In this case it is as if only the superficial perceptual, associative, and conceptual processes have been more or less adequately differentiated. It might also be argued that the constellation of a low $F+$%, *DW*'s, low *P*%, perseveration and blandness speaks for the diagnosis *simple schizophrenia*. The *R* of 26 would, however, be unusual in the record of a simple schizophrenic; even more unusual would be the absence of peculiar verbalizations in a record that is not quantitatively constricted.

WORD ASSOCIATION TEST

The conceptual orderliness of the reactions in this test supports the reasoning regarding the low form level in the Rorschach Test. From a simple schizophrenic we would expect a few clang associations, unrelated or very distant responses, or other deviant reactions. It seems safe at this point to rule out simple schizophrenia as a probable diagnosis, bearing in mind, however, that he is basically withdrawn.

In this record the stimulus words with more or less clear oral connotations (hunger, suck, nipple, beef, table, mouth) systematically elicit one type of disturbance or another, indicating that conflict in the realm of oral-passive needs is conspicuous. The long delayed reaction to *bowel movement* is noteworthy. Inquiry is strikingly unsuccessful in eliciting introspections; this virtual absence of reflectiveness has already been indicated. It is also striking that there is not the least trace of "vulgarity" in the responses; ordinarily this is not expected in the record of a subject with a working class background: this again seems referable to the deferent, socially compliant "front".

THEMATIC APPERCEPTION TEST

Card 1. (Boy with violin.) The theme is retreat from difficulty. This is the popular theme and the only distinctive aspect of the story is its rather cold verbalization: "this business", and so forth. Card 2. (Old woman in doorway.) The theme is trivial; this becomes extreme in the final evasion of serious content: she is worrying about wasting electricity. What is striking here is the sudden appearance of the avoidant tendency; this suggests that his relationship with the mother-figure is especially conflictful. The content of the conflict remains unknown. Card 3. (Old man in graveyard.) The theme, elicited upon inquiry, is a father's grief at his son's death. It is rare that a younger person is the one who has died; whenever such a fantasy occurs, identification with the dead person is suggested; this in turn suggests that fantasies of dying maybe active in the patient. The father-figure is portrayed as a loving person: this is probably a wish. Card 4. (Silhouette of man at window.) The theme is longing for freedom—an obvious self-reference. The reference to loved ones is flat: ". . . out in the *street* with them, something like that." The final statement has a casual, resigned quality.

Card 5. (Heads of embracing couple.) The theme is grief at loss of a son. This is a popular story because of the recent war, but the fact that the son has died once already (Card 3) gives this theme a more personal significance. His description of the husband's lack of empathy is probably a projection of his own lack of empathy. Card 6. (Prehistoric animal, rocky road, bridge.) The theme is conflict between desire for personal safety and desire for possessions. There is also a quality of desperation in the story; he seems to be saying that events will go against him whichever way he turns and that in the end he must be the loser. His lack of empathy is evident in the trivial statement of feelings: ". . . . feels that he's up pretty high." Card 7. (Shadowy photograph of thumb.) The theme is the popular one of a minor cut on the thumb and is unrevealing. Card 8. (Nude couple, older woman with infant.) The theme is getting "another chance" from an authoritative figure after wrong-doing. This is consistent with the diagnostic impression. The expressed difficulty in dealing with this highly charged sexual material indicates psychosexual immaturity, and the blurred perception of the sex of the older woman, with its implication that his own sexual role is uncrystallized, supports this indication.

Card 9. (Two chairs and table set for tea.) The theme is anger over disappointment in social relationships and the instability of interpersonal relationships. This is an unusual theme and appears to express a personal expectation accompanied by strong irritation. Card 10. (Old man on shoulders of another old man.) The theme is a nightmare. Making the story a dream and evading elaboration of the aggressive implications of the picture indicates the superficial denial of aggressions already evident in his generally deferent attitude. It is striking that his first explanation of the murder callously and blandly deals with a trivial disagreement; only when inquiry confronts him with the inappropriateness of such drastic action, does he seek a more extreme cause. He appears to view the world (people) as threatening immediate destruction for the least breach of rapport. The second cause—taking a possession away —has that innocent quality already noted. Card 11. (Old woman facing away from young man.) The theme is escape from an overprotective mother-figure. This is a popular theme: she is very loving, he is sad, she respects his needs, and so forth. No personal significance is indicated. Card 12. (Man grasped by hands from behind.) The theme is the unfairness of the law. The details of the story, like the details in his definition of *habeas corpus*, indicate extensive experience with crime and its consequences. Again, as in the story to Card 6, he seems to feel that there is no way out for him, that he will inevitably "take a beating".

Card 13. (Figure on floor, against couch.) The theme is escape from grief by suicide. The theme is popular. What is striking is the verbalization: "... done something awful bad: might be a prostitute." A consistent adherence to conventional sexual morality (see Word Association Test and Card 8) is clear, and, because it is so singular in this psychopathic context, suggests that a mature heterosexual adjustment has not been achieved. It is noteworthy that he identifies the sex of this figure as female (See Card 8). The idea of death appears again. Card 14. ("Hypnotism" scene.) The theme is unabashed emotional hypocrisy. The dying criminal is said to be "repenting", but when it is added that he is making his last few moments as painless as possible, one wonders about the sincerity of the remorse. In other words, as is often true of psychopaths, he seems to feel that a few moments of penitence can really go a long way in making things "easy". It is not likely that he is aware of these implications because his innocent front is generally well-maintained and he himself probably is not able to tell when he is sincere and when he is acting. Although remorse seems to be absent, it does appear that he longs for a few moments of peace and letting up of pressure (See Cards 6 and 12). Again the idea of death intrudes.

Card 15. (Older man facing younger man.) The theme is the scheming of criminals. Again he seems to know what he is talking about. Guilt is absent. The final bland statement during the inquiry is striking and is reminiscent of the rather detached attitude of the third degree victim in the twelfth story: "If they're guilty, they feel that they got caught doing it and will suffer the consequences." Here is no rage, no explosiveness, no drastic resistance, but only the resigned, detached attitude of a bland criminal. Card 16. (Man on rope.) The theme of crime and escape is becoming perseverative by now, indicating to what extent his view of the world must be dominated by such content. The details of such an escape seem quite familiar to him. Card 17. (Figure at table; bats and owls.) The theme is a nightmare and is essentially conventional. Although the sex of the figure is not sharply defined in the picture, it is usually seen as male; his seeing it as female is still another reflection of a blurred conception of his own sexual role (see Cards 8 and 13) and of a strong, latent feminine identification.

Card 18. (Man on bed; face in pillow.) The theme is again crime and the inevitability of imprisonment. His spoofing about the *layman's* conception of prison life is strikingly bland. Card 19. (Shadowed figure with arms raised.) The theme is fantasies of revenge for punishment. The "Germans" are probably identified with the police. Card 20. (Unkempt man and well-groomed man.) The theme is the unfairness of the law in pressing *all* its charges against a criminal. A little punishment is enough, he seems to feel. Again he expresses a feeling of being hounded and being given no respite. Guilt is absent.

Test Report

Intelligence and Thought Organization: The patient obtained an IQ of 105, 60th percentile, high average range, on the Wechsler-Bellevue Scale. His verbal achievements include a surprising variety of informational references, which, however, are vague, essentially unsystematized and implicitly pretentious. His grasp of conventional judgments is appropriate to his general level and cannot be considered impaired; his answer to "Why are laws necessary?" is quite satisfactory. A concentration impairment is noted, which interferes with his grasp of questions and makes for an occasional irrelevant-sounding response or word-usage, and slight fluidity of thinking. There does not, however, appear to be any basic disorganization or breakdown of communicative ability. He manifests a keen, rapid, overalert grasp of situations, on a level above that of his judgment—a feature frequently found in psychopathic characters. Learning efficiency is poor, reflecting the impaired concentration already noted. Concept formation is essentially intact and appropriate to his general intellectual level; he tends to be cautious and somewhat concrete, but occasionally, when pressed to conceptualize a difficult grouping, he freely fabulates in psychopathic fashion. This tendency is also evident in his attempts to use his vague information to answer difficult questions. The concentration impairment also tends to impair his concepts but this does not appear to be an intrinsic impairment. His verbalizations are orderly, generally concise, and do not indicate disorganization of thought processes.

His independent creative thinking is on a primitive, syncretistic level. His responses in general are reminiscent of those obtained from pre-school children, passing from fragmentary observations to gross and vague conclusions with little attempt to check the conclusions against reality. This poor reality testing does not appear to be of the schizophrenic variety but more akin to what has been observed in the records of psychopaths. Those aspects of the ego which have to do with active understanding and interpretation are weakly developed, rigidly fixated on a global, unarticulated level, lacking in perspective and often arbitrary or fluid.

Emotional Factors: He presents an excessively polite, orderly, and compliant front. This does not appear to be conscious play-acting. In ordinary everyday situations he appears to keep his aggressions under strict control and to assume a passive but watchful role. The passive rapport, however, does not appear to be backed up by readiness for emotional output; in fact he seems to be basically withdrawn and bland. His conception of the world (see below) seems to be one in which object-attachments are of minimal significance. Despite his superficially strict control of impulses, a tendency to impulsivity is indicated and is likely to make its appearance in the sphere of action much as his fabulizing does in the sphere of thought; that is, when he is "on the spot". Inappropriate affect of the schizophrenic variety is not indicated, although there is a striking absence of acute anxiety on the surface.

Conception of Reality: The crux of the problem appears, from the test results, to lie in his conception of the world around him and of his place in it. This conception is one which is so dominated by things criminal that all else recedes far into the background. For him it is a world of thieves and murderers, policemen and courtrooms and prisons, jailbreaks and captures. In specifying which kinds of businesses desire city locations, he mentions jewelry stores first. His Thematic Appercep- tion Test stories deal primarily with crime. He relates the stories bland- ly and the content of the stories gives no indication that he experiences conscious guilt feelings about his criminal behavior. The implication is that he has not drawn completely the conventional line between right and wrong, although he is superficially aware of what other people believe in this connection. He does appear to consider prostitution, insult, and injury of children "wrong", but no moral reaction to thieve- ry and provoked murder is evident. He does, however, feel hard pressed in his dealings with the world and anticipates that in the end he will inevitably be the loser. Direct expression of aggressions in ordinary social situations appears disturbing to him, however, as does sexuality, toward which he reacts naively. This paradoxical picture appears to be resolved in terms of the deviant moral code he has developed and not in terms of any "false front".

His conception of punishment is noteworthy: he does not appear to consider imprisonment a severe punishment; although it leads to escape tendencies, he feels that it is almost an intrinsic part of his life- role—crime is followed by imprisonment. He also appears to believe blithely that a few moments of penitence are worth a good deal of subsequent comfort.

His conception of reality also appears not to include the possibility *for him* of firm object attachments. Here too there is superficial aware- ness that such relationships exist and of the feelings they imply, but he does not appear to identify strongly with them. The only stories where he does participate in an emotional relationship are two in which the son-figure is killed, indicating preoccupation with death. His relation- ship with the mother-figure appears to be especially distressing and his conception of his own sexual role appears to be uncrystallized.

Diagnostic Impression: Psychopathic character disorder with schizoid features.

CLINICAL SUMMARY

Mr. F., a twenty-nine-year old prisoner at a penitentiary, was ex- amined after he had murdered a fellow prisoner. He grew up in large eastern United States cities. His mother, of whom he had been fond, returned to Ireland to see her family when he was nine and died during the visit. He has always been hostile toward his father, a truck driver; however, he denies excessive punishment by the father. He began steal- ing before he was seven years old and has continued stealing ever since.

He was sent to reform school for the first time when he was thirteen and since then has been convicted of crimes more than fifty times. One prison officer described him several years ago as being mean, disorderly, and abusive, often calling the guards "mother-fuckers". A fellow prisoner offered the same description and added that the patient had attacks of rage, was asocial, and moody. He made two suicidal attempts, one by cutting his wrists, and one by swallowing open safety pins. In an argument with a fellow prisoner, he was called a "mother-fucker". He brooded about this all that night and reasoned that he must kill the other prisoner. His reasoning was this: that particular insult is a challenge for a death-struggle in the underworld; the other prisoner knew this and would therefore, in self-defense, try to kill the patient first; this was especially likely because the other prisoner was a convicted murderer; therefore he must kill his potential murderer. The next day, with a knife he had picked up somewhere, he stabbed his opponent ten times, killing him. He reported that he felt a great sense of relief afterwards and the brooding ceased. He said that he did not recall what had happened in the few minutes after the first stab.

The psychiatric examination revealed a neat, polite, calm, and co-operative person. He discussed his criminal history and the murder in a matter-of-fact tone and seemed to derive pleasure from frequently going into great detail about his previous crimes. He expressed no guilt feelings about the murder and felt justified on the basis of the criminal code. If society punished him, he would feel no resentment: "That's what they have laws for." He divides society into a criminal class and a non-criminal class, identifies with the criminal class, and feels, therefore, that he cannot trust anyone and that "a good cop doesn't exist". He discusses his masturbatory activity calmly, feeling that it is normal for a prisoner to masturbate. He has had intercourse only twice and has never been in love. He does not want to be "tied down" by marriage. He has dreams of both heterosexual and homosexual relations, achieves orgasm, and feels gratified during both types of dream. He has been approached by homosexuals but has calmly rejected their advances. He has fantasies of being a rich, dashing fellow and also of being a cultured gentleman. Toward the latter end, he reads books. He wants to better himself socially, and watches and imitates the good manners of others. His discussions of his criminal record, the absence of friendships or family ties, and the murder and its possible consequences were bland throughout. The diagnosis was psychopathic personality, schizoid type.

ACUTE PARANOID SCHIZOPHRENIA: TEST RESULTS

Mrs. L. Age: 37. Education: 3 years high school and business college. Occupation: Housewife. Marital: 15 years; 1 child. Husband: Mailman. Father: Merchant. Early Environment: Small town. Family Position: 4th of 12. Religion: Protestant.

BELLEVUE SCALE

Comprehension

ENVELOPE: Give it to your mail carrier or to the post office (1). THEATRE: Give an alarm. BAD COMPANY: Because of bad influence (2). TAXES: It furnishes money for government and state (2). SHOES: They wear better (1). LAND: Because it's more populated and the demand is greater (2). FOREST: The moss was on the north side of trees (2). LAW: To keep from confusion, to keep within the law. LICENSE: To stay within the law. DEAF: Because they can't hear other people. (?) Can't hear other people say things. (?) People who can't hear would have to learn by other methods than hearing someone else talk (2). RAW SCORE: 12.

Information

PRESIDENT (before Roosevelt): dk. LONDON: +. PINTS: +. RUBBER: +. THERMOMETER: +. WEEKS: I don't know; 300 and something. ITALY: Vienna. WASHINGTON: +. HEIGHT: +. PLANE: +. PARIS: dk. BRAZIL: +. HAMLET: +. POLE: Byrd. VATICAN: dk. JAPAN: +. HEART: +. ALL REST: dk. RAW SCORE: 11.

Digit Span

FORWARD: 3, 4, 5 on first try; fails first series of 6 by omitting digits; passes 7 on first try; fails both series of 8 by omissions. BACKWARDS: 3 and 4 on first try; fails both series of 5 by omissions. RAW SCORE: 11.

Arithmetic

ITEMS 1-4: +. Fails succeeding items, being unable to work on them. RAW SCORE: 4.

Similarities

ORANGE: Fruit (2). COAT: Clothing (2). DOG: Animals (2). WAGON: Vehicles (2). DAILY PAPER: News (1). AIR: dk. WOOD: Burn (1). EYE: Two essential things to the body. (?) One is sense of hearing, other is sight. EGG: Both are seeds. (?) Starting of life (1). POEM: dk. PRAISE: Opposites. FLY: Both part of nature (1). RAW SCORE: 12.

Picture Arrangement

HOUSE: + 3″ (2). HOLD UP: ABDC 12″. ELEVATOR: + 10″

(2). FLIRT: JNATE 60". FISH: EFGIJH 71". "I don't know what I am doing." TAXI: SAMELU 80". "I can't do anything with it." RAW SCORE: 4.

Picture Completion

NOSE: +. MUSTACHE: +. EAR: Hair 10". (?) Ear 20". DIAMOND: One spot 30". LEG: dk. TAIL: +. STACKS: +. KNOB: +. SECOND HAND: Hands 28". WATER: +. REFLECTION: Leg of table. (?) dk. TIE: +. THREADS: dk. EYEBROW: dk. SHADOW: dk. RAW SCORE: 7.

Block Designs

ITEM 1: 9" (5). ITEM 2: 12" (4). ITEM 3: 12" (4). ITEM 4: 15" (5). ITEM 5: 55" (3). ITEM 6: 90" (3). ITEM 7: 195" (3). RAW SCORE: 27.

Object Assembly

ITEM 1: 18" (6). ITEM 2: 78" (6). ITEM 3: 35" (8). RAW SCORE: 20.

Digit Symbol

37 correct; one error—symbol for 3 under a 7. RAW SCORE: 37.

Vocabulary

APPLE: Fruit (1). DONKEY: Animal (1). JOIN: To bring together (1). DIAMOND: Stone. (?) Diamond shape (½). NUISANCE: Bother (1). FUR: Protection for animals (1). CUSHION: Something soft you sit on (1). SHILLING: Money. (?) Not our money. (?) English (1). GAMBLE: Take a chance (1). BACON: Meat. (?) From a hog (1). NAIL: A metal tool. (?) Something you use to put two things together. (?) Two pieces of wood (1). NITROGLYCERINE: Explosive (1). STANZA: A part. (?) Of a sentence. MICROSCOPE: Instrument you look through to enlarge the object. (?) Has many lenses (½). VESPER: Vesper bells. (?) dk. BRIM: Brim of a hat. (?) Edge (1). GUILLOTINE: Something used to cut your head off (1). PLURAL: More than one (1). SECLUDE: Stay in seclusion. (?) Stay away from everything. (?) To stay to yourself (1). CEDAR: A tree (1). TINT: To color anything lightly (1). ARMORY: A suit of armory. FABLE: Story (1). BELFRY: Part of a tower (½). ALL REST: dk. RAW SCORE: 20.

Weighted Scores and IQ's

Comprehension 11	Picture Arrangement 4	Vocabulary 9
Information 8	Picture Completion 6	Verbal IQ: 96
Digit Span 9	Block Designs 12	Performance IQ: 100
Arithmetic 4	Object Assembly 12	Total IQ: 99
Similarities 10	Digit Symbol 9	

LEARNING EFFICIENCY

IMMEDIATE RECALL: (December 6) in the city of Albany (a flood). Somebody (catching cold). SCORE: 7.

DELAYED RECALL: (December 6) (near the town of Albany) (a river) (overflowed). The water came up to the houses. It isn't (drowned), was it? (One man) injured and you said something about a group of men being something. SCORE: 6.

SORTING TEST

Part I

CORK: Adds other cork. "They're alike." Narrow sorting, concrete concept. LARGE FORK: Adds large silver. "A habit of having them like that. (?) Required for a table." Mildly narrow sorting, concrete concept. PIPE: Adds real cigar, matches. "Tobacco and pipe and matches. All required for smoking a pipe." Narrow sorting, concrete concept. BELL: Adds small hammer and hatchet. "All make noise." Loose sorting, syncretistic concept. CIRCLE: Adds red square. "I just thought they did. (?) I can't tell you a reason . . . (?) No reason." This sorting is narrow at the same time as it is a failure, and is peculiar. (Subject asked to try another sorting; adds sink stopper: "They're round." This is a narrow sorting, abstract concept.) TOY PLIERS: Adds all tools, nails, and block with nail. "Tools." Mildly loose sorting, abstract concept. BALL: Adds eraser and sink stopper. "Rubber." Mildly narrow sorting, abstract concept.

Part II

RED: "No. (?) First I thought they were just a conglomeration. (?) Go together because we use them." Syncretistic concept. METAL: "Metal. Wasn't a good reason, was it?" Abstract concept. ROUND: "They all float." False and syncretistic concept. TOOLS: "Tools." Abstract concept. PAPER: "Burn." Syncretistic concept. PAIRS: "Things we use." Syncretistic concept. WHITE: "No. (?) No. (?) Everyone uses them." Syncretistic concept. RUBBER: "Rubber." Abstract concept. SMOKING MATERIALS: "Smoking—what you smoke." Functional concept. SILVERWARE: "For eating." Functional concept. TOYS: "Things we use every day." Syncretistic concept. RECTANGLES: "Things we use every day; can't think of anything else." Syncretistic concept. Patient asks at end of test, "Did I fail them all?"

RORSCHACH TEST

CARD I. Reaction time: 10″. Total time: 150″.

1. (Weeps.) (?) Well, looks like a bat or something. 2. Looks like a figure (center) with eyes (upper middle bumps) and hands up here. I see the legs and the body and I can't see anything else.

SCORES. 1: W F+A P. 2: D FM±H, Eyes.

CARD II. Reaction time: 25". Total time: 150".

Couldn't be anything (aggressively and sobbing)! 1. Two objects together. [(?) Not any certain thing . . . could resemble two bears (head is upper red).] 2. Looks like two faces here (upper middle projection). [(?) Human faces. It all seems so crazy to me. I can't tell you anything about it!]

SCORES. 1: W F+A P Peculiar. 2: Dd F+Hd.

CARD III. Reaction time: 15". Total time: 90".

Looks like two figures standing there holding something in the center. Shall I turn it around and look at it? I still couldn't see anything. I can't see anything else.

SCORE: W M+H P.

CARD IV. Reaction time: 50". Total time: 150".

They get worse all the time, don't they? 1. Well, looks like an object; two arms, this is the head, these are the feet. [(?) Monster, an ape, looked very vicious, was walking, standing up, with arms out.] 2. This here looks like two eyes here, a head of something . . . of an animal (lower middle).

SCORES. 1: W FM+Monster Peculiar. 2: D F+Ad, Eyes.

CARD V. Reaction time: 25". Total time: 150".

1. That could be some kind of an animal that can fly . . . Do animals fly? (?) Birds do. [(?) I thought it could be a bat.] 2. This could be a face . . . same on the other side (upper edge of wings). (?) No, that's all I can imagine on that one.

SCORES. 1: W F+A P Confusion. 2: De F+Hd.

CARD VI. Reaction time: 90". Total time: 300".

Well, I can't imagine anything. 1. I can imagine that eyes, nose, and . . . and . . . whiskers (uppermost tip). 2. You look at it here (base of upper projection) . . . like two little animals. Here is two small objects (tiny light areas near midline) they could be holding—these two animals could be holding them. [(?) Those two animals have bushy tails but these (tiny area) don't, so they're something else.]

SCORES. 1: Do F(C)+Ad. 2: Dr F±A Combination, Peculiar.

CARD VII. Reaction time: 33". Total time: 180".

Why don't you give me something that does resemble . . .? 1. This one here could be a moth (lower third). 2. This looks like a face (on forehead of popular face). 3. Well, I can imagine this is a face (middle ⅓, facing outward).

SCORES. 1: D F+A. 2: Dr F—Hd. 3: D F+Ad.

CARD VIII. Reaction time: 10". Total time: 120".

1. This could be a flower (pink and orange). [(?) Shaped like a flower, has that center; at first I thought a pansy. (?) No.] 2. This could

be something . . . an animal. [(?) I'd say a seal. A seal isn't classed as an animal, is it?]

SCORES. 1: D F+Pl. 2: D F∓A (P) Confusion.

CARD IX. Reaction time: 135″. Total time: 180″.

I can't imagine anything. (Wants to give up at 75″.) (!) I'll make at least a try. At the bottom (outer sections of pink), fishes, bluegills. [(?) Bluegills are round and flat.]

SCORE: (Failure) D F±A.

CARD X. Reaction time: 40″. Total time: 180″.

1. Well, this looks like a face (lower middle). [(?) Oh, of a rabbit.] 2. Well, this looks like two objects here (upper gray); just part of them, just the head and neck. [(?) You mean the name of the objects? Could look like a crab, I'd say.]

SCORES. 1: D F+Ad P. 2: D F+Ad Peculiar.

Summary of Responses

R: 19   EB: 2–0

W 5	F+ 14	A 7	W% 26
D 9	F± 1	Ad 5	D% 47
Dd 1	F∓ 1	H 1	DR% 21
Do 1	F− 1	Hd 4	
Dr 2	M 1+	Plant 1	F% 89-100
De 1	FM 1+, 1±	Monster 1	F+% 88-89
		Eyes (2)	
Qualitative			A% 63
Peculiar 4			H% 26
Confusion 2			P 4 (2)
			P% 21 (32)

WORD ASSOCIATION TEST

WORLD–2″–people. LOVE–3″–people; I didn't mean to say that, that's already said. FATHER–1″–mother. HAT–2″–woman (6″). BREAST–1″–woman. CURTAINS–1″–house. TRUNK–5″–house. [(?) The first thing I thought was clothing.] DRINK–3″–glass (1″– water). PARTY–1″–people. BOWEL MOVEMENT–5″–I thought of a person. BOOK–2″–read. LAMP–1″–light. RUG–2″–floor. CHAIR –2″–table. BOY FRIEND–1″–girl friend. PENIS–3″–woman (I didn't answer that one). DARK–2″–light. DEPRESSED–2″–feeling. SPRING –2″–summer. BOWL–2″–dish. SUICIDE–5″–murder. MOUNTAIN –3″–hills. HOUSE–8″–place to live. PAPER–4″–writing. HOMO-SEXUAL–19″–(shakes head) two persons together (6″–dk.). RADI-ATOR–3″–heating (4″). GIRL FRIEND–3″–young girl (3″–boy friend, young girl). SCREEN–3″–house. MASTURBATE–8″–I can't give you any answer for it. FRAME–2″–around a picture. MAN–8″– sex (9″). ORGASM–8″–I don't know the word. (10″–I don't think I answered.) MOVIES–2″–stars. CUT–3″–blood (4″). LAUGH–1″–

be happy (2"—good time). BITE—6"—well, I thought of bit. WOMEN—6" — ladies (13"). DANCE – 2" – good time. DOG – 1" – animal (7"). DAUGHTER—1"—girl. TAXI – 2" – automobile. MOTHER – 10" – I thought of mother. TABLE—2"—chair. BEEF—2"—cow (3"—animal, no, I said cow). NIPPLE—2"—bottle. RACE—2"—run. WATER—1"—drink. SUCK—5"—suction. HORSE—1"—animal (12"). FIRE—1"—burn. VAGI-NA—7"—blank. FARM—3"—is to live. SOCIAL—1"—gathering. SON (SUN) —3"—moon. TAXES—10"—taxes... well, the first thing I ever thought of was something we have to pay (6"). TOBACCO—1"—smoke. CITY—1"—town. INTERCOURSE—2"—two people. HOSPITAL—2"—sanitarium. DOCTOR—1"—nurse.

THEMATIC APPERCEPTION TEST

CARD 1. (Boy with violin.) Oh, I can't tell you a story about that! (Shakes head.) Just a boy sitting there looking at his violin, dreaming. I wouldn't say he was concentrating—just looking at the violin, dreaming, or asleep. Is that what you wanted? (Dreaming about?) Nothing. (?) He could be dreaming about wanting to go somewhere. (Where?) Swimming or fishing. (Outcome?) It's the darndest thing I ever went through (laughs). I don't know. (Will he go?) He looks too far asleep though.

CARD 2. (Old woman in doorway.) I can't do these things! This is a story of an old woman coming in the house. She will probably sit down and play the victrola a while, and sit down and dream a little and fall asleep. (More about woman?) She's probably a woman that has ... whose sons are all gone or married, she lives alone. (Feel?) She feels very tired about, about ... (?) Well, she's getting very weary.

CARD 3. (Old man in graveyard.) Well in the first place I don't know what these things are (tombstones) ... unless it's supposed to be a cemetery and it's ... er, I guess it doesn't make any difference what I say (laughs). It looks like a man standing alone, praying. Thinking of someone that he once knew. I'll end it now. He is sad. (Thinking?) He is thinking of someone that has died, passed away. (Who?) Someone he cared for, or ... I can't go on with it! I was going to say something, but ... er, nothing doing. (Relationship?) Oh, a friend or buddy. (Outcome?) He leaves the cemetery.

CARD 4. (Silhouette of man at window.) This is supposed to be a man looking out of the window, looking for someone, or dreaming about someone, something that never comes. (Explain?) A girl friend. (Something that never comes?) Maybe she's gotten married and he'll never see her again. (Feel?) He might feel blue for a while. (Outcome?) He would ... Is that a chair here (windowsill)? ... well, he would go and do something else; he would read a book.

CARD 5. (Heads of embracing couple.) Well, it's a picture of a man and his wife. They're very troubled about something. I said they were troubled about something and tried to console themselves over whatever has happened ... Well, that's all I can tell you. (Worried about?) It could be anything. It could be their son, daughter, just any unhappiness. (?) One of them could have gotten married, the other could have gone to war. (Why unhappy over marriage?) They had gone through it themselves and they didn't want to lose their child. (Explain?) There was much unhappiness. (In marriage?) Some people are and some people aren't. (Outcome?) They go on together.

CARD .6. (Prehistoric animal, rocky road, bridge.) What is this (center figure)? Well, it's ... I'll say it's an old castle that hasn't been used for years and years. There are these old ... no, I don't mean that ... these different animals living around in holes in the rocks. Well, that's all I can tell you about it. (Happening?) This lizard—what would you call it?—some sort of ancient animal, looking for food. (Center figure?) Well now, at first it looked like something else, but now it looks like men. This one (on bridge) looks like he's looking over down into the water. (Doing?) They're pushing this log. (Looking at water?) To see if they can escape from this ... from this animal. (Outcome?) They throw this log in the water and then climb down and get on the log. They may get away. (?) By this tunnel of water, or this stream of water.

CARD 7. (Shadowy photograph of thumb.) (Turns card.) Well, it looks like the inside of a ... well, it's a part of a hand. I can see the nail, the fingernail and there's a drop of blood. He might have cut his finger, or ... I can't tell you any more about it. I guess I don't know what it is even. (How cut?) On a branch.

CARD 8. (Nude couple; older woman with infant.) Well, this is a couple that envy this woman that has this baby. They wanted one themselves. Could I change the thought? They didn't want the child and they gave it to this woman to keep and she's going to take care of it. That's all. (Relationship?) They're not related. (?) None of them are related. (Give child away?) Because they weren't married.

CARD 9. (Two chairs and table set for tea.) It's a picture of a room: two chairs and a table set for tea. They've been set there, or put there for a couple to relax. That's all I can say. (More about couple?) Well, they come there to visit and have a little talk. (Who?) Two women or ... I'll leave that like it is, and oh, they just discuss different subjects and laugh and talk.

CARD 10. (Old man on shoulders of another old man.) It's a picture of two old men that lived way up in the mountains. They stayed there quite a long time ... till they became hermits. They just exist ... until they don't know what they're doing. (Explain?) Well, if a person just keeps away from everything—civilization—and do the same ... well, they wouldn't do very much at all, just eating and sleeping ... walking around a little. They just wouldn't know what they were doing. (Happening?) It looks like one of them is pulling the other one's hair. (Led up?) You mean the pulling of the hair? He doesn't know what he is doing. (Outcome?) The outcome is that they just exist until they die.

CARD F 11. (Hag behind young woman.) It's an old man standing behind a young man thinking, or knows what this young man should do, or what he has ahead of him. He is very tired (old man) and the young man has a lot more—I can't explain it. The young man hasn't had the experience and gone through as much as the old man. That's all I think of now. (Relationship?) There is no relationship. I said father and son though, didn't I? (Related?) No. (Happening?) They're both concentrating on life. (Explain?) Well, the old man, as I said, is concentrating on what the young man has ahead of him. (?) Whatever he chooses. (What did old man go through?) He looked like he had gone through suffering. (Explain?) Suffering from living. (?) Working hard. (Else?) No. (?) Well, I thought of other things. The trouble he'd had. (?) Family troubles. (Story!) They lived way out in a lonely place, worked and existed. Nothing much to do, and they became very tired, and that's all.

CARD F 12. (Men unloading boat; girl on bridge.) A picture of boats. The girl is standing over a bridge. The moon is shining. The men look like they're loading—they're unloading the boat. The girl doesn't ... isn't watching them—the men. She's looking into the water. That's all. (Why looking in water?) She hasn't anything else to do, she is just standing there looking into the water. (Thoughts and feelings?) Perhaps she is ready to jump in the water. (Why?) She doesn't want to live any more. (?) Everything ... every happening ... she wasn't satisfied with life. (Happened?) She had lost things ... she had dreamed ... her dream may come true. (?) What she expected of life. (?) Have what other people have. (?) People that have money. (Does she jump?) She was disappointed because she didn't have those things. (Does she jump?) She changed her mind. (Why?) She wasn't ready to die.

CARD F 13 (Boy with book; two girls in background.) This is a picture of a boy studying—a brother of these two girls. He has to be sure of his education—more so than the girls, because he may have to support the family or wife, or he may be studying to keep out of trouble, or to have a good mind. That's all. (Keep out of trouble?) Well, most boys that don't study and try to do the right things, they do what they want to do and it leads to penitentiaries. (Outcome?) He studies and becomes a man of the world.

CARD F 14. (Woman turning away from man.) It's a story about a couple. It looks like he wants to kiss her and she doesn't want to kiss him—she doesn't want to kiss him. It looks like there's something between them ... I don't know ... something that was troubling them. That's all I can tell you about it. (Trouble?) Well, perhaps he's a married man. (Led up?) She shouldn't be with him. (Why did he try to kiss her?) Well, they were keeping company before. (Married man?) He was. (Wife?) She isn't here. (Outcome?) This girl had gotten in trouble with this married man. (?) They just separate. (Happens to girl?) She goes on her own. (Trouble?) She had something to do with this married man. (Baby?) Yes. (?) She goes and puts her baby in the day nursery and works. (Man feel?) He goes back to his wife.

CARD F 15. (Girl leaning against wall, arm outstretched.) Well, this looks like a girl that is very unhappy and troubled and worried and dissatisfied over something or other. She would like to leave ... to go to work ... make her own way. That's all I can tell you. (Trouble?)

The way things are . . . no mother and no family. (Outcome?) She goes to work as a housekeeper and lives with the people she works for.

CARD F 16. (Man at window.) It's a picture of an elderly man standing by a window . . . looking out of a window and thinking, wishing he were somewhere—dreaming of his family. Can't be with them. That's as far as I can go. (Where is he?) He could be in a hotel lobby or in a room. (Why away?) His business keeps him from them. (Outcome?) He doesn't get to go home. (Why?) He has his work to do.

CARD F 17. (Two women struggling on stairway.) This is mother and daughter—or two women. It looks like they're coming down a stairway and this one woman is holding the other with her hands around her neck . . . clutching the other woman by the neck because she had been keeping company with her husband and had gotten into trouble with him. I can't tell you any more about it. (Outcome?) This woman that has tears in her eyes (upper figure) takes the child. (Clutching?) Well, she doesn't kill her, only she'd like to. (Why take child?) It belongs to her husband.

CARD F 18. (Maid in hallway.) That's a maid in the house . . . a room. She's acting very peculiar . . . she has a finger in her mouth and looking out to the side. She's looking at someone. That's the end. (Story!) I'm afraid I can't tell you much story. It looks like she would rather be with someone than at work. (Who?) A guest of the house. (Who?) A man. (Outcome?) She doesn't go with him—she goes on with her work.

CARD F 19. (Woman in bed; dishevelled man standing.) It looks like this man had been drinking . . . had something to do with this young lady . . . to get away from worries. That's all. (Worries?) His family. (Explain?) He'd had much trouble with his family . . . wife . . . wanting to get away for a day or two on a drunk. (Trouble?) She had spent all the money, gotten in debt, was never satisfied with anything that she had, always wanted more. (End?) He goes back to his wife . . . (Why?) He feels that it's his duty to take care of his family.

CARD F 20. (Bearded old man looking down.) An old man sitting in a chair, dreaming of things . . . I'm always saying *things!* . . . dreaming of different people—different ones he had known . . . dreaming of his wife who had passed away, just dreaming. (How wife die?) Old age. (Feel?) He doesn't feel so sad as dreaming—just dreaming. (Outcome?) He gets his pipe and paper and reads.

ANALYSIS OF RESULTS

BELLEVUE SCALE

The scatter opens up several diagnostic possibilities. The Information-Comprehension relationship and the two high Performance scores indicate a strong repressive emphasis in her character and suggest hysterical features. The out-of-pattern Digit Span-Arithmetic relationship indicates low anxiety tolerance and impaired concentration, and suggests either a narcissistic character make-up or schizophrenia. The extreme drops of Picture Arrangement and Picture Completion below the Block Designs-Object Assembly level is distinctively schizophrenic. If this is a schizophrenia, the well-retained Comprehension score implies that paranoid features are prominent since this pattern is very frequent in the overcautious, well-preserved paranoid cases. On the other hand high Performance scores are infrequent in paranoid cases. Regarding duration, the scatter is more typical of an acute condition since Similarities is not relatively low and Block Designs is well-retained. The scatter is not conclusive but it favors the diagnosis acute schizophrenia.

The qualitative analysis of Information renders the diagnosis *schizophrenia* even more probable. She confuses weeks with days on the *weeks* item and offers Vienna as the *capital of Italy*. An hysteric on a very low intelligence level might make these mistakes but this woman has at least an average IQ and has gone to high school and business college. It is more likely therefore that the responses to *weeks* and *Italy* represent disorganization of the memory frame of reference and possibly confusion. It is indicated at the same time that broad interests have not characterized her previous adjustment and that a repressive emphasis may have been characteristic of her pre-morbid adjustment efforts. It might be argued that inertia and confusion have depressed the Verbal level, particularly the Information score, and that the Block Designs and Object Assembly scores reflect her pre-morbid level. Inertia and confusion of such proportions, however, would be more likely to strike at the visual-motor abilities first; furthermore, the item analysis of the Information subtest should have revealed at least one or two passes on more difficult items.

There are no clear peculiarities in Comprehension, Digit Span, Arithmetic or Similarities, although "to keep from confusion" on the *laws* item does have a strange ring to it. In Arithmetic a striking inertia and inability to concentrate are evident. After the first four items she says practically nothing and cannot be persuaded to apply herself or to verbalize her thoughts. This has a depressive quality and depression is likely to be a conspicuous clinical symptom, but the high Block Designs and Object Assembly indicate that there is more to this than depression alone.

In Picture Arrangement she is unable to organize any story on the last two items, again manifesting a blocked, depressive quality. The fact that she correctly answers two Picture Completion items overtime is also depressive-like. The good scores in Block Designs and Object Assembly indicate not only a capacity to work fast (she gets several time bonuses) but also unusual persistence (note the time on the seventh Block Design). Persistence is not one of the shining qualities of depressives; they tend to give up quickly as a rule. In Vocabulary, "a suit of armory" is peculiar.

The essential pathology is not yet established beyond doubt, but a schizophrenia with paranoid and depressive features is the best bet so far. It is conceivable, however, that this is a depression in a woman of hysterical character make-up.

LEARNING EFFICIENCY

The extremely poor efficiency evident in an average score of 6.5 and the dramatic fragmentation of the structure of the story is indicative of either profound depression with inert features or schizophrenia with confused features, or, as appears to be likely in this case, both.

SORTING TEST

Part I of the Sorting Test virtually establishes the diagnosis *schizophrenia* at the same time as it reinforces the indications of depression. Regarding depression, the sortings are mostly quite narrow. Regarding schizophrenia, the syncretistic concept "make noise" and the fluid—confused—sorting which she could not explain ("No reason.") are diagnostic. "A habit of having them like that" on the *fork* item is also peculiar. Depressives have not been found to give such disorganized responses. The responses in Part II are also restricted by depression; the feeble syncretistic answers about *use* are cover-ups for complete failure more than anything else. However, the syncretistic response "burn" and the false response "float" are schizophrenic in quality. The self-depreciations—"Wasn't a good reason, was it?" and "Did I fail them all?"—are typically depressive.

RORSCHACH TEST

The relatively low number of responses, the *Do*, the high $F\%$, $F+\%$, $A\%$, and $P\%$, and the depressive verbalizations with an aggressive tinge[7]) suggest a neurotic depression. However, the *EB* of 2—0 and the $DR\%$ of 21 are atypical in ordinary depressions and suggest that ideational symptom formation is present in a setting of depression. Since there are no color responses and several movement responses the symptoms are likely to be obsessive or delusional in nature rather than phobic. However, the "vicious monster" on IV suggests that fearfulness or

---

7) Card II: "It all seems so crazy"; Card IV: "They get worse all the time;" Card VII: "Why don't you give me something that does resemble...?"

apprehensiveness is conspicuous. There are qualitative notes which settle the diagnostic problem: four peculiar verbalizations and two verbalizations indicative of feelings of confusion. The peculiar verbalizations all consist of referring to animals or persons as "objects". Unusual formulations are rare among depressives, even among psychotic depressives. The two instances of confusion are those in which she asks whether animals fly and whether a seal is an animal. It might be felt that these are questions any flustered person might ask, but this would ignore the total context of test results. It is clear that this is a profoundly ill person who has given evidences that she may be a schizophrenic. When we find in addition that she is questioning simple everyday concepts and relationships, we must infer that she is experiencing feelings of confusion. The absence of color responses indicates extreme withdrawal.

We can assume by now that she is schizophrenic and that depression and confusion are secondary symptoms. We can also decide on the basis of what we have seen so far that this is an acute paranoid schizophrenia: the constricted experience balance with the emphasis on *M*, the generally constricted Rorschach Test record, the absence of florid schizophrenic verbalizations and the well-retained Comprehension score all combine to yield this differential diagnosis. The unusual eyes on the figure on Card I also imply paranoid pathology. If she were not predominantly paranoid, more florid productions could be expected. If she were a chronic case, pure *C* would be conspicuous and *M* would tend to disappear. The Bellevue Scale has already been shown to favor acute schizophrenia.

There is little in the Rorschach Test to facilitate a description of character make-up. The "monster" on Card IV, with its implication of fearfulness, is reminiscent of the hysteric-like pattern in the Bellevue Scale. Otherwise the acute psychosis and the depression cut off more personal expressions.

WORD ASSOCIATION TEST

Diagnostically significant are the perseverations of the words *people, woman,* and especially *house,* and the clang association *bite*-"bit", because responses of these types occur frequently in schizophrenic records and rarely in depressive records. *Love*-"people" is appropriate and her prompt rejection of the response may have content-significance; that is, she may be trying to tell us that it is not true that she "loves people". The multiword responses, because they result from blocking, indicate the depressive features of the illness. Striking responses include *penis*-"woman" and its repression during the recall session, the long delay on *homosexual* and the generalized blocking on words of sexual connotation. All these together would suggest that acute homoerotic conflict is present. Indications of this type of conflict are frequent in the records of paranoid schizophrenics. *Man*-"sex" would itself indicate sexual pre-occupation. The delay in reaction to *suicide,* in the context of depressive mood, indicates a suicidal risk.

THEMATIC APPERCEPTION TEST

The following features of her stories support the diagnosis *paranoid schizophrenia.* Card 1, the non sequitur elicited by inquiry: "He looks *too far* asleep ..." to go anywhere. Card 2, the non sequitur elicited by inquiry: "She feels tired ..." about her sons being gone. Card 3: doubt about the perception of gravestones; in inquiry indicating withholding of ideas. Card 4: the cryptic statement, "Something that never comes;" the emotional non sequitur, "He would read a book;" arbitrary percept (chair). Card 5, inquiry: the elliptical statements, "There was much un-happiness" and "Some people are and some people aren't;" the latter statement is not a meaningful response to the examiner's question. Card 6: perceptual distortion—seeing a stream of water; peculiar verbal con-densation—"tunnel of water". Card 8: the literal interpretation of the word *relationship* during inquiry. Card 10: the incomplete communica-tion of an idea in the statement, "They just exist ... until they don't know what they're doing;" she does not make explicit how the one fol-lows from the other. Card F 11: extreme sexual misrecognition, imply-ing not only confusion about her sexual identity, but the capacity for gross perceptual distortions of reality; the sequence of elliptical state-ments in inquiry; the confusion about whether she had referred to the figures as father and son; the literal interpretation of the word *relation-ship;* the non sequitur at the end—"Nothing to do and they became very tired." Card F 12: "A picture of boats"—a distinctively psychotic overgeneralization; the inadequate explanation of why the girl is look-ing into the water. Card F 13: the elliptical statements—"Studying to keep out of trouble" and "It leads to penitentiaries;" the non sequitur, "He studies and (thereby) becomes a man of the world." Card F 14: the veiled reference to an illegitimate child which required very active probing to be clarified; the inappropriate response to the question about the outcome and the man's feelings. Card F 17: perceptual distortion—seeing tears on one of the faces. Card F 20: emotional discontinuity between present situation and outcome (he reads).

Card 1. (Boy with violin.) The theme is dreaming of happier cir-cumstances. However, the identification-figure is too inert (asleep) to effect any change. Card 2. (Old woman in doorway.) The theme is dreaming of lost love-objects. There are frequent references to "dreaming" throughout these stories—a theme indicating depression and preoccupation. Card 3. (Old man in graveyard.) The theme is the popular one, grief at loss of a love-object. The substitution of "friend or buddy" for wife is unusual; this concern with relationships between men is consistent with already cited indications of strong homoerotic features. Card 4. (Silhouette of man at window.) The theme is endless disappointment. The love-object never materializes. This story has a heavy depressive tone. Card 5. (Heads of embracing couple.) The theme is sadness at loss of love-objects. In this story, as in the second story, the husband-figure is ignored as a love-object and only the children are mentioned. A strong rejection of the husband-figure is implied; this implication is supported by her veiled self-references, in inquiry, concerning an unhappy marriage.

Card 6. (Prehistoric animal, rocky road, bridge.) The theme is the popular one of escape from destruction. Card 7. (Shadowy photograph of thumb.) The theme is the popular one of a cut finger. Card 8. (Nude couple; older woman with infant.) The theme is a significant one of escape from the stamp of sin. Card 9. (Two chairs and table set for tea.) The theme is a relaxed social conversation. It is popular and not revealing. Card 10. (Old man on shoulders of another old man.) The theme is withdrawal from the world. This appears to be a self-reference because of its unusual twist. She describes herself actually as withdrawn, confused and "existing". "Existing" is another way of saying that gratifications are no longer anticipated. The aggressive implications of the picture are avoided, implying denial of aggressions—a very frequent characteristic in paranoid cases.

Card F 11. (Hag behind younger woman.) The theme is suffering and weariness in a stale, profitless world. The perceptual distortion changes the usual mother-daughter relationship to a father-son relationship and suggests that unconsciously she may relate herself to her father-figure as a son. Card F 12 (Girl on bridge; men and boat.) The theme is preoccupation with suicide following loss of love-objects and unfulfilled dreams. The singular formulations indicate that this is a self-reference. Card F 13. (Boy with book; two girls in background.) The theme is the need for financial security and the necessity to live a highly moral life. Financial preoccupations were also suggested in the twelfth story by her reference to the longing for money. Card F 14. (Woman turning away from man.) The theme is adultery on the part of the husband-figure. This may indicate a delusional idea, inasmuch as paranoid schizophrenia seems to be the diagnosis. Card F 15. (Girl leaning against wall.) The theme is despair at the absence of love-objects (see also Cards 4 and 12). By now the expression of this theme speaks clearly for the presence of extreme withdrawal, which the patient is indirectly aware of.

Card F 16. (Man at window.) The theme is separation from the family, an idea which probably preoccupies her. Card F 17. (Two women on stairway.) The theme is again adultery on the part of the husband-figure, and this is probably another regnant preoccupation. Card F 18. (Maid in hallway.) The theme is a significant one of frustrated sexual desire. Card F 19. (Woman in bed; dishevelled man standing.) The theme is again adultery on the part of the husband-figure, but this time the guilt is put squarely on the demanding, extravagant wife-figure. This makes it likely that depressive ideas of personal worthlessness are clinically prominent. Card F 20. (Old bearded man looking down.) The theme is dreaming of past relationships. The death of the wife is not an occasion for grief here (see Card 3 also) and this may relate to the feelings of worthlessness implied in the previous story.

Considering the entire series of stories, it is impressive that not once is a warm, firm interpersonal relationship elaborated, indicating how bleak her world must seem to her in her withdrawn and depressed state.

TEST REPORT

Intelligence and Thought Organization: There appears to be a good deal of intactness of ego-organization present, but sufficient disorganization to indicate a schizophrenic psychosis. Thinking is slowed down, fragmented, and, at times, blocked. Ability to concentrate is devastated and anticipations are feeble. She appears to be extensively preoccupied ("dreaming"). There are traces of confusion and conceptual loosening present. Severe perceptual distortions occur. The good preservation of conventional judgments and the absence of florid psychotic productions indicate that the schizophrenia is predominantly paranoid and allow, therefore, the inference that paranoid delusions are present. It is suggested that a strong repressive emphasis characterized her premorbid adjustment-efforts. Her present IQ is 99.

Emotional Factors: She appears to be extremely withdrawn and depressed. Affective output is minimal. Fearfulness or apprehensiveness is probably conspicuous. Strong feelings of despair and worthlessness are indicated. Aggressions tend to be denied, but veiled aggressiveness can be detected in critical, demanding and rejective statements which superficially appear to be expressions of inadequacy.

Figures and Attitudes: Her picture of the world appears to be one in which love-objects have been lost and dreams have remained unfulfilled; gratifications are minimal and people just "exist". The world seems to have congealed. Preoccupation with morality and sin, money, and suicide is indicated. The husband-figure seems to be regarded suspiciously as an adulterer but the identification- or wife-figure is partly blamed for having driven him to his sinful ways by her demanding, worthless ways. The husband-figure appears to be rejected and the (lost) love-objects are primarily children. A powerful underlying masculine identification is indicated.

Diagnostic Impression: Acute paranoid schizophrenia with conspicuous depressive features.

CLINICAL SUMMARY

Mrs. L. is a thirty-seven-year-old housewife from a small mid-western town, the fourth of twelve children. The scant childhood history obtained from two informants was highly contradictory. She left high school at seventeen for business college and after that worked as a typist. She married at twenty-one after having become pregnant. She vomited throughout pregnancy. She was never demonstrative to her child. Her menses became scanty after the child's birth. She and her husband led a very seclusive life. In the last six months she has become depressed and even more seclusive, neglecting her household, frequently crying, threatening suicide, and being suspicious of her "hostile" neighbors. She believed that they sent dogs to ruin her flowers, and that they looked in through the windows of her house whenever she was alone. She refused to go shopping. She also believed that the radio news had a hidden meaning which only she could understand. When agitated, she would cry and laugh at the same time. During her examination her speech was retarded, she stared away from the examiner, and she would sob and mumble childishly when upset. Her face was expressionless but she was quite alert. She believed that fellow patients talked about her and she "heard them" make "smart remarks". She believes that her marriage disgraced her family and feels no hope for recovery from her "illness". The diagnosis was paranoid schizophrenia with symptomatic depression.

CHRONIC SCHIZOPHRENIA: TEST RESULTS

Mr. R. Age: 18. Education: 10th grade. Occupation: None; "Housemaid in own home." Father: Accountant. Early Environment: Big city. Family Position: 3rd of 5. Religion: Jewish.

BELLEVUE SCALE

Comprehension

ENVELOPE: If it wasn't postmarked I'd put it in a mail box (2). THEATRE: I wouldn't yell. I'd probably get up and walk out or tell the usher about it. (?) I'd tell the usher first (2). BAD COMPANY: People judge you by the company you keep (1). TAXES: To support our government, thereby supporting ourself (2). SHOES: It's flexible and doesn't wear out so easy, I guess (1). LAND: Scarcer. (?) More populated (1). FOREST: I'd use a compass if I had one; if not, I'd look for the nearest stream and follow that to its source (1). LAW: To safeguard our general public (1). LICENSE: So one won't be... have two or three wives, husbands. DEAF: They never heard a spoken word. (?) Speech in man is comparatively new, and a baby, if he hears sounds, he would imitate; so I guess if a deaf person ever heard the sound of speech he could speak but wouldn't exactly know how to go about it and therefore wouldn't speak, I guess (2). RAW SCORE: 13.

Information

PRESIDENT: +. LONDON: +. PINTS: 4. RUBBER: +. THERMOMETER: +. WEEKS: 48. ITALY: +. WASHINGTON: 12 or 22 of February. (?) 22; +. HEIGHT: +. PLANE: +. PARIS: +. BRAZIL: +. HAMLET: +. POLE: +. VATICAN: +. JAPAN: +. HEART: Beats. (?) dk. POPULATION: +. H. FINN +. EGYPT: +. KORAN: +. FAUST: dk. HABEAS CORPUS: Legal term. ETHNOLOGY: dk. APOCRYPHA: dk. RAW SCORE: 18.

Digit Span

FORWARD: 3, 4, 5, 6 on first try; fails first series of 7 by misplacing one digit; fails both series of 8. BACKWARDS: 3 on first try; fails both series of 4 by placing last digit first and repeating the rest forward. Subject was then given 2 additional series of 3 digits and made the same type of error on both. (Did you try to reverse them?) "Yes." RAW SCORE: 10.

Arithmetic

ITEM 1: +. ITEM 2: +. ITEM 3: 12. (?) 25 less 8 is 17. ITEM 4: About 8, no, 9; +. ITEM 5: About 9. ITEM 6: dk. (30") (?) 36. ITEM 7: About 4. (?) 25 into a dollar is 4. (?) 38. (?) 28. ITEM 8: About $650. (?) A guess. (1/3?) 200. (3/3?) $600. ITEM 9: A foot or so, or an inch. I don't know how many feet in a yard. ITEM 10: About 36, I guess. (?) I knew it was much more than 8, and I associated 6 with 8. Maybe it's 32. RAW SCORE: 3.

Similarities

ORANGE: Fruit (2). COAT: Clothes (2). DOG: Animals (2). WAGON: Vehicles (2). DAILY PAPER: Entertainment (1). AIR: One's a liquid, and the other's a gas. (?) Both on earth. WOOD: Alcohol is made from wood. EYE: Parts of the body (1). EGG: Sometimes an egg comes from a seed or vice versa. POEM: Objects of memory. (?) A poet writes a poem from what he remembers, and a statue is in commemoration. PRAISE: Both are given out by human beings. FLY: A fly would land on a tree, and also since trees are dirty, flies may come from trees. RAW SCORE: 10.

Picture Arrangement

HOUSE: + 4" (2). HOLD UP: + 9" (2). ELEVATOR: + 18" (2). FLIRT: JNAET 32" (3). FISH: EFGHIJ 51" (3); insight. TAXI: SAMUEL 60" (3); insight. RAW SCORE: 15.

Picture Completion

NOSE: +. MUSTACHE: +. EAR: +. DIAMOND: The 6 is upside down. LEG: Upper part of shell. TAIL: +. STACKS: +. KNOB: +. SECOND HAND: +. WATER: +. REFLECTION: An arm on the lady. (?) The rest of the chair. (?) Parts of the legs of the table. TIE: +. THREADS: The lamp that holds the bulb. EYEBROW: The rest of the body. SHADOW: Parts of the hill. RAW SCORE: 9.

Block Designs

Cannot do second sample without help. ITEM 1: 18" (3). ITEM 2: 28" (3). ITEM 3: 13" (4). ITEM 4: 200"; confused, planless manipulation of blocks. Bottom 2 correct but cannot get top 2. Helped by examiner after 200". ITEM 5: 107"; makes red center using 4 all-red blocks; corrects: (3). ITEM 6: 200"; starts on corner; if one block does not fit, rejects it and uses another block turned so that it fits his plan instead of manipulating the first one; makes 4 red stripes of 2 blocks each and tries to combine them. ITEM 7: 250"; places 4 corner blocks correctly. "Who would want to make a design like that anyhow!" Cannot go beyond that; gets 4 sides slowly in 230". Builds center outside and puts it in. Thinks he has built different design. RAW SCORE: 13.

Object Assembly

ITEM 1: 20" (6). ITEM 2: 35"; ear reversed. (Correct?) "Yes." (?) "Oh! The ear." (4). ITEM 3: 77"; places thumb and wrist pieces first; index and middle finger reversed; compares with own hand: "Guess it's correct." (?) "Sure it's ok." (4). RAW SCORE: 14.

Digit Symbol

25 correct; 2 reversals of the 2–symbol; miscopies one 2–symbol as W. RAW SCORE: 26.

Vocabulary

APPLE: Fruit (1). DONKEY: Animal (1). JOIN: Get together

or merge (1). DIAMOND: Jewel (1). NUISANCE: Pest (1). FUR: Cloth or skin. (?) From animals (1). CUSHION: Cloth stuffed with material. (?) Used on chairs so you can sit on them (1). SHILLING: Part of a system of ... it's money, English money (1). GAMBLE: Sport. (?) Take a chance (1). BACON: Comes from pigs, it's a food. (?) Meat (1). NAIL: A piece of metal to hold boards together with; a part of a finger (1). CEDAR: Trees (1). TINT: To dye (1). ARMORY: Place where they hold arms. (?) Arms in the sense of munitions and weapons of war (1). FABLE: Story (1). BRIM: Edge (1). GUILLOTINE: Weapon to chop off people's heads (1). PLURAL: More than one, I think (1). SECLUDE: To differentiate and take away from (1). NITRO-GLYCERINE: Chemical used in war; they make bombs out of it (1). STANZA: Verse (1). MICROSCOPE: Instrument with lens so you can see little bugs and germs (½). VESPER: Pertains to religion; it's lights, I think. BELFRY: Tower. (?) Has a bell in it (1). RECEDE: Come back ... the opposite of cede or something. No ... to come back (½). AFFLICTION: Sore, or pertaining to afflict. PEWTER: dk. BALLAST: Weight. (?) Used on ships or balloons. (?) So it won't go up too high, to keep it down (1). CATACOMB: In Rome, tunnels, I think. (?) First Christians used them (1). SPANGLE: Starred, a thing full of stars. ESPIONAGE: A person whose work is spying ... spying (1). IMMINENT, MANTIS: dk. HARA KIRI: To kill oneself, in Japanese (1). CHATTEL: Slave or something like that (½). DILATORY, AMANUENSIS, PROSELYTE, MOIETY: dk. ASEPTIC: Pertains to medicine, to alleviate pain. FLOUT: Hit. TRADUCE: dk. RAW SCORE: 27.5.

Weighted Scores and IQ's

Comprehension 11	Picture Arrangement 13	Vocabulary 12
Information 13	Picture Completion 8	Verbal IQ: 100
Digit Span 7	Block Designs 7	Performance IQ: 85
Arithmetic 3	Object Assembly 7	Total IQ: 93
Similarities 8	Digit Symbol 6	

LEARNING EFFICIENCY

IMMEDIATE RECALL: (December 6) in Albany (a river) (overflowed).... (A man) in trying to (save) (a boy) (cut his hands)... Something about a house. SCORE: 11.

DELAYED RECALL: (December 6) a house ... (a river) (overflowing)... Albany... (in a small town) (near Albany). (A man) trying (to save) (a boy) and he hurt his hand in the process. SCORE: 8.

SORTING TEST

Part I

SINK STOPPER: Adds sugar, all silverware, cigarettes and real cigar. "First I'd put all the food. I associate all of them with food and this (sink stopper) since the sink is in the kitchen." Loose sorting, concrete concept. LARGE FORK: Adds large silver, sugar, candy cigarette.

"Both food and I associate the materials, the tools of eating, with food materials." Loose sorting, mixed concrete and abstract concept. PIPE: Adds real cigar and cigarette, matches, and paper circle "as an ashtray". "When you smoke, smoking makes ashes and you have to light up, that's why the matches." Mildly loose sorting, concrete and fabulized concept. BELL: Adds large pliers and large screwdriver. "This goes on a contraption or on vehicles and the screwdriver is to unscrew it and the pliers are abstract since I don't know the vehicle: may need it for protection." Mildly narrow sorting, concrete concept, peculiar verbalization ("protection"). CIRCLE: Adds ball. "You can use this (red circle) as a wall, and bounce the ball off the wall." Loose sorting, fabulized concept. TOY PLIERS: Adds small tools. "Since that's a toy. (?) I think they're a set. (?) If a person was going to build, he'd use these various objects, and since it was a child, they would be smaller." Mildly narrow sorting, concrete concept. BALL: Adds block with nail. "This time we have a real wall here." (See sorting on CIRCLE.) Loose sorting, fabulized concept.

Part II

RED: "First I gather it was a child eating (toy silverware) and she or it got through with eating and took this (sink stopper) from the sink and then played ball with this (ball), and fooled around with this (paper circle), went to school (eraser), and the child plays with matches." Fabulized concept. METAL: "All tools except for the nails and the lock and the bicycle bell. (All?) All metal." The first is a split-narrow syncretistic concept; the second is abstract. ROUND: "All soft objects I would say, all pliable objects." Syncretistic concept. TOOLS: "Tools of trade." Abstract concept, peculiar verbalization. PAPER: Before cigarette is put out says, "All paper;" then changes to "All from plants." Syncretistic concept. PAIRS: "Two of everything; the cigars, and the sugar and candy and cigarettes all belong together because they are objects of pleasure." (All?) "Objects of pleasure." Syncretistic concept. WHITE: "Paper and cardboard are all from the ground, from plants and trees." Syncretistic concept. RUBBER: "Rubber." Abstract concept. SMOKING MATERIALS: "All come from plants, that includes trees too, and all are objects of pleasure." Syncretistic concept. SILVERWARE: "The same type of tools. (?) The tools you eat . . . needed in eating." Syncretistic and functional concept. TOYS: "Toys or all things a child would play with." Abstract concept. RECTANGLES: "Paper comes from wood and you can also build with wood. That's why there's a nail (in block), and trees are plants and sugar comes from a plant. (All?) All come from the earth." Chain reasoning leading to syncretistic concept.

RORSCHACH TEST

CARD I. Reaction time: 17". Total time: 60".

Well, it's ink, a design in ink. It looks like a very mistreated butterfly. I used to make these when I was a little boy.

SCORE: W F+A P Fabulation Aggression.

CARD II. Reaction time: 50″. Total time: 90″.

Well, that was made with red ink also: design... it is... That's all (wants to give up card). (?) ∨... 1. Well, it looks more like a map than anything else I guess. [(?) In school, I looked at a map of the U. S., the black part is shaped like... wavy outline; red part: maps are different colors.] 2. Or maybe a butterfly or something like that. [(?) It looked something like the other picture that looked more like a butterfly than anything else.] That's all.

SCORES. 1: W F/C—Geog. 2: W F+A.

CARD III. Reaction time: 13″. Total time: 120″.

A cross between a... I'd say a dissected bug enlarged. [(?) I was going to say that because of the red ink, it looked like a map or something, a map and a moth and a butterfly. (?) First this (black) looked like a butterfly. This (middle red) is a more complete one and closer to its size.]

SCORE: W F—A; (W F/C—Geog); (D F+A); Contamination tendency.

CARD IV. Reaction time: 8″. Total time: 60″.

∨ Looks more like an animal that has been flattened out, or a bat or something. [(Sure?) You put the element of doubt into my mind. Yes, I am sure... Complete thing, whole. It's easier to say the first thing that popped into my mind. (?) It was sprawled out.]

SCORE: W F±A Aggression Peculiar.

CARD V. Reaction time: 5″. Total time: 45″.

∧...∨ ∧. That looks more like a butterfly than anything else, or a moth, but it's really an ink blot though, if you want to know what it really is. [(?) Nothing else except it's black. You made it with black ink so consequently it's black!]

SCORE: W F+A P Peculiar Peculiar.

CARD VI. Reaction time: 105″. Total time: 150″.

∨... ∧. Well, very interesting question you asked me. (Note: peculiar verbalization.) (?) It's hard to say what it is. I haven't very much of an imagination to say what it is. I know in all these blot pictures, one side is identical with the other side practically. (?) ∨ It could be a... an enlarged photograph of some kind of bug, butterfly or animal, to use my imagination. I'd just say that. [(?) Bug. (?) I don't know. (?) The extra long great neck, the outer proportions, body.]

SCORE: W F—A.

CARD VII. Reaction time: 30″. Total time: 90″.

(Turns to observer:) What do you think it is? ∨ This... from the distance looks more like a map than anything else because it has the proportions of white and black and fades on the edges. [(?) Eliminating bugs and animals, I came to a map. I enlarged on it so as not to make myself out as a liar. It was also irregular. That's why I thought that.]

SCORE: W ChF Geog Peculiar Peculiar.

CARD VIII. Reaction time: 90″. Total time: 120″.

1. A conflagration of colors, that's what it looks like at first. (Turns card all around.) And then it would be more of a living type of thing than matter type of thing. I don't know. I mean ... maybe it's an animal or bug. An animal would have more color in his system than a bug. [(?) I'd have to be psychoanalyzed because it's in the back of my mind. I think the colors more than anything else. The way they were in order, the plan. (?) I associate that color with the moving around, and animals aren't very stationary. (?) Well, usually anything that's colorful is movable, like a wall would be of one color and that was a series of colors and it was therefore movable and animals are usually very active, not stationary.] I gather this is supposed to be a supreme test because two psychologists are here. 2. (Card shown again.) > Well, these two look more like an animal.

SCORES. 1: W C A Autistic Logic Peculiar Peculiar. 2: (D F+A P).

CARD IX. Reaction time: 60″. Total time: 180″.

That could be a series of blots in colors. That's all. I don't want to get in deep. (Note: peculiar verbalization.) I am no good at explaining. (?) 1. I think it would be more a map, if I'd take it in three colors. It would be more a map, inlets, shapes. 2. If I take a general view or artist's view of it, it'd look more like a dream or a surrealist's job of painting. [(?) I was going to say it was one of Salvadore Dali's dreams. He paints after he dreams usually, and therefore you get the art subject involved in it. Mostly I just tried to be funny or smart there. To get away from the hard labor of defining the hard earlier picture, I put in a bit of sarcastic humor in the next.] (Continuous turning of the card.) (?) If I tried harder, I'd say it was a combination of a few of the other pictures. (Note: reference idea.)

SCORES. 1: W F/C—Geog. 2: W C Dream Peculiar Peculiar.

CARD X. Reaction time: 30″. Total time: 210″.

That could be a little of everything I guess. That could be ... I can't name it. 1. This part (red) we will make believe is a map because it's the largest part of it, and the other parts could be little bugs squashed on the map. This would be a cockroach (side blue) except for the different color. This is a grasshopper (upper gray). 2. Maybe the few yellow ones could be egg spots.

SCORES. 1: (W) D F— Geog. Autistic Logic, Confabulation, Agression; D F—A Absurd; D F—A Absurd. 2: D C Egg spots, Deterioration-C.

Summary of Responses

R: 15 (3)   EB: 0—5.5 (6)

W 11 (2)
D 4 (2)

Qualitative
Fabulation 1
Confabulation 1
Contamination tendency 1
Autistic Logic 2
Perseveration
Absurd 2
Reference Idea 1
Peculiar 12
Deterioration-C 1

F+3 (2)
F—5
F± 1
F/C 2— (1—)
C 3
ChF 1

A 9 (2)
Geog 4 (1)
Dream 1
Egg spots 1

W% 73 (72)
D% 27 (33)

F% 60-73 (61-78)
F+% 44-36 (55-46)

A% 60 (61)
Geog% 27 (28)
P 2 (1)
P% 13 (17)

WORD ASSOCIATION TEST

WORLD — 2.5″ — ground. LOVE — 1.5″ — hate. FATHER (heard FARTHER) — 2″ — near (2″ — mother). HAT — 3.5″ — cloth (6″ — head). BREAST—5.5″—body (5.5″). CURTAINS—2.5″—window. TRUNK—2.5″ —lock. DRINK—1.5″—glass. PARTY—2″—fun. BOWEL MOVEMENT— 4″— (laugh) waste. BOOK—1.5″—words. LAMP—1.5″—shade. RUG— 2.5″—foot (3.5″—feet, floor). CHAIR—2.5″—floor. BOY FRIEND—1.5″ —girl friend. PENIS—8.5″— (laugh) waste. DARK—2″—light (4.5″). DE-PRESSED—1.5″—sad. SPRING—2.5″—fun. BOWL—4″—balls. SUICIDE —2″—death. MOUNTAIN—2″—hill. HOUSE—2″—family. PAPER—2″ —pen (2″—words). HOMOSEXUAL—10.5″—pervert. RADIATOR—4″ —heat. GIRL FRIEND—4.5″—boy friend. SCREEN—2.5″—window. MASTURBATE—17″—pervert again. FRAME—.5″—picture. MAN—1.5″ —woman. ORGASM—4.5″—organism. MOVIES—1.5″—shows. CUT—2″ —blood. LAUGH—2.5″—cry. BITE—2.5″—taste. WOMEN—2.5″—man. DANCE—3″—floor. DOG—1″—house (4″). DAUGHTER—1.5″—son. TAXI—2″—cab (5″). MOTHER—1″— father. TABLE—1.5″ — chair (2″ —lamp). BEEF—2.5″—meat. NIPPLE—6.5″—breast. RACE—2.5″—contest. WATER—1.5″—land (4.5″—glass). SUCK—3.5″—taste. HORSE—4.5″— ground (3.5″). FIRE—4″—flame (10″—dk.). VAGINA—4″—virgin. FARM—2″—help. SOCIAL—6″—socialist. SON—1.5″—daughter. TAXES (heard TEXAS)—3″—state. TOBACCO—2″—cigarette (3.5″). CITY—1″ —town. INTERCOURSE—5″—sexual. HOSPITAL—6″—cripple (4″— doc). DOCTOR—2″—nurse.

THEMATIC APPERCEPTION TEST

CARD 1. (Boy with violin.) This little boy has been told to play the violin which he does not like to play and after playing for quite a while, he sets it down to study it and to think of what makes it work. His mother catches him in this attitude and he is made to practice an extra hour. (Feel?) Being a little boy, he would like to be outside and play and he is pretty much resentful about having to stay and practice an extra hour, having been disgusted with the violin in the first place.

CARD 2. (Old woman in doorway.) Could I make up a name for her? Matilda opened the door to find her long lost sister come home after so many years of rampaging around the world. At first sight both could neither say anything ... say a word, but after a long pause they began to go over their life pretty thoroughly, which they found had been pretty complete. (Complete?) She looks none too young and being her sister would have been none too young; also, she has had many experiences in the cruel, cruel, hard world. (Experiences?) They have both been travellers I assume, since one sister was ... had adventurous experiences, mixed with a little emotional experiences. (Explain?) Hard life and deaths. (Whose?) Of their family or friends, or other associations. I'm afraid my phraseology isn't so hot. (Outcome?) After being home together, they both live happily ever after in a life of reminiscing. Boy, have I an imagination!

CARD 3. (Old man in graveyard.) He came into this world and he knew he was going out some time or other. All of his friends were gone now and thinking of them made him wonder what the eternal resting place would be like, period. That's all. (Led up?) I knew I'd let myself in deep when I started that one! Well, this picture here represents a graveyard and when you think of a graveyard, you think of death, and when you think of death you think of life. (Why in graveyard?) Well, there are many reasons: sadness and remorse, curiosity. (?) Sad and remorseful about being alone in the world and since he was alone he developed a form of melancholia, whatever that means, and so he decided to see the place where his friends rested before he died. (Curiosity?) Whether they were comfortable or not, or ... I did have to say so. (Mean?) Nothing. He was curious about the life, if there was eternal life after death and things pertaining to the soul.

CARD 4. (Silhouette of man at window.) Hmm ... There isn't much to go on in here. Are you going to put that down too? As the siren rang, or sounded from the air-raid alarm, Felix got off his bed, no ... got up and switched the light. He then proceeded to make his rounds and waited for the all-clear period. (Rounds?) Since he was an air-raid warden, he had to see that lights were out in the area that he was supposed to take care of.

CARD 5. (Heads of embracing couple.) Hmm ... ∨ ... Now I'll look at it this way. It looks much better. You wrote that down too. (Gets up and looks at examiner's notes.) The battle was fought continuously for twelve hours. They were so tired after the twelve hours and the fight was so even that the referee called it a draw. (Fighting?) These two people. (Why?) That's an interesting question. They were fighting a grudge-fight ... no, well, it could be. It was their sense of honor that compelled them to fight for twelve straight hours. (?) No, they probably had been acquaintances, but some incident—now I said it: you'll ask me—compels them to fight. Not having known the combatants personally, I wouldn't know what it was. (Any idea?) No, I couldn't ... I have no idea what causes these battles. (Story!) We're getting into another story... all right. Hate, love or any emotion can be the cause of a fight between two persons. (Story!) They were walking down the street one day when they accidentally kicked each other in the shins and that started the whole thing. (Any other cause?) No, not that I know of. (How an honor fight?) Well, their sense of honor was a little off in the first place, so then it was an honor fight. (Mean?) Well, their outlook, their definition of the word. (?) I'm getting myself in deeper. Let's see. How they look on the term, their view of it. (?) They were ready to fight the moment anything happens: that was what was peculiar about their view of it.

CARD 6. (Prehistoric animal, rocky road, bridge.) Ye Gods! What is that thing over there? This sight is too awe-inspiring for me to write anything about, or in other words, I haven't got the imagination that would require a story about it. (See?) Rocks, a cliff formation, part of a prehistoric beast and that's all. (Center figure?) Well, I think I'll just leave it as part of the rocks. (Happening?) They are just waiting there for time to devour them. (Who?) The rocks and animals.

CARD 7. (Shadowy photograph of thumb.) ∨ ... Ha, this is a fine one! What is it? Can you tell me? Oh! This is an enlarged picture of a thumb, I think, or a finger, and if anyone can make up a story about an enlarged picture of a finger, I would like to hear it, period. (See anything else?) Nope.

CARD 8. (Nude couple; older woman with infant.) I refuse to make up a story about this! (Turns card over.) (Why?) That's an interesting question. Because I assume you are a lady and I am too modest or flustered or whatever you call it to make up a story about it. (See?) People. (Kind of people?) Now you are trying to get a story out of me. People that walk around on two legs. (Story?) Well, from the expressions on their face they are very sad about something, and I would be very sad too if I were in that predicament. (What predicament?) Well... er... I couldn't say, because I don't know the predicament. (?) From their poverty. (?) Because they are without clothing, and if they weren't poverty-stricken, they wouldn't be without clothing.

CARD 9. (Two chairs; table set for tea.) In the palatial home of S. Quopsnagle Thorndike, the society editor of "The Daily Blare" had come in person to photograph his prized antiques, which were standing in one corner of the blue-gray room, period. That's all. (Kind of person?) Well, he was a person, he was well-off because he owned these antiques and this palatial room and he also was a leader of society in his community. (Wealthy?) He inherited it from his father who inherited it from his father, and so on down the line. (?) A charitable, well-meaning, conscientious, well-liked person in his community. He is some guy, isn't he! (Funny name?) A name isn't everything. I knew that you would ask me that. I gave him such a name to open new thoughts in my mind which is pretty dull now—for energy food or whatever you want to call it. And please don't ask me what energy food is!

CARD 10. (Old man on shoulders of another old man.) (Patient gets up and looks at examiner's notes again; then reads back of card.)

Harvard Psychological Clinic!.. "Scratch my head," the old man said, and his request was immediately granted. That's all I can do with that. (People?) Old men, if you can call it a picture. (Relationship?) Well, they have only one thing in common, I think, and that is that they are both old and that is the only relationship that I can see. (Led up?) An itchy head. I'm afraid I acted like a smart alec on those first pictures.

CARD M 11. I'm sorry. I cannot do this. (Refuses to continue with test.)

(Test resumed next day.) CARD M 11. (Old woman looking away from young man.) This... her young son was just going off to the army and since he shedded certain obligations... (?) shirked, I meant to say... by going off, her mother felt quite blue about it and the son was torn between two emotions. (?) A sense of duty at home and a patriotic duty to his country. (?) He could be the only son in the family, the only means of support.

CARD M 12. (Man held by hands from behind.) The... as Jim was walking down the street, he happened to be overpowered by an unknown foe, or opponent, since it was a dark street. After being overpowered, the culprit escaped from the scene. (Jim was overpowered.) (?) Well, he happened to be overpowered while he walked down the street because of his dislike in the community, and because someone wanted to overpower him in the community, wishing to do him violence.

CARD M 13. (Figure on floor by couch.) Feeling very sad about life, Bill went to his father's drawer, took out a gun and shot himself. (?) Because he was going to die from a sickness anyway and he felt very sad having the sickness and instead of suffering for months, he decided to shoot himself now.

CARD M 14. ("Hypnosis" scene.) The hypnotist was trying very desperately to get his patient out of the trance which he had put him in. (?) He finally succeeded after many hours of work. (?) He put him into a trance to experiment with the subconscious and since he was an amateur at this sort of work, or a beginner I should say, it was hard for him to get the patient up.

CARD M 15. (Older man looking at younger man.) These two men were to be shot at dawn the next day, the following morning, and they were pondering their fate, and trying to figure out ways of escape, but came the dawn and they were shot. (?) Well, they did something in their civilian life, or in their life previously, that was very bad. They set fire to a group of buildings and many people died and so they were to be shot. (?) Oh, to get revenge on the government.

CARD M 16. (Man on rope.) Jim thought it was hopeless trying to escape but when the opportunity presented itself he succeeded in escaping. That's all. (?) He was a menace to society. (?) In a penitentiary.

CARD M 17. (Figure by table; bats and owls.) Having been lost in the wilderness for eight days, our traveller comes across this cave and he slowly starves to death, being too weak to... to kill any of the animals that live in the cave. The reason why he wanted to kill the animals was to eat, but he was too weak to do it so he starved to death.

CARD M 18. (Man on bed; face in pillow.) Coming home from a very strenuous trip, and having exhausted all his energy, he flops himself on the bed to rest for a couple of hours. That's all. (?) Walking around, trying to get to some place where he didn't succeed in getting so he came back and rested.

CARD M 19. (Shadowed figure with arms up.) The escaped convict was finally trapped and he decided to surrender, instead of going on or be killed in the process of escaping again. (?) For crimes which he did. He robbed several banks.

CARD M 20 (Unkempt man and well-groomed man.) Mr. Witherspoon was being abducted and held for ransom but he finally manages to escape and sets the law on his abductors.

ANALYSIS OF RESULTS

BELLEVUE SCALE

The two most diagnostic features of the scatter are the low Arithmetic and Similarities scores. As a rule, a great drop of the Arithmetic score indicates one of two diagnoses: schizophrenia or narcissistic character disorder. In both cases an extreme impairment of concentration is what is *directly* indicated, but in the latter case this appears to be referable to extremely low anxiety tolerance as part of the narcissistic syndrome, while in the former case this appears to be referable to the effects of withdrawal. In this case, however, narcissistic character disorder is pretty well ruled out by the great drop of the Similarities score, since this pattern is atypical outside of psychotic conditions. A relatively low Similarities score also indicates a *chronic* aspect to the illness and is most typical of chronic *paranoid* schizophrenics. This diagnostic impression is supported by the relatively low Performance level, a pattern distinctively *paranoid* in schizophrenic records. Further support of an indirect or secondary nature is provided by the relatively well-retained Comprehension score: this too is distinctively *paranoid* in schizophrenic records, referring to the good front so often put up by these cases. The only aspect of the scatter which deviates from the usual schizophrenic pattern is the excellent Picture Arrangement score, since the pertinent functions of anticipation and visual organization are generally among the first to be impaired in schizophrenia. On the basis of this well-retained score, it is usually expected that anti-social features will be present. The drop of the Performance scores could also suggest that this is merely a depression, but the great drop of the Arithmetic score would be expected only in psychotic depressions and the good Comprehension score is atypical in that group. This possibility can be more clearly ruled out on the basis of the verbalizations.

In Information, his inability to explain what the heart does, at the same time as he obtains a very good total score on the subtest, has an ominous quality, suggesting loss of previously acquired assets and, therefore, disorganization. "Forty-eight weeks in a year" has this quality too, though to a lesser degree.

In Comprehension, the rambling and wordy response to the *deaf* item also suggests disorganization. The statement, "Speech in man is comparatively new", is irrelevant to the rest of his answer; it also has an intellectualizing aspect and suggests that intellectualizing will be clinically prominent. The wordiness of the response goes far beyond what would be expected from the ordinarily monosyllabic psychotic depressive.

In Digit Span, his inability to reverse to any adequate extent the digits to be repeated backwards strongly suggests psychosis (because of its glaring incorrectness) and extreme rigidity (because essentially he is repeating the numbers as they have been given to him forward). It was established by inquiry that he had been trying to reverse the sequence.

His failures in Arithmetic have both a bland, breezy quality and an inappropriate, arbitrary quality. The breezy quality is seen in prefacing most of his answers with "about" and in answering the 9th item with "a foot or so or an inch". These verbalizations are sometimes obtained from bland psychopaths and do not necessarily indicate schizophrenia. They imply mainly that the subject is announcing boldly his disinclination or inability to get involved in the responsibility of serious mental application. On the 9th item it turns out that he cannot say how many feet are in a yard, which again indicates decline of his intellectual level. On the 10th item his explanation of the response *36* is a classical example of schizophrenic breakdown in communication: "I knew it was much more than 8 and I associated 6 with 8." This explanation makes it even less understandable how he got 36 in the first place; it makes one feel that he should have come out with 68. Equally disorganized is his casual substitution of random associations for arithmetical logic: "I *associated* 6 with 8." One catches a glimpse here of the devious trails his thinking must take in everyday situations and the inappropriate affect or bland- ness that accompanies it.

In Similarities, the first convincingly schizophrenic concept is on *poem-statue*. The concept "memory" is used on two different levels simultaneously, since a poem is written *from* memory and a statue is created *for* memory. On *fly-tree* he first essays a fabulation and then becomes clearly arbitrary: he casually assumes that trees are dirty and reasons that since flies breed in dirt, they may come from trees. This is autistic logic in a clear form: both the premises and the inference are arbitrary. There can be little doubt at this point that this is a chronic schizophrenia.

Nothing of note is elicited in Picture Arrangement, but in Picture Completion the last three responses support the diagnosis. There he names as missing parts items obviously not intended to be included in the first place, such as the girl's body on item 14.

Deterioration of analytic and synthetic abilities is evidenced in the Block Designs subtest: he cannot complete item 4 even with considerable assistance; his attacks on items 4, 6, and 7 are planless; he considers his finally correct reproduction of the seventh design to be a *different* design; and the equivalence of the red-white sides of all the blocks is not recognized. In the light of this qualitative analysis, the low score can be seen to reflect disorganization and not depressive retardation. Some petulance is apparent during the seventh item. The poor perceptual organization implied in his not accepting the seventh block design as correct is also indicated on the *hand* item of Object Assembly, where even with a hint and an attempt at checking, he still fails to recognize a finger-reversal. In Vocabulary, "pertaining to afflict" is inappropriate pretentiousness, as is "to differentiate" for *seclude*. *Gamble*—"sport" has a peculiar association-like quality; *recede*—"... the opposite of cede ..." is arbitrary.

The test results thus far therefore clearly indicate a chronic paranoid schizophrenia, and also point up conspicuous intellectualizing and rigidity, a breezy blandness, and the possibility of an anti-social trend.

LEARNING EFFICIENCY

The average score of 9.5 is pathologically low compared to a Vocabulary score of 12 in the Bellevue Scale. A score of at least 15 or 16 should have been obtained. The only striking qualitative feature is the fragmentation in both recalls of the idea of water entering houses, so that he remembers only "house". Thus learning efficiency also bears the imprint of a chronic psychosis.

SORTING TEST

Schizophrenic looseness of the concept span and concreteness of conceptual thinking are striking throughout the first part of the test. The idea of a wall to bounce a ball off, represented by a piece of paper or small block of wood, is extremely arbitrary. This is the kind of reasoning which, like the "dirty tree" reasoning in Similarities, can prove anything; it occurs frequently in the records of chronic paranoid schizophrenics. We shall see this reasoning reaching a fantastic extreme in the

Rorschach Test. The phrase "food materials" is peculiar. In Part II, there are relatively few abstract concepts formed and some of those are spoiled. Generalized impairment of Part II usually indicates a chronic psychosis, and this finding here is quite compatible with what has been inferred so far. There is a trace of a chain concept on the last item, another typically chronic feature. The frequent syncretistic concepts suggest expansiveness of thinking, and the response "all soft" to the *round* item, because it disregards the metal bell, is arbitrary as well as syncretistic.

RORSCHACH TEST

The test is distinguished most of all by its abundance of deviant verbalizations and reasoning[8]). These in themselves indicate schizophrenia. The low R, the high $A\%$ and the perseverations suggest the usual coarctation of a *paranoid* schizophrenic; the absence of M and emphasis on pure C together with the low $F+\%$ indicate that dramatic, systematized delusions are probably no longer present, and that inappropriateness of affect and behavior, and impairment of reality-testing are conspicuous. The high $W\%$ suggests, however, that expansive ideation is still conspicuous, though the absence of M indicates that these ideas are probably loose and shifting. This is the picture of a chronic, probably paranoid, schizophrenia.

Card I: "Mistreated butterfly" suggests similar feelings about himself. Card II: his attempt to return the card after a brief description, even though he has already offered an interpretation on Card I, indicates a basic weakness of anticipations. Card III: a cross between a map and a moth and a butterfly is a confabulation, but is nipped in the bud. This restraint of verbalization has a paranoid quality. Card IV: a "flattened out" bat has an aggressive quality. "You *put* the element of doubt into my mind" is an aggressive, paranoid verbalization. Card V: the defiant assertion, "but is really an inkblot", also has a paranoid quality in that it has the tone of someone being led into a trap and trying to protest. When his verbal aggressiveness breaks through in inquiry, it comes out in a peculiar, petulant verbalization: "You made it with black ink so consequently it's black!"

Card VI begins with a peculiarly bland and aggressive verbalization, ". . . . very interesting question you asked me". The long delay may be an expression of the blocking effect of anxiety stimulated by this heavily shaded card. Card VII begins with a peculiar and again ag-

------

8) The reader unfamiliar with schizophrenic verbalizations in the Rorschach Test should benefit from a detailed study of this most instructive record.

gressive question—asking an observer what he thinks it is. The phrase "proportions of white and black" is a somewhat clouded communication. His explanation about the process of elimination in arriving at "a map" is a confusing communication of what has happened: if he is taken literally, it sounds as if he were saying that what is not a bug or animal is a map, actually he is saying that his anticipation, based on previous cards, of seeing a bug or animal was not satisfied, but that he did notice a resemblance to a map. The anticipation itself is arbitrary in paranoid fashion and is based on the same kind of autistic logic as the more florid schizophrenic response on Card VIII. "... So as not to make myself out a liar" does not quite communicate the rationale of "enlarging on it", and is a paranoid anticipation that others will unjustifiably question his sincerity and that he must therefore prove them wrong at once.

Card VIII begins with the peculiar verbalization: "conflagration of colors". There follows a most classical instance of autistic logic: like the "dirty tree" reasoning in Similarities, it mixes in arbitrary premises and arbitrary deductions from these premises. He ends his verbalizations with another paranoid inference about the importance of the test. Card IX begins with a paranoid statement, "I don't want to get in deep", and goes on to an expansive formulation about taking "a general view or artist's view". He confesses spontaneously on inquiry that he has been trying to be "smart", but it is clear that this is said in self-defense. His defective reality testing is glaring here: he verbalized the autistic logic on VIII casually, but felt that this not too peculiar response on IX was arbitrary. Paranoid cases will be cautious about expressing arbitrary ideas, but because their reality testing is so impaired, they will invariably be unsuccessful in getting through a *battery* of tests without yielding patently schizophrenic responses. On Card X, autistic logic again comes to the fore in his choice of the *map* area. A confabulation is then developed—"bugs squashed on a map"—which, like the flattened out bat on Card IV, has an aggressive quality. Subjects who see things as squashed, smashed, and flattened out in this test are usually characterized by intense pent-up aggressions. Defective reality testing is apparent in the two absurd form responses. Blunting of affect is implied by the pale, pure C, "egg spots".

The records of chronic schizophrenics are not always this clear diagnostically, but to a greater or lesser extent they partake of the same features: pure C replacing M, low $F+\%$ and a massing of deviant verbalizations and reasoning.

WORD ASSOCIATION TEST

Vagina—"virgin" has a clang-association quality even though the content of the response is still sexual. *World*—"ground", *horse*—"ground", *hospital*—"cripple", and *rug*—"foot" are more or less distant associations. Otherwise the responses are quite orderly, and, in itself, the record is not diagnostic. Not infrequently chronic schizophrenics who are well-preserved yield such diagnostically ambiguous records. We have already seen in the previous tests evidences of deterioration from a premorbidly higher level of functioning; in the light of the results in the Word Association Test we must nevertheless conclude that a semblance of a good front is maintained by this patient and that his decline will not be too conspicuous clinically.

Striking responses include hearing *father* as "farther" (an implicit avoidance), *penis*—"waste" and its delay, the delay on *homosexual* and *masturbate* and the moralistic response to the latter, and the delays on *nipple, intercourse* and *hospital*. In general the sexual words are the most disturbing, suggesting particularly acute conflict in this area.

THEMATIC APPERCEPTION TEST

Peculiar paranoid verbalizations, many of which might pass at first hearing as merely facetious, occur throughout this record; only some of the more instructive peculiarities will be discussed.

Card 1. The theme is the popular one of wanting to get outside, away from the violin, but the mother is described as a punitive figure, punishing him not for behavior but for an attitude. Card 2. The theme is reminiscing about a full but hard life, and is elaborated facetiously: "rampaging" and "cruel, cruel, hard world". The idea of a cruel, hard world even though introduced facetiously, probably expresses his own view of the world. "Adventurous experiences, mixed with a little emotional experiences" is a peculiar formulation, and the inference that they were both travellers since one sister had already been described as such is an instance of autistic logic. The restriction of the theme to sisters implies a strong feminine identification. Card 3. The theme is preoccupation with death. Paranoid thinking is evident in "I knew I'd let myself in deep...." The story is replete with non sequiturs. Autistic logic is apparent in: "... when you think of a graveyard you think of death, and when you think of death you think of life." Moreover his response is irrelevant, since he was asked, "What led up to it?" and he replied with an account of his subjective experience in making up the story. A similar irrelevancy is, "To the story I told you". "Melancholia" has an intellectualizing quality. "Whether they were comfortable or not" is clearly an absurd idea. This one story is sufficient to indicate serious disorganization. The concern with death and afterlife probably indicates a current preoccupation. Card 4. This theme of an air-raid was conventional during the war. Concern with what is being written down is widespread among paranoid cases.

Card 5. Paranoid and other peculiar verbalizations are frequent here; in turning the card upside down he is clearly being "perverse". The noteworthy theme is a fight without a victor. This indicates unusually intense aggressive feelings, since the picture is almost invariably seen as involving affection or sorrow. "Not having known the combatants personally" is flippant and evasive, and further inquiry makes it clear that he is resisting exploration of motives for aggression. "You wrote that down", "That's an interesting question", "Now I said it, you'll ask me", and "I'm getting myself in deeper" are hostile and paranoid verbalizations, and make their appearance when he is pressed to deal with the aggressive impulses in the story. A disorganized reaction to this stress is evident in "... hate, *love*, or *any emotion* can be the cause of a fight". When confronted with the discrepancy (based on fluidity) between the initial fight for honor and the later more trivial fight, he rigidly defends both ideas and tries to reconcile them by attributing poor judgment to the characters in the story. This is clearly a paranoid technique: it is as if to say, "I am not mixed up; they are mixed up". The readiness to fight is reminiscent of the aggressive content in the Rorschach Test, and suggests the presence of strong, poorly controlled (pure *C*'s), aggressive impulses. The original theme of a fight for honor may be expressive of strong conflicts with his conscience. A moralistic note was already sounded in the Word Association Test. On the other hand, the implication that the figures are two *men* instead of man and woman, and the statement that they might be fighting because of love, suggest that this story may be an expression of acute conflict over homoerotic impulses which has not yet been decided ("a draw"). The long delay on *homosexual* in the Word Association Test comes to mind here. The fluidity of the tale makes it difficult to piece together the underlying fantasy.

Card 6. He begins with a flippant evasion but finally states the theme of slow decay with time—an unusual statement and probably expressive of a personal feeling. Card 7. Here he becomes openly negativistic and refuses to do more than describe the picture. Apparently this very unstructured stimulus for a story represents too much of a threat to this paranoid subject. Card 8. He is evasive throughout the discussion and finally escapes from the sexual implications of the picture. In view of the general description of this patient thus far developed, this appears to be a clear instance of paranoid "shutting up".

Card 9. Here he is again flippant and evasive. The excessive use of this defense is by now obviously characteristic of his adjustment-efforts and gives the psychological picture an anti-social coloring. The suggestion offered by the high Picture Arrangement score finds good support. "Energy food" slipped out but was rejected at once. Chronic paranoid schizophrenics often manifest a pseudo-awareness of their own peculiarities and try to sift their verbalizations for those which should be rejected. They are never completely successful at this. The peculiarities they let pass and the fact that peculiarities continue to make an appearance indicate that a sound appreciation or genuine awareness of the rules of logic and communication has been lost. "To open new thoughts in my mind" fails as a communication since it does not quite explain the flippant name he used.

Card 10. He avoids the aggressive implications of this picture and is in a hurry to leave the disturbing situation. His absolute refusal to deal with the picture suggests paranoid fears of being attacked. Card 11. He refuses to continue when confronted with this picture, presumably because of its oedipal implications. Card 11. (Test resumed.) The theme is guilt over breaking away from the mother-figure—a popular theme. The slip "*her* mother" is suggestive of the feminine identification already inferred. "Shedded" obligations is less of a slip and more of a pathological word misusage. Card 12. The theme is being overpowered by unknown forces in a hostile world. The vague, general formulation indicates that this is a personal feeling, since the more casual, popular story would have remained concrete. Moreover he feels no need to state a concrete motive for the assault, such as robbery, which is usually done when the story involves aggression. Granting this, and the general impressions thus far, the theme expresses paranoid apprehensiveness and feelings of estrangement from the community. Inappropriate affect is evident in the juxtaposition of casual and dramatic words: "He happened to be overpowered."

Card 13. The theme is suicide as an escape from the lingering death of illness. He is probably expressing a feeling of despair regarding his own illness. The response "cripple" to *hospital* in the Word Association Test may relate to the same feeling. Suicidal fantasies are suggested. Card 14. The theme is the danger of psychotherapy and mistrust of the ability of the doctor (as part of his general mistrustfulness). Card 15. The theme is punishment for wanton aggressiveness. Note, however, that the men do not feel guilty even though they killed "many people". The idea of taking revenge on a government is somewhat vague, indicating his inability to face concrete motives for aggressive acts; it also is somewhat inappropriate. The "government", may, however, represent the authoritative father-figure. The message in this story may be the following: I hate people and would like to destroy them (particularly my father?) ; I will be destroyed whatever I do and I will therefore take my revenge in advance. Card 16. The theme is popular.

Card 17. The theme is inability to act in one's own behalf and the threat implied by that inability. The "starving to death" idea is not common and the story probably expresses a personal fear. Card 18. The theme of fatigue is popular. The statement, "Walking around; trying to get some place where he didn't succeed in getting", is inappropriate in its switch from the casual walking around to the serious, though vague, implication of failure. A note of discouragement is sounded here. Card 19. The theme is the popular one of a captured criminal. Card 20. The theme is again the idea that crime does not pay. He seems well aware that he must hold his aggressions in check, but, as we have seen, they do break through in irritability and negativism at least, and possibly even in violence (3 C's in the Rorschach Test).

It is noteworthy that no perceptual distortions occur, since they are frequent in the records of chronic paranoid cases. There is hardly an indicator which occurs without fail in all members of one nosological group. This absence of distortions, like the orderly word associations, is probably a manifestation of the "good front".

Test Report

Intelligence and Thought Organization: The present IQ of 93 appears to be the result of a process of schizophrenic deterioration. The premorbid IQ appears to have been at least in the bright normal range. Concentration, concept formation, learning efficiency, and independent judgment appear to be impaired. However, grasp of superficial conventional judgments and social situations is well-retained and this suggests that a fairly good front may be sustained. Behind this front his thinking is simultaneously pathologically fluid and pathologically rigid, and arbitrary and expansive in a paranoid manner. Disorganized and pretentious intellectualizing is prominent. Although he tries to be cautious and correct, his defective reality testing betrays him and clearly psychotic reasoning makes frequent appearances.

Emotional Factors. Inappropriate and blunted affect and the potentiality for violent aggressive outbursts are conspicuous. There is a good deal of blandness present but he still experiences acute anxiety when confronted with sexual or aggressive material. He tries to cover his upset by sarcasm and aggressive facetiousness; these failing, he becomes surly, petulant, and negativistic. Premorbidly, he appears to have relied heavily on compulsive and intellectualizing defenses; these defenses are still conspicuous but they now have a feeble, scattered quality. Conflict over homoerotic impulses is indicated.

Figures and Attitudes: He appears to be preoccupied with death and the after-life, to feel himself irrevocably involved in a process of slow "decay" or "starvation". The world is viewed as threatening, overpowering, and unjust, and he thinks of himself as ineffectual in his own defense. A wantonly destructive wish for revenge is evident, however. Suicidal preoccupation and a strong latent feminine identification are also indicated.

Diagnostic Impression: Chronic paranoid schizophrenia.

CLINICAL SUMMARY

Mr. R. has been extremely orderly from an early age. He has been a stammerer since the age of three, and since that time self-consciousness about this symptom has led him to shun the company of others. At the age of fourteen, he suddenly became restless, excitable, and confused, stated that his mother was "to blame for everything", and was preoccupied with Hitler's persecution of the Jews (the patient is Jewish) and with Einstein's theory of relativity. Paranoid ideas about poisoned food and secret panels developed. After two weeks he became moody, mute, and then suddenly snapped out of this state. Five weeks later he had a similar attack, again followed by a brief period of mutism and sudden remission. This was followed by a period of excitement and later by a period of listlessness and generalized disinterest. At the end of about a year he resumed school for two years but attended sporadically, being troubled by apathy and a concentration impairment. He left school after finishing the tenth grade, seemed greatly worried and stammered more conspicuously. He spent a year at a school for speech correction which he apparently enjoyed; his speech improved. Upon returning home he again became apathetic and seclusive, spending all his time in his room, listening to the radio and reading books on varied subjects, including philosophy and mystery stories. In this period he attempted suicide several times by hanging from the head of his bed, but since these attempts failed he gave up the idea of suicide. Two months ago he tried to enlist in the armed forces but was rejected; he was upset and his seclusiveness increased. The patient came here at the age of eighteen, four years after his first "break".

His initial approach to the hospital and interviews here was characterized by reserve, pointed deference, suspiciousness, evasiveness, and seclusiveness. He was also self-depreciatory, feeling himself to be worthless. In interviews he often avoided personal questions, answering in intellectual generalizations. He worried about the war, being opposed to killing, and feeling that for that reason he would not even work in a defense plant. On the other hand he didn't care "if the world goes to hell". He was loath to criticize his parents and evasive about sexual matters. He expressed mixed feelings of curiosity and revulsion toward intercourse and stated that he had obtained much of his sexual information "through deduction". He described a "mental stammer" which made it difficult for him to think things through. Florid psychotic symptoms were not, however, evident during his examination, and in some situations he was able to give the impression of an "inhibited, neurotic boy" who could be congenial. Once in the hospital, he soon became aggressively dominant and critical toward other patients and later developed mild paranoid ideas about hospital practices here. He read heavily, including the great novels. His enthusiasms for new activities were quickly mobilized but just as quickly gave way to disinterest. After some months he began public high school again; the strain imposed by this return to the community and by the anticipation of his hospital physician's imminent departure for military service appears to have been the precipitating factor of another psychotic break. This began with somatic complaints but soon gave way to confusion, to hyper-activity, grandiose delusions about his own identity and about the war, to ideas that some patients were German spies, and finally to violence.

SCHIZOPHRENIC CHARACTER: TEST RESULTS[9]

Mr. V. Age: 19. Education: High school. Father: Broker; divorced from mother. Early Environment: Big city. Family Position: Younger of 2. Religion: Protestant.

BELLEVUE SCALE
Comprehension

ENVELOPE: What would I do? . . . Mail it. (?) Post office box.

---

[9] Unfortunately, the Thematic Apperception Test was not administered to this patient. Nor was it possible to administer this test to the patient with the Paranoid Condition (see p. 233). and to the Inhibited Normal Subject (see p. 268).

(?) In any chute. I'd just go to the post office and mail it (1). THEATRE: I'd just get up and yell fire... Warn everybody. (?) That's what I'd do—I wouldn't know. (Else?) I'd probably be so excited I wouldn't know what to do. Maybe I'd just leave and when I got to an exit, yell fire. BAD COMPANY: Bad influence (2). TAXES: To keep the country going (2). SHOES: Most durable, soft thing, I guess (1). LAND: Light in the city? (Land!) In the city, it's more thickly populated; naturally, it's more expensive. (?) Land is worth much more: you could build an apartment house or store, make more money—at least in New York if you have a house, it's fabulous, so expensive to keep up (1). FOREST: Probably by the sun or stars... I don't know. I'd just walk and walk and try to go straight; try to find a star I remembered. (Sun?) I wouldn't know—you read stories... by the stars or moon... I guess the sun wouldn't help you. LAW: To make the country follow a decent track. (?) If there were no laws, everybody would do what they want, there wouldn't be any justice—be lots of criminals. LICENSE: Uh—never knew—never really thought about it. I suppose just to make it legal and so they'd have a record of it (1). DEAF: I don't know. Well, they can't hear, wouldn't know what to say (1). RAW SCORE: 9.

Information

PRESIDENT: +; (Who was president before Roosevelt?) I had it in American history: Teddy Roosevelt or Coolidge. THERMOMETER: Thing you... registers the weather, or in your mouth, the temperature; +. RUBBER: Plant... tree... or bush, or something. (?) Plant... in Borneo or South America and Dutch East Indies; +. LONDON: +. PINTS: 4... (?) No, never good at arithmetic... maybe 2. (?) 2. WEEKS: +. ITALY: +. JAPAN: +. HEIGHT: +. PLANE: Well, those two brothers, the Wrights... They really didn't. Da Vinci back in 1200 had some designs; +. BRAZIL: +. PARIS: +. HEART: Pumps blood to the rest of your body, keeps you going (with finger, traces outward from heart on his chest); +. HAMLET: +. POPULATION: +. WASHINGTON: July 4th... No, Washington's birthday is February 22 (slight laugh). I was thinking of Independence Day; +. POLE: Byrd... (smiles)... I don't know. EGYPT: +. H. FINN: +. VATICAN: +. KORAN: dk., what is it? FAUST: Wagner. HABEAS CORPUS: Something in a law court. (?) I heard it but I can't place it... Have it in a trial... corpus... I don't know. ETHNOLOGY: dk. APOCRYPHA: The fifth part of the Bible... The earliest part of the Bible. (?) Earliest. (?) No, I can't remember. RAW SCORE: 18.

Digit Span

FORWARD: "I'm no good at this." 3, 4, 5, 6 on first try; fails both series of 7 by adding extra digits. BACKWARDS: "Oh god!" 3 and 4 on first try—some difficulty with series of 4, repeats forward first; fails first series of 5, passes second by repeating series forward first. Tries series of 6, gives only a few digits and says, "I don't know. I'm terrible at these things. I hate numbers." RAW SCORE: 11.

Arithmetic

Comments, "I hate arithmetic." ITEM 1: +. ITEM 2: +. ITEM 3:

+. ITEM 4: 12 ... no 9; +. ITEMS 5, 6, 7: +. ITEM 8: 300, I guess. 2/3 of 400 is 275 ... I don't know. (More or less?) Less I guess. 2/3 ... (?) More. (?) I don't know if it's more or less. First thing to do would be to take 2/3 of 400. ITEM 9: 3, I guess. (?) I'm sure I can't do this. I never used to do my homework. I'd divide 10 into 150. That would be 15 I guess, then divide 15 by 5, get 3. (?) Oh! feet and yards. There are 3 feet in a yard, aren't there? ... so it would be 9 (90"); +. ITEM 10: One man I guess; no 1½. It doesn't make any sense. Only need 1½ I guess. (?) About 40 I guess. (More or less?) More. (1 day?) 6 times 8 is 48, no ... 8 times 8 is 64, that's right 48; divide 48 by 2 is 24. (?) 48 for 1 day ... (More or less?) Oh, so you'd need 2 times 48 is 96 (205"). RAW SCORE: 8.

Similarities

ORANGE: Fruit (2). COAT: Clothes (2). DOG: Animals (2). WAGON: Wheels, they both have wheels (1). DAILY PAPER: News (1). AIR: Traveling, I guess; both substances or whatever you call them. (?) Substances. (?) I immediately think of traveling because I like to travel; used to travel a lot when I was little. WOOD: Well, alcohol is made out of wood, isn't it? EYE: Part of your face (1). EGG: Egg and seed ... both the beginnings of something. Seed is necessary for the egg ... give to the mother so that the egg comes out. (Necessary for egg?) For the chicken, the hen has to be fed. POEM: Something that was written in the past or done in the past. They don't ring a bell at all. (?) I always thought of a statue commemorating a person in the past, and a poem is old. PRAISE: I wouldn't have the vaguest idea. (?) I suppose in order to be praised, you have to be punished. (?) Or vice versa. (?) If you're praised you're usually punished too. (?) I don't know, I really don't know. I better not say anything. FLY: Both nature I guess ... part of nature (1). RAW SCORE: 10.

Picture Arrangement

HOUSE: + 5" (2). HOLD UP: + 7"; snickers while telling the story (2). ELEVATOR: + 7" (2). FLIRT: JNAET 20"; "It's quite amusing." (3). FISH: EFGHIJ 47"; "Diver is down there to scare up some fish." (3). TAXI: MLEUAS 55"; "It doesn't make any sense whatsoever. He hailed a taxi, had a dummy with him. It starts to lean over to him in the cab and he's rather surprised and gets out. (Was hailing taxi first picture?) Yes. (Sure?) No ... it didn't make much sense to me." RAW SCORE: 12.

Picture Completion

NOSE: +. MUSTACHE: +. EAR: +. DIAMOND: +. LEG: +. TAIL: The tail, if a pig has a tail; +. STACKS: +. KNOB: The number on the door or something there ... the latch ... or door handle; door handle; +. SECOND HAND: Minute hand (points to second hand). (?) The minute hand, the little one; +. WATER: +. REFLECTION: (looks closely) She's powdering her reflection it looks like ... A table leg gone, and she's missing an arm. (?) Looks ridiculous. (?) She doesn't seem to be powdering anything; anyway, the reflection is wrong. I don't see the arm (60''). TIE: +. THREADS: I don't know anything about bulbs so I wouldn't know whatever it's supposed to be. (?) I never looked at a light bulb—it has a queer shape (points to the tip); no screws down here (50''). EYEBROW: +. SHADOW: +. RAW SCORE: 13.

Block Designs

ITEM 1: 13''; moves slowly, no hurry (4). ITEM 2: 18'' (3). ITEM 3: 13'' (4). ITEM 4: 34'' (3). ITEM 5: 53'' (3). ITEM 6: 142''; tries fitting blocks in diagonally, persists (3). ITEM 7: 300''; tries diagonal fitting again, turns head to side and looks at design from left side, builds around periphery, puts block in place and rotates it till it fits, makes two errors; "There it's done; it's amazing! Is it wrong? (?) (Checks carefully.) Yes, as far as I can see. (Check again!) Oh, no. This is supposed to be red." Corrects, then mixes up all the blocks. RAW SCORE: 20.

Object Assembly

ITEM 1: 49''; tries arms in wrong sockets, then reverses; tries to put them in at wrong angle, turns one over, pushes it in. "Is it wrong?" Looks carefully and corrects. While examiner writes, turns arm over again to wrong side and then back in a provocative manner (6). ITEM 2: 58'' (7). ITEM 3: 53''; "I suppose it's a hand." Two fingers reversed; "It doesn't look right at all." Corrects, then mixes up pieces by pushing them away from him (7). RAW SCORE: 20.

Digit Symbol

42 correct; no errors. RAW SCORE: 42.

Vocabulary

APPLE: A fruit (1). DONKEY: Animal (1). JOIN: To put together (1). DIAMOND: Jewel (1). NUISANCE: Pest (1). FUR: (grimaces) Sable or mink . . . animal. (?) Pelt (1). CUSHION: Pillow (1). SHILLING: You mean how much it's worth? (?) A coin. (?) About 25 cents, 50 cents in English currency (1). GAMBLE: Try your luck, take a chance; to dissipate. (?) Throw away ($\frac{1}{2}$). BACON: Pig . . . Oh no, what does it mean? . . . Something to eat. (?) Off a pig (1). NAIL: You could call it . . . something you hammer into something to put it together (1). CEDAR: Kind of a tree (1). TINT: . . . Kind of a color, shade of a color (1). ARMORY: Guns, place where guns are kept, armor is stored (1). FABLE: Myth (1). BRIM: Edge (1). GUILLOTINE: Something you cut your head off with . . . the French (1). PLURAL: . . . The plural of a word is . . . the . . . two . . . two things, in double: . . . car, cars ($\frac{1}{2}$). SECLUDE: To hide away (1). NITROGLYCERINE: Explosive (1). STANZA: A line in poetry ($\frac{1}{2}$). MICROSCOPE: To look at something, at a little ant or something, magnifies it. (?) Something you look down, see germs or something (1). VESPER: Evening services (1). BELFRY: In a tower . . . the bells. (?) Bell tower (1). RECEDE: Sink away, sink down. (?) To go down, go away. (?)

Just go down, sink away—the water recedes in the drain (½). AFFLIC-TION: An illness or wound (½). PEWTER: China, some kind of china. BALLAST: Something to do with a boat, bottom of a boat. I don't know what it is. CATACOMB: Underneath the earth, place where the Jews hid in old Roman days; a refuge. (?) Refuge. SPANGLE: An earring, something that shines and hangs on something, sort of a jingle or bob; don't know what you call it (½). ESPIONAGE: Spies, spy rings. (?) Secret service (1). IMMINENT: Prominent. (Spelled.) ...Impeccable. (?) Of worthy character. (Sure?) Yes, I suppose so. MANTIS: Kind of animal, praying mantis, locust or something (1). HARA KIRI: Japanese suicide (1). CHATTEL: To talk, to babble. (Spelled.) dk. (?) Thought it would be like chatter; a fob maybe, to hang on a watch. DILATORY: Studious. (?) When someone studies hard; don't think I know what it means. AMANUENSIS: dk. PROSELYTE: Something in the Bible; dk.; parasite it sounds like. MOIETY: dk. ASEPTIC: Something to clean a wound; dk. FLOUT: Float? (Spelled.) Oh, to show. TRADUCE: To understand. (?) To comprehend; no, I was thinking of translate; maybe to make simpler. (?) Make it easier. (Sentence?) He traduced it easily. RAW SCORE: 27.

Weighted Scores and IQ's

Comprehension 8	Picture Arrangement 11	Vocabulary 12
Information 13	Picture Completion 13	Verbal IQ: 105
Digit Span 9	Block Designs 10	Performance IQ: 106
Arithmetic 10	Object Assembly 12	Total IQ: 107
Similarities 8	Digit Symbol 10	

LEARNING EFFICIENCY

IMMEDIATE RECALL: There was a terrible (flood) in Albany about December 6 and all those bridges were sort of washed away and there was a great flood and 400 people were homeless and a little man, I mean a (little boy) was drowning or something and (a man) tried to (help) him and (his hands were cut). SCORE: 7, after subtracting 1 for "bridges washed away" and 1 for "400 people were homeless".

DELAYED RECALL: Well, there was a terrible (flood) in this (town) (10 miles) (from Albany) and (the streets were flushed with water) and (14 people) lost their lives and (600) were killed—I mean were made homeless and it was all very grim and tragic and then this little (boy) had cut his hand—no!—was drowning and the (man) tried (to help him) and he (cut his hands) trying to pull the boy under the water. Oh yes, and this happened (a week before) (December 6). SCORE: 10, after subtracting 1 for "600 made homeless", 1 for "all very grim and tragic", and 1 for "pull the boy under the water".

SORTING TEST

Part I

(Forced, inappropriate laughter throughout test.) MATCHES: Adds all smoking materials. "I suppose this is a cigar too (rubber cigar).

You need matches to light the cigarette, cigar and pipe." Adequate sorting, concrete concept. LARGE FORK: Adds all silverware and sugar. "All on the table." Mildly loose sorting, concrete concept. PIPE: See first sorting. BELL: Adds lock. "Reminds me of a bicycle." Narrow sorting, concrete concept. CIRCLE: Adds index card and cardboard square. "They are all paper." Mildly narrow sorting, abstract concept. TOY PLIERS: Adds all tools and nails. "They're all mechanical things and could be in a tool box. (?) For fixing a car." Much later, patient says, "This (block with nail) goes with it too. I didn't see it, obviously (laughs)." Adequate sorting; first concept is close to an abstract definition, second is concrete. BALL: Adds sink stopper and eraser. "All the rubber things." Mildly narrow sorting, abstract concept.

Part II

RED: (laughs) "I wouldn't know; let's see. I haven't the vaguest idea (laughs)." Failure. METAL: "All iron or tin or something. (?) All metal of some sort." Abstract concept. ROUND: "It's just a mixture of odd things. I wouldn't know." Failure. TOOLS: "I thought immediately they're all dangerous, but they're all mechanical, used in a home or shop. (?) Dangerous things you could kill somebody with (laughs)." Syncretistic concept, then functional concept. PAPER: "Paper." Abstract concept. PAIRS: "All in a couple—pairs." Abstract concept. WHITE: "Doesn't ring a bell at all. (?) No." Failure. RUBBER: "All rubber." Abstract concept. SMOKING MATERIALS: "The matches light all of them, the matches are necessary." Concrete concept. SILVERWARE: "They're three plastic and three silver ones of the same kind, red plastic and silver. (?) All silverware." Split-narrow to abstract concept. TOYS: "Well, the knife, fork, spoon and the two rubber things and the hammer and screw driver. (?) Three separate things. (?) No." Split - narrow failure. RECTANGLES: "Don't know . . . doesn't represent anything, to me anyway." Failure. Patient blandly comments, "I'd love to know what this test meant. Do I ever know?"

RORSCHACH TEST

CARD I. Reaction time: 9″. Total time: 75″.

Oh, I saw this in that movie. 1. Looks like a bat. 2. An ant or something; no, no. [(?) Just thought the whole thing looked sort of like an ant, but it really didn't.] 3. Oh, yes, two faces on either side (nose is upper side wing). [(?) A sinister face, sort of grim. (?) Human.] 4. Sort of a figure in the middle (lower center). [(?) A shadow. (?) Just the bottom. (?) Just a figure, kind of sort of like a woman's figure.] That's all I can see.

SCORES. 1: W F+A P. 2: W F−A Orig Absurd. 3: D F∓Hd Fabulation. 4: Dr F±Hd.

CARD II. Reaction time: 11″. Total time: 150″.

1. Looks like two disagreeable people sticking their tongues out at each other, sitting opposite each other. [(Disagreeable?) The tongues, and the red signified disagreeableness or anger.] That's all I can see in

the thing. (?) > 2. It could be two cows, two little cows rubbing their
noses together, the dark part. I don't know ... two dogs, two little
animals and they're very nice looking little things. [(?) I don't know,
they just looked nice: little furry animals. I've always liked dogs. (?)
The darkness (Nice?) Don't know, they just struck me like that. (?) Just
dark and they looked as if they would be furry. I can't explain it.]

SCORES. 1: W M+H P; D C Anger Fabulation Aggression Symbolic. 2: D FC'+Ad P Fabulation.

CARD III. Reaction time: 11″. Total time: 130″.

1. Two very gay people, sort of leaning over warming their hands
at a fire. < ∧ That's all. I don't know what the red means. [(?) They
looked as if they might be running; kind of happy. (?) Sort of a bowl.
I don't know what it could be; just looked like a fire, or a stove; some
coal burning.] 2. These two here could be two birds shot down (side
red). They look like chickens. It doesn't make any sense though. They
look as if they're falling. [(?) Just the way they were heading down,
with wing down, head at bottom, tail.] That's all (laughs).

SCORES. 1: W M+H P Fabulation. 2: D F+A Aggression.

CARD IV. Reaction time: 20″. Total time: 120″.

1. First, they look like two little skunks (half of card, omitting
bottom center D and upper side projections) ; long bushy tails (lower
side), very graceful. [(?) Just the bushy tail first struck me. (?) Sort
of the growth at the end. First the card looked pleasant and then sinister
because of the snake heads (see 3rd response). (Growth?) Shadow, sort
of shaded.] 2. It looks like they might be sea horses, unicorns (same
area as skunk but without lower sides). [(?) They looked so graceful,
without the shadow of the tail, if you didn't notice the bushy tail (can't
point out head of skunk or sea horse).] No, they don't look like skunks
at all. That's all I can see. No, I can't see anything. 3. The two heads
could be snakes maybe (upper side projections). [(?) Looked very ugly,
long, slimy looking. (?) Because it was so black.].

SCORES. 1: D FCh—A Fabulation. 2: Dr F—A Fabulation. 3: D FC'+
Ad Fabulation.

CARD V. Reaction time: 20″. Total time: 120″.

1. When I first saw it, I thought they were two figures lying in a
forest, two women with long hair (side figures). [(Forest?) The bodies
were sort of light and when I first looked at them, it looked as if all the
dark hair was sort of woods (whole side D) .] 2. That looks like a butterfly too, the middle (only the center section) and the butterfly has some
beautiful jewels on top (usual antennae), very attractive, rather pleasant
(sigh). [(?) Just the center, and the head was very pretty. (?) The
wings might have been sort of dark. (Jewels?) Sparkling; I don't know,
just struck me like that, little sort of stones in the head.] That's about
all I can see.

SCORES. 1: D MC'+H—Forest Contamination. 2: Dr FC'±A (P)
Confabulation.

CARD VI. Reaction time: 5″. Total time: 135″.

1. Looks like a fur rug, one of those sort of luxurious bear rugs, spread out on the floor. [(?) Just the way it was sort of out (gestures, arms out). I saw one hanging in a store once and I wanted it. (?) The lines in it, the round lines.] 2. The top though, looks sort of like a ... looks like a jewel too, looks like diamonds on the white part, and looks sparkling as if it has stones in it again (tip of upper D). [(?) I've always liked diamonds. The pavement in New York on a bright day sort of sparkles. (?) The chips of stone, sun lighting it. This looked like that. (?) The contrast with the black in center and the white.] The bear's sort of a soft and nice, woolly, furry beast; sort of the thing you might have hanging on the wall.

SCORES. 1: D FCh + Ad P Fabulation. 2: Dr C′F Jewels Fabulation.

CARD VII. Reaction time: 22″. Total time: 195″.

1. Mm ... I don't know why they look like two little figures, two horses, very elegant figures, standing on their heads (upper two thirds); might be lions, looks as if they're laughing. Just these two. [(?) Looked sort of like a gay smile, both looked very happy, both little girls (see second response), or lions, or horses, having fun, frolicking.] I don't know what the other is. I don't know why I always think of animals. I don't know, these two don't strike me at all (lower thirds). Can you look at it upside down? ∨ 2. From this side, it looks like two little girls playing, with no heads (upper two thirds). [(?) They look as if they're wearing high stockings and skirts little girls wear; sort of Alice in Wonderland stuff. (Happy?) The way the dress is flying and their figures, might be clapping their hands.] ∨ I still can't make out that (lower one-third). That's all that strikes me.

SCORES. 1: D F∓A Fabulation. 2: D M + H Incompleteness.

CARD VIII. Reaction time: 10″. Total time: 135″.

1. When I first looked at it, it looked like two intestines, two stomachs, you know, those anatomical charts. [(?) The whole thing. (?) I don't know, I've really never studied one; just struck me. (?) It's silly. (?) It was colored, colored part might be stomach or what do you call it?] 2. And then my second look at it, it looks like two frogs (side pink). They're sort of holding on to someone's hands, each one is holding on to somebody's hand (sides of upper gray-green). 3. It might be a man (upper gray-green) swimming under water and the frogs are shaking hands with him. [(?) It looks like he's swimming in water. I didn't notice any head.] ∧ ∨ That's all it looks like.

SCORES. 1: W C/F Ats. 2: D F∓ A (P). 3: D M−H Orig Confabulation.

CARD IX. Reaction time: 22″. Total time: 115″.

(Picks up card, laughs.) I like it. It's very nice. 1. It might be ... looks like a fountain and water (middle space); very elegant picture. [(?) In the middle it was sort of greenish. (Water?) Sort of a sea-green looking (fountain not really seen).] 2. Or it might be a champagne glass (space). [(?) Looked as if the champagne glass was being crushed by more solid things in life (colored areas), and the violin (see third response) was sort of stuck under the water, sort of Lost Genius. (Glass?) The whitish color.] 3. Or this might be a violin here (lower part of center space). It looks very pretty. I like the color. ∨ That's all.

SCORES. 1: S C Water Confabulation. 2: WS FC′+Obj Confabulation. 3: S F∓Obj Confabulation Contamination Symbolic.

CARD X. Reaction time: 27″. Total time: 285″.

(Laughs.) This is very complicated. 1. It looks like two women in pink nightgowns (pink). They're very bitchy; they don't like each other. They're fighting over something. [(?) Pink sort of symbolizes a woman.] 2. And there's green on the bottom, sort of signifies envy. 3. Then these two crabs (side blue) look as if they're fighting: the two women and the two crabs. [(?) The crabs looked angry at each other and that symbolized that the women were mad at each other.] The two heads up here (upper gray) could sort of symbolize the heads of the women; don't look like them. [(?) The two heads at the top looked sort of like crabs too.] And the women aren't ordinary women. They're very beautiful. [(?) Graceful pose.] Yes, and these arms, they look as if they might be ready to smack one another. 4. And these two things are laughing (middle yellow). They're people laughing at them. [(?) Might be two lions. (Lions or people?) People; I think they're people. Might be two men. Lions could signify males: two husbands maybe.] 5. And this just makes them look rich for some reason (lower green). [(?) The way the thing was draped. (?) It was green and expensive looking. It looked like a curtain over a French window.] That's all I can see.

SCORES. 1: DM/C+H Fabulation Aggression Peculiar; DC Woman Symbolic. 2: D C Envy Symbolic. 3: D F+A P Fabulation Aggression. 4: D Ms−H Orig, Absurd; D F+A. 5: D FC+Obj Fabulation.

Summary of Responses

R: 31   EB: 7–8

W 6	F+ 4	A 10	W% 19
D 19	F± 1	Ad 3	D% 61
Dr 4	F∓ 4	H 7	DR% 19
S 2+1	F− 2	Hd 2	
	M 3+, 1−	Obj 3	F% 35-81
Qualitative	MC′ 1+	Ats 1	F+% 45-64
Fabulation 15	M/C 1+	Water 1	
Confabulation 6	Ms 1−	Envy 1	A% 42
Contamination 2	FC 1+	Anger 1	H% 29
Absurd 2	C/F 1	Female 1	P 6 (2)
Symbolic 5	C 4	Jewels 1 (1)	P% 19 (26)
Peculiar 1	FC′ 3+, 1±		Orig 3−
Aggressive 5	C′F 1		Orig% 10
Incompleteness 1	FCh 1+, 1∓		

WORD ASSOCIATION TEST

HAT—1.5"—coat. LAMP—1.5"—chair. LOVE—5"—women (laugh).
[(?) I was just trying to think. I thought of the book *Sons and Lovers*
which I just read; no, *Women in Love*, a D. H. Lawrence book.] BOOK
—2"—writing. FATHER—4"—father? uh... mother. [(?) I was just
trying to think about what would be suitable to say.] PAPER—1"—
desk (3"). BREAST—2"—body (1"—woman). CURTAINS—3"—drapes.
TRUNK—1.5"—key. [(?) I had a trunk once and I'd keep losing the
key, I kept losing the key. I always lose keys.] DRINK—2"—alcohol.
PARTY—3"—fun. SPRING—2"—beauty. BOWEL MOVEMENT—6"—
uh (laugh) constipation. [(?) I'm always constipated.] RUG—2"—floor.
BOY FRIEND—1"—girl friend. CHAIR—4"—uh... couch. [(?) Just in
a room, kind of. (?) Sitting in the anteroom. (Image?) Yes. (Others?)
No... yes; on FIRE because my mother's aunt had been burned in a
fire. I saw a picture of that, that sort of stuck in my mind for some
reason.] SCREEN—3"—door. PENIS—2"—man. RADIATOR—2"—heat.
FRAME—1.5"—picture. SUICIDE—2"—death. MOUNTAIN—5.5"—uh...
tall. [(?) I always imagine a mountain as being tall; I pictured that,
a snowy mountain.] SNAKE—2"—death. [(?) I always hated snakes.]
HOUSE—6.5"—family. [(?) Sort of a happy home, the idea.] (1"—
home, family). VAGINA — 2" — woman. TOBACCO — 2" — cigarette.
MOUTH—2"—lips. HORSE—2"—animal. MASTURBATION—2"—ado-
lescence. WIFE—1.5"—husband. TABLE—4"—wood (3"). FIGHT—4"—
excitement. [(?) I thought of watching a fight I once saw, it was sort
of exciting. (Image?) No.] BEEF—2"—meat (3"). STOMACH—4"—
body (3"). FARM—1.5"—country. MAN—1.5"—woman. TAXES—2"—
money. NIPPLE—1.5"—breast. DOCTOR—4"—uh... sickness. DIRT—
2"—filth. CUT—3.5"—bruise (2"—wound, bruise). MOVIES—3.5"—
cinema (he shrugs). COCKROACH—4"—dirty (he grimaces). [(?)
You know a little cockroach in one's bed (grimace). I remember in
Mexico there was some.] BITE—2"—chew. DOG—1"—cat. DANCE—3.5"
—fun. [(?) What I do at a dance.] GUN—1.5"—shooting. WATER—3.5"
—ocean. [(?) I always like the ocean. (Image?) Yes, ocean beating on
the rocks.] HUSBAND—1"—wife. MUD—1"—dirt. WOMAN—1.5"—man.
FIRE—3"—death. [(?) I thought of that aunt who was burned up in a
fire, and then you know all these awful stories in the newspapers about
these hotel fires.] (Did you say fair? Can't remember that one—country).
SUCK—4"—hmm... mouth (1.5"—lips). MONEY—3"—rich. MOTHER
—1"—father. HOSPITAL — 1" — sickness. GIRL FRIEND — 3.5" — girl
friend? boy friend. TAXI—1.5"—cab. INTERCOURSE—4"—hmm...
man and woman. HUNGER—3"—stomach (3").

ANALYSIS OF RESULTS

BELLEVUE SCALE

The scatter is distinguished by the equality of the Performance and
Verbal levels. This suggests a character problem rather than an acute
illness, since the latter usually more or less depresses the average Per-

formance level. Hysteria might have been suggested if the Information and Comprehension scores were reversed in position, but, as they stand, there is no evidence for the retarding effects of a strong repressive emphasis on verbal-intellectual development. Psychopathic character might have been suggested if the Information and Vocabulary scores were lower; 13 is in the superior range and a score so high is not likely in a clear-cut psychopathic case. The 3-point discrepancy between Vocabulary and Similarities suggests that the condition is one of long-standing. The 5-point discrepancy between Vocabulary and Comprehension indicates poor judgment.

In Information he starts right off with flashy detail and self-references. Going into unnecessary detail, in itself, would suggest obsessiveness but the self-reference on the *president* item and the dating of Da Vinci at 1200 on the *airplane* item betray this verbalization as pretentious rather than pedantic. By now hysteria is ruled out, since the last thing to expect from the usual hysteric is intellectual pretentiousness. On the *Washington* item, even though he spontaneously corrects the response "July 4th", the mere occurrence of this answer has a malignant quality. It cannot be excused as impulsiveness only, even though it is impulsive. When the memory frame of reference becomes so fluid that the most commonplace connections are abandoned, the possible presence of a psychosis must be considered. Thus far a character disorder is strongly indicated and it is likely that it possesses psychotic features.

In Comprehension he demonstrates striking egocentricity on the *envelope* and *theatre* items. There is an implicit self-reference on *land* (referring to his home town). Impulsive guessing and low anxiety tolerance are evident in the poor performance on the last three Arithmetic items. He is alternately self-depreciating, irresponsible, and rejecting in this difficult situation. In Similarities the self-reference on the *air-water* item, the fabulation on the *egg-seed* item and the irresponsible, impulsive answers to the *praise-punishment* item are noteworthy. His use of the concept *past* on the *poem-statue* item, in two different senses simultaneously, indicates disorganization.

In Picture Arrangement, his bland snickering and his comment, "Quite amusing", suggest generalized blandness, as does the careless discrepancy between his story and his sequence on the *taxi* item. In Block Designs and Object Assembly his destruction of his finished product and the spiteful spoiling of the mannikin after it was accepted as correct hint at an inclination to aggressive, negativistic acting-out.

The impulsive and bland association-like responses in Vocabulary are inappropriate: *bacon* is a good example of this. There is fluidity evident on *recede* where "sink" changes from a verb to a noun in the course of inquiry, on *traduce* where he goes from "translate"[10]) to "understand" to "make simpler", and on *dilatory* where he apparently recalls the phrase "diligent student" and reasons, syncretistically, that diligent means studious. The clang-like guesses on *chattel* (chatter), *dilatory* (diligent), *flout* (float), *imminent* (eminent, despite spelling), *proselyte* (parasite) are of the type found in character disorders and psychopaths.

In summary, it appears so far that the diagnosis narcissistic character disorder will not embrace all the indications, although it could take care of the bland, impulsive, irresponsible features. The very poor judgment and the fluidity of associations, memories and reasoning speak for a schizophrenic condition. More conclusive evidence is needed for the latter conclusion.

LEARNING EFFICIENCY

The devastated learning efficiency is a conclusive indication of schizophrenia, since there is no reason to believe that severe depression, mental deficiency, or organic brain damage is present. In general the distortions and recombinations are confabulatory in nature; the emotional connotations are done up in grand style. The psychopath, whose tests are analyzed in this chapter, had poor learning efficiency, but the drop below his Vocabulary level was not so great and the structure of the story was fairly well-retained.

SORTING TEST

In Part I, his concepts are mainly concrete although a capacity for using abstract concepts is indicated. No loosening is evident here. Part II is very poor, however, and indicates therefore that this is a condition of long standing. A depressive could do so badly or perhaps an unintelligent person, but he is neither of these. A schizophrenic background for this impairment is suggested by his response to the *tools* item in Part II: "Dangerous things you could kill somebody with," followed by bland laughter. This cannot be excused as only an expression of aggressiveness, which is undoubtedly involved, because the formal aspect of the concept is so arbitrary as to imply that it took schizophrenic inappropriateness of affect to allow the aggressive thought to make its appearance just then. The breezy irresponsible answer on the *round* item—"It's just a mixture of odd things"—is more typical of non-psychotic character disorders.

---

10) Probably taken from the French verb *traduire*.

There can be little doubt at this point that this is a schizophrenia; whatever doubts remain will be put to rest by the Rorschach Test record. What needs to be decided is whether this is an acute or chronic condition, and what the distinguishing features of the psychosis are. On the basis of the impaired Part II of the Sorting Test, the well-retained Performance level in the Bellevue Scale and the blandness, the condition appears to be a chronic one; on the basis of the numerous features suggestive of a character disorder it is likely that this is not a schizophrenia which falls into any of the classical subgroups, but that it is a psychosis so closely interwoven with the character make-up that the diagnosis *schizophrenic character* is warranted. Aggressive acting-out, involving basically defective reality testing and blandness, and confabulatory thinking are likely to dominate the clinical picture.

RORSCHACH TEST

The summary of scores supports, and in itself could establish, the diagnostic picture already arrived at. The record is replete with fabulations and confabulations, symbolic reasoning, contaminations, and fluidity. Hardly a response is untainted by egocentricity or fantastic elaboration. Reality testing is weak (low $F+\%$, $M-$, absurd percepts) and affect is labile and inappropriate (4 C's, lavish reactions to the cards). A Rorschach Test record of this type could be obtained from an acute schizophrenic, but the blandness running throughout this and the other tests and the indications of chronicity in the other tests eliminate this possibility. Nor could this be a chronic stage of a more usual schizophrenic process, since that would require a flatter record (less M and generally less florid productions). The pervasiveness of the fantastic elaborations suggests that this type of thinking is thoroughly interwoven and well-established in all aspects of life. The frequency of affect-dominated and symbolically-rooted connections suggests that paranoid reference ideas are likely to be present or to develop.

When fantastic responses are as dominant as they are here, it is implied that a sharp distinction between fact and fantasy in everyday affairs is no longer maintained, that bizarre ideas are likely to be casually accepted, and that vivid fantasying is generally conspicuous. The 4 C responses and the virtual absence of FC responses indicate that impulsive acts will occur and that the affects accompanying these acts and their consequences will be inappropriate. The relatively widespread presence of aggressive responses indicates that many of these impulsive acts are likely to be aggressive; a good part of the aggressions is likely to be absorbed in fantasy, however. The 3 S's on IX indicate conspicuous negativism, and are reminiscent of his behavior during the administration of the Bellevue Scale.

Fluidity of affective experience is indicated on Card IV where the "graceful skunks" take on a sinister quality once the snakes are perceived, and on Card X where the "bitchy women" soon become graceful and beautiful as well. These indications plus the 4 C's suggest that mood swings will be conspicuous. Fluidity of ideas is indicated by many responses; one good example is the "people laughing" response on Card X: upon inquiry, they turn out to be lions; he covers up quickly with a symbolic connection—"Lions could signify males". Another example is the "envy" response on Card X: the same lower green area later becomes symbolic of wealth in the context of the same confabulation. The many M's indicate how sharp and creative he is likely to be in some of his thinking, probably frequently transcending in brightness the level implied by his IQ.

The "crushed champagne glass" and "Lost Genius" on Card IX probably express subjective feelings, of a partly contradictory nature to be sure, but nevertheless hinting at deep feelings of despair. The "pleasant" skunk on Card IV seems to express somewhat the same contradiction in his self-conception as "champagne glass" and "genius" on Card IX. A rejection of women as hostile figures is suggested on Card X.

WORD ASSOCIATION TEST

Because the reactions are generally orderly, this test suggests that some front of appropriateness may be present; in the light of the Rorschach Test results we can see that it is not likely to be sustained very well. The responses to *love, bowel movement,* and *trunk* are noteworthy. Most striking however are the indications of vivid aggressive fantasies in his reactions to *house, fire,* and *snake.*

Test Report

Intelligence and Thought Organization: It is indicated that this is a person whose overall intelligence level (IQ of 107) is below the superior level to which he can rise and that this discrepancy is one manifestation of a weakness of ego integration. There are marked fluctuations in the quality of his reality testing, ranging from the sharp and creative to the absurd and fantastic. Judgment is exceptionally poor, with respect both to grasp of conventional ideas and to independent action. The distinction between fact and fantasy is poorly maintained. Unrealistic ideas and actions are likely to be numerous. Bland, recklessly impulsive confabulations with a pretentious quality characterize much of his thinking.

Thoughts merge with each other or replace each other fluidly and his capacity for sustained concentration is weak. Thoughts in general are also dominated by more or less inappropriate, easily stimulated, intense affects; they are largely egocentric and concrete. Arbitrary relationships between ideas or events, based on emotional or symbolic meanings rather than logical coherence, are the chief results of his integrative efforts; this suggests that paranoid reference ideas are likely to be present.

Emotional Factors: Affects have an intense, volatile quality and are released with trigger-fast impulsivity and minimal critical restraint. His emotional lability reflects on the one hand a potentiality for marked mood swings, fears and impulsive acting-out, and on the other hand a basic instability of object-attachments, inappropriateness of much of his affective experience and a basically narcissistic orientation to the world. Deep feelings of despair are indicated. His tolerance for anxiety-arousing situations is low and he characteristically tends to avoid them. For the most part he appears to be bland with respect to his highly deviant thoughts and behavior. Strong pent-up aggressions are indicated and, although the aggressions appear to be absorbed to a large extent in fantasy, the poor controls implied in his impulsiveness probably permit aggressive, anti-social outbursts. He appears to be particularly aggressive toward women. The confabulatory quality of his thinking plus the impulsiveness plus a capacity to put up a fair front of coherence suggest that he may superficially resemble a psychopath, but the schizophrenia should nevertheless be clear upon closer inspection.

Diagnostic Impression: This appears to be a schizophrenic character disorder distinguished by fluid and fantastic thoughts, inappropriate emotional lability, mood swings and impulsiveness, and blandness with respect to his violations of logic, fact, and prohibition.

CLINICAL SUMMARY

Mr. V., a nineteen-year-old son of a wealthy California family, was referred for examination because of inability to settle down after discharge from the army, anti-social behavior, and quarrels with his mother. He states that he came to please her.

His parents were divorced when he was two years old and since then he has been the responsibility of his mother. His mother has always been interested mainly in a gay social life and has had many lovers, which the patient knows about. She gave him little attention, sending him to boarding schools and going abroad for a long period. His attitude toward her is openly ambivalent. The father is described by the patient as lazy and worthless and the patient desperately hopes not to become a man of his father's type.

He has had temper tantrums from an early age whenever he has not been able to get his own way. He has never had close friends and has engaged extensively in vivid fantasying. The fantasies perseveratively deal with his mother's romances and with wealth. His behavior has been described as insolent and snobbish. His grandiose fantasies were bolstered when he won a prize for a composition in school. Since then he has had little use for education and has been considering himself a potentially great man. In one series of arguments with his mother he smashed furniture and tried to set fire to the apartment. He got his father drunk so he could gather information about his mother's liaisons and then confronted her with this information to torment her. Sexual relations have generally been avoided. His school history is one of destructive behavior, infringement of rules, and expulsions. His army history is one of frequent AWOL's, snobbish rejection of fellow soldiers and final neuropsychiatric discharge after eleven months. His work plans afterwards were exceptionally confused and irrealistic. He now has grandiose plans about becoming rich by writing and then living a notorious, daring life, and has given no thought to the problems and obstacles involved in this undertaking. He is emotionally labile, frequently giving way to irritable outbursts and mild depression. He complains of always having felt a "colossal emptiness and loneliness" because of his poor social relations. He describes his utterly narcissistic orientation to people in a strikingly frank (bland?) manner. He is hostile to his father, mother and brother, and cannot take orders from anybody. He worries about accidents happening to him and is therefore in a hurry to become a success before an accident makes this impossible. His vivid fantasies appear to color his percepts, attitudes, plans and behavior in many areas. The diagnosis was schizophrenic character disorder. The test results indicate this diagnosis more strongly than the initial clinical findings.

PARANOID CONDITION: TEST RESULTS

Mrs. P. Age: 50. Education: High school. Occupation: Housewife; was accountant. Marital: 24 years; no children. Husband: Engineer. Father: Farmer. Early Environment: Farm. Family Position: Oldest of 3. Religion: Protestant.

BELLEVUE SCALE
Comprehension
ENVELOPE: Mail it (2). THEATRE: I would notify an usher (2). BAD COMPANY: It's a trend toward living the same kind of a

life, get bad yourself (2). TAXES: It's part of their government duties; goes to keep up schools, roads and everything that one enjoys (1). SHOES: Let's see . . . durable, better for the feet. I don't know. I never heard that question before (1). LAND: Well, I suppose more conveniences to offer, trading centers are closer, and you have more things to enjoy in the city than in the country, so it would cost more (1). FOREST: If I could see the sun, I would figure it out from that, and they say there is moss on the north side of trees. (?) You would know about what time of day it was and you know the sun's direction at that time: it rises in the east and sets in the west (2). LAW: To make good citizens out of us; to keep the unruly under control (1). LICENSE: To make the court record and make it legal (1). DEAF: They never catch the sound. I don't know. I've never thought about that. If they can't hear, they'll have to learn how to talk some other way (2). RAW SCORE: 15.

Information

PRESIDENT: +. THERMOMETER: +. RUBBER: +. LONDON: +. PINTS: 4. (?) 2 pints in a quart, 4 quarts in a gallon. WEEKS: +. ITALY: +. JAPAN: +. HEIGHT: +. PLANE: dk. BRAZIL: +. PARIS: About 3,000 miles. Is that right? +. HEART: Oh, I don't know. Circulates the blood, I guess; +. HAMLET: +. POPULATION: About 10 million I expect. Some of these are guesses. I don't know the exact population. WASHINGTON: 14th of February. Let's see: Lincoln is the 12th. It's the 22nd. I was thinking of Valentine's Day; +. POLE: Byrd. EGYPT: Asia. H. FINN: I should know that maybe, but I can't think of it. VATICAN: It's in Rome. It's the temple for a part of their religious government, isn't it? (?) Catholic church; +. KORAN: I don't know, but I know what Korea is: it's a country. FAUST: I can't think of it, but I know. HABEAS CORPUS: A procedure in court. I don't know. I've never been in court. ETHNOLOGY: Would that have something to do with ethnoid treatment. (?) I just heard doctors talking about ethnoid treatment. APOCRYPHA: dk. RAW SCORE: 14.

Digit Span

Forward: passes 3, 4, 5, 6, 7 on first try; fails both series of 8—digits in jumbled order, new ones inserted, some left out. "I can't get that one and I used to do all kinds of numbers." BACKWARDS: passes 3, 4, 5 on first try; fails first series of 6; fails first series of 7, with one incorrect digit; fails both series of 8. RAW SCORE: 14.

Arithmetic

ITEMS 1-8: +; very fast. ITEM 9: 15 yards a second. In 1/5 of a second, it would be 3, no, would be 9 feet (27″). You tax me; I haven't been in this sort of stuff for 40 years; +. ITEM 10: ++ (6″). RAW SCORE: 11.

Similarities

ORANGE: Fruit (2). COAT: Wearing apparel (2). DOG: Animal (2). WAGON: Vehicles (2). DAILY PAPER: Means of news (1). AIR: Elements (1). WOOD: How do you mean? . . . Fuel or . . . (?) Fuel. (Or what?) I didn't know (1). EYE: Two of the senses (2). EGG: Food.

POEM: Both ... I don't know. A poem is literature and a statue is art. Both educational. PRAISE: If you mean how they are alike, I don't know. (?) (Shakes head.) They seem opposite to me. (?) (Shakes head.) FLY: They are supposed to be outside (laugh) but flies aren't always. (?) A fly and tree, how are they alike? ... I don't know. (?) No, one is a pest and one is a pleasure. I don't get the connection. RAW SCORE: 13.

Picture Arrangement

HOUSE: + 4″ (2). HOLD UP: + 8″ (2). ELEVATOR: + 25″; what is this thing, something on the street? (?) Freight elevator from a basement (2). FLIRT: AJNET 73″; I don't know what this is supposed to be. Are these officers (chauffeurs)? This one is colored and this one isn't (woman). Oh, this is just the back of her head. Now I know, I see now (2). FISH: JFHEGI 52″; aren't these two (pictures) alike? (?) It's about a fisherman. He didn't seem to be satisfied with what he caught so he threw his bait bucket back into the water. TAXI: SALEUM 69″; (laughs) seems like this fellow was carrying his friend in and was getting weary so he hailed a taxi and put her in and so for some reason, you can guess, they got together and he looked out the back window to see if anybody was watching (1). RAW SCORE: 9.

Picture Completion

NOSE: +. MUSTACHE: +. EAR: +. DIAMOND: +. LEG: +. TAIL: +. STACKS: +. KNOB: +. SECOND HAND: +. WATER: +. REFLECTION: Leg of the chair. (?) Her right arm. TIE: +. THREADS: +. EYEBROW: +. SHADOW: +. RAW SCORE: 14.

Block Designs

ITEM 1: 6″; uses one hand throughout (5). ITEM 2: 9″ (5). ITEM 3: 11″ (4). ITEM 4: 16″ (4). ITEM 5: 47″; works smoothly and systematically, checks carefully before stating she is finished (4). ITEM 6: 75″; gets the idea of the stripes in 15″, completes smoothly and quickly (4). ITEM 7: 138″; builds design systematically in rows, no errors (4). RAW SCORE: 30.

Object Assembly

ITEM 1: 14″ (6). ITEM 2: 67″; reverses ear and corrects spontaneously (6). ITEM 3: 50″ (7). RAW SCORE: 19.

Digit Symbol

58 correct; no errors. RAW SCORE: 58.

Vocabulary

APPLE: Fruit (1). DONKEY: Animal (1). JOIN: To connect (1). DIAMOND: Gem (1). NUISANCE: Bother, or something aggravating (1). FUR: An animal's coat (1). CUSHION: Pillow (1). SHILLING: English money (1). GAMBLE: To take a chance (1). BACON: Meat (1). NAIL: Used in construction, a piece of small steel (1). CEDAR: Tree or lumber (1). TINT: To color (1). ARMORY: A training station. (?) Used in military training (½). FABLE: A story with a moral (1).

BRIM: Part of a hat. (?) Surrounding the crown. GUILLOTINE: Method of punishment. (?) Well, it's made of wood, put their head, legs and arms through it and proceeded with the punishment that way. PLURAL: More than one (1). SECLUDE: To hide (1). NITRO-GLYCERINE: A drug given sometimes as a heart stimulant; also it's an explosive (1). STANZA: Part of a poem, group of lines (1). MICRO-SCOPE: An instrument to use in bacteria study, and in laboratory work (1). VESPER: Hymn (1). BELFRY: Part of a church, usually in the steeple where the bell is anchored (1). RECEDE: To draw away from (1). AFFLICTION: That is . . . pertains to a human being when some part of their body doesn't function correctly; an invalid or something (½). PEWTER: Metal (½). BALLAST: dk. CATACOMB: dk. SPANGLE: Spangle? Oh, that's a . . . it's a drop of some kind, or a bead used in different kinds of paraphernalia. (?) It could be little metal gadgets with some means of fastening them on (1). ESPIONAGE: Discrete, destructive ideas against one's own country. (Discrete?) What they do is maliciously, . . . what they do they don't want anybody to know. IMMINENT: Friendly. (?) dk. MANTIS: dk. HARA KIRI: Death by suicide (1). CHATTEL: Would that mean personal possessions or property? (1) DILATORY: Not very ambitious. AMANUENSIS, PROSELYTE, MOIETY: dk. ASEPTIC: Sterile (1). FLOUT: Well, I'll guess. Unkind? TRADUCE: I don't know how to tell that one. (?) No. RAW SCORE: 27.5.

Weighted Scores and IQ's

Comprehension 13	Picture Arrangement 8	Vocabulary 12
Information 10	Picture Completion 14	Verbal IQ: 120
Digit Span 13	Block Designs 14	Performance IQ: 131
Arithmetic 15	Object Assembly 11	Total IQ: 127
Similarities 11	Digit Symbol 14	

LEARNING EFFICIENCY

IMMEDIATE RECALL: (December 6) (last week) (a river) rose (10 miles) (from Albany) and (came into the houses) and 10 people were killed and (600) were injured and a small (boy) was (caught) (under a bridge) and (a man) (cut his hands). SCORE: 16.

DELAYED RECALL: Well, let's see. (December 6) (last week) (a river) (overflowed) going into . . . well anyway, (it rose into the streets) and (houses) in a (small town) (10 miles) (from Albany). (14 people) were (drowned) and (600) were ill from (the cold) and (dampness), and a small (boy) was (caught) (under the bridge) and (a man) (cut his hands). SCORE: 19.

SORTING TEST

Part I

LARGE SPOON: Adds large silver, sugar, matches ("You might smoke."), index card ("Is this a check? I guess it might be. I forgot the cigarettes.") "Well, it tends to set up a table. It's the furnishings for a table service. (?) Well, if you ran a restaurant, that (index card) might be for a check." Loose sorting, fabulized concept. PIPE: "Where's your tobacco? (Looks at examiner questioningly.) Well, I guess I'll have to play I'm in a cigar store." Adds all smoking materials. "There! Well, I bought all these things; I might have to pay the check (adds index card). (Laughs.) Well, it's what you'd find at a tobacco counter in a store, a tobacco bar perhaps I should say." Loose sorting, fabulized concept. BELL: ("I suppose some toys for a boy.") Adds toy tools, paper square, ball, lock ("The lock for the bike."), block with nail, nails. "Well, they're play toys for a boy." Loose sorting, abstract and fabulized concept. CIRCLE: ("That looks like school, doesn't it?") Adds chalk, eraser, paper square. "If they're kindergarten age, they'd use the blocks perhaps (refers to paper square). They're things used by kindergarten children, used in kindergarten by them especially." Mildly loose sorting, concrete and fabulized concept. TOY PLIERS: ("That's the thing! I don't know what it is. I'll do the same as I did before.") Adds all toy tools except the hammer. "Well, this is a youngster's tool set. (Reject hammer?) I think that belongs with the nails, more in proportion to it. A child this small wouldn't use nails, if any." Narrow sorting, concrete and fabulized concept. BALL: Adds all toy tools except hammer. "Toys for a small youngster." Narrow sorting, abstract and fabulized concept. TOY FORK: ("Well, I haven't been placing anything for little girls, have I?") Adds small silver and paper square. "These are toys a very young girl would use. (Square?) A block." Mildly loose sorting, abstract and fabulized concept.

Part II

RED: "I don't think they do. (?) Well, one is for a kitchen sink, and I don't see how the others would fit in." Failure. METAL: "They don't. These could be combined (silverware), and these (lock and bell) for the bicycle, and these for a tool kit." Split-narrow failure. ROUND: "They don't!" Failure. TOOLS: "They really don't. They could all be in a tool kit but one's for children and one's for adults." Concrete, split-narrow concept. PAPER: "They don't. (?) Yes, the matches and cigarettes, and these (cards) are toys." Split-narrow failure. PAIRS: (laughs) "Why? I wouldn't think they do. They're mostly useful things, but I wouldn't say that they belong together." Failure. WHITE: "Because they're all white, I guess." Abstract concept. RUBBER: "They don't. (?) Because they're not the same color. (Other way?) You mean because these two are rubber (ball and sink stopper). . . . Oh, this is too . . . Oh, all four are." Near failure, abstract concept. SMOKING MATERIALS: "All pertain to smoking." Abstract concept. SILVERWARE: "Kitchenware." Abstract concept. TOYS: "They don't. (?) They're all toys but this (small hammer) . . . but I guess you can use this for a toy." Split-narrow tendency, abstract concept. RECTANGLES: "I guess because of the shape, either rectangles or square." Abstract concept.

RORSCHACH TEST

CARD I. Reaction time: 12″. Total time: 80″.

Well, it doesn't look like much of anything. 1. It looks like a creation of bones of some kind. [(?) I guess it was the heavy appearance, over and under the shadow. (Creation?) I didn't mean ... maybe I didn't mean creation, some kind of an object, I guess. (whispers) I've got a back ache.] (Returns card.) (Else?) 2. Oh there's a shape similar to a butterfly, I guess, maybe. I don't know. Is it supposed to be some specific something?

SCORES. 1: W ChF At. 2: W F+A P.

CARD II. Reaction time: 3″. Total time: 92″.

1. Clowns. What else do you want to know? (?) It just looks like two clowns. [(?) Oh, I guess it was the coloring and the way they were setting there; it looks like they were in some kind of a pranking mood or something (laughs).] (Else?) 2. Well, the center could be a ceiling light, a chandelier I guess. [(?) Well, the shape of it and it seemed like it had a glow of light under it and one above I believe. (?) The red coloring, is that what you mean?] That's all I see.

SCORES. 1: W MC+H P. 2: S F+Obj; D CF Light.

CARD III. Reaction Time: 70″. Total time: 172″.

(Laughs.) It doesn't look like anything to me. (Laugh ... sigh.) I wouldn't know (sigh) ... (?) 1. No, I guess it wouldn't be men in dress clothes. That's about what I could think of. (Else?) Well, I've told you what I ... what it impresses me as being. (Looks at card again.) 2. That might be part of a lady (lower middle D). [(?) Well, it looked like an evening gown across here.] 3. That (upper red) looks like it could be some entertainers. I don't know. [(Entertainers?) Those little red figures on the sides. (What made it look like that?) Well, it was the position they were in. (?) A graceful position. (Anything else to make them look like entertainers?) (sigh) Well, due to the fact that if those were men in evening clothes, and that was a lady in an evening gown, they would naturally be in some place where there was dancing or entertainment. That would be the way I would interpret it.]

SCORES. 1: (W) D M+H P. 2: D F±Hd. 3: D Ms+H Confabulation.

CARD IV. Failure: 130″.

That doesn't impress me as being anything ... uh, uh ... I don't get anything out of that. (?) I just don't see anything to it. (?) Nope (sigh). (?) No.

CARD V. Failure: 125″.

(Smile.) That doesn't mean anything either ... to me (Smiles, shakes head, picks up card.) It doesn't make a picture for me. I don't know what it's supposed to be. (?) No sir! (sigh).

CARD VI. Failure: 150".

(Laughs, shakes head, picks up card.) I'm sorry, I don't know what those ... They don't mean anything to me. (Laughs.) ... Doesn't mean anything to me (sweetly). ... Still doesn't ... (?) (Sighs, picks up card.) Uh, uh, ... it doesn't. I don't get any picture out of it myself. (Possibly suggest?) No, sir! (?) No, sir!

CARD VII. Reaction time: 175". Total time: 205".

Well, I don't see anything in that. That doesn't make a picture for me. (?) No, sir! I don't know. (?) It doesn't suggest anything to me. (?) No, sir, I don't ... I do not. (?) Well, I don't know. That might be two people down there (sigh) (light part of lower middle Dr). [(Can you describe them?) No, you mean they were standing? I don't know what you want to know.] (?) No, I guess not.

SCORE: (Failure.) Dr F+H.

CARD VIII. Reaction time: 50". Total time: 135".

< ... > ... Hm! Well, the only thing I get out of this, it might be an animal (side pink) some place in the trees (upper gray-green) or animals, in fact. [(Trees?) I guess the shape, perhaps the way the branches came out. (?) Oh, I don't know; they could have been tigers or bears, I guess.] That's all I get. I don't get anything more out of that. (?) That's all I see. (?) (Smiles sweetly.) No, sir!

SCORE: D F+A P; D F+Pl Combination.

CARD IX. Reaction time: 58". Total time: 150".

Well, I don't see anything ... > ... uh, uh ... < Looks a little like it might be a deer right here, a deer head (in shading of green to orange). That's all I get out of it ... It looks gentle ... That's all I see. (?) (Drums fingers on chair.) I don't see anything else. (?) (Shakes head.) (?) That's all.

SCORE: D F+Ad.

CARD X. Failure: 300".

I don't get any certain something out of this. (Smiles sweetly.) I just don't. (Puts card down.) ... It doesn't make a picture for me. (Keep looking!) ... It just doesn't suggest anything to me ... Well, I can't even imagine any thing out there .... (laughs). Well, I don't see anything. (?) Well, you want me to just make up something? (Laughs sweetly.) I don't see ... it doesn't suggest any definite thing to me at all.

CARDS IV, V, VI and X were readministered at the end of the test: on IV, after 60", she saw a cowhide, using shading as a determinant (W FCh+Ad P); on V, after 25", she saw a butterfly (W F+A P); she again failed VI; and on X she saw "the coloring of flowers" (W C Pl).

Summary of Responses

R: 12 (3)   EB: 3—1.5 (3)

W 3 (4)	F+ 6 (1)	A 2 (1)	W% 25 (47)
D 7	F± 1	Ad 2 (1)	D% 58 (47)
Dr 1	M 1+	H 4	DR% 17 (13)
S 1	MC 1+	Hd 1	
	MS 1+	Obj 1	F% 58-83 (53-80)
Qualitative	CF 1	Pl 1 (1)	F+% 100-100
Failures 4 (1)	C (1)	Light 1	
Combination 1	FCh (1+)		A% 33 (40)
Confabulation 1	ChF 1		H% 42 (33)
			P 4 (2)
			P% 33 (40)

WORD ASSOCIATION TEST

HAT—2.5"—wearing apparel. LAMP—2"—light. LOVE—1.5"—affection (1.5"—devotion). BOOK—2"—reading (1"—object, reading, literature, dk.). FATHER—5"—devotion. [(?) Just finding the word I thought suited my father.] PAPER—2"—literature. BREAST—3"—meat. [(?) Thought of chicken sandwich.] CURTAINS—2"—house. TRUNK—2"—travel. DRINK—2"—water (deep sigh). PARTY—1.5"—fun. SPRING—1.5"—season (deep sigh). BOWEL MOVEMENT—7"—(laugh) natural procedure, I guess. [(?) (laugh) First I started to say bathroom... (laugh) then I decided to change it.] RUG—2"—floors (1.5"—house, floor). BOY FRIEND—2"—man. CHAIR—1.5"—object (7"—cheer? I thought you said chair before. Cheer is happiness). SCREEN—1.5"—window. PENIS—2"—anatomy (sigh). [(?) Well, part of a man's anatomy. (?) Just the... my husband's, I guess. (Image?) Probably; dk.] RADIATOR—1.5"—fire. FRAME—3"—picture. SUICIDE—4"—destroy yourself (deep sigh). MOUNTAIN—5"—(startled) **mountains, nature.** [(?) Thought of rock formation made by nature. (Image?) Yes.] SNAKE—2" —reptile (sigh). HOUSE—2"—living (7"). VAGINA—1.5"—anatomy. TOBACCO—4"—vegetable (laughs), plant. [(?) I was thinking of plants really, my mental picture association was of the tobacco fields, I guess.] MOUTH—2.5"—(deep sigh) body. [(?) Oh, just that it was in the head and that's part of the body.] HORSE—1"—animal. MASTURBATION—2.5"—childhood. WIFE—2"—woman. TABLE—2"—furniture (2"—house). FIGHT—2.5"—quarrel (3"—anger). BEEF—1"—meat. STOMACH—1.5"—anatomy. FARM—2"—land. MAN—3"—(deep sigh) husband. [(?) Well, *naturally*, he'd be the first one I'd think of.] TAXES—2"—expenses. NIPPLE—2"—bottle. DOCTOR—1.5"—friend. DIRT—3"—dust (smile). CUT—15"—I don't know (shakes head); I don't know what you call that. Cunt, wasn't it? MOVIES—1"—show. COCKROACH—1"—bug. BITE—2" —(deep sigh) teeth (3"—mouth, teeth). DOG—1"—animal. DANCE—2"—fun. GUN—3"—weapon. WATER—2"—liquid. HUSBAND—2"—(deep sigh) love. MUD—1"—dirt. WOMAN—5"—(deep sigh) uhm... friend, I guess. [(?) My relationship with women would be my friends.] FIRE—

4″—destruction. [(?) Fire burning a house or it could be a fire in a furnace.] SUCK (heard SULK) —3″—impatience. MONEY—2.5″—method of paying bills. MOTHER—2″—(sigh) love. HOSPITAL—1.5″—sickness (3″—illness). GIRL FRIEND—1.5″—chum. SUCK—1.5″—nibble. TAXI—2.5″—transportation. INTERCOURSE—3″—human relations. HUNGER —8.5″—(laugh) wanting of food (2.5″—desire for food).

ANALYSIS OF RESULTS

BELLEVUE SCALE

The high Arithmetic and Picture Completion scores suggest over-alertness, possibly with paranoid coloring. It is true that she has worked as an accountant and that, consequently, the Arithmetic score may be high on an occupational basis. Picture Completion is, however, also high, quite high for a fifty year old woman, and this makes the inference possible. With Information being the lowest Verbal score, with Comprehension well above it, and with Block Designs and Digit Symbol being excellently retained, the scatter takes on an hysterical (repressive) or narcissistic (avoidant) coloring. Since this pattern is frequent in women in either of these two categories, it will be necessary to scrutinize the qualitative features as well as the other tests for differential diagnostic indications. A clue is provided by the well-retained Digit Span score: this score is much less likely to drop in narcissistic cases than in hysterical cases.

Her answer to the first Information item is suggestive of the low anxiety tolerance and strong avoidant tendencies of a narcissist: she makes a stab at reflection, but quickly retreats and waves aside the need for further effort even though she senses that her answer is incorrect. She is at the same time cautious and asks for reassurance, saying, "I think!" on *height,* "Is that right?" on *Paris,* "A guess", on *population,* "Isn't it?" on *Vatican,* and, to top it off, pointing out on the *habeas corpus* item that she has never been in court. This last remark might represent the concrete orientation of a naive person, but it could also represent the defensiveness of a suspicious person. The qualitative features of Comprehension, Digit Span, Arithmetic and Similarities do not appear to shed any light on the diagnostic problem.

Picture Arrangement makes an important contribution. On the *elevator* item she has difficulty recognizing the elevator at first. Age does not excuse this, since we know she has a nearly perfect score on Picture Completion. Perceptual misrecognitions or distortions often stem from a paranoid background. On the *flirt* item she at first thinks that the chauffeurs are policemen and that there are two different women in the story. Both errors represent not only perceptual arbitrariness but imply a drastic breakdown of the *anticipation* function. A king sitting in the rear of a limousine with two uniformed men up front: this is the context from which the anticipation, *chauffeurs*, springs in almost all subjects. When the details of the pictures are studied in isolation, however, there can be no anticipations based on mutual implications of details, and the grossest misinterpretations become possible. Similarly, seeing two different women in the *flirt* sequence implies that she was reacting to the head or forepart of the woman in isolation from the rest of her body and the remaining pictures in the sequence; otherwise it would be quite apparent that it was the same woman and it could be anticipated that she had turned around. Perceptual distortion reaches an extreme on the *taxi* item where the half of a dummy is transformed into a whole, live person. The story she tells implies that the woman is drunk, a most unusual idea and very likely an interpretation that stems from personal problems in this area. But tracing a distortion to its source does not lessen the importance of the fact that a distortion occurred. We can tentatively assume that she is preoccupied with intoxication and gay parties, but we can also be rather certain, on the basis of the massing of errors in this subtest and the indications of overalertness in the scatter, that a significant paranoid trend is present. The qualitative aspects of the remaining subtests do not contribute significantly to the diagnostic picture.

Thus far then this appears to be a possibly narcissistic woman with a noteworthy paranoid trend; addiction may be also involved.

LEARNING EFFICIENCY

Learning efficiency is well-retained. In the immediate recall she intensifies the aggressive implications of the story by speaking of people killed and injured. This is a fairly frequent error and usually implies strong pent-up aggressions.

SORTING TEST

In Part I we find a classical demonstration of the egocentric conceptual orientation so frequently found in women of narcissistic character make-up. The sortings are loose and the concepts concrete and fabulated. Since the fabulations are all based on self-references or references to the family, and since no clearly disorganized thinking has yet been evident, it is not likely that schizophrenic impairment of concept formation is involved. On the *spoon* item the "check" is the boldest fabulation. On the *pipe* item she guesses, "I'll have to play I'm in a cigar store". The arbitrary formulation, "tobacco bar", is reminiscent of the arbitrary story of a drunk in Picture Arrangement. The *bell* makes her think of a boy, the *paper circle* of school, the *toy pliers* of a boy again and the *toy fork* calls to her attention her neglect of little girls.

In Part II, however, where she is no longer free to follow her whims but must commit herself to an interpretation of the sortings of the examiner, she becomes quite cautious, failing or nearly failing 8 of the 12 items. It is evident at the same time that she is capable of forming abstract concepts and it is this which gives the failures an air of caution rather than inability. A depressive or neurasthenic might fail many items and yet give abstract concepts, but her performance in Part I and the previous tests contra-indicate these diagnoses. If the extensive fabulizing in Part I happened to be done by a schizophrenic, Part II would certainly have been equally fabulized. It seems necessary therefore to consider her thinking in Part I representative of extreme egocentricity and her thinking in Part II representative of paranoid overcautiousness.

RORSCHACH TEST

The question posed by the summary of scores is this: what kind of case can combine in one record 4 to 5 failures, 11 to 14 responses, 4 M's and a confabulation? Failures tend to accumulate in the records of severe depressives, blocked schizophrenics, organics, hysterics with a primitive cultural background, occasionally in severe addictions, and in paranoid conditions. Depression, organic brain damage and blocked schizophrenia are ruled out by the preceding results; hysteria can be ruled out by the EB of 4-to-1.5 or 3, which has too many M's both in an absolute sense and relative to the amount of color; severe addiction, when it does make for many failures, usually restricts the record to ordinary or vague forms and tends to eliminate the M's. Paranoid condition is therefore the most likely diagnosis. Not all persons with paranoid conditions yield records of this type, but when a record of this type is obtained it implies a paranoid condition in the patient.

What is the rationale of this diagnostic pattern? A record with a relatively high number of M's implies unusually active ideation, and, in a clinical case, always suggests ideational symptoms as well. "Active ideation", however, implies that productivity should reach at least the average level, if not significantly exceed it. The question then becomes: what factors can restrict the potential productivity of an ideationally active person? Two factors stand out: depressed mood in an obsessive person or paranoid overcautiousness. Assuming that the depressive-obsessive syndrome can be ruled out (as it can in this case) we end up with a picture of a person whose thinking can be sharp and creative but who, consciously or unconsciously, is "holding back". In this connection note the perfect form-level. Ideational symptoms mixed with such restraint suggests paranoid symptoms. The presence of a confabulation, with its implication that even in this overcautious setting arbitrary relationships can be elaborated, makes it all the more likely that paranoid symptoms are present.

The diagnosis paranoid *schizophrenia* must be considered in these cases. Failures occasionally pile up in the records of *chronic* paranoid schizophrenics, but there has been no evidence for such far-progressed disorganization in the preceding tests. Also, the scatter of subtest scores in the Bellevue Scale contra-indicates an *acute* paranoid schizophrenia: the Performance level is high and there is no great scatter. Let us examine the confabulation before reasoning further. It occurs on Card III, is not spontaneously offered, and is elicited only during inquiry. This is a saving feature, suggesting that widespread disorganization is not present. The essence of the confabulation is that the men, the woman (represented only by the top of her gown), and the entertainers are woven into one scene. The men and the entertainers alone might have passed as a combination response, but when she says, "That would be a lady in an evening gown," it becomes clear that she is spinning a fantasy at too great a distance from her initial percepts and therefore overruling their conventional implications in order to work out an arbitrary relationship.

To return to the summary of scores, we also note that the color distribution favors *CF* and *C* over *FC*. This is in accord with the inference of narcissistic features, since the emphasis is not on adaptiveness. Her verbalizations, facial expressions and the quality of her voice during the test, especially during her failures, were observed to be sweet and smiley. Pitting these qualitative notes against the color distribution, we can conclude that a front of adaptivity is cautiously maintained but that genuine warmth and intensity of social feelings are lacking. One *FC* is just enough for a pretense at good rapport.

WORD ASSOCIATION TEST

The following groups of responses are noteworthy: (1) *penis*—"anatomy" and *vagina*—"anatomy". The content of these responses represents an avoidance of the sexual connotations of these words; this avoidance indicates either inhibition or coldness. In terms of the personality picture elaborated thus far, coldness is the more likely implication. Responses such as "childbirth" or "urination" often have the same implication. (2) *Drink*— "*(deep sigh)* water"; *mouth*— "body"—a mildly distant response—and the false recall, "anatomy"; *bite*—"*(deep sigh)* teeth" and the near miss in recall; *suck* (misheard as *sulk*); *hunger*—delay of 8 seconds. This piling up of disturbances in reaction to words with oral connotations indicates intense conflict over oral needs and is frequent in addicts' records. There is now even more reason to suspect addiction. (3) *Man*—"husband. (?) Well *naturally* he'd be the first one I'd think of!"; *husband*—" (deep sigh) love". The lady protests too much here and may be doing the same thing in *father*—"devotion" and *mother*—"love". In other words she is too ready to emphasize feelings of love and devotion in the "appropriate" areas. A paranoid attitude probably underlies these responses.

The strongest indication of all regarding paranoid pathology is mishearing *cut* as *cunt*. This distortion can be referred back to the arbitrariness of anticipations revealed in Picture Arrangement. Mishearing is an active, not a passive, process; a person reconstructs a pattern of sounds, using whatever anticipations of meaning are stimulated by the immediate situation. Under no circumstances is there reason to anticipate that so tabooed a word for the female genitals will be used as a stimulus-word by the examiner. Many possibilities can come to mind, but so long as a person's anticipations are at all in tune with the immediate situation and the social relationships it involves, certain possibilities rarely come to mind; if they do, they are ordinarily promptly rejected. If the automatic controls fail, and if the possibility is not rejected on a conscious level, we can conclude that the most arbitrary anticipations can occur in the subject's mental life, and, because arbitrary anticipations are so typically paranoid, we can conclude that some form of paranoid state is either imminent or present. This sometimes applies to men as well as to women, but especially to women because of the doubly intense cultural pressure to which they are subjected in this respect. Sexual preoccupation is also indicated by the mishearing.

TEST REPORT

Intelligence and Thought Organization: This is a woman of superior overall intelligence (IQ—127) whose thinking manifests two main pathological trends: marked egocentricity on the one hand and paranoid overalertness, caution, and arbitrariness on the other. Distorted anticipations, and distorted visual and auditory perceptions are conspicuous. When she senses that she is being put on the spot, she appears characteristically to inhibit expression of her ideas and may even resort to dissimulation. There is no evidence of schizophrenic disorganization, but paranoid ideas are apparently well-developed and encroach upon reality testing. General, wordly interests are poorly developed.

Emotional Factors: She appears to be a narcissistic woman, with little capacity for warm and firm object-attachments, with low anxiety-tolerance and a tendency toward impulsiveness. She maintains a rigidly smiling front of compliance, which hardly conceals her intense, underlying negativism. Strong conflict over acceptance of passive needs is indicated and addiction is likely. She appears to react coldly to sexuality but is apparently preoccupied with it.

Diagnostic Impression: Paranoid condition in a woman of narcissistic character make-up.

CLINICAL SUMMARY

Mrs. P. was referred because of alcoholism and paranoid ideas. She had been a compliant, considerate child but has never had a close friend. She did well in school, got along with classmates of both sexes, but was "independent" and confided in no one. At the age of twenty, intercourse with a young man she was engaged to led to a pregnancy. At her father's advice, she had an abortion performed. The parents were disappointed in her but were sympathetic. She was married at the age of twenty-five to an engineering student, and gave up working after she went into what appears to have been a state of anxiety and depression "from overwork". She was afraid to become pregnant "because" she feared insanity on her husband's side of the family. They adopted a child to whom she gave much attention. The husband showed her little affection or recognition of her efforts to be a good and helpful wife. He required much "mothering", and was often so busy working that he neglected her and the home. Following an operation in the pelvic region, ten years after the marriage, she became frigid. Her husband began having affairs with other women then and she criticized his lack of sexual desire during the next ten years. When the war broke out and the adopted child left for the army, she became overtly suspicious of her husband's infidelity. She gathered evidence against him by having a detective follow him, and blamed her "nervousness" on him. She claims, however, that she had suspected infidelity since shortly after the marriage. She threatened to leave him and he promised to remain faithful, which he seems to have been since then, but her accusations did not cease. She became moody and began drinking; when intoxicated she would even accuse other persons of infidelity. She became seclusive, lost interest in her friends and watched her husband "like a hawk". She talked incessantly of the sexual affairs of people she knew as well as of her own marital difficulties. She made occasional scenes and wept often.

She presented a neat and gracious appearance during her examinations here. She minimized the amount of drinking she had done, claimed to have used alcohol as an "escape" and blamed all her difficulties on her husband's lack of "kindness". She refused to give some information, suspected that her husband was trying to commit her, and initially thought of each psychological test as a test of "commitability". She also suspected her husband of taking dope, of having an illegitimate child and of trying to do her out of some money. Her attitude was alternately conciliatory and retributive. The diagnosis was paranoid state with symptomatic alcoholism.

INCIPIENT SCHIZOPHRENIA: TEST RESULTS

Mrs. E. Age: 27. Education: High school. Occupation: Waitress; Office work. Marital: Twice; first: few months; second: 3 years. Second husband died a year ago; 2 children, one died last month. Husband: Mechanic. Father: Clerk. Early Environment: City. Family Position: Older of two. Religion: Protestant.

BELLEVUE SCALE

Comprehension

ENVELOPE: Put it in the nearest mail box (2). THEATRE: For a minute I wouldn't do anything. I'd think what I'd do, then I'd tell the usher or somebody, I'm not sure, or I'd just get panicky. With me it has to happen first (2). BAD COMPANY: Because of the bad influence, because you become bad too (2). TAXES: If you don't pay taxes, there won't be any money for the government to operate on. It takes money for everything (2). SHOES: Well, because they're pliable, long wearing (1). LAND: I don't know ... must be so many people, so much competition; the more people, the more land costs (2). FOREST: I don't know. I think probably I'd watch the sun (1). LAW: If we didn't have laws, it would be a sorry state of affairs, even though many of the laws are bad. People would steal, kill, wouldn't pay attention to other people (1). LICENSE: (sigh) I really don't know, but of course that's a small tax, and then the moral side to it: people just don't go off and live together. DEAF: If they can't hear, they can't tell how to make the sound. They could see lips, but don't hear (1). RAW SCORE: 14.

Information

PRESIDENT (before Roosevelt): dk. LONDON: +. PINTS: +. RUBBER: +. THERMOMETER: +. WEEKS: +. ITALY: +. WASHINGTON: February ... dk. HEIGHT: +. PLANE: +. PARIS: 1000 miles. BRAZIL: +. HAMLET: +. POLE: Byrd. VATICAN: He is the highest in the Catholic order. JAPAN: +. HEART: +. POPULATION:

dk. H. FINN: +. Egypt: +. KORAN: Bible of India. FAUST: Dante. HABEAS CORPUS: To have in case of death. ETHNOLOGY: dk. APOCRYPHA: dk. RAW SCORE: 14.

Digit Span

FORWARD: passes 3, 4, 5, 6 on first try; fails first series of 7; fails both series of 8 by reversing digits. BACKWARDS: passes 3 and 4 on first try; fails both series of 5. RAW SCORE: 11.

Arithmetic

ITEMS 1–3: +. ITEM 4: 8 (6″). (?) 9 (10″). ITEMS 5–9: +. ITEM 10: 7500 feet (30″). (?) 9 feet (60″). RAW SCORE: 8.

Similarities

ORANGE: Fruit (2). COAT: Wearing apparel (2). DOG: Animals (2). WAGON: Means of transportation or getting around (2). DAILY PAPER: You get news, information (2). AIR: Both necessary to life (2) WOOD: I don't see how they are the same. EYE: Senses (2). EGG: You might say that's what life comes from, beginning of life (2). POEM: They please the senses: the beautiful pleases the eye; a poem pleases the ear, the inner kind (1). PRAISE: Both might induce you to do better (1). FLY: I don't see how they could be the same. (?) I don't see it. They are just not the same to me. It couldn't be they are both living things (2). RAW SCORE: 20.

Picture Arrangement

HOUSE: + 7″ (2). HOLD UP: + 8″ (2). ELEVATOR: + 8″ (2). FLIRT: JNAET 32″ (3). FISH: EFGHJI 63″. TAXI: SAMUEL 105″; insight (3). RAW SCORE: 12.

Picture Completion

NOSE: +. MUSTACHE: +. EAR: +. DIAMOND: No picture (5″). (?) No diamond in the middle (15″). LEG: In here, something (shell). TAIL: +. STACKS: +. KNOB: +. SECOND HAND: +. WATER: +. REFLECTION: Leg on table. (?) +. TIE: +. THREADS: +. EYEBROW: +. SHADOW: +. RAW SCORE: 13.

Block Designs

ITEM 1: 8″ (5). ITEM 2: 12″ (4). ITEM 3: 11″ (4). ITEM 4: 17″ (4). ITEM 5: 24″ (6). ITEM 6: 80″; correct start and good performance; only one error, spontaneously corrects (4). ITEM 7: 116″ (4). RAW SCORE: 31.

Object Assembly

ITEM 1: 15″ (6). ITEM 2: 4ι″ (7). ITEM 3: 95″. "This is very odd looking. I can't imagine what it is." Two fingers reversed; recognizes (4). RAW SCORE: 17.

Digit Symbol

67 correct. RAW SCORE: 67.

Vocabulary

APPLE: Fruit (1). DONKEY: Animal (1). JOIN: Make two things . . . put them together (1). DIAMOND: Jewel (1). NUISANCE: Annoyance (1). FUR: Coat on an animal (1). CUSHION: Something soft to put under your head (1). SHILLING: English term for a coin (1). GAMBLE: Bet (1). BACON: Meat from pigs, hogs (1). NAIL: Small metal spike (1). NITROGLYCERINE: Ingredient used in making dynamite (1). STANZA: Verse (1). MICROSCOPE: I can only describe it. You use it to see things that would be invisible to the naked eye (1). VESPER: A word used in church, some sort of mass (½). BRIM: Edge (1). GUILLOTINE: Something that was used centuries ago to cut off people's heads (1). PLURAL: More than one (1). SECLUDE: Alone (1). CEDAR: Tree (1). TINT: Color, shade (1). ARMORY: Place where arms are kept (1). FABLE: Story (1). BELFRY: A high place in a church where bells are (1). RECEDE: To go back (1). AFFLICTION: Ailment (½). PEWTER: Dishes are made of pewter (½). BALLAST: Used for weight in boats and balloons; something heavy to throw out as you go higher up (1). CATACOMB: I think a series of caves, underground (½). SPANGLE: Little shiny things used for decoration on clothing (1). ESPIONAGE: How am I going? . . . I know what it means . . . spying (1). IMMINENT: Close, near by (1). MANTIS: Bug, praying mantis (½). HARA KIRI: That's what the Japanese call suicide (1). CHATTEL: Not a servant, more like a slave (½). DILATORY: Opening. AMANUENSIS, PROSELYTE, MOIETY: dk. ASEPTIC: Something to cleanse of germs. FLOUT: The way a person acts towards another person. TRADUCE: dk. RAW SCORE: 32.

Weighted Scores and IQ's

Comprehension 12	Picture Arrangement 11	Vocabulary 14
Information 10	Picture Completion 13	Verbal IQ: 120
Digit Span 9	Block Designs 14	Performance IQ: 120
Arithmetic 12	Object Assembly 9	Total IQ: 122
Similarities 16	Digit Symbol 16	

LEARNING EFFICIENCY

IMMEDIATE RECALL: (December 6) (last week) (a river) (overflowed) (10 miles) (from Albany). (Water flowed in the streets). 12 people were (drowned), (600 people) (caught cold) as a result of (the dampness). (A man) who (rescued) a small (boy) who was (caught) (under a bridge) (cut his hands). SCORE: 21.

DELAYED RECALL: (December 6) (last week) (a river) (overflowed) in a (small town) (10 miles) (from Albany). (Water entered the houses). (14 people) (were drowned), (600) (caught cold) as a result of (the dampness) and (cold weather). In (saving) a small (boy) who was (caught) (under a bridge) (a man) (cut his hands). SCORE: 20.

SORTING TEST

Part I

BALL: Adds bell, small silverware, sugar, index card, and paper circle, block with nail, small tools, nails. "All children's things. A child can write on the paper, or can cut out. Children like sugar." (Notices imitation cigar later. "I thought this was real. I'd put it with these baby things.") Loose sorting, concrete concept. LARGE FORK: Adds large tools, large silver, cigar, cigarette, pipe, matches, corks, eraser. "These are all a grown person's things, a man's things." Loose sorting, concrete concept. PIPE: Adds cigar, cigarette, matches. "To smoke." Mildly narrow sorting, functional concept. BELL: Adds ball, rubber cigar and cigarette. "A child plays with these." Mildly narrow sorting, concrete concept. CIRCLE: Adds index card, eraser. "When I see these, I imagine a little child writing, cutting up, erasing. Though I don't see any pencil, still I put these together in my mind." Mildly loose sorting, concrete concept. TOY PLIERS: Adds hammer, screwdriver, block with nail, nails. "All practically . . . all belong to the same category, when the child is making something . . . playing, doing things daddy would do." Mildly narrow and mildly loose sorting, concrete concept. BALL: See first sorting.

Part II

RED: "I don't know how, unless because they all belong to the same family." Syncretistic concept. METAL: "All metal." Abstract concept. ROUND: "I can't see that they are all rubber, so I don't know. Because they are all round?" Abstract concept. TOOLS: "All instruments of work." Abstract concept. PAPER: "Paper." Abstract concept. PAIRS: "I see a father and son. I see a father and his little boy when I look at these (long story about activities of father and son involving the sorted objects)." Fabulized concept. WHITE: dk. "I can't imagine. The only thing is they all afford pleasure; this you write on, might enjoy smoking, and everyone likes sugar." Syncretistic concept. RUBBER: "Rubber." Abstract concept. SMOKING MATERIALS: "Smoking, to smoke with." Functional concept. SILVERWARE: "Eating utensils." Abstract concept. TOYS: "A child's toys." Abstract concept. RECTANGLES: "All square." Abstract concept.

RORSCHACH TEST

CARD I. Reaction time: 25″. Total time: 150″.

It looks like a . . . not a human, but some queer thing dressed like a man (center figure). His boots are down here, his belt, his coat. It's a belt with a buckle, like a uniform. Looks more like a monster than a man . . . hands up here. The rest is just background, as though he might be coming out from rocks (sides) some place. It looks as though he would jump at somebody. [(?) It looked like craggy rocks . . . coming out of the mouth of . . . not exactly a cave but some place in the mountains.}

SCORE: W M(C)+H—Monster—scene; Fabulation Aggression.

CARD II. Reaction time: 4″. Total time: 300″.

1. Looks like two bears (laughs). They have their noses tied together. Their noses are bent (giggles a little) up here and tied together. 2. These look like feet on the heads of the bears (upper red). These are legs attached to the feet (light red area merging into black). [(?) Spurs on, like a chicken, like a fighting cock.] ∧ ... ∨ ... > 3. This looks like an animal (black) standing on the edge of water and there is a reflection in the water. I don't know what kind of an animal ... here is the nose, eye. < Here is another animal (other side). It rushed up to something and skidded to a stop. There's a scared look on his face: maybe this red thing scared him (upper red). 4. This thing (upper red) looks like a creature you might find in another world, not ever in this. Here is the head and eye; the head is raised up and the rest is like a caterpillar, drags behind it. It certainly scared this animal.

SCORES: 1: D F+Ad P. 2: D F±Ad Orig Fabulized-combination. 3: D F+A Fabulation. 4: D F∓A Combination Fabulation.

CARD III. Reaction time: 10″ Total time: 180″.

1. At first glance it looked like two cannibals beside a pot. ∨ 2. Two African natives (all black); they have their arms uplifted. 3. These look like trees (upper red). The wind is blowing them. I see a coconut dropping. 4. This is a very strange looking head (arm of popular figure is nose, leg of popular is neck). Here is the eye, the skull going up to a top, and whiskers. 5. And a growth on the end of the nose (lower middle D), like a little bush.

SCORES. 1: W MC′+H P. 2: W MC′+H. 3: D F+Pl Fabulation. 4: D F−Hd Orig. 5: D F+Pl Fabulized-combination.

CARD IV. Reaction time: 12″. Total time: 330″.

(Pushes back in seat.) 1. Hmm ... that's a horrible looking monster, something seen in a nightmare. Here are his huge feet, legs; head right here. I see his eyes, eyebrows, wrinkles on his forehead, his nose (all in upper middle). These (upper sides) serve as arms for him, not really arms but they grow out where arms ordinarily would be. (Enjoys task as a child might.) [(?) It just had a fiendish face. There was nothing human. It was more like you would imagine the devil looked like.] ... ∨ 2. Here is a creature. Ah, maybe he lives in the ocean. He is not frightening in appearance although he's very odd looking. He might frighten some people. Here are eyes (in lower middle). Light is reflected on them. His horns ... here are two big ones, two smaller, and two more. All this is his body. 3. This looks like the head of some prehistoric animal (upper side projections, white space included as mouth) and he is in a fight with something.

SCORES: 1: W FM(C)+A—Devil Fabulation Aggression. 2: W FC′∓ A Fabulation. 3: Ds F−Ad Fabulation Aggression.

CARD V. Reaction time: 1″. Total time: 420″.

1. Looks like a bat. ∨ Still looks like a bat. > (Covers half.) 2. I see Satan's face as clear as it just can be (upper edge contour, toward

middle); his pointed beard, his eyes as plain as can be. $\vee$ 3. Just this part here looks like legs and feet and this is lace trimming on whatever is being worn (upper middle Dd). I think these must be bloomers with lace on them (covers that part). 4. These look like two snakes looking at each other (lower middle Dd). 5. I can also imagine two birds with all their feathers behind them, all their plumage. $\wedge$ 6. This is a bird's head and long neck stretched out on the ground, dead as dead (lower, thin side projection). 7. Here are two girls facing each other. They have very high headdresses; they have lace collars. These are their extremely fancy gowns, much material.

SCORES. 1: W F+A P.   2: De F+Satan. Dd F(C)+Hd   Orig. 4: Dd F+Ad. 5: W F+A Orig. 6: Dr F—Ad Orig. Fabulation Aggression Peculiar. 7: W M(C)∓H Orig.

CARD VI. Reaction time: 33″. Total time: 480″.

1. That's the very queerest looking thing. I don't know whether to call it a bird or not (upper D). These are its wings. It looks like a carved thing, like a totem pole... feelers, and the feet are right down here (tiny gray spots in upper center). Head is here... head you might see on an insect or something like that. 2. This is a ghost (central area), without this top (upper projection), like you see in cartoons in movies; here are the two eyes (tiny light gray areas). [(?) Just looked like it... wrapped up in a sheet... like the shape.] 3. When I first looked at these, they looked like doctors in surgical outfits in conference (at base of upper projection). The more I look at it, they look like men in uniform. They work in another planet—not here—or in the future. $>$ 4. Here is a woman. Here is her fancy hair curls. She is blond, looking at her foot stretched out here (lower side projection is head, upper side is foot). Looks like a sponge in her lap. Maybe she is going to take a bath. $\vee$ 5. This is an animal very similar to a bear. He is running from something, running on his hind feet... afraid of something... something is chasing him (each side is one bear).

SCORES. 1: D F+A—Obj. 2: Dr F—Ghost Orig. 3: Dr F+Hd Orig Fabulation Peculiar. 4: Dr MC′+H Orig Fabulation. 5: D FM+A Orig Fabulation Aggression.

CARD VII. Reaction time: 10″. Total time: 660″.

1. (laughs) This is an old man with an extremely hooked nose, tall cap, like a dunce cap, bent back, hands behind his back. Here is his seat, knee over here, funny looking (seat is chin of popular head; knee is neck of popular head; nose is outer tiny bump at base of upper projection). $>$ 2. Here is... they are partly disguised things you might see in clouds. This is the female, this is the male, and he is kissing her on the forehead... strange shapes. (Male face is lower contour of middle one-third; female face is outer half of upper edge of lower one-third). 3. This is a lady, maybe a colonial lady with white wigs they used to wear. She is dressed in an elaborate gown (middle one third; side projection is head and neck; gown is bulk of area). $\wedge$ 4. Here are two women (popular; upper two-thirds). They also have elaborate hair-dresses,

like women used to have in the king's court. These women are rather elderly, not young. They look like a lot of people that have their teeth out. Their noses and chins start to meet almost. They are arguing. One is pointing in one direction, and the other is pointing in the other. That makes me think of myself. I am two people. One part of me wants to do one thing, the other the other. One is the right way; the other the wrong. That's why it makes me think of me. ∨ 5. There are girls. dressed for very much snow, cold weather (upper two-thirds). They have on some kind of hood. She is jumping down. She has on a coat with a full skirt. She has on high boots or leggings—I don't know which they are—and mittens. Caught her right in the middle of the jump. She is in mid-air.

SCORES. 1: D M—H Orig. 2: De F+Hd Orig. 3: D MsC'+H Orig. 4: D FM+Hd P Fabulation Self-reference. 5: D M(C)+H.

CARD VIII. Reaction time: 18". Total time: 480".

∧ ... > Hmm (smiles). 1. This is an animal (side pink). It is not a very pleasant animal either. This is his reflection in the water down here. ∨ 2. This is something ... you only see it in your imagination, some creature (upper gray-green). Here is the head (upper tip), long snout, looks very bony. 3. (Whirls card around.) < This is a totem pole (side projection of upper gray). I see the different heads, part of body, arms hanging down. Here's a head, here's another one, here's another. They're not all facing in the same direction. 4. This is another thing. It looks very fierce. I see his mouth drawn down at the corners, see his feet; no body; eyes, horn or ears; nose (upper center space: lower segments are feet; upper outer segments are horns). 5. These are two old gray-beards, very wise, deep in thought. They have some great problem on their minds (upper gray-green; two heads back to back).

SCORES. 1: D F+A P Fabulation. 2: D F—A Orig. 3: Dr F—Obj—Hd. 4: S FM∓A Orig Fabulation Fabulized—combination Aggression. 5: D FC'∓Hd Fabulation.

CARD IX. Reaction time: 15". Total time: 480".

1. > This is a great huge animal rushing along away from something (green; head is outer edge). It is in a great hurry. 2. ∨ This (orange) looks a little bit like Santa Claus, but he isn't quite as fat and he has a very surprised look on his face, amazed. His eyes are just popping. < 3. This is a deer I think (shading of green to orange). I see his soft eye here, very gentle. These are antlers; he must be coming out of water. [(Water?) Just gives the impression, just the picture.] > 4. This is a man (pink). He is elderly, well-to-do. I just have that impression. 5. ∨ These are two people dressed in very strange costumes (upper half orange; usual clown hat is one leg, other leg is uppermost orange projection to center, head is bell-shaped orange projection to center—below the usual antlers) and they are very mad at each other. They have their faces all screwed up in anger. They are going to wade into each other to show each other what's what. They are very young, almost children. > 6. Here is (green) ... I don't know if it might be a man on another planet. It doesn't look

like ours. He has been knocked down and is terribly frightened. Whatever it is that knocked him down, he is afraid it will kill him. His
mouth is open in fear. The expression in the eyes is nothing definite,
like something drawn in a hurry (face is outer contour of green). [(?)
He is down on hands and feet.]

SCORES. 1: D F + A Fabulation Aggression. 2: D M+H Fabulation.
3: D F+Ad Fabulation. 4: D F+Hd Fabulation. 5: D M∓H Orig,
Fabulation Aggression. 6: D M±H Orig, Confabulation Aggression.

CARD X. Reaction time: 9″. Total time: 780″.

1. (laughs). Here are funny looking creatures. These (side blue) are
sitting on tree limbs. 2. These (upper middle gray) are standing on
rocks. They (side blue) are making a big noise, flinging their arms
around like monkeys only they are not . . . just acting like them . . . The
more I look at them, the more they look angry about something, arguing. These two (upper middle gray) are the angriest of them all, about
to exchange blows. 3. These are part animal, part human. This part is
a woman with arms (outer part of side sepia and partly into outer
yellow), this is animal (bulk of side sepia). She is as graceful as a gazelle.
[(Belong together?) Yes, it is all one.] 4. This is some snail-like thing.
These are the antennae here, tiny feet parts, very little (entire lower
green, feet are tiny projections at bottom). 5. This down here is a
princess, queen, has a crown on and long gown. She has four legs (one
side of lower green; four legs are four tiny projections at bottom).
6. Here these look like, I don't know whether it's a man or woman
(inner yellow, vague articulation). They are dressed in aviator's costume, helmets. They're clinging to the side of a cliff (pink). [(?) I don't
know how they can stay there. It seems they have the power of flying.
They are hardly holding on to that cliff, these cliffs.] ∨ 7. These are
two females (pink), not really human, but look . . . faces are so ugly,
look more like animals, but they have long hair, dresses; very haughty.
[(?) Posture and female expression.] > Now it looks like they're knocked
unconscious, lying down, head turned to the side. > 8. This is an
animal's body with a woman's head (side yellow; head is outermost
projection). ∨ 9. Here is . . . I think it's a man (rabbit head). He is
sitting down. This is his support (lower green). He has his arms clasped
above his head. 10. Here is a sheep and carrot in his paw (upper green).

SCORES. 1: D FM∓A Fabulation Aggression. 2: D F+A Fabulation Aggression. 3: D Ms+H−A Orig Fabulized−combination. 4: D F∓
A Orig. 5: Dr Ms−H Orig Confabulation. 6: D Ms−H Orig Confabulation. 7: D M + H Fabulation Aggression. 8: D F−H−A Fabulized−com-
bination. 9: D Ms+H Orig. 10: D F+A Fabulation.

Summary of Responses

R: 51   EB: 18.5−0

W 8	F+ 17	A 16 (2)	W% 16
D 32	F± 1	Ad 6	D% 63
Dd 2	F∓ 2	H 17	DR% 21

Dr 6
De 2
S 1
s (1)

Qualitative
Fabulation 24
Confabulation 3
Fab-comb 5
Combination 1
Peculiar 2
Self-reference 1
Aggression 12

F− 7
M 2+, 1±, 1∓, 1−
MC' 3+
M(C) 2+, 1∓
Ms 2+, 2−
MsC' 1+
FM 2+; 2∓
FM(C) 1+
F(C) 1+
FC' 2∓

Hd 7 (1)
Devil 1 (1) $F\%$ 53-100
Monster (1) $F+\%$ 70-69
Ghost 1
Pl 2 $A\%$ 43
Scene (1) $H\%$ 47
Obj 1 (1)   P 5
P% 10
Orig 9+, 3±, 3∓, 7−
Orig% 43

WORD ASSOCIATION TEST

WORLD−3.5″−cold. LOVE−2″−hate. FATHER−1.5″−mother. HAT − 1.5″ − coat. BREAST − 2″ − head. CURTAINS − 2″ − window. TRUNK−2″−suitcase. DRINK−1″−water. PARTY−3″−fun. BOWEL MOVEMENT−3.5″−bathroom. BOOK−1.5″−read. LAMP−2″−light. RUG−3.5″−cup (4″−I don't remember that one, might be cup). CHAIR −1.5″−sit. BOY FRIEND−2″−friend. PENIS−3.5″−body (6″). DARK −1.5″−light. DEPRESSED−4″−down. SPRING−1.5″−up. BOWL−1.5″ −dish (6″). SUICIDE−2.5″−dead. MOUNTAIN−2″−hill. HOUSE−2″ −live. PAPER−2″−write. HOMOSEXUAL−3″−wrong. RADIATOR− 2″−heat. GIRL FRIEND−2″−love (3″−friend, love). SCREEN−2.5″− door. MASTURBATE−2.5″−no. FRAME−2.5″−window. MAN−1.5″− woman. ORGASM−4″−sexual. MOVIES−2.5″−like. CUT−2″−blood. LAUGH−4.5″−tooth (10″−dk.). BITE−3″−tongue (6″). WOMEN− 1.5″−girl (2″−men). DANCE−2″−lovely. DOG−1.5″−cat. DAUGHTER −2.5″−baby. TAXI−2.5″−car. MOTHER−3″−father. TABLE−2″−sit. BEEF−2.5″−eat. NIPPLE−1.5″−bottle. RACE−2″−go. WATER−1.5″− drink. SUCK−2″−bottle (2″−nipple). HORSE−1.5″−cow. FIRE−2″− heat. VAGINA−2″−women. FARM−3″−far (8″). SOCIAL−1.5″−people. SON−1.5″−brother. TAXES−2″−country. TOBACCO−1.5″−smoke. CITY−2″−town. INTERCOURSE−4″−women. HOSPITAL−2″−sick. DOCTOR−1.5″−good.

THEMATIC APPERCEPTION TEST

CARD 1. (Boy with violin.) (Mouth twitches. Begins after 90″.) This little boy is sitting at the table looking at his violin. From the seriousness of his expression, I think a lot is going through his mind. I think he wishes passionately to be able to play as well as his father could or someone close to him. Because he cannot play as well as he likes . . . it makes him depressed, makes him feel perhaps he will never be a great player. Is that enough?

CARD 2. (Old woman in doorway.) This old woman has heard a noise and she is investigating it. When she opened the door, a very strange sight greeted her eyes. She is startled . . . She is startled. Is that enough? (See?) A very bedraggled man stood there across the room from her. He had climbed through the window. His clothes were dripping wet and the water dripping down formed pools around his feet. The old lady entered and shut the door behind her. The man at once began to explain, "I was coming through your fields and I fell into a pond. I came up to the house and thought no one was home. For two days, I had had nothing to eat and when I came to the front door, it was locked. I decided I would climb through the window and try to find some food." Naturally the old lady, who possessed a very kind heart, fed the poor man and sent him on his way with his pockets full.

CARD 3. (Old man in graveyard.) This old man has come to the cemetery in a dead night. He is quite alone in the world. His family is gone. They have passed on one by one, his dear wife being the last to leave him. He feels that he just can't go on; that he makes nightly visits here, seeking comfort and solace: there isn't any. That's just the reason he is here.

CARD 4. (Silhouette of man at window.) This man has left his own home and come to a large city. He is full of ambition. Tonight, he has turned out all his lights and is standing at the open window, looking out over the town and thinking, "Some day soon, I will be an important part of all this." (Outcome?) I don't know. I'd have to make a big long story out of it.

CARD 5. (Heads of embracing couple.) It's awfully hard for me to make up these stories. I need more practice. (Story?) I think the man is a soldier and the girl is his wife. (Looks up, embarrassed smile.) I imagine his wife. He is home on a three-day pass. They have had so much to talk about. Now the time has come for him to leave her, and he holds her once more in his arms, whispering tender words of love in her ear. She knows she must have courage to go on without him close by her side, and she only prays that his courage too will be high. (Outcome?) No outcome.

CARD 6. (Prehistoric animal, rocky road, bridge.) Let's call this man John. This will be about him. John invented a flying ship that carried him to a new planet. After he landed his ship, he got out and explored the country. Running across a herd of strange creatures, who proved themselves friendly, he managed to capture one and teach it to carry him about, much as a horse would on Earth. One day, while carrying on his exploring while mounted on his strange steed, he entered some entirely new country consisting mostly of huge cliffs filled with caves. Strangely enough, there seems to be a pathway that led up the side of one of these cliffs. Immediately he and his mount started up this path. When they reached a level place and he saw ahead of him what appeared to be a bridge spanning the chasm between the cliffs . . . I see another man whom I didn't see before. I wonder how I'll get him in the story. Let's see . . . what was the last? Dismounting, he proceeded to investigate, when suddenly he heard a hissing sound behind him. Turning, he beheld a monster emerging from one of the cliffs—no, from one of the caves behind him. Whirling, he leaped on his horse—put horse in quotation marks—and started to dash across the narrow bridge. Suddenly, before him, he saw a man running frantically. With a swift command, he ordered his mount to pause long enough for the fleeing man to get astride, and then they went tearing off up the side of the cliff, following the path. They finally stopped for breath, they dismounted, and looked down. They saw this. What they saw was a creature that possessed a long heavy body, four short legs that ended in webbed feet, a long neck with short horns all along it and a head like a lizard. This queer-looking animal was waddling down the pass. The two men heaved sighs of relief and then turned to one another (closes eyes) with questions. What did I call this man? . . . John learned the other man had also invented a flying ship which had carried him to this planet. He too had been exploring on this day and was examining some stones on the bridge when he looked around and saw John fleeing from the beast behind him. The two men became fast friends, and after . . . upon completion of their exploring, they returned to Earth with much valuable information about the new planet. (Total time: 22 minutes.)

CARD 7. (Shadowy photograph of thumb.) I can't make out just what this is . . . , ∨ Upside down it looks like a finger. I can't tell what this is (drop). It seems this thing here looks like a pair of spectacles (in black area). That's all I could tell. I just can't make anything out of that.

CARD 8. (Nude couple; older woman with infant.) I don't think I can make a story out of this. It just doesn't suggest anything to me, just too puzzling. Here is a woman with a baby in her arms and she is looking at a young man and a young woman. The young woman seems to be leaning on the young man for comfort and the young man must be making conversation with the woman, the one with the baby. (Happening?) I don't know. That's what's so puzzling. I can't figure it out. I wasn't really talking or saying anything. I was just in conversation with myself. The baby belongs to the young woman and the young man. This other woman, the one holding the baby, must be the young man's mother, but I don't think I can make any more of a story. (?) Well, looking at this picture suggests to me that there is something dramatic about it, something they are expecting to happen . . . or already happened, something terrible. If I could think . . . have a lot of time . . . I could write this out in all the details. I could probably . . . it's awfully hard . . . just the highlights . . . maybe the next one will be easier. (?) Well, it might be that the baby is taken away from the parents.

CARD 9. (Two chairs; table set for tea.) (Smiles, mumbles "two cups", glances up at examiner.) The table appears to be set for two. Somebody is going to have tea. This must be a beautiful home. This corner looks like it's part of a very beautiful home, such a lovely tapestry. Just tea. They will have tea and pleasant conversation and then . . . that's the end.

CARD 10. (Old man on shoulders of another old man.) (Patient shakes head, becomes grim, sighs slightly, doesn't look up, doesn't really look at card for a while, then takes it again; swallows. Begins after 60".) I couldn't make a story out of that. I think that all symbolizes something. It's not just a story. It's a big idea but not for a story. It all suggests something forceful, dynamic, but I can't make a story. I've had no experience in interpreting something like this. I can't tell what led up to it or the outcome. The only thing I can do is interpret it and tell what it means. Two old men—maybe this old man on the top signifies wisdom. The one on the bottom must signify work, hard work. In the background there appears to be smokestacks. That could mean our many factories and plants. There is a tree in the corner and it seems to be storm-tossed. I think that means the war our country is in, and these smokestacks mean all our industries at this time. This man on the top signifies the courage and... wisdom and courage our country means. The old man at the bottom: our whole war effort. (Significance in position of men?) Yes. The war effort would come to nothing if it wouldn't be wisdom behind it all. People could have worked their fingers to the bone if they wouldn't have had a definite purpose... a wise purpose ... The hardest part is to put into words what I am thinking. In other words I am tongue-tied. I have a lot of thoughts. It's hard to utter them.

CARD F 11. (Hag behind young woman.) (Shakes head, swallows.) The old woman must be either the mother or the grandmother of the young woman. The young woman has a strong face. She has lots of character. The old woman has a sly expression on her face or around her mouth. If it wasn't for that expression on her face, I might try to interpret it. I can't imagine why she looks that way. The old woman looks like she worked hard all her life. (?) I don't know, just can't imagine. If this old lady had a different expression on her face, say one of worry... (?) Then I'd say she must be cherishing a lot of ambitions for this girl. Maybe she would be hoping the girl would do things she always wanted to do. Maybe her ambitions would be realized in this woman.

CARD F 12. (Men unloading boat; girl on bridge.) This is a little village, right on the edge of the sea. I think it must be midsummer: the sun looks so hot. The men in the corner here are very busy carrying a cargo from the ship to the wharf and passing under the eyes of a foreman. I don't recall what the proper word would be, so I say foreman. There is a young girl on the bridge, looking down on the wharf. There is a huge warehouse in this picture and the men must be very busy to carry their burden into this warehouse. They might have just returned from a long voyage under a hard master. The young girl has worked hard all morning. Now she is just resting, standing on the bridge, looking down at the waters, looking forward to the day when her sweetheart will come back from a voyage on the sea. They will be married and will live happily ever after.

CARD F 13. (Boy with book; two girls in background.) Two sisters and a brother. They are studying under a private teacher, a tutor. They have been studying hard for several hours and the two sisters have finished their lessons, but the boy is going on with some more difficult ones. He is listening intently to what his teacher is telling him, and it is of such interest that the two sisters have remained behind to hear. When the two girls leave this room, they will go to their separate recreations, the older girl to her embroidery and the younger one to her dolls. The boy will study until late afternoon.

CARD F 14. (Woman turning away from man.) The man is not of much account. The girl has been in love with him for a long time, against her better judgment, but finally she has decided to end the matter ... or I might better say, to end the affair. So she goes up to the young man's apartment to tell him this is the last time she will see him ... this is goodbye. He pleads with her and wants to take her in his arms and kiss her, but she is afraid that ... (looks up) if she kisses him, all her firm resolve will weaken, so she pushes him away. Shall I make an ending to the story? I think I should leave it right there, don't you? I think I shall leave it right there. That seems to be a good ending to me.

CARD F 15. (Girl leaning against wall; arm outstretched.) This poor girl (emotion in voice) ... she is suffering mental tortures. She and her husband have been living on a farm and they have been very happy, (looks up, smiles) but suddenly the husband becomes ill. She calls the doctor and there seems to be little hope (chokes) for the young man's recovery (emotional). She is sick with dread, praying that she won't be left all alone (puts card down, scared). (?) Well ... he recovers and she finds more happiness in him than ever before.

CARD F 16. (Man at window.) The man is a detective. He has been hired by a wealthy banker who was worried about the actions of his only daughter. He is afraid she has seen a group of young people who are a bad influence on her, but his daughter refuses to tell him anything about her comings and goings, so he feels that the detective is the only means of solving this case. The detective is looking at a window after following the girl to a house on the outskirts of the city, and he sees that the girl is in the midst of a group of young people who are not actually criminals but dangerously close to it. The girl just ... the girl loves adventure and this group of people provide new thrills for her. The detective informs the father. The father takes the girl on a trip and provides new and less horrible activities for her, thus diverting her mind from the activities of the past.

CARD F 17. (Two women struggling on stairway.) Once there was a young married couple and the wife was very much in love with the husband, but suddenly (swallows) she became very suspicious of his very peculiar behavior. She followed him several times and learned he was seeing another woman. She was consumed with jealousy. One night, she went to the other woman's house and upon finding her quite alone —no, I want to change that—and attempted to reason with the woman, begging her not to see him any more. The woman laughed in her face and taunted her. Our young woman became blind with fury and proceded to strangle the other woman, but luckily the husband entered in time to prevent a great tragedy. He realized what he had done and went back to his wife with remorse in his heart and remained always faithful. That was a great lesson to him.

CARD F 18. (Maid in hallway.) (Begins after 2 minutes.) The maid is one of a large staff of servants. One night, three men came to visit Mr. Barnes. They all went into the library. Upon hearing loud

voices, the maid tip-toed to the end of the hall to see what was the cause
of the disturbance. The three men were threatening Mr. Barnes. She
stood for a moment wondering what the best course of action would be.
Then she went after the butler. After listening a few minutes, he decided
to call the police. The three men had been trying to threaten Mr. Barnes
to relinquish certain business ventures he had undertaken. I think I'll
end it there.

CARD F 19. (Woman in bed, dishevelled man standing.) (Begins
after 2 minutes.) After several years of steady drinking, the man has
become a worthless, sodden mess, doesn't amount to two cents now
(smile). His wife has remained loyally by his side. One night when she
tries to reason with him, he flies into a drunken rage and kills her. Now
he doesn't know what to do. He is completely sobered up by the terrible
thing he has done. I guess I'll end it there.

CARD F 20. (Bearded old man, looking down.) That old man is
thinking of many things that made up the long years behind him. He
now has grandsons in the army and he is thinking of them. No, he is
thinking how proud he is of them. He is tired of the many battles he
has taken part in.

ANALYSIS OF RESULTS

BELLEVUE SCALE

The scatter has several striking features: (1) Information is clearly
below Vocabulary and somewhat below Comprehension, suggesting that
a repressive emphasis has dominated intellectual development; (2) Similarities is clearly higher than the remaining Verbal scores, an unusual
pattern and one frequently indicative of a paranoid trend; (3) Object
Assembly is relatively low, indicating that strong tension is probably
present; (4) the excellent score on Digit Symbol appears referable to
her generally excellent Performance abilities and to special secretarial
training. Scatter of this type is not infrequent in the records of hysterics and patients with character disorders.

The qualitative material does not clarify the diagnostic picture:
her verbalizations are not unduly impulsive, flippant, pedantic, or disorganized. In Comprehension she prefaces several responses with "I
don't know", suggesting a characteristic self-deprecating attitude. The
verbalizations "... because you become bad too" on the bad company
item and "... wouldn't pay attention to other people" on the laws item
have a naive, childish quality. In Similarities the response to the poem
—statue item has a sensitive quality: "... pleases the senses ..." Otherwise the verbalizations are conservative and unrevealing. Their con-
servativeness contra-indicates the diagnosis character disorder.

LEARNING EFFICIENCY

Learning efficiency is excellent and leads one to expect that no very profound illness is present.

SORTING TEST

Suddenly malignant features appear. In Part I there are two loose sortings, and a concrete conceptual attitude appears to dominate a persisting abstract attitude. Loose sortings with fabulated concepts which center around the family and home also occur in the records of patients with narcissistic character disorders. There are, however, two considerations which make it clear that this record speaks more for the egocentricity which goes with developing disorganization than for the egocentricity of a narcissist: (1) if this were a narcissistic character disorder, we would expect low anxiety tolerance and avoidant tendencies to be clear in the Bellevue Scale, and they are not; (2) her verbalizations in the Sorting Test have a decidedly autistic quality—"When I see these things I imagine a little child ..." and "I put these together in my mind," and in Part II, "I see a father and son." In Part II the syncretistic concept, "All afford pleasure", heightens the impression of acute sensitivity at the same time as its looseness suggests disorganization. Her perseverative use of content dealing with parent-child relationships suggests special preoccupation in this area.

The good preservation in the Bellevue Scale and the Learning Efficiency test suggests that if these inferences about disorganization are valid, this patient must be in an early stage of disorganization. The diagnosis *incipient schizophrenia* must be considered.

RORSCHACH TEST

If we put together the *EB* of 18.5-to-0, the 22 original responses, the 24 fabulations and 3 confabulations, there can be little doubt that this is an extremely withdrawn, fantasy-ridden person, whose fantasies become inseparable from perceived reality. The dreamy quality of those few verbalizations in the Sorting Test take on more meaning now: when she said "I see ..." she was indicating that rich imagery probably pervades her present thinking. The Rorschach Test record is a gold mine of dreamy, physiognomic responses and verbalizations.

Card I: "... more like a monster than a man" is noteworthy. On Card II her giggling about the bears' noses suggests how actively she must be participating in her fantasies and how inappropriate her affect can seem to an observer. The highly projective "scared look" on the animal, together with "jump at somebody" on Card I, indicates an apprehensive, fearful attitude. Card IV: the "monster" response is again expressive of a phobic tendency, even though she describes the response with an air of childish glee. The glee refers essentially to the extensive withdrawal into fantasy and to external blandness (note the absence of shading). The deliberation about exactly how frightening the second response is again indicates how immersed she can become in her fantasies and how the fantasies intrude into her dealings with reality. Card V: the lace on the bloomers and the fancy gowns suggest that a good part of her fantasying is taken up with glorified images of herself.

CARD VI: the changing of the doctors to men from another planet before her very eyes indicates the fluidity of her perception of reality and the likelihood that feelings of unreality are present. The bear being chased suggests apprehensiveness again. Card VII: the organization of the first M is fantastic; it is a striking M— and therefore a response with malignant implications. The self-reference is noteworthy: little gestures (as by the two women) become symbolic of her own feelings—a paranoid-like reaction. Obsessional doubting with moral content is also implied; obsessive phenomena would be expected (in addition to fantasying) on the basis of so many M's being present. Card VIII: the "graybeards" response is an excellent example of autistic fabulation. Card IX: the "soft eye, very gentle" description of the deer emphasizes her sensitivity. The "knocked down" man response goes beyond the ordinary fabulation and becomes elaborate fantasy or confabulation. The relative unimportance of reality as compared to the spinning of dreams is evident. Card X: the aviators response is noteworthy. In her fantasy she sees the aviators clinging to the side of a cliff; more careful observation indicates that this is not a tenable idea, but she does not reject the fantasy; instead she reinterprets the reality situation to fit her fantasy more neatly. Loss of distance from the fantasies is clear. They are experienced so intensely that they overrule reality considerations. The fluidity of her fantasies is evident in the reinterpretation of the two women in the seventh response as "unconscious" once the card is turned sideways. Each slight change apparently can stimulate a new fantasy. In a sense *she* knocked the women unconscious, having disliked them from the first. The frequency of the theme of being pursued, attacked, knocked down, and unconscious suggests a basically terrified reaction to the world about her as well as a tendency to elaborate aggressive fantasies. A childish and acutely sensitive quality is also evident in these responses, as well as in her more cheerful productions.

It is surprising to find so many *M*'s in the record of a person with a Verbal IQ which is barely in the superior range, and with relatively immature concept formation in the Sorting Test, since all these *M*'s would ordinarily suggest that we are dealing with a highly gifted and intellectually active person. In this case it appears that her creative assets are completely at the disposal of her vivid fantasy life and have not been focused on active dealings with reality problems.

The extensiveness of the withdrawal into fantasy, the absence of adaptive efforts or other emotional output, and the apprehensiveness and terror indicate the imminence of a psychotic break. The relative orderliness of the Bellevue Scale and the Learning Efficiency test, as well as the absence of bizarre schizophrenic verbalizations in the otherwise *dilated* Rorschach Test record, indicate that this is not yet an acute schizophrenia, but rather falls into the group of incipient schizophrenias. Fantasies rather than delusions are in the foreground for the time being. The pervasiveness of the fantasying suggests that it is an ingrained character trait; the occasional arbitrary lengths to which the fantasies go suggest, however, that she is slipping into a schizophrenia. Her frequent evaluative comments, physiognomic percepts and generalized emotionality in the course of this test, when seen in the light of a complete absence of color responses, indicate that she is trying to maintain a last grip on reality-oriented feelings but that her efforts are already artificial and exaggerated.

WORD ASSOCIATION TEST

Farm—"far" has a clang-association quality, and *laugh*—"tooth" and *rug*—"cup" are conceptually distant. These deviant responses are not so striking or so numerous as to indicate serious disorganization; the entire record therefore supports the inference that considerable preservation of organization is still present and that this is not yet a full-blown schizophrenia. *World*—"cold" is understandable in terms of the withdrawal implied by the *EB* of 18.5-to-0. The cool response *boy friend*—"friend" is in marked contrast to the responses *girl friend*—"love", *intercourse*—"women" and *women*—"girl"; however, *homosexual*—"wrong" is also present: a strong but ego-alien homoerotic trend is indicated. *Masturbate*—"no" is noteworthy. *World*—"cold", *depressed*—"down", *homosexual*—"wrong", *dance*—"lovely" and *doctor*—"good" are affective, evaluative reactions and tie in with impression of naivete and dreaminess. The remaining deviations, delays, and recall errors are mild and not especially significant.

THEMATIC APPERCEPTION TEST

Card 1. The theme is depression at not being able to make dreams come true. In terms of what has already been inferred, this most likely is a personal feeling. The reference to equalling the father is noteworthy but must be amplified in later stories before being interpreted. Card 2. The theme is kindness of the mother-figure. This may well be an expression of a wish, since this is the subject who said "cold" in association with *world* (see also Card 11). At the beginning, she tries to avoid facing the cause of the "startle", and, when asked to continue, she turns to a gentle theme. Characteristic avoidance of any unpleasant thoughts is suggested. Card 3. The theme is loneliness and the absence of love-objects in this world; not only the wife, but the entire family is gone. The phrase "in a dead night" has a poetic yet nonsensical quality. She also seems to feel that there is no solace to be found anywhere. Card 4. The theme is dreams of success (at returning to the community?). Her avoidance of stating the outcome has a hint of the despair that has been clearer in previous stories; the avoidance implies that not even in a relatively unimportant situation can she forget the complexities and disappointments of life.

Card 5. This theme was especially popular during the war: the soldier taking leave of his wife. She expresses a wish for courage to go on in the face of the frustrations encountered in reality. Again she avoids the outcome. Card 6. This is a tale fanciful to the point of dreaminess, which is built around the common theme of escape from destruction. The final characterization of the monster as a comical rather than threatening beast probably expresses a general hope that her fears are unfounded, and that all her distress will prove to be silly and unnecessary. Card 8. She blocks dramatically throughout the story. Ordinarily this suggests intense sexual repressions and this may apply here also. We know, however, that she is a widow who has recently lost the younger of her two children, and her anticipation that "something terrible" is involved suggests that this picture has touched on intense feelings associated with her own unfortunate sexual and familial situation, and that she cannot face these feelings at all. The loss of the child is conventional, and, having been elicited by great pressure, would ordinarily have suggested little personal meaning; knowing her reality situation, however, we can assume that she is expressing her sense of loss associated with the recent death of her child.

Card 9. The theme is conventional and the striking thing is her naive, delighted participation in this "lovely" and "pleasant" scene. Card 10. The theme is a symbolic one, superficially dealing with war, but indicating a strong concern with finding wisdom in order to live an effective life. She seems to be saying, "I must find out what I am to do or I shall come to nothing." The freely symbolic thinking has a fantastic quality, and is quite consistent with the implications of the Rorschach Test results. It is also noteworthy that her initial reaction was blocking, presumably in response to the aggressive implications of the picture, and that her final story, though dealing with aggression (war), is on an abstract plane and negates the aggressive action in the picture itself. Characteristic extreme denial of aggressions is implied. Her final statement about inability to express her (highly emotional) thoughts is noteworthy. Card 11. Here again she avoids the aggressive implications of the picture, going so far as to apologize for the old woman— "... she worked hard all her life"—and finally ignoring the sly look altogether. The switch from a sly (hostile) mother to a helpful, encouraging mother probably represents a switch from her actual mother-figure to her ideal and longed-for mother-figure. She also implies that there is something going on (in her) that interested persons should worry about.

Card 12. The theme is "looking forward to the day when her sweetheart will come back from a long voyage on the sea". Her husband, it will be remembered, died a year ago, and, as indicated here, she appears to be immersed in gratifying as well as terrifying fantasies. Card 13. The theme is intense interest in learning, a theme reminiscent of the concern with wisdom on Card 10 and the wise old graybeards on VIII of the Rorschach Test. Card 14. Again she is most unwilling to follow through on a fantasy about an unpleasant event. She appears to be expressing a personal concern with the frailty of her defenses against sexual stimulation. Card 15. The theme is the "torture" associated with loss of a loved husband-figure. Her acute emotional distress makes it clear that she is talking about herself and the happy ending is clearly a wish. The emotional lability she manifests is of the same type as that seen in the Rorschach Test: it implies loss of distance from her fantasies and a desperate clinging to feelings which are on the wane. An hysteric could appear equally labile in the course of telling this story, but the total context of responses rules out hysteria as a diagnosis.

Card 16. This appears to be a statement of a wish for an omnipotent father-figure who will look after her and rescue her from the "horrors" of her past. The dreaminess of this patient renders it unlikely that the specific content of the story relates to anti-social acting out. Card 17. The theme is the popular one of a jealous wife's attack on a rival and the ultimate return of the husband to his wife. Special emphasis is put on the identification-figure's attempts to be reasonable in the face of distress. Card 18. This story is unusual since this picture usually elicits casual themes. In this story she fantasies herself as the rescuer of the father-figure. Card 19. This theme of a drunken murder is frequent, but the victim is usually a pick-up or girl friend and not a wife. The story suggests an underlying conception of the husband-figure as an aggressor. We have already seen (Card 5) how her conscious orientation to him is filled with love. Card 20. The man is thinking of the many battles he has taken part in. Probably she is expressing her own feelings about how difficult life has been for her.

Test Report

Intelligence and Thought Organization: This woman appears to be living in a dream-world. Fantasy with vivid imagery is all-pervasive and colors perception of reality so strongly that very likely she loses distance from her thoughts and is unable to distinguish fantasy from reality. In fact, in a clash between fantasy and reality, she tends to give priority to fantasy and to reinterpret reality so as to fit it in well with her fantasy. Reality testing therefore appears to be seriously impaired, though more by lack of concern than by arbitrary distortion. There are, however, traces of loosening of conceptual and associative processes. The records contain peculiar verbalizations with a highly poetic quality, communicating a wealth of emotional experience but little sense. Percepts are fluid and feelings of unreality are likely to be present. She is bright—her IQ of 122 falls in the superior range—but her thinking is in many ways naive and childish. A repressive inclination probably inhibited her verbal-intellectual development.

Emotional Factors: Extreme emotional withdrawal is indicated, but affects are intense and finely modulated and are not flat. They emerge primarily in the context of vivid fantasies, and by their extravagant and forced quality they indicate that she is desperately clinging to a capacity to experience reality-oriented feelings which is on the wane. Because of this increasing distance from reality and immersion in fantasy, her affective display is likely to seem inappropriate; however, the inappropriateness will refer to the objective situation and not to the thought content; schizophrenic *disharmony* of affect does not appear to have developed yet. She appears to have low tolerance for the anxiety associated with consciously admitting aggressive feelings and tries desperately to avoid facing aggressively-toned situations. Her fantasies are nevertheless filled with aggressive as well as glorified and gratifying situations. Basically her mood appears to be depressed, but she can get so immersed in pleasing fantasy as to experience the glee of a delighted child. Sexual inhibition is indicated.

Figures and Attitudes: Her fantasies appear to center around several main themes: being buffeted about and feeling terrified in a cold, threatening world; being lovely and lavishly dressed; finding the wisdom to make her life meaningful; waiting for the return of lost love-objects. She appears to feel that her dreams have not been fulfilled, that the world is empty of love-objects. She tries to restrict her fantasies to pleasant events only, but feelings of apprehensiveness, fearfulness, and loneliness keep intruding, and aggressive fantasies do emerge. It appears that she longs for an omnipotent father-figure to rescue her from her "horrible" life and precarious position; she seems to conceive of her mother as hostile, although consciously she denies this.

Diagnostic Impression: Incipient schizophrenia.

CLINICAL SUMMARY

Mrs. E., twenty-six years old, reared in a middle-sized town in Nebraska, had frequently been whipped, between the ages of three and thirteen, by her critical, punitive father. Her mother was a timid woman, who tried to defend the patient from these attacks. The girl was in constant terror of her father and was chronically unhappy. At an early age she began to avoid other girls because she was sensitive to their criticisms. Up to the age of fourteen, she was occasionally enuretic during the day. At the age of seventeen, she ran away from home and worked as a waitress in an establishment catering to hoboes, but had no sexual experiences. Her father finally persuaded her to return home, and from that time on, he lost his grip on her. She began to date frequently and drank "a lot of liquor", but did not have intercourse till she married an army sergeant when she was eighteen. He proved to be like her father and their marriage was unhappy. She discovered that he was unfaithful and attempted suicide with an overdose of sedatives. They were soon divorced, and although she resumed drinking, this gradually decreased till at present she detests even the odor of alcohol, feeling ashamed of the false happiness she sought in drinking. She had several jobs before she married again, this time a man whom she loved and who was gentle and affectionate. He was killed in an automobile accident the day before she gave birth to their second child, but she was told of this a day after the birth. There was no emotional display at this news, perhaps because she was under sedation, but during the subsequent months she tried to prevent herself from "going to pieces"; she reported, however, that she felt "dazed" for several months afterward. This was one year ago and since that time she has felt no sexual desire.

She came spontaneously to the Clinic after learning about it from the telephone directory, because she wanted to be "made into an entirely new person". In the course of her examination it became evident that she really wanted to be transformed into a man. She was dissatisfied with herself, having been unhappy most of her life, feeling friendless and different from other people, and being unable to sustain interest and enthusiasm in any undertaking and unable to manage her finances competently. Her second child had just died but she did not show the expected grief reaction. She presented a child-like appearance and showed little change of expression during her interviews except for an occasional shy but friendly smile. She complained of having lacked energy for the last few years, being easily fatigued, feeling faint, and having cardiac palpitations. She also reported that for the last six years she had frequently been preoccupied to the extent of not hearing remarks directed at her and once being hit by a car as a result of preoccupation while crossing a street. She reported periods of stubbornness and impulsive decisions and actions. There was a fear of falling and also a fear of being attacked in the dark. After being thwarted she would fantasy for hours what she should have said. She engaged extensively in fantasying, portraying herself as a brave and generous heroine or else taking pleasant excursions. When she would read of someone in the paper she did not like, she would picture herself shooting that person. Her dreams were vivid, some very pleasant and some nightmarish. In some of them men turned into women. She reported that she confused her dreams with reality and there was also indication of vague feelings of depersonalization.

The diagnosis was mixed neurosis in a schizoid personality, but in the staff discussion the possibility of a psychotic break was considered. She moved to a different state shortly after her examination, and several months later suffered an acute schizophrenic break. The details are not known.

INHIBITED NORMAL SUBJECT: TEST RESULTS

Mr. J. Age: 34. Education: High school. Occupation: Was teacher, now telephone lineman. Marital: 10 years; no children. Father: Farmer. Early Environment: Farm. Family Position: Oldest of 4. Religion: Catholic.

BELLEVUE SCALE

Comprehension

ENVELOPE: Drop it in the nearest mail box (2). THEATRE: Go to the box office and notify the manager (2). BAD COMPANY: One bad apple spoils the rest of the sack (2). TAXES: In order to have protection from the government, to maintain the government, we should say (2). SHOES: Protection, comfort, large amount available, durability (2). LAND: Because it is scarcer; more money can be made out of the same amount of land (1). FOREST: Locate my direction by the sun or moss on the trees, and then travel according to my direction. (?) Sun rises in the east, and moss is on the north side of trees (2). LAW: For the protection of the general public (1). LICENSE: So they may have a record (2). DEAF: Because you learn to speak by hearing other people speak (2). RAW SCORE: 18.

Information

PRESIDENT: +. LONDON: +. PINTS: +. RUBBER: +. THERMOMETER: +. WEEKS: +. ITALY: +. WASHINGTON: +. HEIGHT: +. PLANE: +. PARIS: +. HAMLET: ┐. POLE: +. VATICAN: +. JAPAN: +. HEART: +. POPULATION: +. H. FINN: +. EGYPT: +. KORAN: +. FAUST: Beethoven. HABEAS CORPUS: You have the body or right to a trial by jury in a case. ETHNOLOGY: dk. APOCRYPHA: dk. RAW SCORE: 21.

Digit Span

FORWARD: 3, 4, 5 on first try; fails first series of 6; fails both series of 7 by reversals. BACKWARDS: 3, 4 on first try; fails first series of 5; fails both series of 6 by reversals. RAW SCORE: 11.

Arithmetic

ITEMS 1–8: +. ITEM 9: ++ (2″). ITEM 10: ++ (4″). RAW SCORE: 12.

Similarities

ORANGE: Fruits (2). COAT: Clothing (2). DOG: Animals (2). WAGON: Vehicles of transportation (2). DAILY PAPER: News (1). AIR: Necessities of the body (1). WOOD: Both are derived from a tree. EYE: Sources of information to the body (1). EGG: They're the beginning of new products, egg of a chicken, seed of a plant (1). POEM: Both tell a story (1). PRAISE: Both given for a deed performed. FLY: Both things of nature (1). RAW SCORE: 14.

Picture Arrangement

HOUSE: + 2″ (2). HOLD UP: + 5″ (2). ELEVATOR: + 5″ (2). FLIRT: AJNET 24″ (2). FISH: EFGHIJ 60″; insight (3). TAXI: SAMUEL 19″; insight (6). RAW SCORE: 17.

Picture Completion

All correct. RAW SCORE: 15.

Block Designs

ITEM 1: 13" (4). ITEM 2: 10" (5). ITEM 3: 17" (3). ITEM 4: 25" (4). ITEM 5: 34" (5). ITEM 6: 96". Upper row correct, uses all-white block for stripe in center, corrects (3). ITEM 7: 130". Careful, smooth performance (4). RAW SCORE: 28.

Object Assembly

ITEM 1: 28"; one arm raised (5). ITEM 2: 15" (10). ITEM 3: 31"; two fingers reversed (4). RAW SCORE: 19.

Digit Symbol

51 correct; no errors. RAW SCORE: 51.

Vocabulary

APPLE: Fruit (1). DONKEY: Animal (1). JOIN: Fasten together (1). DIAMOND: Stone. (?) Precious stone (1). NUISANCE: Troublesome (1). FUR: Skin of an animal (1). CUSHION: On a chair. (?) To sit on (1). SHILLING: Money, English (1). GAMBLE: Game of chance (1). BACON: Meat of a hog (1). NAIL: Fastener for wood (1). CEDAR: Type of tree (1). TINT: Slightly colored (1). ARMORY: A building where army supplies are stored (1). FABLE: Ancient story (1). BRIM: Edge (1). GUILLOTINE: Method of punishment, capital punishment. (?) Cuts off head (1). PLURAL: More than one (1). SECLUDE: Separate (½). NITROGLYCERINE: Explosive (1). STANZA: Part of a poem (1). MICROSCOPE: Instrument for looking at small objects. (?) Magnifies (1). VESPER: Evening. (?) Evening church service (1). BELFRY: Top of a church. (?) Place where the bell is kept (1). RECEDE: Draw back (1). AFFLICTION: Weakness of a body (½). PEWTER: Type of metal used in dishes (1). BALLAST: Something to build up under a rim or a track (½). CATACOMB: Ancient home for the religious in the early period of Christianity (1). SPANGLE: dk. ESPIONAGE: Something to harm a government or home country. (?) Talking or acts. IMMINENT: Immediately (½). MANTIS: Insect (1). HARA KIRI: Method of self-destruction. (?) Used by Japs (1). CHATTEL: Movable property (1). DILATORY: Something that enlarges or changes. AMANUENSIS, PROSELYTE, MOIETY: dk. ASEPTIC: Something that you take easily, as a disease. FLOUT: To show prominently or display. TRADUCE: dk. RAW SCORE: 31.

Weighted Scores and IQ's

Comprehension 16	Picture Arrangement 14	Vocabulary 13
Information 15	Picture Completion 15	Verbal IQ: 130
Digit Span 9	Block Designs 13	Performance IQ: 125
Arithmetic 17	Object Assembly 11	Total IQ: 130
Similarities 11	Digit Symbol 12	

LEARNING EFFICIENCY

IMMEDIATE RECALL: December 6, which was (last week), (a river) (overflowed). (14 people) (drowned) and (600) were injured.

(A man) (cut his hand) in (saving) (a boy) who was (caught) (under a bridge). SCORE: 16.

DELAYED RECALL: (December 6) (last week) a (river) (overflowed) in a (small town) (10 miles) (from Albany). (It overflowed in the houses). 16 (drowned), (600) (caught cold) from (the dampness) and (cold weather). (A man) (cut his hand) (rescuing) (a boy) from (under a bridge). SCORE: 18.

SORTING TEST

Part I

PIPE: Adds all smoking materials. "All connected with smoking." Adequate sorting, abstract concept. LARGE FORK: Adds all silver, sugar, bell. (Subject also had the idea of "putting all the metal together".) "Dinner table. (?) Silverware, and sugar, and the bell to call the butler." Loose sorting, concrete concept. BELL: Adds lock and large tools. "Bicycle and tools for it." Inadequate sorting, concrete concept. CIRCLE: Adds cards, matches. "All paper." Adequate sorting, abstract concept. TOY PLIERS: Adds all tools and lock. "Tools." (All?) "I expect I just wasn't thinking about it." (Removes lock.) "I was thinking of tools." Mildly loose sorting, abstract concept. BALL: Adds all rubber items. "Rubber." Adequate sorting, abstract concept.

Part II

RED: "Various shades of red." Abstract concept. METAL: "All metal." Abstract concept. ROUND: "They aren't metal." Syncretistic concept. TOOLS: "Tools." Abstract concept. PAPER: "Paper, at least part of them." Abstract concept with split-narrow quality. PAIRS: "By two's: pairs." Abstract concept. WHITE: "White." Abstract concept. RUBBER: "Rubber." Abstract concept. SMOKING MATERIAL: "Smoking equipment." Abstract concept. SILVERWARE: "Silverware, serving for two people. I should have said eating utensils, because the red ones (plastic) are not silverware." Abstract concept. TOYS: "Household equipment, household tools." Syncretistic concept. RECTANGLES: "Squares." Abstract concept.

RORSCHACH TEST

CARD I. Reaction time: 12". Total time: 75".

You mean what the shape makes you think of? A butterfly, or a moth of some kind... It still looks like a butterfly to me. (?) That's the only thing I can see on it.

SCORE: W F + A P.

CARD II. Reaction time: 25". Total time: 90".

< ... ∧ ... A couple of animals' heads, probably calves or cows, something of that sort. ∧ ... < ... ∧ That's about all for that (?) No, that's what it looked like at first, and I can't see any change.

SCORE: D F + Ad P.

CARD III. Reaction time: 30″. Total time: 90″.

A man's neck, red necktie, white shirt, this being the neck and shoulders going out (center space and middle red). [(?) It was shaped like it, coming out, ... looking at the whole thing; like a bowtie of a full dress suit. (?) The color was more prominent in the center part of each side piece, corners tip back to the neck. (?) I would think of it as black but since it was red on there ... (?) Color didn't make me think of a necktie.] That's the only thing I can see on it. (?) That's it.

SCORE: DS F(C)C′+Obj.

CARD IV. Reaction time: 70″. Total time: 105″.

Is there a top or bottom to these? ... ∨ It looks like a worm (lower middle D) under a couple of twigs on a branch of a tree. [(?) It looked like a branch or leaf, bark. (?) Looked like a leaf curled there to me. (?) Like it was curled toward me (light gray on boot is curled part). (?) Shape of bark, not like the color, sort of a dead leaf you might see. (?) A dead leaf ...]

SCORE: W F(C)±A−Pl Combination.

CARD V. Reaction time: 80″. Total time: 135″.

∧ ∨ ∧ ∨ ∧ ∨ That looks like a butterfly to me with the wings stretched out of proportion. I don't know why all of them run to birds and butterflies to me, but that's the way it runs. > ∨ < Any way I look at it, it still looks like a butterfly.

SCORE: W F+A P.

CARD VI. Reaction time: 30″. Total time: 100″.

∨ > Look like a cross-section of a volcano we studied in school many years ago, in illustrations with the top here and showing different strata in the low part of the earth. [(?) It went down a ways, then a sort of a light spot there, and deeper there were darker marks and lines.]

SCORE: W ChF Geol.

CARD VII. Reaction time: 80″. Total time: 165″.

∧ ∨ ∧ < ∨ ∧ 1. The only thing I can see if that were covered up (covers lower center Dr with finger) would be clouds. 2. There could be some people up here and buildings (on forehead of popular), but it doesn't fit in with my cloud theory. [(?) Heads of people ...] It's darker up here like thunder clouds ... > ∨ This is like a steeple on the building (refers to second response). Will you tell me what they really represent?

SCORES. 1: W Ch Clouds. 2: Dr F−Scene Fabulized-combination Tendency.

CARD VIII. Reaction time: 15″. Total time: 120″.

1. A pair of animals here, opossums or some similar animal, out here in the red (side pink). 2. This looks like a fellow's breastbone (upper central space), the starting of his ribs in the white. [(?) It could

be the backbone or breastbone and start of the ribs. (?) Like that white part and space between the ribs.] ∧ ∨ < ∧ 3. That white (same area as 2) in here could be a skull of a cow or a buffalo ... or did you want the whole thing? [(?) Triangular shape, white.]

SCORES. 1: D F+A P. 2: S FC'+At. 3: S FC'+AAt.

CARD IX: Reaction time: 25". Total time: 120".

∧ < ∧ 1. This red down here looks like a man with his hands folded on his chest, with a mustache, hair pretty well tousled. < 2. This green looks like a woman on a washtub, washing clothes on a washboard. [(?) Head, hands sticking out to tub, knot on back of apron.] (?) That's about the size of it.

SCORES. 1: D F+Hd. 2: D M+H.

CARD X. Reaction time: 75". Total time: 150".

∧ ∨ ∧ It looks like it might be a rabbit's head here (lower middle), taking these green parts off. < > ∨ That's all I see on that. Just different colors, but I can't make out any forms on it. (?) I don't see a thing.

SCORE: D F+Ad P.

Summary of Responses

R: 14   EB: 1–0

W 5	F+ 6	A 5	W% 36
D 6	F− 1	Ad 1	D% 43
Dr 1	M 1+	H 1	DR% 21
S 2 (2)	F (C) 1±	Hd 1	
	F (C) C' 1+	Obj 1	F% 50-86
Qualitative	FC' 2+	At 1	F+% 86-92
Combination 1	ChF 1	Cl 1	
Fabulized-combination	Ch 1	Geol 1	
Tendency 1		Scene 1	A% 43
		Pl (1)	H% 14
			P 5
			P% 36

WORD ASSOCIATION TEST

WORLD − 1.5" − domination. LOVE − 1" − hate. FATHER − 1"− mother. HAT−3"−cap. BREAST−2"−chest. CURTAINS−2"−shades (3" −drapes, screens). TRUNK−1"−suitcase. DRINK−1"−water. PARTY− 1.5"−fun. BOWEL MOVEMENT−2.5"− (he whispers) shit. BOOK− 1.5"−story (1"−read). LAMP−4"−lamp? shade (2"−light). RUG−1.5" −carpet. CHAIR−1"−settee. BOY FRIEND−2"−pal (1"−girl friend). PENIS−2.5"−lady (20"−don't remember). DARK−2"−night (1"− light). DEPRESSED−1"−sad. SPRING−1.5"−summer. BOWL−2"−pipe (10"−table). SUICIDE−1"−kill. MOUNTAIN−1.5"−valley. HOUSE

—1.5″—live   (2″—home). PAPER—1″—write. HOMOSEXUAL—10″—I just can't think of any word. RADIATOR—1″—car (1″—water). GIRL FRIEND—4″—party (1″—boy friend). SCREEN—1.5″—window (3″—shade). MASTURBATE—2.5″—habits (3″). FRAME—2″—screen. MAN—1.5″—woman. ORGASM—4.5″—never heard of it. MOVIES—1″—show. CUT—2″—doctor. LAUGH—1.5″—joyous   (2″—happy). BITE—1.5″—sting. WOMEN— 1″ — men. DANCE — 2″ — party. DOG — 1.5″ — rabbit. DAUGHTER — 1.5″ — father (1″ — son). TAXI — 1″ — car (3″ — ride). MOTHER—1.5″—daughter. TABLE—1″—eat. BEEF—1.5″—eat. NIPPLE —2″—baby. RACE—2″— speed. WATER—1″ — drink. SUCK — 2″ — baby (2″—drink). HORSE—1″—ride (1″—speed). FIRE—1″—burn. VAGINA —1.5″—woman. FARM—2″—live stock. SOCIAL—2″—social, enjoyment (1″—contacts). SON—1″—father. TAXES—1″—pay. TOBACCO—1″—smoke. CITY—2″—people. INTERCOURSE—1.5″—sexual. HOSPITAL—1″—sick. DOCTOR—1.5″—sick.

ANALYSIS OF RESULTS

BELLEVUE SCALE

The scatter indicates that the subject's development has been characterized by strong intellectual "drive" and suggests therefore that the character make-up is primarily obsessive. This history of intellectual drive is indicated in two ways: first, he has only a high school education yet his Information score is in the very superior range; second, the Vocabulary and Similarities scores, which are generally more responsive to limitations imposed by a poor cultural background, are below Comprehension and Information, which are most easily pushed up by special application. In other words, the scatter indicates that this man has struggled to expand the scope of his thinking beyond that characteristic of his cultural milieu. The high Comprehension score would also suggest a special interest in social conformity and, therefore, possibly an inhibiting, strict moral code. The perfect Arithmetic and Picture Completion scores indicate unusual alertness, perhaps over-alertness. The relatively low Object Assembly and Digit Symbol scores may reflect a mild depressive trend or the temporary lowering of efficiency by tension. Looking ahead to the time and error notes on Object Assembly, we see that the scores are not due to slowness at all but to errors, indicating that tension may be readily stimulated in this man. That the errors are not due to impulsiveness and carelessness is evident in the remainder of his test performance, where his responses are precise and careful. The drop of the Digit Span score 6 points below Information indicates a somewhat greater readiness to anxious reactions than would be expected in an "ideally normal" person. The anxiety, however, does not appear to get out of hand, as can be inferred from the indications of excellent overall efficiency.

In Information he passes *all* of the first 21 items; there is no spottiness of achievement or dramatic temporary inefficiency. Despite only a high school education he knows what the Koran is, indicating that cultural interests are probably active; however, they are not so active as to have greatly broadened him—he fails the last four items. His verbalizations in Information, Comprehension, and Similarities are neither pedantic nor impulsive, but are neat and to the point. In Comprehension there is again no unevenness of achievement; he reaches his level smoothly. In Similarities his relatively low score is obtained by conventional passes and conventional failures; there is no trace of arbitrariness, strain, or looseness. He goes through the Performance subtests smoothly. Vocabulary achievement also appears to be even and there are no striking temporary inefficiencies.

LEARNING EFFICIENCY

Learning efficiency is good: the average score of 17 is appropriate to the Vocabulary score of 13. There are no striking qualitative features present.

SORTING TEST

The loose sorting with the *fork* in Part I and the syncretistic concept, "They aren't metal", in Part II indicate a schizoid personality component. Concepts based on the *absence* rather than presence of attributes are obviously overinclusive and are distinctively schizoid. In certain incipient or full schizophrenics these concepts become more numerous and far-fetched: "All not alive", "All without intelligence", and the like. The very good overall retention of an abstract conceptual level suggests that these two loosenesses refer only to a schizoid trend and not to disorganization. Moreover, the loose sorting in Part I is not extreme; it does not involve altogether arbitrary and rare inclusions and does not include a great number of extraneous objects. It therefore does not have the malignant implications of a more absurd or overinclusive sorting. Also, there so far has been no other evidence of disorganization. Some incipient schizophrenics, however, could have come this far through the tests without doing anything more deviant than he did. Although an obsessive make-up has been indicated in the Bellevue Scale, it is noteworthy that so far no signs of overmeticulousness or pedantry have appeared, suggesting that his obsessiveness does not reach pathological proportions and thereby impair his efficiency.

RORSCHACH TEST

Most striking in the summary of scores are the relatively low R for a man of his intelligence and the extremely coarctated EB of 1–0. These features might be referable to depression, but the relatively high $DR\%$ of 21, the relatively low $F\%$ of 50-86, and the $A\%$ of only 43 contra-indicate this diagnosis. In addition, the previous tests offer no convincing evidence of depression. These features could be due to a neurasthenic condition, but we have already seen the excellent efficiency maintained by this man and are in no position to consider this possibility seriously. Inhibition suggests itself and is quite consistent with the findings thus far: it would encompass the discrepancy between IQ and productivity, the high Comprehension score, the constricted EB, and the high $F+\%$ (caution). Furthermore the shift away from color to the $F(C)$ and FC' responses indicate an unfree, anxious, compliant adaptivity, and general weakness of self-assertiveness (no CF), which also would fit in well. Striking inhibition of emotional and intellectual self-expression is therefore indicated.

In a coarctated record, an EB of 1-0 can be considered to represent a clear-cut M-prevalence; M-prevalence is characteristic of the records of obsessives. The tendency to a fabulized combination—a frequent type of response in obsessive records—is also noteworthy. Inhibition probably stopped it in its tracks. The occurrence of $2+2$ space responses in this setting of inhibition and obsessiveness suggests active doubting, a tendency to dwell too long on the opposite side of the question, and to be hesitant about accepting casual matters at face value. The two strong shading responses in this brief record suggest that anxious reactions will also be clinically conspicuous; this has already been suggested in the Bellevue Scale.

The generally delayed reaction times followed by well-integrated responses are further indications of the cautious but competent manner of approach. His only M occurs on Card IX; it is quite frequent that persons who give only one or two relatively rare M's but one on III prove to be obsessive clinically. The single response on Card X can be understood as an expression of his basic difficulty in coping with strong emotional experiences and his retreat to the safe and conventional in such situations; his opening question on Card I, "You mean what the *shape* makes you think of?" has the same implication.

At this point we might ask whether pathology can be ruled out, and, if so, whether we can predict at all what type of pathology would be likely to develop if he were to become ill. Regarding present pathology, we have seen that he has maintained a high level of efficiency in the more intellectual tests, that his verbalizations have been more or less precise, that arbitrariness has not been manifest. Thus, although inhibition, obsessiveness, and schizoid features have been indicated, these appear to be rather character traits than symptoms, and rather restrained than pathologically conspicuous traits. If he were to become ill, however, we would expect him to manifest extreme tension (because of the prominent inhibitory defenses), exacerbated obsessiveness, an a more conspicuous withdrawal tendency (no colors in the Rorschach Test, schizoid features in concept formation).

WORD ASSOCIATION TEST

The use of such words as "domination" and "joyous" is distinctive of the intellectualizing, obsessive features already noted in the Bellevue Scale. Persons not especially concerned with ideas cannot think of these literary words when under the time-pressure of this test; only where one characteristically tosses such terms about in one's mind are they available for immediate delivery in a test like this. This seems especially true here because of the subject's limited cultural and educational background. His whispered answer to *bowel movement*, his blocking on *homosexual*, his ignorance of *orgasm*, and the accumulation of mild disturbances on most words with sexual connotations (or words following them) reinforce the impression of strong inhibition, and suggest that sexual inhibition in particular may also be conspicuous.

Test Report

Intelligence and Thought Organization: This appears to be an intelligent, obsessive man with strong intellectual interests. His thinking is conventional and well-organized, and bears the imprint of a poor cultural background, especially in a relative weakness of verbal concept formation. His grasp of conventional judgments is excellent. It appears, however, that creative application of his intellectual assets is hindered by generalized inhibition and mild obsessive doubting. His intelligence functioning, despite its high level, has little sparkle. His concepts are occasionally loose in schizoid fashion. His IQ is 130.

Emotional Factors: Inhibition is striking. He appears to be totally unfree in expressing affective reactions of any type or in coping with strong affects once they are stimulated. His adaptivity is of an anxious, cautious, compliant variety and he is likely to be weak in self-assertiveness. He appears susceptible to mild attacks of anxiety and tension but these do not seriously disrupt effective functioning; when ruffled he appears to intensify his inhibitory efforts and to proceed with utmost caution. Inhibition in the sexual sphere is likely to be conspicuous. In addition to defense by inhibition, defense by intellectualization and defense by withdrawal are probably prominent.

Diagnostic Impression: No serious pathology is indicated. This is an inhibited, obsessive and mildly schizoid man who is functioning on a good level of efficiency.

CLINICAL SUMMARY [11])

Mr. J.'s father was a farmer who dominated J.'s mother strictly and expressed "violent feelings" freely. His mother was easy-going and affectionate to the children. J. was an excellent student throughout his school years. He was "shy" in school and claims to have gotten into less than the average amount of trouble; he was anxious to please his teachers and was afraid of being "bawled out". He dreamed of becoming a doctor but began teaching in rural schools upon completion of high school and taught for fourteen years before becoming a telephone lineman. He was especially anxious to get away from farm work, preferring his "bookworm" habits.

His adaptivity was of an anxious and cautious nature during his interviews. He would not talk about himself spontaneously and preferred to answer specific questions. J. described himself as resisting expression of strong feelings, being ashamed of his father for that tendency; he feels himself to be more like his mother. He seemed to be disappointed in himself for not having made fuller use of his assets, as by becoming a doctor. He enjoys hunting and fishing, reading and light classical music. He is politically conservative. Financial management is essentially his wife's responsibility. They have not been able to have children, for some unestablished cause, and are currently planning to adopt a child. After ten years of marriage, they are "still in love". He enjoys working under a good boss. Though he holds grudges against fellow workmen, he has been unable to bring his complaints to the attention of anyone in authority except in a very indirect way. He is described by his supervisor as an intelligent, level-headed worker and not much of a talker; he has never been observed to be angry or blue, although an

---

11) Because this subject was a "control" in an experiment that did not require intensive history-taking or interviews, this summary is somewhat superficial relative to those offered on the patients in this chapter.

impression of some brooding was obtained. In general he keeps to him-self. In his work he is cautious about making decisions when there is room for doubt. The general impression was of a passive, inhibited, somewhat anxious man with intellectual leanings.

Chapter Four

BRIEFER CASE STUDIES

In this chapter ten additional cases will be discussed. Some of these belong to the same diagnostic group as a case in the previous chapter, and have been included to indicate another form of appearance that the same illness may take in test results. Others represent types of illness frequently encountered in clinical work, but not discussed in Chapter Three. As in Chapter Three, the test records have been chosen with an eye to presenting diagnostic prototypes. Because the results of the full battery of tests are not included, the emphasis in the following analyses will be primarily on diagnosis.

ANXIETY STATE WITH DEPRESSION: TEST RESULTS

Dr. C. Age: 43. Education: M.D. Occupation: M.D. Marital: Single. Father: Merchant. Early Environment: City. Family Position: ?. Religion: Jewish.

BELLEVUE SCALE

Comprehension

ENVELOPE: Put it in the post office box. (?) Letter box (2). THEATRE: Give the alarm without trying to create too much excitement. BAD COMPANY: Association with bad company infiltrates our own personality and it's in a way contagious (2). TAXES: One of the necessary means of supporting our government and all that it provides for us (2). SHOES: Comfort, resistance to wear (1). LAND: There are more people that need it; same old story of demand (2). FOREST: Watch the sun where it was setting or rising. (?) It would give me the direction (2). LAW: To regulate human society and behavior (2). MARRIAGE: It's a legal state and it forms a record for all future time (2). DEAF: Because they have to first hear the sound before they can imitate it (2). RAW SCORE: 17.

Information

PRESIDENT: +. LONDON: +. PINTS: 4, no 2; +. RUBBER: +. THERMOMETER: +. WEEKS: +. ITALY: +. WASHINGTON: +. HEIGHT: +. PLANE: +. PARIS: +. BRAZIL: +. HAMLET: +. POLE: +. VATICAN: +. JAPAN: +. HEART: +. POPULATION: +. H. FINN: +. EGYPT: +. KORAN: +. FAUST: Grenot. HABEAS CORPUS: +. ETHNOLOGY: Study of birds. APOCRYPHA: dk. RAW SCORE: 22.

Digit Span

FORWARD: 3, 4, 5, 6 on first try; fails both series of 7 by omitting digits. BACKWARDS: 3, 4, 5, 6 on first try; fails both series of 7 by omitting digits. RAW SCORE: 12.

Arithmetic

ITEMS 1–7: +. ITEM 8: $525. ITEM 9: + + (12″). ITEM 10: + (20″). RAW SCORE: 10.

Similarities

ORANGE: Fruits (2). COAT: Wearing apparel (2). DOG: Animals (2). WAGON: Means of conveyance (2). DAILY PAPER: News dispensers (1). AIR: Chemical elements. WOOD: Alcohol is derived from wood. EYE: Parts of the body. (?) Special senses (1). EGG: Both elements from which life will spring, one in an animal and one in a plant (2). POEM: Expression of art (2). PRAISE: Both estimations of one's behavior (1). FLY: Both products of nature (1). RAW SCORE: 16.

Picture Arrangement

HOUSE: + 6″ (2). HOLD UP: + 5″ (2). ELEVATOR: + 14″ (2). FLIRT: AJNET 47″ (2). FISH: EFGHIJ 67″ (3). TAXI: ASMELU 59″; no insight. RAW SCORE: 11.

Picture Completion

NOSE: +. MUSTACHE: +. EAR: +. DIAMOND: One spot (35″). LEG: +. TAIL: +. STACKS: +. KNOB: +. SECOND HAND: +. WATER: +. REFLECTION: Leg on table. (?) Right arm. TIE: +. BULB: The connection (in filament). EYEBROW: dk. SHADOW: dk. RAW SCORE: 10.

Block Designs

ITEM 1: 6″ (5). ITEM 2: 13″ (4). ITEM 3: 12″ (4). ITEM 4: 25″ (4). ITEM 5: 48″ (4). ITEM 6: Has difficulty copying direction of diagonals, makes wide stripes using all-white blocks. Design incomplete at time limit. ITEM 7: Places an extra all-red block in center of top row; "I haven't got enough blocks. I'll have to change my tactics." Corrects error; eight blocks correct at time limit; completes design in 275″. RAW SCORE: 21.

Object Assembly

ITEM 1: 40" (6) . ITEM 2: 76"; uses ear-piece as skull-piece; corrects (6) . ITEM 3: 58" (7). RAW SCORE: 19.

Digit Symbol

56 correct; 2 reversals of the 2-symbol. RAW SCORE: 57.

Vocabulary

APPLE: Fruit (1). DONKEY: Animal (1)   JOIN: To become part of (1). DIAMOND: Precious stone (1). NUISANCE: An annoyance (1). FUR: Pelt of an animal, worn by women mostly (1). CUSHION: A soft... usually felt or cotton put in as pads for seats or beds (1). SHILLING: Coin, English (1). GAMBLE: Betting on various things of chance (1). BACON: Meat from hogs (1). NAIL: An instrument used in building. (?) Used to join planks together (1). CEDAR: A type of lumber gotten from the cedar tree (1). TINT: A type of color, light color (1). ARMORY: Place where arms are usually stored (1). FABLE: A story, usually for children (1). BRIM: The edge (1). GUILLOTINE: An instrument designed during the French Revolution by a man whose name was very similar. It beheads people. I'd like to do that to a few people I know in this world, Mr. Hitler in particular (1). PLURAL: Meaning two of anything. (?) Two or more (½). SECLUDE: To hide away (1). NITROGLYCERINE: A chemical which has explosive qualities; also used as a drug (1). STANZA: A part of a poem or verse or even song (1). MICROSCOPE: An instrument used for the magnification of objects in medicine, geology, crime detection (1). VESPER: A type of religious service. (?) Usually in the evening (1). BELFRY: The part of the church in which the bells are placed (1). RECEDE: To withdraw (1). AFFLICTION: Some type of deformity or disease (½) . PEWTER: A type of material from which kitchen or dining room utensils are made. (?) Alloy (1). BALLAST: dk. CATACOMB: Geological formation of some type. SPANGLE: A decorative glistening type of material that's put on dresses (1). ESPIONAGE: Done in secrecy by spies in the military. (?) Undermine the security of a country. (?) Wrecking plants, etc... IMMINENT: Certain to happen (½). MANTIS: dk. HARA KIRI: Form of suicide in Japan (1). CHATTEL: Connected with a mortgage. (?) They can come and take your furniture. (?) Other type of mortgage is on land and this one is on material. DILATORY: Delay (1). AMANUENSIS, PROSELYTE, MOIETY: dk. ASEPTIC: Sterile (1). FLOUT: To boast, show off. TRADUCE: dk. RAW SCORE: 30.5.

Weighted Scores and IQ's

Comprehension 15	Picture Arrangement 10	Vocabulary 13
Information 15	Picture Completion 9	Verbal IQ: 128
Digit Span 10	Block Designs 10	Performance IQ: 117
Arithmetic 13	Object Assembly 11	Total IQ: 124
Similarities 14	Digit Symbol 14	

RORSCHACH TEST

CARD I. Reaction time: 8″. Total time: 90″.

1. It could be some type of insect. It is symmetrical so it couldn't be a blot . . . too symmetrical. If it weren't for these blank spaces, it would be an insect, bat, or some developmental stage of a butterfly or . . . what exactly, I do not know. 2. (covers half) Maybe a map . . . not all produced on the other side. [(?) Irregularities, indentations, . . . the openings are like lakes.]

SCORES. 1: Ws F+A P.   2: Ws F—Map.

CARD II. Reaction time: 15″. Total time: 90″.

1. It might be some type of flower. The pattern is exactly symmetrical as some type of plant, flower maybe. [(?) Two colors, some little projection like it might be the pollen-bearing stalk. Its nice pattern is not unlike a bloom.] . . . ∨ 2. It could be an insect too, again. [(?) Projections, mouth, feelers (lower red) . . . very nice, like an insect, butterfly would be.] That's all I can say about that.

SCORES: 1: W FC∓Pl.   2: W F+A.

CARD III. Reaction time: 90″. Total time: 150″.

I just never have seen anything like it . . . coming apart now, not joined together. I don't know of anything, plant or animal, that it could represent. I do not know . . . (?) It looks like it's taking the form of two human beings, facing each other, feet, body, head. [(?) Feet are sharp, pointed like leaves.]

SCORE: D M+H P.

CARD IV. Reaction time: 7″. Total time: 75″.

That looks to me like a rug that has been made out of the skin of a big bear. [(?) Color, texture, short neck and big head, short tail.] No . . . I don't think of anything else . . . that fulfills that exactly. (Exact description of card.) Yes, sir, I really believe that's a hide of an animal.

SCORE: W FCh+Ad P.

CARD V. Reaction time: 20″. Total time: 90″.

1. That looks to me like the fur of a fox or a small animal. That's what I think it is. [(?) Shape, color, texture. (?) The symmetry, two sides had back legs, front legs on it are parts I associated with them. I think that's all I could say to support my view.] 2. It could be a butterfly, now that I come to think of it, but it looks much more like the hide of an animal.

SCORES. 1: W FCh∓Ad.   2: W F+A P.

CARD VI. Reaction time: 10″. Total time: 90″.

Hmm, I think that's definitely an animal, the type I don't know because of the long neck. I see the hide, the feet; the head and neck are quite unusual . . . Maybe even a deer, short tail, short legs and neck a little bit too long. (?) I don't think it could be anything else but an animal . . . a hide of an animal. [(?) Just the parts I mentioned. (?) No.]

SCORE: W FCh + Ad P.

CARD VII. Reaction time: 65″. Total time: 120″.

Hmm (groan) . . . (Picks up card and holds it far off . . . sigh.) I have no idea . . . I think that's very puzzling. I don't know . . . I imagine it's also some sort of animal . . . of a different shape and size, that is hard to skin. It looks like fur to me. All I can think of is an animal. [(?) Having seen hides before. (?) The back part was covered, projections could be feet, color and texture.]

SCORE: W ChF Ad.

CARD VIII. Reaction time: 15″. Total time: 90″.

This looks like an animal to me, the pink part, four feet . . . an animal, and the coloring in between I don't know. Definitely these pink figures look like an animal. The others are just a decorative scheme, but no special object than the animals on each side.

SCORE: D F+ A P.

CARD IX. Reaction time: 45″. Total time: 120″.

∧ . . . ∨ . . . ∧ ∨ . . . Might be some embryological study in the brain. I am not very familiar with it . . . the forebrain (pink), midbrain (green), hindbrain (orange). [(?) Spinal cord (midline) at the end of it; the symmetry; different shapes of different parts; suggestion of a cord.] No, I don't know what it could be. That got me. I do not know. Suggests nothing else.

SCORE: W F—Ats.

CARD X. Reaction time: 7″. Total time: 90″.

I think this is a part of the nervous system, very definitely. Here comes the spinal cord, lateral ventricles in the spinal cord (upper middle gray). This probably is some neurological cell (side blue). I don't know the anatomy of the brain enough to discuss it with you but this is brain.

SCORE: W F—Ats.

Summary of Responses

R: 13   EB: 1—.5

W 11	F+ 3	A 4	W% 85
D 2	F— 3	Ad 4	D% 15
s (2)	F± 1	H 1	
	M 1+	At 2	F% 54-92
Qualitative	FC 1∓	Pl 1	F+% 57-58
Circumstantiality	FCh 2+, 1∓	Geog 1	A% 62
Exactness	ChF 1		H% 8
			At% 15
			P 6
			P% 46

ANALYSIS OF RESULTS

BELLEVUE SCALE

The scatter is indicative of anxiety (Digit Span drop) and depression (drop of four of the Performance scores and of the Performance IQ). Neither the anxiety nor depression appears to be extreme since a scatter of 3 to 4 points below Vocabulary is not great. The high Verbal level suggests that the character make-up is primarily obsessive-compulsive.

The verbalizations in Information and Comprehension are not especially revealing. "Grenot" for Gounod on the *Faust* item suggests rather poorly developed cultural interests for a person with his educational background. In Similarities, the phrase "news dispensers" is somewhat stilted and therefore has an obsessive quality. In Block Designs, the incapacitating effects of tension are indicated on the seventh item when he builds a row of 5 blocks, losing the logical implications of 16 blocks and a square design. In Vocabulary, there is another stilted verbalization: "betting on various things of chance." Note also "infiltrates our own personality" on *bad company* in Comprehension.

RORSCHACH TEST

The presence of only 13 responses, the $A\%$ of 62 and the $P\%$ of 46 are indicative of depressive features because the Bellevue Scale has indicated a high level of intelligence and has therefore implied that greater productivity and variety would normally be present. Depressive features almost invariably cut down productivity and variability. The almost complete restriction of responses to more or less gross W's, the presence of 4 shading responses in such a short record, and the relatively low $F+\%$, are all diagnostic of the anxiety state. They indicate that the reduced responsiveness associated with the depressive features is dominated by an anxious quality, and that he is restricted to gross, often inaccurate perceptions and judgments. The coarctated EB in the context of superior intelligence indicates the rigidity of inhibitory defenses. The solitary $FC-$ suggests that adaptive efforts are continuing despite the incapacitating features already mentioned, but that these efforts are likely to be forced and unsuccessful. The 15% At does not suggest bodily preoccupation since the subject is a doctor, and since medical interests are known to increase the $At\%$ significantly.

Turning to the verbalizations, we find striking attention to detail throughout the record: he is concerned with symmetry and asymmetry, with exactness and with the "perfect" response. Compulsive circumstantiality and perfectionism are pervasive. Yet these strenuous efforts bring little gain; this is essentially much ado about nothing, for he ends up by seeing a couple of animal skins, butterflies and brains, a map, a flower and a person. When the productivity appears to be greatly decreased and the responses groan under the heavy burden of profitless compulsiveness, a decompensation of a compulsive character make-up is indicated. These decompensations generally yield a symptomatic picture of anxiety, tension, and depression; the basic pathology is the increasing ineffectiveness of compulsive defenses despite the relatively greater and more rigid reliance on them in the face of the resulting anxiety.

The verbalization on III—"It looks like it's taking a form of two human beings . . ."—is a spontaneous description of a perceptual-associative process and is distinctively obsessive.

TEST REPORT

Intelligence and Thought Organization: This appears to be an intelligent man whose thinking is dominated by obsessive-compulsive features. Although in more familiar situations (Bellevue Scale) his thinking appears to be neat and precise, in less familiar and more threatening situations (Rorschach Test) empty perfectionism and circumstantiality become apparent. His productivity and efficiency appear to be significantly lowered. His present IQ is 124.

Emotional Factors: Decompensation of compulsive defenses appears to have taken place, with a resulting state of anxiety, tension, and depression. Exacerbation of compulsive features and intensification of inhibition are also noted. Adaptive efforts are forced and unsuccessful.

Diagnostic Impression: Anxiety state with depressive features in a decompensating compulsive character.

CLINICAL SUMMARY

Dr. C. was a forty-three year old man from Arizona, unmarried and with no hobbies. He appeared to be a compulsive, hyperconscientious person. He had built up a handsome income in private practice by working at a terrific pace and for long hours. In the Army he found himself with little to do but fill out forms. He became increasingly discouraged and exasperated with the enforced idleness, and became irritable and provocatively aggressive. When he spoke of his difficulties he was quite tense, tears came to his eyes, his voice rose almost to a scream, he beat on the arms of his chair and cried, "I can't stand it!" The diagnosis was anxiety state with mild depression in a compulsive personality.

NEURASTHENIA: TEST RESULTS

Mr. C. Age: 43. Education: 1 year High school. Occupation: Barber. Marital: 17 years; 2 children. Father: Tailor, died when patient was 5. Early Environment: Small town. Family Position: Youngest of 4. Religion: Protestant.

BELLEVUE SCALE

Comprehension

ENVELOPE: Mail it (2). THEATER: I would get up quietly and notify the management (2). BAD COMPANY: Will get you into trouble and send you downhill (1). TAXES: To maintain the government (2). SHOES: To be comfortable, for long wearing (1). LAND: More valuable on account of the location, near populated area (1). FOREST: Locate the sun and try to arrive at my direction from the sun (2). LAWS: To protect the people (1). LICENSE: (laughs) I never had given thought to that; revenue and to keep a record (1). DEAF: Unable to hear the spoken word and learn to talk (2). RAW SCORE: 15.

Information

PRESIDENT: +. LONDON: +. PINTS: 4. RUBBER: +. THERMOMETER: +. WEEKS: +. ITALY: +. WASHINGTON: +. HEIGHT: 5,2. PLANE: +. PARIS: +. BRAZIL: +. HAMLET: +. POLE: +. VATICAN: +. JAPAN: +. HEART: +. POPULATION: +. H. FINN: +. EGYPT: Asia. KORAN: Near Japan. FAUST: dk. HABEAS CORPUS: dk. ETHNOLOGY: dk. APOCRYPHA: dk. RAW SCORE: 17.

Digit Span

FORWARD: gets 3, 4, 5 and 6 on first try; fails both series of 7. BACKWARDS: gets 3 and 4 on first try; fails first series of 5 and 6; fails both at 7. RAW SCORE: 12.

Arithmetic

All correct; no time bonuses. RAW SCORE: 10.

Similarities

ORANGE: Fruit (2). COAT: Clothing (2). DOG: Animals (2). WAGON: Vehicles (2). DAILY PAPER: Both present news (1). AIR: Both contain oxygen; both necessary for life (2). WOOD: Both burn (1). EYE: Both take care of one sense (2). EGG: Both reproduce (1).

POEM: Statue presents the likeness and the other the feeling of any-thing. PRAISE: dk. (?) dk. FLY: No likeness. (?) No. RAW SCORE: 15.

Picture Arrangement

HOUSE: + 6" (2). HOLD UP: + 6" (2). ELEVATOR: + 12" (2). FLIRT: AJNET 17" (2). FISH: IJEHGF 49"; no insight. TAXI: SALEUM 35"; no insight (1). RAW SCORE: 9.

Picture Completion

NOSE: +. MUSTACHE: +. EAR: +. DIAMOND: +. LEG: Eyes. TAIL: +. STACKS: +. KNOB: +. SECOND HAND: +. WATER: +. REFLECTION: +. TIE: dk. THREADS: +. EYEBROW: dk. SHADOW: dk. RAW SCORE: 11.

Block Designs

ITEM 1: 9" (5). ITEM 2: 36" (3). ITEM 3: 17" (3). ITEM 4: 23" (4). ITEM 5: 42" (4). ITEM 6: has the principle of the stripes but makes errors; design not complete at 150". ITEM 7: starts with center, uses all-whites; finally corrects; difficulty on sides; design not complete at 195". RAW SCORE: 19.

Object Assembly

ITEM 1: 15" (6). ITEM 2: ear reversed; 18" (4). ITEM 3: tries various arbitrary combinations; only the thumb is in place at 180" (1). RAW SCORE: 11.

Digit Symbol

47 correct; no errors. RAW SCORE: 47.

Vocabulary

APPLE: Fruit (1). DONKEY: Animal (1). JOIN: To put together (1). DIAMOND: Stone. (?) It's valuable (1). NUISANCE: An undesir-able conduct (½). FUR: Covering of a fur-bearing animal (1). CUSHION: Soft article to lay on or... (1). SHILLING: English money (1). GAMBLE: A game of chance (1). BACON: The side of a hog (1). NAIL: Galvanized article used in building (1). NITRO-GLYCERINE: Explosive (1). STANZA: In poems, a part of a poem (1). MICROSCOPE: A delicate instrument whereby bacteria is seen, its size is magnified (1). VESPER: A song, church song (1). BRIM: Edge of (1). GUILLOTINE: A thing where they destroy a man's life; used in France (1). PLURAL: More than one (1). SECLUDE: To hide (1). CEDAR: Tree, timber (1). TINT: To color (1). ARMORY: A place maintained by the government for military purposes (1). FABLE: Untrue story (1). BELFRY: Part of a building containing the bell (1). RECEDE: Retreat (1). AFFLICTION: A human ailment (½). PEWT-ER: An old metal used for tableware (1). BALLAST: A weight. (?) Usually used in ships (1). CATACOMB: A place built in rock, used by ancient people. (?) Rooms (½). SPANGLE: dk. ESPIONAGE: Under-cover work in military operations. (?) Undercover (½). IMMINENT:

To be close, friendly. MANTIS: dk. HARA KIRI: dk. CHATTEL: When I take a lien on something you have. DILATORY: dk. AMANUENSIS: dk. ALL REST: dk. RAW SCORE: 28.

Weighted Scores and IQ's

Comprehension 13	Picture Arrangement 8	Vocabulary 12
Information 13	Picture Completion 10	Verbal IQ: 118
Digit Span 10	Block Designs 9	Performance IQ: 103
Arithmetic 13	Object Assembly 4	Total IQ: 113
Similarities 12	Digit Symbol 11	

RORSCHACH TEST

CARD I. Reaction time: 6″. Total time: 90″.

Looks like the skeleton of something ... of some animal, of some deep sea animal.
SCORE: Ws F—AAt.

CARD II. Reaction time: 50″. Total time: 120″.

1. Hm ... (smiles) ... A candle (upper middle Dd). 2. Bears, reaching up on a table or counter (just the black).
SCORES. 1: Dd F∓Obj. 2: D FM+A P.

CARD III. Reaction time: 55″. Total time: 120″.

Well, that looks like two people trying to pick up the same object ... and I don't see anything in the red part of the picture: doesn't represent anything.
SCORE: W M+H P.

CARD IV. Reaction time: 60″. Total time: 90″.

You are supposed to look at it just as it is? That again looks to me like some kind of deep sea animal; some species ... I don't know what, couldn't name it.
SCORE: W F∓A.

CARD V. Reaction time: 13″. Total time: 60″.

Well, that looks like a bat or butterfly ... that's all.
SCORE: W F+A P.

CARD VI. Reaction time: 90″. Total time: 180″.

Hm ... well, that again looks to me like the top side or back part of a sea animal ... the hide or skin off it. [(?) Just looked like it.]
SCORE: W F∓Ad.

CARD VII. Reaction time: 100″. Total time: 120″.

I don't make a thing out of that ... (Try.) ... The only thing I can compare that to is the picture of ... the lower part here (lower one-third) ... of the lungs ... No, I can't make a thing out of that picture.
SCORE: D F—Ats.

CARD VIII. Reaction time: 70″. Total time: 165″.

1. These two objects here look like animals of some kind (side pink). 2. This part here looks like the top of a tree (upper gray-green). [(?) Shape.] 3. This part here in the center looks like the picture of a vertebra I saw (upper center). 4. This is the lungs (center blue). 5. This is the lower part of the body (pink and orange). [(?) Just continuing it down.]

SCORES. 1: D F+A P. 2: D F+Pl. 3: D F+At. 4: D F−Ats. 5. D F∓At.

CARD IX. Failure: 120″.

Hm, Jesus! .. I can't make anything on that ... I never saw anything like that that I know of ... I wouldn't have any remarks on that, I just don't know.

CARD X. Reaction time: 55″. Total time: 150″.

1. Well, this might be a rabbit, a long-eared fellow (lower middle). 2. That reminds me of a couple of cherries (center orange). [(?) Just looks like it. (?) Shape.] 3. These look like bugs on a straw (upper gray). And that's all I make of that picture.

SCORES. 1: D F+Ad P. 2: D F+Food. 3: D F+A Combination.

Summary of Responses

R: 16   EB: 1.5—0

W 5	F+ 7	A 5	W% 31
D 10	F− 3	Ad 2	D% 62
Dd 1	F∓ 4	H 1	
s (1)	M 1+	At 5	F% 88-100
	FM 1+	Obj 1	F+% 50-56
Qualitative		Pl 1	
Failure on IX		Food 1	A% 44
Delayed reactions			H% 6
Combination 1			At% 31
			P 5
			P% 31

Summary of Responses

BELLEVUE SCALE

The scatter suggests tension and the visual-motor retardation of a depressive or of a sluggish neurasthenic. The retardation is seen in the drop of the Performance level below the Verbal level (Verbal IQ is 118, Performance IQ is 103). Tension is seen in the especially striking drop in Object Assembly—a subtest especially vulnerable in the presence of tension. The fact that this man has had only one year of high school education and obtains clearly above average scores on most of the Verbal subtests suggests that he is or was a man of noteworthy "drive" toward self-betterment, and therefore suggests prominent compulsive features.

RORSCHACH TEST

The number of responses, 16, is low for a person of his intelligence and suggests that tension and depression or sluggishness may be cutting down productivity. However, the $A\%$ and $P\%$ are not unduly high and instead there is a high $At\%$ of 31. In a coarctated record, the presence of even a few anatomy responses indicates significant bodily preoccupation. The low R, the coarctated EB of 1.5—0 and the high $F\%$ of 88-100 suggest generalized inhibition, lack of "drive" and warmth (no colors), and ruminativeness (1.5 M). The low $F+\%$ indicates noteworthy reduction of intellectual efficiency. The lack of "drive" is particularly impressive since the Bellevue Scale has already indicated that strong efforts toward achievement have been conspicuous in his psychological development. At present, on Card III, he can say only that the men are *trying* to lift something—probably an expression of feelings of inadequacy.

We end up therefore with a picture of a bright, compulsive man whose efficiency, productivity and "drive" appear to be pathologically reduced by inhibition, tension and sluggishness. Emotional output is minimal and his responsiveness has a flat quality. In addition, a ruminative inclination and conspicuous bodily preoccupations are indicated. This is the typical test picture of a neurasthenic condition in a compulsive personality. It represents a type of decompensation different from that described in the case of anxiety and depression discussed in this chapter. There, acute anxiety and intensification of compulsive attempts to regain control were indicated; here we find a more apathetic and flat quality, and bodily preoccupations are more prominent.

CLINICAL SUMMARY

For the past two years this patient has had many somatic complaints, most of which refer to his back and inguinal region, and which he believes are due to some type of prostatic disease. In addition he has become acutely anxious, despondent and irritable and has had frequent crying spells. He strenuously resisted efforts to demonstrate that his complaints had no physical basis. Premorbidly he had been a compulsive worker and successful business man.

NARCISSISTIC CHARACTER DISORDER: RORSCHACH TEST

Mrs. D. Age: 36. Education: High school; finishing school. Occupation: Housewife. Marital: 6th marriage. Husband: Manufacturer. Father: Finance. Early Environment: Big city. Family Position: Only child. Religion: Protestant.

CARD I. Reaction time: 18″. Total time: 75″.

What it might look like... 1. A crab, I guess (grimace). [(?) The shape of it. (?) Shape of it was the shape of a crab! (?) I don't have too much information on crabs... I don't know. (?) It comes in on the center and goes out like a crab (laugh).] It looks like ink has been spilled (gestures)... 2. A map. [(?) I've seen others like that. (?) From the outline of it. (?) No... shadowed like some maps.] (smile) It doesn't look like much else to me. 3. A butterfly... no... I guess a butterfly, vaguely.

SCORES. 1: W F∓A. 2: W ChF Geog. 3: W F+A P.

CARD II. Reaction time: 25″. Total time: 120″.

(Grimaces.) Holy Smoke!... (laughs) I'm going to repeat myself. 1. It looks like the other one, like a butterfly. [(?) The shape... all-over shape. (?) No. (?) No.] ... Or... I don't think I'm going to be helpful to you. I can't see anything in it. Can I leave off parts of it? 2. I guess it could be two little puppy dogs if you try real hard (black). [(?) Sitting down, side view, little eye. By a stretch of the imagination, it could have a collar (stripe in shading). (Where is the collar? As the examiner extended the card to her, but before she looked at it, she answered.) On its neck.]

SCORES. 1: W F±A. 2: D F(C)+Ad P.

CARD III. Reaction time: 35″. Total time: 120″.

(Grimaces, laughs, looks at examiner.) (What could it look like?) You mean just wildly? I suppose it could be two people... Awful! Something is in their hands, I don't know, baskets or... [(?) (grimaces) I did well to think they look like people, vaguely,... long-necked people. (?) Men.] (Look like anything else?) Not to me. (?) Some more? (plaintive tone) Do I have to look at it the same way... I can turn it around? ... ∨ ... ∧ (?) I guess I just don't have imagination.

SCORE: W M+H P.

CARD IV. Reaction time: 20″. Total time: 90″.

(Grimaces.) ... ∨ ... ∧ (laughs) Frankly, that could look like a cow... kind of flattened out. [(Flat?) (patient demonstrates) Looked like it had been cut in two.] ... (sighs) ... (waves hand)... (Else?)... (shakes head).

SCORE: W F±A Aggression.

CARD V. Reaction time: 50″. Total time: 90″.

They're certainly uniform, aren't they? ... (laughs) ... (shakes head) ... Is there such a thing as a rabbit with wings? (laughs) ... > ∨ ... (whisper) You can just take it away.

SCORE: W F + A Fabulized-combination.

CARD VI. Reaction time: 35″. Total time: 110″.

(Grimaces ... covers top of card.) Without that it could almost be an aerial map with a big highway, or a river running straight through it. [(?) Oh, it has dark places on it which could be elevations, dark lines could be a highway. I never saw a river that straight ... its shadings.] (Else?) I still can't see anything else. (?) I have no ideas about it.

SCORE: D ChF Geog.

CARD VII. Reaction time: 30″. Total time: 120″.

(Grimaces even before card is presented.) ... (laughs) 1. It looks like two little animals with long ears, looking at each other, standing on something. [(?) Kind of perched, weren't standing; like fluff. (?) (laughs) Fuzzy. (?) It was kind of light, wasn't a direct line, sort of wandered around. (Light?) Light in color.] ... < ∧ ... (Hands card back.) ... (Else?) It don't mean anything ... I just stop. (?) 2. It looks like something kids cut out with paper and unfold. (Coughs: "Pardon me.") (?) No.

SCORES. 1: W FC′+A (P). 2: W F−Cutout.

CARD VIII. Reaction time: 45″. Total time: 120″.

A terrific sameness here ... to me ... > (?) (Covers sides of card, ... sighs.) ... < ... ∧ ... Looks like two little animals climbing up something. I seem to be stuck on the animal idea. [(?) (grimace) I don't know very much about animals but it looked like a little, long animal with feet (laughs cutely). (Kind?) Not dogs, not squirrels; no tail. I don't know. I never looked at a rat real close but that ... you'll have me dreaming things in a minute.] I'm just very sorry, I don't see anything. (?) You don't want me to make something up? (?) (shakes head) There just isn't.

SCORE: D F+A P.

CARD IX. Failure: 140″.

(Sighs, whistles.) ... I wish you wouldn't do this to me! ... It just doesn't look like anything I ever saw before ... (sighs ... drums fingers) ... (?) I'm keeping at it but it looks just the same ... (?) Not to me ... just rather pretty colors.

CARD X. Reaction time: 40″. Total time: 120″.

Well! ... (looks at wall pictures) ... (tilts card). Very wildly, it could be flowers; only the colors make me think that ... no shape. [(?) I told you, no ... just the color.] ... ∨ ... (laughs) ... (?) Really that isn't much because it doesn't look an awful lot like that to me ... I'm just no help.

SCORE: W C Pl.

Summary of Responses

R: 13   EB: 1—1.5

W 10	F+ 3	A 7	W% 77
D 3	F— 1	Ad 1	D% 23
	F± 2	H 1	
	F∓ 1	Pl 1	F% 54-77
Qualitative	M 1+	Cutout 1	F+% 71-80
Failure IX	C 1	Geog 2	
Fabulized-Combination 1	F (C) 1+		A% 54
Aggression 1	FC' 1+		H% 8
	ChF 2		P 4 (1)
			P% 31 (38)

ANALYSIS OF RORSCHACH TEST RESULTS

It seems better to begin this analysis by reviewing the content of the record before discussing the summary of scores. On Card I she makes a face as she offers her first response and then gestures as she describes the blot. At once there is a suggestion of histrionic behavior. Inquiry into the "crab" makes clear that she is strongly resistive to reflective thinking: after mentioning the shape vaguely, she resists efforts to get her to describe the shape, and even attempts a false confession of ignorance before she finally gives in and offers a futile formal articulation. This avoidance of reflective thinking is characteristic of most narcissistic character disorders and is part of the syndrome of low anxiety tolerance, a passive-demanding orientation, excessive reliance on the defense of avoidance, and inability to reflect on thinking and behavior. Avoidance and retreat into passivity (feigned ignorance) are prominent in this example.

On Card II, the "Holy Smoke!" and the accompanying grimace are even more histrionic. "I don't think I am going to be very helpful to you" is so inappropriately sympathetic that utter lack of insight into her difficulties is indicated. "If you try real hard", she says as she gives a popular response. So far this is the best articulated of her responses, the previous four having been more or less gross, "lazy" W's. They are lazy because this woman's IQ is 121, superior intelligence range, and if there had been genuine drive in her it would have shown itself in more articulated, creative responses. The records of many narcissistic characters, especially when addiction is present, consist almost entirely of vague and popular responses, despite an intelligence level that could be the basis for a much richer record. The inability to apply assets constructively because of the passive, narcissistic orientation is what is implied. During inquiry she expresses her irritation in a flippant manner, deliberately misinterpreting the question in order to make the examiner feel foolish.

Histrionics continue on III, especially in the mock-plaintive question, "Some more?" and in the variety of expressive movements and sounds on IV. On V she whispers dramatically, but for no good reason, "You can just take it away". The fabulized combination on V is a strained W, and probably refers to a sterile "quality ambition" or pretentiousness. (Note the high $W\%$.) On VIII we find the key to the whole record: "A terrific sameness here." The first fully chromatic card and a distinctive one in a formal sense as well, and yet it looks like all the rest to her. This bit of verbalization demonstrates how little emotional participation has been involved in her previous responses. Everything looks alike when a person can invest affect in nothing, when there is a basic coldness and distance from people and objects. Chronic ennui can therefore be expected to be a conspicuous symptom. It is quite clear by now that we are dealing with an extremely narcissistic woman and that her continuous display of affect is shallow play-acting.

On IX, the most difficult "emotional situation", she can do nothing at all, indicating how little capacity she has for coping with affects once they must be faced. On X she finally gives a color response, a pure C. Note that this is the first and only color response, another bit of evidence of the shallowness of her affective display (otherwise color would have appeared sooner and more frequently) and her narcissistic orientation (otherwise a more balanced color distribution would have been present).

Turning now to the summary of scores we can understand the high $W\%$ as an indicator of empty pretentiousness, especially when we consider the creative poverty implied in only 13 responses, 1 M and a high $A\%$ and $P\%$. The color distribution bespeaks a cold narcissistic character make-up and the failure on IX represents her low tolerance for anxiety- and affect-arousing situations. There is, however, one unusual feature: the two shading responses. Shading tends to be absent from the records of narcissistic character disorders, especially when R is low, indicating the characteristically weak reflectiveness. This may be a hopeful sign but we must remember that there was no break in her test behavior which could be construed as an effort to admit and cope with anxiety. The remaining tests will have to decide this issue. (In this case the rest of the battery confirms the Rorschach Test results by indicating that her narcissistic defenses are so rigidly maintained that sustained, sincere efforts to work on herself would be most unlikely. It is, in fact, evident that there is no genuine acceptance of the fact that anything is wrong.)

CLINICAL SUMMARY

Mrs. D. is currently on the verge of divorcing her sixth husband. She comes with a history of addiction to alcohol and barbiturates. In her interviews she was evasive, misleading, inclined to be histrionic and to exaggerate incidents; she falsely denied any alcoholism at present.

PSYCHOTIC DEPRESSION: THEMATIC APPERCEPTION TEST

Mrs. S. Age: 51. Education: High school. Occupation: Housewife. Marital: 26 years, 2 sons. Husband: Merchant. Father: Merchant. Early Environment: Big city. Family Position: Oldest of 3; both siblings dead. Religion: Jewish.

CARD 1. (Boy with violin.) A boy looking at a violin ... What led up to it? I guess a string broke, is that it? What the outcome will be? He'll stop playing. (Feel?) He feels sad.

CARD 2. (Old woman in doorway.) A lady looking for someone ... What led up to it? The silence of the music I guess. The outcome will be ... she will look for the absent member. (Who is absent?) The one who played the music. (?) The grandchild, I guess. (Why looking for him?) There wasn't any music now. (Where did he go?) Out the door. (?) Because there wasn't any music. (Feel?) He ought to be practising, I suppose.

CARD 3. (Old man in graveyard.) He's looking at tombstones ... a ghost looking at tombstones. (How come?) I don't know why. (Whose tombstone is he looking at?) A member of his family. (Which?) I don't know. (?) A child. (How die?) Fever. (Feel?) He wants to see his child. (?) Sad.

CARD 4. (Silhouette of man at window.) Gazing out the window ... looking at the sky ... What else do you want me to tell you? ... That's all I can see. (Happening?) It's dark in the room. (Why at window?) To see the sky. (Feel?) Restful.

CARD 5. (Heads of embracing couple.) His mother is petting him ... What else do I say? (Story!) He's ... I don't know why. (Make up!) I don't know what to make up ... He was scolded in school I guess. (Why scolded?) Didn't get his lessons. (Outcome?) He will teei better. (Mother feel?) Sad.

CARD 6. (Prehistoric animal, rocky road, bridge.) It's a scene...
scenery... just a bridge, a little bridge, scenery... that's all. Some
rocks by the side. (See anything else?) Just a narrow road. (Else?) That's
all. (Sure?) I thought I saw the sky. (?) No, I didn't see it... I don't
know what that is (the dark gray).

CARD 7. (Shadowy photograph of thumb.) I don't know what this
is... (?) I don't know what it is... (?) I don't know. (It's a thumb.)
Well, I guess so. (Story!) Well, it's just a thumb. (?) I can't see anything.
(?) A piece of the... call it nail if you want to (drop of blood). That's
all I see.

CARD 8. (Nude couple; older woman with infant.) That's the
members of the Bible but I don't know much about the Bible so I don't
know who they are... a mother holding her child... other people,
members pleading with her. (Why pleading?) I don't know. (?) Consent
to their love. (Led up?) I don't know. (?) Their love led up to it. (?)
She doesn't approve. (Why not?) Thinks they're too young, I guess. (?)
They plead for it and gain her consent... no, I don't think they do.
She don't approve. (Outcome?) They marry. (Feel?) Hard toward her.
(Role of the baby?) I don't know.

CARD 9. (Two chairs, table set for tea.) Table with tea for two...
the guests haven't arrived... be there later on. (Led up?) I don't know.
(Guests?) A couple, I don't know who... who are in love, I guess. (?)
To declare their love. (Mean?) To one another. (Outcome?) It will
all be arranged satisfactorily.

CARD 10. (Old man on shoulders of another old man.) Ghosts in
the sky... That's all I can see. (Happening?) One is trying to grab the
other one, snatch him. (Why?) 'Cause he... I don't know why. (?)
'Cause he just died. (Who?) This... grandson (bottom figure)... All
I know. The top one is the grandfather. (How die?) Fever. (Why
snatching him?) Snatch him to heaven. (Successful?) Yes.

CARD F 11. (Hag behind young woman.) Picture of a mother...
What else? (Story!) She's lost her child... buried her. (Mother?) The
youngest one in the picture. (Other?) Death. (What happened?) Died.
(How?) Fever. (Mother feel?) Sad.

CARD F 12. (Men unloading boat, girl on bridge.) Walking across
the bridge... That's all I know. (Who?) The lady. (Why?) I don't
know. (?) I don't know. (?) A flood underneath. (Girl thinking?) She's
thinking it's lonely. (Feel?) Frightened. (Why?) She's afraid she can't
get across. (Outcome?) She gets across.

CARD F 13. (Boy with book, two girls in background.) Listening to
a lecture... on how to study their lessons... They will study. (Who's
lecturing?) The preacher, I guess. (Why?) So they should study.

CARD F 14. (Woman turning away from man.) Asking for a kiss...
having it refused... pleading for it. (Led up?) I don't know. (?) She's
a single girl. (?) He doesn't receive it. (Relationship?) Friends. (Girl
feel?) Shy. (?) She likes him.

CARD F 15. (Girl leaning against wall, arm outstretched.) Sobbing ... because she's left alone ... wants her friend to come for her. (Led up?) I don't know. (?) Fuss, I guess. (?) Lover's quarrel. (Over what?) I don't know. (?) She wanted to go some place. (?) The one she loves the best. (?) He doesn't come. (?) She's left alone. (?) She cries. (?) Never comes back. (?) Sad. (Always sad?) Not always.

CARD F 16. (Man at window.) Gazing out the window at his son ... What else do I see? ... Wanted him to play well ... and be a good child. (Playing?) Ball. (?) He thinks he should watch over him. (Why?) The child isn't behaving. (?) He's just young.

CARD F 17. (Two women struggling on stairway.) Mother choking her child ... because he won't mind. He's been disobedient ... That's all I know. (?) Hasn't obeyed in school. (?) Didn't study his lesson. (Mother feel?) Sad, worried. (Outcome?) He's punished and he'll obey. (Happening in picture?) Looks to me like she's strangling him. (Mother feel?) Worried. (Why?) About punishing him.

CARD F 18. (Maid in hallway.) The maid ... looking at something that was left in the room ... (What?) I don't know. (?) A package. (?) She thinks it belongs to somebody.

CARD F 19. (Woman in bed, dishevelled man standing.) The man ... You'd be surprised at what I'm really thinking about ... (What?) Has nothing to do with the picture. (?) I don't know what this is ... (?) ... A man getting run out of town ... All I can make out of it ... Disobeying the laws. (?) He was a bad citizen. (What makes you think so?) Just his expression, and the way he was dressed. (What else in picture?) On a bridge, isn't it? ... Looked like a bridge to me. (How come bad citizen?) I don't know. (?) He was raised wrong, bad family. (?) He's run out of town. (Outcome?) He gets in more bad company. (Feel?) He felt ... desperate. (?) He'd do anything to escape.

CARD F 20. (Bearded old man, looking down.) Father Time ... I guess I'm all wrong ... Didn't get any of the pictures right! ... How did I do? ... The troubles of the world. (See on card?) Father Time. (Troubles?) The war; might as well make it modern. (Thinking?) All the deaths. (Feel?) Sad.

ANALYSIS OF THEMATIC APPERCEPTION TEST RESULTS

The briefness and barrenness of the spontaneous verbalizations and the responses to inquiry are indicative of severe blocking or retardation of thought processes and therefore point to a profound depression. At the beginning (see Card 1) she tries painfully to comply with the instructions, but by the time she reaches Card 5 ("What else do I say?") a retreat into inert passivity is evident. Attempts to elicit free fantasy are ineffective.

Card 1. The theme, stated with simple finality, is that one gives up in the face of even minor difficulty: "He'll stop playing." The boy feels "sad". Card 2. The theme is a continuation of the first, but is overshadowed by the idea of "a lady looking for someone ... the absent member". This vague, general statement—"absent member"—for a very concrete, specific idea indicates an expression of a personal feeling. Here the implicit feeling is loneliness after loss of the love-object. The poignant statement, "the silence of the music", expresses the emotional tone of the entire set of stories. Card 3. The theme is grief at loss of a love-object—in this case, the child. Card 4. This is essentially description. In terms of the depressive tone of the record, the "restful" feeling probably is longed for. Card 5. Here the mother is affectionate to the child but feels sad because he has not fulfilled his responsibilities. This idea has already been hinted at on Card 2 and will become even clearer later on. The theme is concern with moral responsibility.

Card 6: description. Card 7: description. Card 8. The theme is ambivalence toward children-figures. The ambivalence has already been seen in the contrast of Card 3 (death of child) and Card 5 (petting the child) and will become still clearer in later stories. The overt vacillation in this story is striking. The children are seen as rejecting the mother. The naive realism and peculiar wording in "members of the Bible" are psychotic and indicate religious preoccupation. Card 9. The theme is love without complications. This picture ordinarily elicits more casual stories about chatting or business, and the intrusion of the idea of nicely arranged love probably expresses a wish. Card 10. The theme is the death of a child, another expression of hostility. She avoids the aggressive implications of the picture, first by saying nothing and second by changing the idea of "snatching" to "snatching to heaven". Such a turnabout is clearly indicative of rigid efforts to deny aggressive impulses which are breaking through to expression. The opening statement, "ghosts in the sky", has a decidedly superstitious quality, since it is stated without qualification. On Card 3 she saw "a ghost looking at tombstones"—a similarly superstitious statement. The expression of such ideas in a record which as a whole appears to be that of a psychotic depressive suggests, however, that this is not mere superstition, but that normally unconscious, primitive, magical fantasies are breaking into consciousness. Preoccupations or delusions with this content—ghosts— are likely to be present.

Card 11. The theme is again death of a child. It is not unlikely that this indicates the presence of the frequent delusion of psychotic depressives that they have destroyed their children in some way. Since this patient is in her fifties, it is likely that essentially she is talking more directly about her relationship with her children than about that with her mother. Card 12. The theme is loneliness, apprehensiveness, and despair. At the end she says, "she gets across", but in this very depressive setting, the statement can be regarded as no more than a feeble wish. These feeble wishes are not infrequent in depressive records; what gives them away as such is the context of utter gloom from which they emerge. A hopeful person would not have gotten in that spot in the first place. Moreover, describing the water as a *flood* indicates the tendency to exaggerate the aggressive, destructive implications of situations or events. Card 13. Moral responsibility is again the theme. The sudden intrusion of a "preacher", where a parent or teacher is usually sufficient, is all the more indicative of the central role of morality and guilt in this illness. Card 14. This is the popular theme of rejecting "improper" advances; when, however, she states that the kiss is refused even though the girl likes the man, the strict moral code is again evident. Card 15. The theme is loneliness because of the absence of the love-object. This story is similar to that on Card 2; it has the same vague, general formulation. Despair is evident when she says that he "never comes back". It is evident at this point that she feels herself to be an abandoned woman and an unworthy one because of her hostile feelings.

Card 16. Moral responsibility is again a primary concern: the child must be "a good child" (even if it spoils his fun). Card 17. The theme is extreme hostility and consequent guilt stimulated by irresponsibility. By this time, the strictness of her moral code is glaring. The gross misrecognition of sex indicates a projective trend and, in the setting of a depressive psychosis, suggests that there may be a paranoid coloring to her delusions. The destructive impulses directed toward the child-figure are also striking. Card 18: description. Card 19. Her initial evasiveness (about sexual, "improper" ideas?) has a paranoid quality, as does the gross perceptual distortion involved in seeing the room as a bridge. This distortion in itself would suggest that some form of psychosis is present. Not discerning the woman in bed is a further distortion and suggests unusually intense repression and evasion of sexual material. The theme is punishment for wickedness. At this point, the moralistic verbalizations throughout the inquiry require no elaboration. Card 20. The spontaneous self-criticisms and expressions of helplessness are typically depressive, especially because they are so inappropriate to the Thematic Apperception Test instructions and situation. "The troubles of the world" is enough of a story for her.

In summary, this seems to be a psychotic depression with paranoid features. The patient appears to be preoccupied with problems of moral responsibility, religious ideas and superstitions, wickedness and guilt. Intensely ambivalent feelings toward the children-figures are expressed; the children are seen as hostile but she seems to imply that the mother's (her own) hostility has earned her this. At the same time she tries to deny her aggressive feelings and appears to project them. She expresses feelings of loneliness, apprehensiveness and despair: the great love-object will never return. Extreme inertia, retardation, and passivity are evident.

CLINICAL SUMMARY

Mrs. S. has always been extremely passive. She has had several previous periods of depression and each time has been helped out of the depression by courses of shock therapy. At present she accuses herself of having completely mismanaged her life, of having "done wrong", and of being old and ugly. She is agitated, pulls her hair, and despairs of any improvement. She has attempted suicide several times and just before admission, in a paranoid rage, tried to choke her husband. The diagnosis was psychotic depression.

ACUTE SCHIZOPHRENIA, UNCLASSIFIED: TEST RESULTS

Mrs. J. Age: 24. Education: 4 months college. Marital: 6 years; 1 girl. Husband: Mechanic. Father: Farmer. Early Environment: Farm. Family Position: Oldest of 3. Religion: Protestant.

BELLEVUE SCALE

Comprehension

ENVELOPE: Mail it. (?) Mail it in the box (2). THEATRE: Yell fire. BAD COMPANY: Because you don't care for them or don't like them. TAXES: To keep the government going (2). SHOES: I don't know. That's just what they've always made them out of. (?) So you can wear them and they protect the feet. LAND: More people there. (?) Have to have more space (1). FOREST: Try to look for the sun. (?) That would tell you your directions (2). LAW: To keep the country substantial. (?) To keep it firm. LICENSE: So they can have a record (2). DEAF: I don't know. (?) Well, if you can't hear, you can't talk. (?) Well, you couldn't hear anything (1). RAW SCORE: .10.

Information

PRESIDENT: +. LONDON: +. PINTS: +. RUBBER: A shrub. THERMOMETER: +. WEEKS: dk. ITALY: dk. WASHINGTON:

dk. HEIGHT: +. PLANE: +. PARIS: dk. BRAZIL: +. HAMLET: +. POLE: dk. VATICAN: dk. JAPAN: +. HEART: +. ALL REST: dk. RAW SCORE: 10.

Digit Span

FORWARD: Passes 3, 4, 5, 6, 7, 8 on first try; fails first series of 9, passes second series. BACKWARDS: Passes 3, 4, 5 on first try; fails both series of 6 by omissions. RAW SCORE: 14.

Arithmetic

ITEMS 1-3: +. Fails all other items, after long silent pauses and inability to work. RAW SCORE: 3.

Similarities

ORANGE: Fruit (2). COAT: Clothing (2). DOG: Animals (2). WAGON: Something to ride on (1). DAILY PAPER: News (1). AIR: dk. WOOD: dk. EYE: To hear and see. EGG: A seed is something that grows and an egg is something that hatches. (?) A seed grows and an egg hatches, grows. ALL REST: dk. RAW SCORE: 8.

Picture Arrangement

HOUSE: + 10" (2). HOLD UP: + 15" (2). ELEVATOR: + 32" (2). FLIRT: AJNET 22" (2). FISH: IGEFHJ 21"; no insight. TAXI: LMEUAS 33"; no insight. RAW SCORE: 8.

Picture Completion

NOSE: +. MUSTACHE: +. EAR: +. DIAMOND: Picture in the middle. LEG: +. TAIL: +. STACKS: dk. KNOB: +. SECOND HAND: +. WATER: Someone to hold it. REFLECTION: dk. TIE: This is not connected up here (top of head). THREADS: dk. EYEBROW: dk. SHADOW: His hand isn't right on the cane. RAW SCORE: 7.

Block Designs

(Patient fails to get second demonstration without help.) ITEM 1: 13" (4). ITEM 2: 33" (3). ITEM 3: 80"; places 2 diagonals correctly, cannot complete design independently. ITEM 4: 80"; disregards square contour, places all blocks in a row, then places 2 blocks together to form top of design, but remaining 2 blocks are placed at upper outer corners of each of these; all blocks are red-white and yield a vague impression of a V. ITEM 5: 78" (3). ITEM 6 and 7: unable to make any progress in allotted time. RAW SCORE: 10.

Object Assembly

ITEM 1: 21" (6). ITEM 2: 79"; ear reversed (4). ITEM 3: 59"; two fingers reversed (4). RAW SCORE: 14.

Digit Symbol

25 correct; no errors. RAW SCORE: 25.

Vocabulary

APPLE: A fruit (1). DONKEY: An animal (1). JOIN: Put together (1). DIAMOND: A ring, or a stone (½). NUISANCE: Something that pesters (1). FUR: The covering of an animal (1). CUSHION: A pillow (1). SHILLING: Money that they have in Europe (1). GAMBLE: Take a chance (1). BACON: Meat. (?) Pork (1). NAIL: Nail a picture up, or nail a garage or a house together. (?) A piece of steel. (?) You pound it in (½). NITROGLYCERINE: Explosive (1). STANZA: dk. MICRO-SCOPE: Something you look through. (?) Look through things and look through people. VESPER: An evening service in church (1). BRIM: Edge of a hat (½). GUILLOTINE: A way of death in a foreign country. (?) Killing somewhere. (?) Beheading (1). PLURAL: You add an *s* to it. (?) More than one (1). SECLUDE: dk. CEDAR: A tree (1). TINT: Color (1). ARMORY: That's where they have their barracks for men. (?) They have dances in it sometimes. (?) It's a building, they keep things in there for national defense (½). FABLE: An old-fashioned story, a long time ago (1). BELFRY: The tower, isn't it? (?) It's where the church bell rings (1). RECEDE: dk. AFFLICTION: You're affected some way. (?) If you have an affliction, you can't hear, your arm hurts, or something (½). PEWTER, BALLAST, CATACOMB: dk. SPANGLE: When something spangles, it lights. (?) It's different little things you have on your dress. (?) Little round things that glimmer (1). ESPIONAGE: A spy (½). CHATTEL: A chattel mortgage. ALL REST: dk. RAW SCORE: 21.

Weighted Scores and IQ's

Comprehension 9	Picture Arrangement 7	Vocabulary 9
Information 8	Picture Completion 6	Verbal IQ: 86
Digit Span 13	Block Designs 5	Performance IQ: 73
Arithmetic 3	Object Assembly 7	Total IQ: 78
Similarities 7	Digit Symbol 6	

LEARNING EFFICIENCY

IMMEDIATE RECALL: A lot of water covered the houses up; and (a boy) went (under a bridge), and he almost drowned and (a man) (saved) him and he (cut his hands). SCORE: 8, after subtracting one for "covered the houses up".

DELAYED RECALL: There was a high water and it washed (into the houses) and there was a little (boy) and he was washed down the stream and (a man) (saved) him and he (cut his hands). SCORE: 4, after subtracting one for "washed down the stream"

ANALYSIS OF RESULTS

BELLEVUE SCALE

There are two striking features in the scatter: first, her general level, when considered against the background of her educational status, is strikingly low; second, the relatively extremely high Digit Span and relatively extremely low Arithmetic scores. The fact that her present IQ of 78 is in the borderline defective range indicates that either a profound depression or a schizophrenia with accompanying depression is present; only these two conditions could so lower her general level. Whichever it is, it is unlikely that the low IQ represents deterioration; because the level is totally lowered, an acute incapacitating condition of confusion, retardation, and withdrawal must be suspected. If this were a chronic case, there would be greater scatter and clear evidences of the approximate premorbid level. Neither is present in this case. The Digit Span-Arithmetic relationship provides the diagnostic clue; it is an extreme "out of pattern" [1]) relationship and is distinctively schizophrenic. If it were less striking, and there were no discrepancy between IQ and educational status, this pattern would indicate a schizoid make-up. The fact that the Performance level is still lower than the Verbal indicates depressive features in the schizophrenia. The scatter therefore indicates an acute schizophrenic condition, which has greatly impaired intelligence functioning—especially the ability to concentrate—and which probably involves depression and confusion.

In Information the failures on such easy items as *weeks, Washington's birthday* (she couldn't even name the month) and *rubber* are noteworthy, especially when she knows who wrote Hamlet and who invented the airplane. There are no bizarre answers. Such incapacity suggests depressive retardation, or schizophrenic blocking and withdrawal or confusion. One of the latter possibilities is most likely in terms of the scatter. In Comprehension she also fails easy items (*fire, bad company, shoes*) and yet gets full credit on the difficult *license* item. This pattern of item-failures is distinctively psychotic. "To keep the country substantial . . . firm" is a peculiar verbalization. No unusual verbalization or reasoning is again evident until she says the picture is missing from the playing card in Picture Completion. In Block Designs she fails item 3 yet passes item 5, again indicating psychotic unevenness of efficiency. In Vocabulary the only striking verbalization is on *microscope*: ". . . look through things and look through people." This is probably a derivative of a delusion.

––––––––

1) "Out of pattern" because Digit Span is usually below Arithmetic; the usual pattern is understood to imply that although passive attention (Digit Span) may be impaired by anxiety, active and effortful concentration (Arithmetic) is still possible. In schizophrenia this capacity for voluntary, active, and sustained application to problems is often lost.

LEARNING EFFICIENCY

Learning efficiency is profoundly impaired along with the other intelligence functions. In the immediate recall the loss of structure of the story is evident by her starting in the middle and introducing the idea of the boy *going* under the bridge. The delayed recall also begins in the middle of the story and this time an extreme distortion—"washed downstream"—is introduced. It is noteworthy that in both recalls the people drowning and catching cold are ignored, suggesting a particular sensitivity to and denial of aggressions.

In summary, this appears to be an acute schizophrenia with depressive features. Extreme blocking, confusion, and withdrawal are likely to be conspicuous. The entire level of intelligence functioning is lowered and psychotic unevenness of efficiency is indicated. It is difficult to estimate the premorbid intelligence level beyond saying that it was at least average.

CLINICAL SUMMARY

Symptoms first appeared six months ago, after her daughter developed a rash about the genitalia. She worried excessively for several months, ate and slept poorly, and lost weight. She then developed the delusion that she had some terrible disease, that her daughter had caught it from her and that other people might also catch it from her. With this delusion as a focus, she developed increasingly expansive ideas of reference, feelings of guilt, and depression, fearfulness and suspiciousness. She wanted to kill her daughter and herself and made several attempts at suicide. Some temporal disorientation, agitation, and incoherence were noted. She was diagnosed acute schizophrenia, unclassified.

ACUTE SCHIZOPHRENIA, UNCLASSIFIED: RORSCHACH TEST

Miss N. Age: 14. Education: High school sophomore, Father: Farmer. Early Environment: Farm. Family Position: Youngest of 4. Religion: Protestant.

CARD I. Reaction time: 35". Total time: 300".

1. Looks like . . . oh gosh, most anything it seems like . . . like some organ in the body. [(?) A woman's organs are different from a man's. I studied it in school. Looked like some sexual organ thing in the abdomen.] 2. It looks like it could be a face, some kind of a funny face, watermelon face (eyes and mouth are inner white spaces). 3. It could be a short tree, small tree, kind of wide. [(?) It had a trunk, looked trimmed

down, and fluffy.] 4. Kind of like a woman without a head (center D).
[(?) Like somebody who cut her head off, someone cut it not because
she was mean but to get rid... maybe she wanted to get rid of her
head.] 5. These on either side (upper side projections) look like they
could be wings... The more you look at it, the more different it seems to
get. Now it looks like a cat, a little cat that's angry (reference to second
response). 6. Women, nuns (side figures). [(?) They're bowing down
(facing outward). They could be holding some small child or food
(upper side projections).]

SCORES. 1: W F— Sex. 2: WS F + Face Fabulation Aggression Confusion. 3: W F∓Pl. 4: D F + H Confabulation Incompleteness. 5: Do
F + Ad. 6: D M + H Fabulation.

CARD II. Reaction time: 13″. Total time: 300″.

1. Oh well, these could be, these red ones... candles, fire. [(?) Fire
because it's red.] 2. Both of these people (black) holding up a candle,
and this down here (lower red) might be the shadow from the candle.
[(?) I can't see the head. They're bowing down, maybe all covered
up... women, all of them dressed in black, dress or robe it could be.
(Shadow of candle?) If it would be the shadow of the candle, would
it be black?] 3. These might be faces, turning or something, looking at
each other (usual profiles in upper red). 4. This down here (lower
red) could be a butterfly, big wings and things, and in the middle...
and butterfly's legs. 5. That might be some organ of the body too,
another sexual organ (all except red). I'm not sure. I don't know. It
may be all of it but the white spaces. [(?) Male (points to white space
for location).] 6. This is like a temple too here (upper middle Dd).
They (refers to second response) might be ringing a church bell. 7. This
other part would be shadow, darkness (black areas are figures of the
ringers and the shadow).

SCORES. 1: D CF Obj. 2: (W)D MC′±H (P) Combination Peculiar
Confusion. 3: Do F + Hd. 4: D F + A. 5: DS F— Sex Absurd Homoerotic.
6: Dd + Arch Contamination. 7: D Ch Darkness Contamination.

CARD III. Reaction time: 27″. Total time: 240″.

Ah! (as if it were an agreeable surprise) Well, let's see. 1. That looks
like some kind of men, Indians without feathers. It looks like... no,
it looks kind of like women. 2. But I don't know what that would be.
It looks kind of like a ribbon you wear in your hair (middle red). It
looks like they (refers to first response) are getting some water from a
pool. 3. It looks like a pig of some kind (lower back of popular figure,
facing out). 4. This (upper red) is like somebody was going to shoot it
(the pig) in the eye. It looks like it might be the fire, each one of these.
[(?) Because of the war. They could be a long time ago, ... bow, torch.
If it was fire of guns, I don't know if it would be red; it's kind of
powdered.]

SCORES. 1: W M + H P Peculiar Homoerotic. 2: D F + Obj. 3: Dr
F∓Ad. 4: D C Fire Confabulation Contamination Confusion Incoherence.

CARD IV. Reaction time: 45″. Total time: 240″.

(Sighs, smiles, becomes serious.) 1. Hm, that looks like two people, this white (lower middle) ... under a tree (W), or just in the darkness (W), probably. [(?) Just sitting under the tree. They could be Adam and Eve, or might be two women to me. (?) Because it's black.] 2. Oh, this (W) looks like ... this black space here ... a big man, big shoes on each foot, trying to kill them (white figures). He's not really mean. He looks like what you would expect Hell would look like. [(?) It doesn't look it now. Looks like some kind of nightmare now, going along, walking with his feet out. (?) Looked like Jehova's Witnesses.]

SCORES. 1: W F∓Pl; W C′ Darkness; S Ms+H Orig Fabulation Homoerotic. 2: W M+H Contamination Confabulation Aggression.

CARD V. Reaction time: 25″. Total time: 210″.

1. Well, these (side figures) look like some people lying down, awful tired probably, look more like shepherds laying down, resting. Might be two small children too, both of these. 2. Somebody (middle D) helping them. [(?) Might be Nature. Nature probably would help them. In a way, that might be God.]

SCORES. 1: D M+H Fabulation. 2: (W) D M+Nature–God Confabulation Contamination.

CARD VI. Reaction time: 75″. Total time: 150″.

Looks like ... > does it matter which way you turn it? ∧ ∨ Seems like they are getting harder all the time; hard to describe. Oh! 1. They could look like ... could look like a tree (W) and this (upper wings) a bush in the back. [(?) Shape of a tree, leaves; no distinct outline; a shadow painting of it.] 2. They look on each side like little children (each half of card). [(?) Nose, arms (lower side projection), feet (upper side projection). Looked like someone was holding them up. They may be up in the tree: maybe they lived there; just sitting there; might be resting.]

SCORES. 1: W FCh+Pl. 2: D M+H Orig Contamination Confabulation.

CARD VII. Reaction time: 10″. Total time: 270″.

1. Looks like dancers (W), swinging around, like there are lots of arms and legs (side and upper projections). [(?) Holding one arm up (upper projection); the face is held down, can't be seen.] 2. Might be two dogs with pug noses (upper third). 3. Down here each side looks like a shadow (lower third) and in the middle it looks like ... hm ... looks like two people, a couple of wise men (lower middle, light gray) kind of a small part of a tree (lower middle, dark midline). [(Shadow?) Just the darkness.] 4. ∨ More like ... dancers (upper two-thirds) this way than the other way. Sky up there (lower one-third), clouds; like each has one leg, other one is up. [(Head?) Can hardly see it.]

SCORES. 1: W M–H. 2: D F±Ad (P). 3: D Ch Shadow; Dr Ms+ H Combination Fabulation; Dr F– Pl Combination. 4: D M+H; (W) D Ch Cl Confabulation.

CARD VIII. Reaction time: 10". Total time: 180".

1. I think it could be a flower; looks kind of like a rose (lower pink and orange, and side pink). [(?) Oh, I like flowers. I had some roses at home. It's petals of it remind me of a pink rose; pink-orange; could be orange blossoms. (?) I always thought pink refers to roses and it was orange.] 2. In a way these on each side look like bears crawling around... I guess that's all.

SCORES. 1: D C Pl Self-reference Incoherence. 2: D F+A P.

CARD IX. Reaction time: 40". Total time: 240".

Hm . . . this seems to look like different colors, don't seem to remind me of much in particular. 1. These two men on top, they could be wise men (orange). 2. And these down here—trees (green), not really a tree: bush, leaves. [(?) Leaves are zig-zaggy; smaller on bottom and spread out; green-shaded.] 3. ∨ This on the bottom might be . . . oh, to look at it right now . . . a cat; maybe eyes (orange). Not the color of it. It's mad, kind of foaming at the mouth; it spits when it is mad. This could be the nostril; no feelers (face in inner projections; arbitrary). 4. Ha ha, looks more like a dress than anything else: sleeves on each side; a jacket (pink).

SCORES. 1: D M+H Fabulation. 2: D CF Pl. 3: D F—A Orig Absurd Fabulation Aggression. 4: D F+Obj.

CARD X. Reaction time: 4". Total time: 330".

1. Looks like a bunch of spiders; all different kinds of small animals; looks like they (side blue) are holding up something (side green) they are going to eat. [(Bunch of spiders?) Only it's blue; some call them black widow spiders. (Others?) No.] 2. More like a shell (lower side orange); a little animal, might be in a shell. 3. This looks like bugs (upper gray) holding up . . . more like princes that ride around on horses: these are just standing. This is a temple, castle (upper gray shaft). It looks like they are holding it up. 4. This looks like two plums, grapes (middle orange). 5. This here is some sort of animal: more like a rabbit than anything else (lower middle). 6. The sides here would be . . . I don't know what they would be . . . this yellow here looks like a peach: see it? Not the shape of a peach, just the color of it: light yellow (middle yellow). 7. If it's not a peach, it's a little like a wolf too, a dog (middle yellow).

SCORES. 1: DW F+A P Fabulation. 2: D F(C)∓Food. 3. D Ms∓H Orig; Dr F—Arch Confabulation. 4: D F+Food. 5: D F+Ad P. 6: D C Food, Deterioration—C. 7: D F+A.

Summary of Responses

R: 45   EB: 13–6.5

W 9 (3)	F+ 12	A 5	W% 20 (27)
DW 1	F− 5	Ad 5	D% 62
D 28	F± 1	H 13	DR% 13
Do 1	F∓ 3	Pl 6	
Dd 1	M 8+, 1−	Obj 3	F% 47-80
Dr 4	MC′ 1±	Sex 2	F+% 62–69
S 1 (1)	Ms 2+, 1∓	Arch 2	
s (1)	CF 2	Darkness 2	A% 22
	C 3	Shadow 1	H% 29
	F(C) 1∓	Face 1	P 4 (2)
Qualitative	C′ 1	Fire 1	P% 9 (13)
Fabulation 7	FCh 1+	Nature 1	Orig 2+, 1∓, 1−
Confabulation 6	Ch 3	God (1)	Orig% 9
Contamination 5		Cl 1	
Confusion 3		Food 2	
Incoherence 2			
Absurd 2			
Self-reference 1			
Symbolic 1			
Peculiar 2			
Deterioration-C 1			
Combination 3			
Aggression 3			
Homoerotic 3			
Incompleteness 1			

ANALYSIS OF RORCHACH TEST RESULTS

Card I. A sex response embracing the entire card is rarely seen except in schizophrenic records; coming as the first response, it suggests overwhelming sexual preoccupation. The confabulation in the fourth response resides in speculation that the woman *wanted her head cut off;* the response indicates that she characteristically directs her aggressions against herself, since she could as well have blamed the decapitation on someone else. It may also be implied that estrangement of the head from the rest of the body has taken place: castration fantasies are often behind such developments. Her verbalization after the fifth response, "the more you look at it, the more different it seems to get", is a statement about the instability of appearances and indicates confusion and feelings of unreality. Introspective subjects often verbalize the coming about of responses in this manner; when, however, the subject is naive—as this one appears to be—and when the record as a whole is clearly schizophrenic, this type of verbalization refers to perceptual fluidity in a setting of disorganization.

Card II. Confusion is again indicated when she asks whether the shadow of a candle would be black. This calling into question of everyday facts indicates that the delivery into consciousness of commonplace images is no longer automatic, and, therefore, that she is constantly required to reorient herself effortfully to details of reality in order to retain any degree of meaningful contact with the world around her. The use of the word *shadow* when she meant to say *reflection* in itself indicates confusion, but the greatest confusion results when she accepts the inappropriate verbalization and ponders its applicability to reality. Seeing the black areas and enclosed white space as the male genital organ implies not only a blurred concept of her sexual identity since this area is generally said to resemble the female genital organ, but, by its extreme arbitrariness, indicates profound impairment of reality testing. In the fifth response, she sees the upper middle *Dd* as a temple and concludes that the men must be ringing a church bell. One area stands for two ideas which are fused—a classical contamination. A further contamination occurs when the black areas are shadows in the scene of the bell-ringers at the same time as they are the bell-ringers.

Card III. The fourth response is confabulated because she associates fire with gunfire, links gunfire with hunting, and concludes that someone is going to shoot the pig; it indicates confusion because she wonders about the color of gunfire; it is incoherent because communication breaks down completely during inquiry. She is asked why it looked like gunfire and she responds not with a reference to the perceptual process but with an association to the idea of gunfire. Incoherence increases when the Indians (first response) are brought into it ("bow") without transition. The response is contaminated because the Indians occupy the same area as the pig they are killing.

Card IV. The first response is confabulated because there is no perceptual warrant for assuming that the big man is trying to kill the two people. It is contaminated because the man and the tree his victims are under (or the darkness) are the same area. It is fabulized because it assumes that the two people could be Adam and Eve. Again, as on Card I, she denies the aggressiveness of the aggressor—"not really mean". The references to Adam and Eve and to Hell suggest religious content in her delusions. The repeated reference to "in the darkness" probably expresses a subjective feeling of confusion and separation from the world.

Card V. The second response is confabulated because the physiognomic impression of tiredness leads to the idea that the central figure must be helping out, and this leads to the idea that Nature would be the logical helper, presumably because these were shepherds. The idea of somebody helping little children is probably expressive of a wish to be ministered to. The reference to God is noteworthy.

Card VI. The second response is a contamination because the foliage of the tree and the children sitting in the tree occupy the same area. The idea, "a tired child up a tree", may also be expressive of subjective feelings of helplessness and confusion. In this connection note the "tiredness" on Card V and the babe in arms in the sixth response to Card I.

Card VII. The $M-$ in the first response, based on the global impression of "lots of arms and legs", in itself strongly suggests schizophrenic breakdown of reality testing.

Card VIII. Inquiry into the first response elicits an incoherent verbalization as well as a pathologically egocentric expression—it looked like flowers because "I like flowers". The incoherence is not extreme, however, and appears to be based on a kind of primitive logic: since it is orange, it must be an orange blossom. The pure C preceding the popular response indicates that inappropriate affective display is likely to precede any grasp of the most obvious aspects of situations.

Card X. The third response is confabulated because the princes are holding up their castle.

Analysis of the summary scores indicates that this is an acute, mixed schizophrenia. It is *schizophrenia* because of the clear-cut contaminatory, confabulatory, and confused thinking. It is *acute* because of the many M's and the greater emphasis on M than on color in the EB, and the relatively well-retained $F+\%$. It is *mixed* because of the florid quality of the schizophrenic thinking. An exclusively paranoid case would give a more coarctated, covertly disorganized record.

The many M's in this setting of disorganization indicate that delusions are present; the pure C's and the relatively low $F\%$ and $A\%$ suggest that excitements and bizarre impulsive behavior are likely to occur. The confusion about identity of sexual organs and the sensitivity to loss of parts of the body indicate that homoerotic conflict is intense.

In summary, the Rorschach test results describe an acute schizophrenia in which florid delusions, excitements and panics, and impulsive bizarre acts are likely to be conspicuous. Extreme inability to admit aggressive feelings and strong feelings of helplessness and confusion are indicated. Acute homoerotic conflict and doubt about her sexual identity appear to be significant background factors. Thinking is fluid, confused and autistic to the point of incoherence. Capacity for rapport is minimal. Her delusions probably involve clearly sexual, destructive, and religious content.

CLINICAL SUMMARY

Three weeks prior to her examination here, following a mild sexual advance by a boy, the first she had experienced, she was disturbed and soon became excited. Silliness and incoherence, delusions with paranoid coloring, misidentification of persons, shifts in personal identity, confusion, inappropriate affective displays, and suggestions of hallucinatory experiences developed rapidly. She was in the midst of this break when she was tested.

ACUTE PARANOID SCHIZOPHRENIA: RORSCHACH TEST

Mr. J. Age: 46. Education: BBA. Occupation: Corporation executive. Marital: 7 years, 1 child. Early Environment: Small town. Family Position: Only child of father's second marriage; 4 step-brothers. Religion: Protestant.

CARD I. Reaction time: 10″. Total time: 180″.
Moth. (Else?) . . . I wouldn't know.
SCORE: W F+A P.

CARD II. Reaction time: 6″. Total time: 300″.
1. A couple of clowns, two people with their left hands together . . .
2. A face, mouth open (eyes: upper red; mouth: space).
SCORES. 1: W M+H P. 2: WS F−Hd.

CARD III. Reaction time: 40″. Total time: 240″.
(Slight smile.) Two people; like Franklin Roosevelt's chin . . .
SCORE: D M+H P.

CARD IV. Reaction time: 15″. Total time: 120″.
Scottie dog (ears are upper side projections, eyes in center shading).
SCORE: W F±Ad.

CARD V. Reaction time: 10″. Total time: 60″.
Butterfly . . . bat.
SCORE: W F+A P.

CARD VI. Reaction time: 14″. Total time: 120″.

Fur rug because it is a... arms, leg... (?) Looks like an animal skin.

SCORE: W F + Ad P.

CARD VII. Reaction time: 35″. Total time: 90″.

Two women. They have their genital organs together (lower middle Dr).

SCORE: W M±H P; Dr F + Sex Contamination, Homoerotic.

CARD VIII. Reaction time: 40″. Total time: 75″.

It looks like a couple of racoons on each side.
SCORE: D F + A P.

CARD IX. Reaction time: 90″. Total time: 180″.

Well, the faces are like donkeys (lower contour of orange).
SCORE: Dr F−Ad.

CARD X. Total time: 120″. "Nothing." Failure.

Summary of Responses

R: 11   EB: 3−0

W 7	F + 5	A 3	W% 64
D 2	F − 2	Ad 3	D% 18
Dr 2	F ± 1	H 3	Dr% 18
S (1)	M 2 +, 1±	Hd 1	
		Sex 1	F% 73-100
			F + % 75-82

Qualitative
Contamination 1
Homoerotic 1
Failure on X

A% 55
H% 36
P 7
P% 64

ANALYSIS OF RORCHACH TEST RESULTS

There are several aspects of the summary of scores which indicate depression: the low R and one failure, the high $A\%$ and $P\%$. The presence of 3 M's, however, indicates that there is more to the case than depression, since a depression which would be severe enough to limit R to 11, would also be severe enough to eliminate the possibility of giving any more than 1 M. The same argument would eliminate low intelligence as the background of this meager record. In this setting, an EB of 3−0 suggests either an obsessional neurosis with severe emotional inhibition and depression or an acute paranoid schizophrenia with depression. In the latter instance the absence of colors would speak for extreme withdrawal rather than inhibition. The problem is resolved when we note the presence of a contamination. On Card VII he sees two women (W) with their genital organs together. This is a contamination because the lower middle Dr has first been seen, as it frequently is, as a vagina, but then changed to two vaginas because there are two women there. In other words, the meaning of the idea has been contaminated by another idea which logically should be distinct from it. The sexual content of this contamination indicates that sexual delusions are probably present; furthermore, the clearly homoerotic aspect of the sexual content suggests that preoccupation with homosexuality is involved. Strained ideas or percepts with homoerotic implications are not infrequent in the records of paranoid schizophrenics.

Diagnostic Impression: Acute paranoid schizophrenia with conspicuous depressive and homoerotic trends and sexual preoccupation.

CLINICAL SUMMARY

Mr. J. had become progressively more seclusive, indecisive, and irrealistic during the last ten years. Since his recent and first frankly psychotic break, symptoms have included delusions of reference and persecution, periods of agitation and fearfulness, depression and indecisiveness, some hallucinatory experiences, seclusiveness and personal disorderliness, near-mutism, periods of confusion, and feelings of unworthiness. The diagnosis was paranoid schizophrenia.

SIMPLE SCHIZOPHRENIA: TEST RESULTS

Mr. G. Age: 18. Education: College sophomore. Father: Clerk. Early Environment: Small town. Family Position: Only child. Religion: Protestant.

BELLEVUE SCALE

Comprehension

ENVELOPE: Put it in the mail box (2). THEATRE: Probably holler fire. BAD COMPANY: With bad company you will probably do what they do; a bad influence (2). TAXES: To keep the government going (2). SHOES: Leather will bend easily and is durable (1). LAND: More value to it, not so much land (1). FOREST: If I had a compass, I'd follow it, try to find the way out like I got in. LAWS: To govern the people (1). MARRIAGE: Like in California, have to take a medical exam; to prove that they're married. DEAF: When you are deaf, you cannot hear the sound of others; if you can watch lips, you might be able (1). RAW SCORE: 10

Information

PRESIDENT: +. LONDON: +. PINTS: +. RUBBER: +. THERMOMETER: +. WEEKS: 53. ITALY: +. WASHINGTON: +. HEIGHT: +. PLANE: +. PARIS: 3252; +. BRAZIL: +. HAMLET: David Copperfield. (?) Shakespeare. POLE: Byrd. VATICAN: A city. JAPAN: +. HEART: +. POPULATION: +. H. FINN: +. EGYPT: Western Hemisphere. (?) Europe. KORAN: dk. FAUST: dk. HABEAS CORPUS: dk. ETHNOLOGY: Study of words. APOCRYPHA: dk. RAW SCORE: 15.

Digit Span

FORWARD: Gets first series of 3 and 4, second series of 5 and fails both of 6; simple errors. BACKWARDS: Gets first series of 3 and 4, and fails both of 5. RAW SCORE: 9.

Arithmetic

ITEMS 1: +. ITTEM 2: +. ITEM 3: 14¢ (8″) (?) 16¢ (15″) (?) 17¢ (25″). ITEM 4: 6 (10″). (?) 9 (17″). ITEM 5: +. ITEM 6: 44 (13″). (?) 34 (25″). (?) 36 (40″). ITEM 7: +. ITEM 8: $225 (60″). ITEM 9: 3 feet (40″). (?) 50 (80″). ITEM 10: 20. (?) 24. (?) 41. (?) 5.5 times as many. RAW SCORE: 4.

Similarities

ORANGE: Same vitamins, have seeds. COAT: Made of same kind of material; the coat can match the dress. DOG: Can both grow, can both be the same color, can eat the same food. WAGON: Both carry people, have wheels (1). PAPER: Gives news ... well, of the war (1). AIR: Both have molecules ... both have oxygen. (?) Oxygen (1). WOOD: There is wood alcohol; both have air in them. EYE: You can see something and hear something if they are close enough. EGG: Egg has an inside yolk, same as center of a seed. POEM: Poem can represent a statue. PRAISE: You can punish somebody and also praise them later. FLY: dk. RAW SCORE: 3.

Picture Arrangement

HOUSE: + 6″ (2). HOLD UP: + 8″ (2). ELEVATOR: + 5″ (2). FLIRT: ATENJ 11″. FISH: EFGHJI 34″. TAXI: SAMELU 25″. RAW SCORE: 6.

Picture Completion

NOSE: +. MUSTACHE: +. EAR: +. DIAMOND: The 9 is upside down. LEG: +. TAIL: +. STACKS: +. KNOB: +. SECOND HAND: +. WATER: +. REFLECTION: dk. TIE: +. THREADS: Filament, socket. EYEBROW: Ear. SHADOW: Cane's handle. RAW SCORE: 10.

Block Designs

ITEM 1: 11″ (4). ITEM 2: 15″ (4). ITEM 3: Said "finished" with one error but spontaneously corrected it; 23″ (3). ITEM 4: 40″ (3).

ITEM 5: Studies finished design for 5″ "to be sure"; 65″ (3). ITEM 6: No semblance of correct solution at 150″; "Sure is a mess!" ITEM 7: Design only partly reproduced at 420″; "Does anyone ever get it the first time?" RAW SCORE: 17.

Object Assembly

ITEM 1: 27″ (6). ITEM 2: 32″ (8) ITEM 3: 43″ (8). RAW SCORE: 22.

Digit Symbol

56 correct; no errors. RAW SCORE: 56.

Vocabulary

APPLE: Fruit (1). DONKEY: Animal (1). JOIN: Putting together (1). DIAMOND: Stone. (?) Polished, valuable (1). NUISANCE: Annoyance (1). FUR: Hair on an animal (1). CUSHION: Pillow, sit on it (1). SHILLING: English money (1). GAMBLE: Take a chance (1). BACON: Food. (?) No (½). NAIL: Wire material to put two things together (1). CEDAR: Wood (1). TINT: To color (1). ARMORY: The guard is there, and guns (½). FABLE: dk. BRIM: Like brim of a hat. GUILLOTINE: King. PLURAL: Two (½). SECLUDE: Include. NITROGLYCERINE: Explosive (1). STANZA: One verse in a poem (1). MICROSCOPE: Used to magnify small objects (1). VESPER: Church, where you drink wine. BELFRY: Where the bell is kept (1). RECEDE: Giving something... no... to quit (½). AFFLICTION: Two things don't go together. PEWTER, BALLAST, CATACOMB, SPANGLE: dk. ESPIONAGE: Unamerican activity, like sabotage. IMMINENT: Valuable. MANTIS: dk. HARA KIRI: dk. CHATTEL: Talk a lot; no—that's chatter. ALL REST: dk. RAW SCORE: 18.

Weighted Scores and IQ's

Comprehension 9	Picture Arrangement 6	Vocabulary 8
Information 11	Picture Completion 9	Verbal IQ: 85
Digit Span 6	Block Designs 8	Performance IQ: 96
Arithmetic 4	Object Assembly 13	Total IQ: 90
Similarities 3	Digit Symbol 13	

RORSCHACH TEST

CARD I. Reaction time: 15″. Total time: 90″.

1. That could be leaves, couldn't it? [(?) Shape. (How many?) One leaf. (?) And the color, brownish; an old leaf, partly deteriorated.] 2. Could be an X-ray. [(?) Ridges in it could be bones.] 3. Something like blood seen through a microscope. [(?) You could see the corpuscles, like red and white corpuscles.]

SCORES. 1: W FC′∓Pl Peculiar Peculiar. 2: W ChF At. 3: W ChF Blood Peculiar.

CARD II. Failure: 135″.

I don't know what that is... I don't have any idea... I don't have any idea what this would be... I don't know... It doesn't suggest anything.

CARD III. Failure: 120''.

(Shakes head.) I wouldn't have any idea what that could be... black and red ink (strained laugh). Are they supposed to be something? I don't know. Don't look like anything to me. Black and red ink daubed on paper... I sure don't know.

CARD IV. Reaction time: 30''. Total time: 90''.

Well, it could be a hide of an animal, couldn't it?... I don't know... That's all I know about that. [(?) The color, different color schemes; shape of an animal: more like a rug.]

SCORE: W FCh+Ad P.

CARD V. Reaction time: 20''. Total time: 60''.

The... that looks something like a bat, doesn't it?... That's all I know about that.

SCORE: W F+A P.

CARD VI. Failure: 120''.

(Shakes head.) I don't have any idea about this one either... are these supposed to be pictures?... I have never seen anything like it.

CARD VII. Failure: 120''.

I don't know what this is... have no idea... If I had an idea what to try to represent... I don't have any idea.

CARD VIII. Reaction time: 35''. Total time: 90''.

...These look like animals (side pink)... That's all I know about that one.

SCORE: D F+A P.

CARD IX. Failure: 120''.

I don't have any idea. Are they animals? Are they? (What do you think?) I don't know what they are. They don't look like anything to me. I am positive; I have never seen anything like it.

CARD X. Failure: 150''.

Whew! I don't have any idea what that could be... I sure wouldn't know... I don't know.

To test the severity of the blocking indicated by the many failures, the test was readministered. On Cards I and II he saw nothing; on Card III he saw "the head of a bird of some kind", referring to the head of the popular figure (Do F+Ad). On Card IV he saw "some leaves" because "they looked like oak leaves; shaped that way and the color, the ridges in it (W FCh∓Pl)." On Card V he saw nothing new. On VI, he thought "it could look something like a hide of a long-necked animal" because of "the color, 1 mean a wolf or animal of that color, light, tawny (W FCh + Ad P)." On VII, he said, "That looks like a cloud in the sky, lots of rain in it—shaded over here (W Ch Cl) ." On VIII he saw nothing new. On IX he finally saw "something like a man's head" in the lower pink (D F + Hd) . On X he said, "Looks like small leaves right there in the inside yellow. (?) It has the shape—zig-zagged—and a brownish color (Dr FC+Pl) ."

Summary of Responses

R: 6 (6)   EB: 0—0 (.5)

W 5 (3)	F+ 2 (2)	A 2	W% 83 (67)
D 1 (1)	FC (1+)	Ad 1 (2)	D% 17 (17)
Do (1)	FC' 1+	Hd (1)	DR% 0 (8)
Dr (1)	FCh 1+ (1+, 1∓)	Pl 1 (2)	
	ChF 2	At 1	F% 33-67 (33-75)
	Ch (1)	Blood 1	F+% 100-75 (100-78)
		Cloud (1)	
Qualitative			A% 50 (42)
Peculiar 3			H% 0 (8)
Decay 1			At% 8
Failures 6			P 3 (1)
			P% 50 (33)

ANALYSIS OF RESULTS

BELLEVUE SCALE

The scatter indicates a schizophrenia with chronic features. The great drops in Arithmetic and Similarities are the diagnostic indicators. Some organic cases have such drops but they would not be expected to obtain superior scores on Object Assembly and Digit Symbol, the latter two being particularly vulnerable to impairment by organic factors. The big drop of Similarities is indicative of chronicity as are the two high Performance scores. The scores on Object Assembly and Digit Symbol, in a setting of schizophrenia, indicate blandness. The relatively low Vocabulary score together with the good psychomotor efficiency suggests *simple* schizophrenia as the diagnosis. Since the patient reached the second year of junior college, it must be presumed that his low scores reflect the decline of intellectual abilities associated with chronic schizophrenia.

The qualitative features bear out the diagnostic hypothesis advanced above: *David Copperfield* wrote Hamlet (despite the subsequent correction); Egypt is in the *Western Hemisphere*; Paris is 3252 miles from New York; there are 53 weeks in a year. All these combine to indicate serious disorganization of the memory frame-of-reference. Conceptual disorganization is manifested in the following: *orange and banana* have the *same* vitamins; *dog and lion* can both grow, can be the same color, can eat the same food; *air and water* have molecules; *wood and alcohol* have air in them; *eye and ear* are alike because you can see something and hear the same thing if it is close enough; *praise and punishment* are alike because you can punish somebody and praise them later. These are syncretistic or concrete and fabulated concepts: if one grants his conceptual premises, anything can be related to anything else, since there are infinite possibilities of superficial, non-essential similarities of attributes and infinite possibilities of concrete contexts in which things may co-exist. The responses to *fable, guillotine, seclude, affliction, imminent,* and *chattel* in the Vocabulary subtest also support the inference that there has been a decline of intellectual abilities.

RORSCHACH TEST

The summary of scores indicates extreme blocking (6 failures, 6 spontaneous responses) and flatness of ideational and emotional experience (*EB* 0--0). The 3 shading responses and the 3 additional shading responses indicate that he still feels anxiety and is not completely bland. In fact, 6 shading responses out of the final total of 12 suggest a persisting anxiety state of the dull, oppressive, restless, vaguely uneasy variety so often observed in chronic schizophrenics and one which might well flare up into acute panics. The disorganization already evident in the Bellevue Scale would speak for highly inappropriate precipitating factors and manifestations of these panics. The high $F + \%$ is deceptive; it does not reflect good reality testing at all It is based on a very few responses and these are gross, more or less common ones, of the type to which blocked or retarded subjects are usually restricted. In addition there are three peculiar verbalizations: one where he refers to Card I as "brownish", a second where he speaks with unwarranted specificity of "red and white corpuscles" on Card I; and a third where he spontaneously says "leaves" on Card I when he means only one leaf. The last type of verbalization is not unusual in schizophrenic records; often the verbalizations are in the plural—"bats" or "butterflies"—when only one is seen. These verbalizations are peculiar because they reflect a breakdown in interpersonal communication. The coming about of the response may be conceived as follows: the patient is referring to an associative process set off by his percept—thinking of leaves because he saw a leaf—but he offers a report of the subsequent association as a statement of the percept itself. On Card I "... couldn't it?" has a naive quality; in this setting it suggests inappropriate, childish dependence. The *FC* elicited during readministration of the test suggests that vestiges of adaptive efforts are present and that this may be a docile, subdued schizophrenic. The response, "deteriorated" leaf, on Card I has a special implication: responses referring vividly to decay, rot, deterioration, or spoiling generally express subjective feelings of decay and worthlessness, and often refer to masturbatory guilt.

Test Report

Intelligence and Thought Organization: The level of intellectual functioning appears to have suffered a marked decline. The present IQ is only 90, dull normal range, and premorbidly—to judge from his fund of information—was at least in the high average range. Memory and concept formation appear to be disorganized, and ability to concentrate is profoundly impaired. Striking blocking is also indicated.

Emotional Factors: Emotional experience in general appears to be flat. Acute flare-ups of anxiety with bizarre features are likely to occur, but he is probably passive and subdued for the most part. Feelings of decay and worthlessness are likely to be present.

Diagnostic Impression: Simple schizophrenia.

Clinical Summary

Mr. G., an eighteen year old boy from a small midwestern town, was raised strictly by an overprotective, domineering, neurotic mother. The father appears to have been fairly tolerant. The mother tried hard to keep her son "a good boy", which he was until the onset of the illness. He was not socially active and was home much of the time. He wanted to study aviation after completing high school but his parents would not give permission. About one year ago, after a year of college in which he did average work on the whole, he finally obtained permission and began taking flying lessons. He soon wanted to join the army but his parents persuaded him to return to college. He reported to a girl friend that, while flying, something had "popped in his head". During the past few months he has felt that something is the matter with his heart, has had difficulty in concentrating, and has frequently held his head in his hands and rubbed his eyes. He has also seemed confused. (The rubbing and confusion were apparent during his clinical examination also. Some questions had to be repeated, there were sometimes long pauses before answers were given, and his memory for dates and events of the last year was clearly mixed up.) About two weeks before his examination here he became confused and went to sleep on the floor of his house. He was awakened by the sound of fire engines and went into the street feeling dazed. He developed numb sensations in the back of his head and in his chest and fainted upon re-entering the house. He was unconscious for about five minutes. When he came to, he asked who had hit him. He continued feeling dazed and confused and could not concentrate. His conversation wandered. One evening, several days later, he was found standing in the bathroom in a dazed condition and had to be helped back to bed. He cried for several minutes. Since then he has felt wobbly when walking, has been unusually thirsty and his hands shake. He has been hearing music from afar in his ears and has heard a vague mumbling of men's voices. He reports that during the past year there has often been a numbness in his arms and legs. His conversation has rambled during interviews, and he has occasionally laughed or grinned inappropriately as he talked about his illness. The diagnosis was simple schizophrenia.

SCHIZOPHRENIC CHARACTER: WORD ASSOCIATION TEST[2])

Mr. W. Age: 24. Education: College sophomore. Occupation: None. Marital: 1 year. Father: Lawyer. Early Environment: Big city. Family Position: Younger of 2. Religion: Protestant.

HAT—3"—girl. [(?) My wife's name is Hattie and I call her Hat often. (Image?) Yes.] LAMP—1"—shade. LOVE—1.5"—hate (he shrugs). BOOK—2.5"—sheet. [(?) I don't know—might have had shit in mind, I'm not sure.] FATHER—1"—mother. PAPER—2"—weight. BREAST—2"—nipple. CURTAINS—1"—shade. TRUNK—1.5"—elephant. DRINK—2"—whiskey. PARTY—2"—orgy. [(?) The parties I've attended; the word *orgy*, for me, has neologistic value. In our gang, we would call anything an orgy.] SPRING—2"—bird. [(Image?) No; I remember thinking of *leap* after I said *bird*.] BOWEL MOVEMENT—2"—leap. [(?) The word was a carry over from *spring*.] RUG—3"—furniture (he shrugs). BOY FRIEND—2"—fire. [(?) I don't know. I think I was thinking of the previous one, *fire* after *furniture*. (?) I haven't the faintest idea, perhaps rug ... wrapping oneself in a rug when on fire.] CHAIR—3"—mess (he shrugs and smiles). [(?) What was the word before? (?) I think *mess* was in reaction to *boy friend*. I think ... hard to say. (Connection?) No idea.] SCREEN—3"—air. PENIS—2"—ejaculation. RADIATOR—3"—heat. FRAME—2"—window. SUICIDE—1.5"—

---

2) Due to lack of time, the recall part of the test was not administered and a number of inquiries were omitted.

escape. [(?) What word did it come after? . . . I got emergency reactions with *boy friend,* a desire to escape. (Did you have a subjective feeling then?) Yes, I was trying to determine how to meet it. I was trying to think of as far-fetched things as possible, and was also trying to shock you: the two are completely contradictory. I was trying to drag these thoughts to the level of verbalization.] MOUNTAIN—2.5"—breast. [(?) I associate mountains with breasts. (Image?) I had an image of the breast coming out of the earth, a great big monster one.] SNAKE—1.5"—penis. [(Image?) I think afterwards. (?) A phallus.] HOUSE—3.5"—live. VAGINA—2"—cavern. TOBACCO—1"—smoke. MOUTH—3"—embarrassed. [(?) What word comes before it? (!) And before that? (!) I think my response was waiting to come out when it would be least appropriate. (?) It was not conscious, it was fore-conscious. (?) There was a block there. (?) I don't know. I must have thought it was appropriate then.] HORSE (heard WORSE)—4"—better. MASTURBATION—2.5"—guilt. WIFE—1"—spirit [(?) It's another word I had on tap from the time you said *horse.* (?) I love to ride and gallop and I laugh wildly.] TABLE—3"—filibuster. [(?) Here also I had resentment against you for causing emergency reactions (reports body trembling). Nothing would come—wait, one way of tabling something is to filibuster. (?) Thought of it just now.] HORSE—5"—fury. [(?) The same feeling as on *wife.*] FIGHT—3"—cataclysm. BEEF—1.5"—stew. STOMACH—2"—sensation. [(?) I had an image that was half kinesthetic and half eidetic—two stomachs pressed together. (?) Male and male.] FARM—3"—eat. MAN—3.5" —woman. TAXES—2"—death. NIPPLE—2"—tree. [(?) I saw a tree outside the window.] DOCTOR—2"—bills. DIRT—2"—eat. [(?) I thought of Pearl Buck's *The Good Earth.* (Connection with eat?) I don't know.] CUT—2"—wound. MOVIES—2"—emergency. [(?) I had that word on tap. I did think of a fire—the Wechsler-Bellevue question. (Image?) Yes. (?) It's too vague to be recalled.] COCKROACH—3.5"—disease. BITE—3"—hard. DOG—3"—sheep. DANCE—5"—intercourse. GUN—2"— phallic symbol. WATER—2"—drink. HUSBAND—1"—wife. MUD—2.5" —wet. WOMAN—2"—man. FIRE—3.5"—joy. [(?) I don't know. (?) The idea of *horse* and *spirit* was there in the background.] SUCK—2"—cock. MONEY—1.5"—power. MOTHER—2"—hate. [(?) I have an ambivalent attitude toward her. I couldn't think of anything to say. The feeling was directed more towards you at the time. The feeling was: My God! Is nothing sacred? What is he going to say next?] HOSPITAL—3"—patient. GIRL FRIEND—2"—boy friend. TAXI—2"—movie. INTERCOURSE— 4"—grass (he shrugs) . [(?) It's nice on the grass sometimes, and I was looking out the windows.] HUNGER—2.5"—satiate.

ANALYSIS OF WORD ASSOCIATION TEST RESULTS

This test is included partly to indicate how wild the associations of a schizophrenic character can become, and partly to offer a collection of examples of schizophrenic responses, any two or three of which may occur in the Word Association tests of other schizophrenics whose test results are less spectacularly diagnostic. This subject was a twenty-four year old psychology student at a large western university, who had had several months of non-psychoanalytic therapy but had wanted to be psychoanalyzed and had done some reading of Freud's basic works. The record will be analyzed primarily from a diagnostic point of view and a number of responses with significant content will be ignored.

Hat-"girl": the response is conceptually distant in two ways; in the first place the conventional concept *hat* is ignored, and in the second place the intervening thought is *wife,* which is not verbalized; instead he apparently goes on to think, "My wife is a girl (female)," and says, "Girl." *Book-*"sheet": inquiry was made because of slight delay in responding. He reports that a clang association either led to the word *sheet* or followed it. This in itself would be strongly diagnostic, but when, in addition, a "vulgar" word reaches conscious expression in this innocent context, the response takes on an even more malignant quality. It suggests that consciousness is crowded with normally repressed or restricted ideas, and, because of his blandness about this and other responses, that these ideas are highly intellectualized. To make matters worse, as we will see later on, there is no reason to be sure that this thought process occurred originally; the word *shit* may well have come to mind only during inquiry. This only adds to the schizophrenic quality of the responses since it implies pathological fluidity of memories. *Bowel movement-*"leap": this is a characteristically schizophrenic perseveration from the previous stimulus word *spring. Boy friend-*"fire" is a similar perseveration, but this time conceptual distance is also involved. After he had said "furniture" in his response to *rug,* his thoughts apparently raced along to the idea *fire.* In this instance a destructive rather than a sexual idea occurred in an innocent context, but the schizophrenic quality remains the same. In this test, when sexual or aggressive ideas intrude into consciousness regardless of the immediate context of ideas, disorganization is indicated. The explanation "wrapping oneself in a rug" makes the association even more arbitrary and extravagant.

Chair-"mess": at this point he seems to be blandly falling back on perseveration as a basis for explaining unrelated answers; whether or not this is really perseveration is less important than the fact that by asking, "What came before?" he casually admits, in effect, that he has a disordered mind and cannot control his own associations. His introduction of *boy friend-*"mess" in this connection sounds potentially meaningful, but its conceptual distance, its absence of important mediating ideas, is still diagnostic. *Suicide-*"escape": again he seeks for an explanation by perseveration but this time fails. He then rationalizes the response in terms of a desire to avoid or "escape" the entire testing situation. The further explanation is of a type indicative of strong obsessive features in that he has a dim awareness of unverbalized feelings and images playing into the association process and attempts to capture them.

Mountain—"breast": this follows from a fantastic image and is probably based on psychotically elaborated oral fantasies. Snake—"penis" makes clear the fact that intellectualized psychoanalytic information is used indiscriminately. *Vagina*—"cavern" is made of the same stuff, as are *dance*—"intercourse" and *gun*—"phallic symbol" later on.[3]) *Mouth*—"embarrassed": in this instance he seeks to establish a perseveration from *two* words back, an even more peculiar quest. His explanation implies that the word was hovering about because it expressed his general reaction to the test and that he therefore had to get it out. But to express it regardless of the current context of ideas is distinctively schizophrenic. It is not too certain that this was the actual thought process leading to the response—"embarrassed" may be expressive of a reaction to psychotic oral fantasies of the *mountain*—"breast" type after all. This unreliability of explanation is indicated by the fact that from this point on he abandons perseveration as an explanatory principle and falls back on hovering ideas or words "on tap". With a subject as fluid as this, inquiry is like digging in loose sand.

Wife—"spirit": here he says the idea was "on tap" since he heard the word *horse*. This is indicative of fluidity of memories since he did not hear the word *horse* when it was first called out and actually heard it for the first time two words after he heard *wife*. The actual idea associated with *horse* has a "wild man" quality and is indicative of dramatic, more or less bizarre acting-out behavior. *Table*—"filibuster" is extremely distant conceptually, if his explanation can be trusted. Ordinarily it would be trusted but we cannot be certain of this here because so many of his explanations have an after-thought quality, and may be confabulations rather than more or less accurate introspective reports. Again it must be stressed that the fact that these explanations are offered at all is indicative of a schizophrenia in which bland intellectualizing of highly autistic thinking and bizarre behavior is conspicuous. *Horse*—"fury": this is apparently the direct expression of his emotional reaction to horseback riding, but again the response is conceptually

---

3) Even subjects who are well-versed in the field do not ordinarily give this type of association.

distant. It does not communicate to the examiner the fabric of ideas and feelings woven around the idea *horse*. The response takes for granted considerable knowledge on the part of the examiner and does not respect his almost complete ignorance of the patient's subjective experiences and attitudes. Such a response is clearly indicative of the breakdown in the system of communication of ideas and feelings which characterizes schizophrenic conditions. The elliptical verbalizations in the Thematic Apperception Test of the acute paranoid schizophrenic discussed in Chapter Three have the same implication. The "resentment" against the examiner expressed calmly during inquiry as one determinant of the response is noteworthy more for its pathologically intellectualized quality than for its intensity.

Stomach—"sensation": inquiry elicits clearly peculiar thinking. He reports that his image was "half eidetic", again demonstrating inappropriate intellectualization of psychological concepts. The content of the image is clearly homoerotic and is reminiscent of his connection of the words "mess" with *boy friend*, "embarrassment" with *mouth*, and, later on, of "cock" with *suck*. *Nipple*—"tree": surprisingly, he makes no attempt to rationalize this unrelated response. This response implies an evasion, a refusal to cope with the oral connotations of the stimulus word. A better organized subject is not expected to resort to an unrelated response as a means of escape. *Dirt*—"eat": a conceptually distant association mediated by a thought of Pearl Buck's book. The content is probably expressive of another bizarre schizophrenic fantasy.

Movies—"emergency": here he reports that an idea was "on tap" which had been stimulated the previous day while he was taking the Comprehension subtest of the Bellevue Scale. Carryover of ideas stimulated by previous tests is not infrequent in the records of schizophrenics. In this instance the explanation is unreliable, since "emergency" has also been thrown about as a description of disturbed reactions in the course of this test. *Bite*—"hard" probably relates to the many other bizarre reactions to oral words. In general these have a perverse, sadistic, and fantastic quality. *Fire*—"joy": a conceptually distant association; he links the response with a hovering perseveration of the *horse* and *spirit* ideas although he does not explain how words which give rise to ideas of fury can also give rise to ideas of joy. In schizophrenic style, he assumes the presence of certain contents of awareness in the examiner and regards his actually incomplete communication as fully adequate. It may also be, however, that he is confabulating here: his thinking is so disconnected and so removed from the usual conceptual rules governing thinking that he cannot accurately and immediately relate his responses to the stimulus words. Inquiry therefore poses an intellectual problem and he blithely free-associates to find the solution to this problem. Finally, he may be expressing sadistic pleasure here: feelings of joy at destruction. *Mother*—"hate": he blandly relates this to "ambivalence" toward his mother—a one-sided expression of ambivalence to be sure. He blandly offers another determinant: his "hate" for the examiner because the examiner has been probing into sore spots.

This test record yields a psychological portrait of a person whose thinking and memories are extremely fluid, whose affects can be both inappropriately intense and bland, and whose intellectualizing reaches the limits of bizarreness. The content of his responses indicates a strong, possibly overt homoerotic trend, impulsive and bizarre acting-out, extremely autistic and perverse fantasies—especially in the oral area—and intense sadistic impulses.

CLINICAL SUMMARY

This patient's history includes enuresis up to the age of fifteen, few friends, homosexual as well as heterosexual relations (he prefers the former), some impulsive stealing, a bizarre and exhibitionistic attempt at suicide with a homosexual lover, a bizarre homocidal attempt on a homosexual rival, a suicidal gesture during one of his frequent arguments with his wife. Following his homocidal attempt he was hospitalized and given eighty insulin shock treatments. He told his history blandly during his examination. He reported compulsive "undoing" rituals, a feeling that he was being watched even though he denied believing this was true, and destructive fantasies. Intellectualizing and basic withdrawal behind a veneer of warmth were evident throughout his examination. He was diagnosed as an ambulatory schizophrenic or schizophrenic character.

INCIPIENT SCHIZOPHRENIA: RORSCHACH TEST

Miss B. Age: 33. Education: M. A. in Music Education. Occupation: Teacher; social work student. Marital: Single. Father: Skilled tradesman. Early Environment: Big city. Family Position: Youngest of 3. Religion: Jewish.

CARD I. Reaction time: 7". Total time: 75".

1. It might look like a bat ... bat in flight, I might add. 2. Or it might be two witches doing a devil's dance (side figures). [(?) This looked like the shadow of them (upper side projections), so much larger

and the same general shape. The color was somewhat lighter too, if I remember the color correctly.] I don't know ... can't make anything much more out of that.

SCORES. 1: W F+A P. 2: D MC′+H Peculiar.

CARD II. Reaction time: 8″. Total time: 120″.

It looks like it might be two old men with these skull cap things on their heads, playing this clap game ... what's it called? ... knee to knee. [(Old?) They seemed to be sitting down, knees together for support, shoulders hunched over.] Also, it looks like it might be two soldiers pretty well mutilated and bleeding pretty badly. [(?) The legs seemed to be bleeding and heads were bashed up and bleeding too.] It might be two old hags having a terrific quarrel; long beak noses, mouths partly open, going to town on each other.

SCORE: W M+H P Fabulation; D CF Blood Aggression Aggression.

CARD III. Reaction time: 10″. Total time: 120″.

1. It looks like two men who are dressed in old-fashioned, high stiff collars, playing ... what's that English game? ... cricket or croquet or something. They have their hands holding something, and about to hit. 2. Maybe that red butterfly (center) is what they're trying to hit ∨ ... 3. Upside down it looks like a butterfly that's been completely dismembered (all of black). [(?) This would be part of the wings (leg of popular figure).]

SCORES. 1: W M+H P. 2: D FC+A Fabulized-combination Aggression. 3: W F−A Aggression.

CARD IV. Reaction time: 8″. Total time: 100″.

1. It looks like it might be a pair of seven-league boots of fairy tale fame, great big things with fancy thing at the knee ... ∨ 2. Upside down, it looks like it might be an old-fashioned candelabra hanging from the ceiling with two whatchamacallit ... It looks like it might be hanging in an old, dirty castle and not cleaned for a long time. [(?) Various shades of what might have been dust, some parts dirtier than others.]

SCORES. 1: W F+Obj. 2: W FCh∓Obj Orig, Fabulation.

CARD V. Reaction time: 5″. Total time: 70″.

This looks like it might be a nice moth with wings spread out and antennae well formed, going off in flight. [(Nice?) Its smoothness, the way the wings were spread out, in almost perfect balance.] ∨ Upside down it looks more like a bat. (Hands card to examiner.) (Else?) ... ∧ ... No.

SCORE: W F+A P Fabulation.

CARD VI. Reaction time: 8″. Total time: 180″.

1. This might be a part of the human skeleton or backbone, pretty well noticeable (all except upper D). I'm sure it's just the back: there is not enough variety of contours in the middle section for it to be the

328 CLINICAL APPLICATION OF PSYCHOLOGICAL TESTS

front. [(?) It had a dark vertical backbone coming down and rotundity that might be part of the back. (?) Two sets of what might have been arms or legs, *and* legs.] 2. It looks like it also might be, the smaller figure on top looks like it might be a butterfly suspended on a rod of some kind. 3. The bottom could be some larger type of insect. 4. I don't know if it would be a fungus growth, something of that sort growing on this piece of twig perhaps (twig is upper D). [(?) It doesn't have a particularly definite shape and yet it's varied in color, speckled quality to it.] ∨ 5. Upside down it looks like it might be some kind of a torch. Somebody just finished whirling it around so it's wider in the middle part than on top or bottom. [(?) Extended bits of what might be flame, after twirling the torch. (?) Narrow and pointed.]

SCORES. 1: D F (C)∓At. 2: D F+A. 3: D F−A. 4: W Ch Fungus. 5: W F∓Torch Orig.

CARD VII. Reaction time: 23″. Total time: 160″.

1. It looks like it might be two little Scotties hopping off in opposite directions but heads turned toward each other (upper two-thirds). 2. It might be two airplanes (dark lines in lower middle Dr) coming out from under the clouds (rest of blot) into the clear blue sky (center space). [(Clouds?) Uneven shape and flimsiness. (?) Shadings.] 3. It might be a mask of some kind with devil's horns (upper Dr) on it, that could be fitted on to someone's face and brought close together (two sides), meet at nose or something... (mumbles). [(?) If it were a mask and brought closer (the two sides) there would be a place for eyes, nose and mouth (eyes are by the jaws of the popular head, nose and mouth in lower space.)] ∨ 4. Upside down it looks like two ballet dancers on their toes, dancing off back to back in opposite directions and yet not so far apart. Heads practically touch, arms suspended. [(?) Had a decorated headpiece.]

SCORES. 1: D F+A (P). 2: Dr F−Obj; Ws ChF Clouds Fabulation. 3: WS F−Mask (Devil) Orig. 4: W M+H.

CARD VIII. Reaction time: 15″. Total time: 120″.

1. This pink one looks like a very pretty butterfly. [(?) Shape and coloring... and then it seemed to suggest four wings, two on each side, one overlapping the other. They seemed to be moving in an upward direction toward the top of the tree. (?) Antennae, the antennae were facing in that direction. (?) The two animals on the sides (see second response) were also going, what seemed to me, toward the top of the tree, so it seems logical that the butterfly would follow in the same direction.] 2. These look like moles climbing up a tree, getting into the branches of a tree. [(Tree?) Color and spreading branches, leaves overlapping so as to get the impression of one mass (gray-green and blue). It came up to a point and was tapered.] ...∨... I don't know... Seems to me once I've gotten an impression of something... If I started out with something else...

SCORES. 1: D FC+A Reference Idea. 2: D F+A P; D FC+Pl Combination.

CARD IX. Reaction time: 40″. Total time: 225″.

1. My first impression is that it's a mass of gnomes or elves or little animals, the green particularly, all going off to the perspective point (upper center). [(?) These green edges (outer) give me the feeling of individuality, but all massed together and moving in the same direction. (Any in particular?) No. (Look like gnomes?) The shading of the coloring for one thing. (?) Some was light and some dark, one might be behind the other and the unevenness of the outer edges giving the impression of limbs or loose garments.] I don't know if I'm saying it right, at the perspective point where two devils are doing a weird dance; don't know if they're devils (orange) , . . . waving arms, peaked hats. Gnomes and things could be coming out of a cauldron with a fire burning (lower red). [(?) The color and unevenness of the outward edges. (?) Got the shape of a cauldron more than the actual contours. (Red area is fire.) (Where cauldron?) Below it, giving it this shape (demonstrates roundness going below pink). I was placing fire in it to have that shape. Cauldron isn't there.] 2. ∨ Upside down it might be two chickens (orange) and two . . . two ducks with some other kind of animal (green) standing on their head, on top of whom is standing a large bird (red) of which we can see only the bottom portion, legs and part of wings, so that each bird doesn't have its head showing because of the other standing in front of it. The bottom ones could be hens with a big broad breast (lower contour of orange). The green ones look like ducks, and I don't know what the other is (red) . [(Ducks?) I think the web-like feet. (?) Tapering kind of tail.]

SCORES. 1: Peculiar; (W) D M—Gnomes Orig Peculiar; D M+H; D CF Fire Confabulation Contamination Tendency. 2: (W) D F±A; D F—A; D F±Ad Confabulation.

CARD X. Reaction time: 38″. Total time: 195″.

1. It looks to me like this might be all varieties of insects gnawing at human skeletons bleeding to death or have bled to death . . . blood all around (pink) . . . they're gnawing on them, chewing them to pieces. [(?) Round part of back in through the head. (One skeleton?) Yes.] 2. Looks to me like two rats on top (gray) have already gnawed at the back of the neck (gray shaft), practically dismembered it from the rest of the body. [(Rats?) Seemed to be gnawing with particular vigor. (?) Color and shape. (?) Grayish.] 3. And these two, whatever kind of insects they are (side blue), seem to be hitting the side and shoulder part of it with trees, parts of trees (upper green). [(?) Some kind of flying animal or thing, had tentacles and wings spread. (Tree?) Shape of it I think . . . It looked like a branch or log. (?) And the color.] 4. Some seem to already have had a good meal and are running off (orange and sepia). [(Kind?) Squirrel (orange); big tail and brownish-reddish color, or a mouse. (Other?) Something of the mouse family, mole or rat (sepia) . (?) Largish nose, had last pick at the body.] 5. These two worms (lower green) are picking at the remnants of the backbone (rabbit head) . . . ∨ . . .∧. [(?) Seemed to be crawling, wiggling, might have been a green variety of . . . of . . . caterpillar.]

SCORES. (W) Confabulation Oral Aggression. 1: D F—Ats; D C Blood. 2: D FC′+A Fabulation. 3: D F∓A (P); D FC∓Pl Confabulation. 4: D FC±A; D F±A. 5: D FC+A.

Summary of Responses

R: 37   EB: 6—6.5

W 12 (2)	F+ 6	A 16	M% 37 (38)
D 24	F− 6	Ad 1	D% 65
Dr 1	F± 3	H 4	Dr% 3
S (2)	F∓ 2	Obj 3	
	M 4+, 1−	At 2	F% 46-86
Qualitative	MC′ 1+	Cl 1	F+% 53-62
Fabulation 6	FC 4+, 1±, 1∓	Pl 2	
Confabulation 4	CF 2	Bl 2	A% 46
Contamination Tend. 1	C 1	Fire 1	H% 11
Peculiar 3	F(C) 1∓	Fungus 1	P 5 (2)
Combination 2	FC′ 1+	Torch 1	P% 14 (18)
Aggression 5	FCh 1∓	Devil Mask 1	Orig 2∓, 2−
Oral Aggression 1	ChF 1	Witch 1	Orig% 11
Reference Idea 1	Ch 1	Gnome 1	

ANALYSIS OF RORCHACH TEST RESULTS

The summary of formal scores has only a few features which suggest pathology. There is nothing striking about the manner of approach; the *EB* and color distribution appear rich and well-balanced, the content is fairly well-distributed. There are, however, the F+% which is low for a dilated record with so many *M*'s and so low a DR%,[4] the 4 confabulations, the contamination tendency, the reference idea, 3 peculiar verbalizations and one *M*−. With the dilated *EB*; this massing of deviant responses and verbalizations suggests an acute, full-blown schizophrenia. However, there is only one pure *C* as against 6 *FC*'s, and 2 *CF*'s; pure *C* is ordinarily more conspicuous in the records of acute schizophrenics. Clearly inappropriate affect is therefore not likely to be manifest, the symptoms are likely to be mainly ideational in nature, and, in view of the entire set of results, they are likely to merge imperceptibly into delusions. With so many *M*'s obsessive ideas are probably present, but with an *M*− and 3 confabulations, paranoid ideas are also likely to be present.

Card I: Two witches should be doing a witch's dance, not a devil's dance. The mixed metaphor quality should not be dismissed casually;

------

4) When the DR% is high, an F+% somewhat lower than 65% can still be acceptable as not indicating impaired reality testing.

it is indicative of some degree of disorganization until proved otherwise by the complete absence of supporting indications. Card II: The initial response has a playful, though subdued, quality, but quickly gives way to two re-interpretations with highly aggressive content. It is as if the controls over aggressive fantasies were quite fragile and served only to effect a slight delay. The "mutilated soldiers" is a fantasy indicative of morbid, sadistic preoccupations. The "quarreling old hags" is a type of response not infrequently found in the records of paranoid subjects; its content suggests a hostile conception of and relation to other women. Card III: Again an initial attempt at play gives way quickly to an aggressive fantasy, which this time is arbitrarily conceived. Men do not use cricket sticks to kill butterflies. A generally sadistic orientation becomes evident. The third response continues in the aggressive vein, but this time brings in the idea of bodily mutilation. This type of content has been found in general to be indicative of subjective feelings of having been mutilated, which feelings often refer to castration fears or fantasies. Card IV: The candelabra in an "old dirty castle" has a symbolically sexual quality, but cannot be safely interpreted in this context. It may imply feelings of worthlessness. Card V: A "nice" moth expresses a noteworthy degree of sensitivity.

Card VI: "Fungus growth" continues the motif of worthlessness and decay. Fungus, rot, and the like, have an especially morbid quality and occur most frequently in schizophrenic records. Milder expressions of these feelings are seen in "withered" leaves or branches, "worn and tattered" clothing, and so forth. Whirling objects (5th response) have been found to occur with great frequency in the records of subjects with acute homoerotic conflicts. Card VII: The symbolic-like "two airplanes coming out from under the clouds" is seen in the area frequently interpreted as a vagina. Symbolic-like responses in "sexual" areas occur mainly where paranoid pathology is involved. For example, one man in a paranoid state saw "a gun emplacement in a strategic position" in this same area. Paranoid pathology is also suggested by overabstract W's of the type that require considerable perceptual reorganization before they fit the assigned content. Seeing Card I as the letter A, or Card VII as a shoelace, has that quality. Similarly the "mask" in this record would be a mask if a number of perceptual alterations were performed. It seems rather likely by now that a paranoid trend is conspicuous. So far, however, there has been no indication that this is a fully developed paranoid schizophrenia. The dilated EB would be most unusual in all but the grandiose forms of that illness. A paranoid state or an incipient schizophrenia with paranoid features is the more likely diagnosis. Pervasive, morbid preoccupations are also evident (witches on Card I, mutilated soldiers on Card II, dismembered butterfly on Card III, dirty candelabra on Card IV, fungus growth on Card VI and devil's mask on Card VII).

On Card VIII the first conclusive indication of a noteworthy degree of disorganization appears in the inquiry into the "butterfly" response. Here she states that it seemed to be moving upward and her explanation of this appearance includes the totally unrealistic connection between the upward motion of the animals on the side and the butterfly. This reference idea is also indicative of paranoid thinking. However, she threw in first the more acceptable idea about the direction of the antennae, suggesting that frank, incautious paranoid reasoning is not characteristic.

Card IX: The global impression, "a mass of gnomes ... moving in the same direction", is a malignant $M-$, since its reality-testing aspect is exceptionally feeble. The confabulation of a scene involving devils, gnomes and a cauldron is the second malignant response on this card; the near confusion between or contamination of the fire and the cauldron is the third, and the confabulated tower of animals is the fourth. The placing of the cauldron below the fire is especially arbitrary and indicates how, once a vivid fantasy holds sway, subsequent reality considerations recede into the background to a pathological extent and become subservient to the fantasy.

Card X: Her most morbid and confabulated response bursts forth here: the fantasy of devouring or being devoured is so intense that reality testing breaks down and the global impression of "skeletons" and "blood all around" becomes dominant; only the examiner's reality-oriented inquiry brings her to check the blot more carefully and realize that it can sustain only one skeleton and only one bloody area (the pink).

Differential diagnosis: This could be the record of an acute schizophrenic or an incipient schizophrenic. There are certain hints of preservation in this record, favoring the latter diagnosis. The remainder of the results of the battery of tests were, with one or two exceptions, quite orderly. There was no great scatter or peculiar verbalization in the Bellevue Scale; learning efficiency and concept formation were well-retained; and there were no strikingly inappropriate word associations.[5] Because the Rorschach Test is, as a rule, so sensitive to the presence of disorganization, and because the other test results do not match

----

5) The TAT was not administered.

the Rorschach Test's florid quality, it is unlikely that a fully developed psychosis is present. Incipient schizophrenia is therefore the more cautious diagnosis. Morbid preoccupations with sado-masochistic content and paranoid thinking appear to be the most dramatic symptoms of imminent disorganization. Adaptive efforts are still being made and extensive withdrawal has not yet taken place; inappropriate affect should not be conspicuous in the clinical picture.

Clinical Summary

This patient manifested no signs of disorganization in her clinical examination. It was noted that she tended to project the blame for her history of educational, vocational and social failures, and that she appeared to be defensively withholding material during the interviews. The chief symptoms were anxiety and depression, irritable outbursts and a withdrawal tendency. The test results make a significant contribution to the clinical understanding of this case.

Chapter Five

CONCLUDING REMARKS

In the course of reviewing the completed manuscript and discussing it with several colleagues, I have become aware of several problems implied in the manner of presentation. The reader may find a summary of these considerations helpful in building up his perspective of the contents of this book.

I have selected and organized the material conservatively. There were several bolder avenues of attack I chose not to take, partly because I did not feel that I could follow through on them with sufficient conviction, and partly because I could not entirely free myself from the diagnostically-oriented setting in which I wrote this book.

Chapter Two, the chapter of diagnostic summaries, could also have been written primarily in terms of the indications of various personality characteristics, and only secondarily in terms of diagnostic implications. Thus, there could have been sections on indications of anxiety, compulsiveness, modes of coping with aggressive impulses, and so forth. As it is, the reader will have to hop around among the discussions of the various groups in order to gather together all the references to any major personality characteristic. The index should be of some help here. The validational studies which would back up a chapter on personality characteristics are, however, woefully lacking, and any such presentation at this time would inevitably have been even more loaded down with *maybes, sometimes,* and *howevers* than this one is. This book was written at The Menninger Clinic where, for a long time and to a large extent out of historical necessity, a great emphasis was placed upon diagnostic specificity and accuracy in the test reports. I think now, upon completion of this book, that this diagnostic emphasis made it unusually difficult to organize experience under other headings than diagnostic ones. The reader may have noted in Chapter Two that the introduction to the test results of each group has two main parts: the psychiatric syndrome on the one hand and the psychological test syndrome on the other. This split reflects the same diagnostic emphasis; otherwise I might have offered a unified description of each clinical condition in which the contributions of both clinical and test findings were combined.

This same difficulty stood in the way of another possible approach to the material in this book. In the case studies in Chapters Three and Four there are no attempts to integrate the final test report and the summary of clinical findings. The clinical summaries have been included mainly to give the reader a rough idea of the kind of person who could give each particular set of test results. This, however, is only the beginning of the job; ultimately it will be necessary to peg each conclusion from the test results into its appropriate hole in the clinical picture of the patient—confirming, amending, or amplifying the detailed clinical impressions and not merely the clinical diagnostic impression. But here, too, the limitations imposed by our own *diagnostic* emphasis plus the general absence of research data in this area precluded an attempt of this sort at this time. The contributions of test results to problems of therapy and prognosis were also not discussed here for these reasons among others.

There are several respects in which the reader may find some compensation for the shortcomings discussed in the above paragraphs. First, I have attempted to call to the reader's attention the role of the analysis of verbalization in any type of testing, whether it be oriented to diagnosis only or to personality description only. The patient's style of verbalization is that aspect of our test results which is closest to his everyday functioning and least dependent upon the particular artificial situation in which we have involved him. This style of verbalization, because it is so ingrained and so expressive of the ways in which the patient has attempted, and is attempting, to cope with himself and with the world around him, often yields the clues to the most significant relationships and implications in the test results. And although the testing situations can be called artificial with respect to real life situations, they elicit by their very artificiality dramatic and, therefore, instructive exhibitions of style of verbalization. A sensitivity to the dynamic implications of the nuances of verbalization appears to be indispensible in diagnostic or descriptive analysis of test results.

Secondly, the reader may find this volume's deficiencies offset by the presentation of the results of a *battery* of tests applied to a *wide variety* of cases. The juxtaposition of these various records offers the reader an opportunity to appreciate the great potentialities of these psychological tests used simultaneously.

Finally, I should like to point to the attempt that has been made in these pages to verbalize the step-by-step process of interpretation of test results and the elaboration of differential diagnostic arguments. It is important to the future of the practice of clinical testing that our methods of analysis be presented in publications with as great care as our conclusions. Only if these analytic principles are exposed to general view and thereby to general criticism can we hope to refine them, render them more communicable, and reclaim them as much as possible from the realm of private insights and "art".

Appendix

Scoring Symbols for the Rorschach Test

AREA OF RESPONSE

W: all or nearly all of the blot.

D: portions of the blot which are relatively large, clearly set off, and frequently interpreted.

Dd: small but not tiny areas, clearly set off from the bulk of the blot.

Dr: tiny areas, or relatively large areas which are neither clearly set off nor frequently interpreted.

De: interpretation of a contour line.

S: a relatively large white area in or around the blot.

s: a relatively small white area.

Do: interpreting an area frequently seen as part of a larger area, and retaining the same content for the smaller area as it would have in the larger, frequent interpretation.

DW: reasoning from a part of the blot to the entire blot without checking the conclusion against the actual appearance of the entire blot.

DETERMINANTS

F: an interpretation based solely on the formal configuration of an area.

F+:   a form response of acceptable or superior accuracy.

F−:   a form response of inferior accuracy; may be vague or arbitrarily organized.

F±:   a basically acceptable form response with some minor inaccuracy.

F∓:   a basically inaccurate form response with some saving features.

M: a response in which a complete or nearly complete human figure is seen in action or in some position of tension.

FM: an M response with weak emphasis on motion or tension, with animal-like features stressed, or with animals in human-like activity.

Ms: an M response using a relatively small area.

FC: a response using form and color, with color subordinate or equal to form as a determinant.

CF: a response using form and color, with form subordinate to color.

C: a response based on color alone.

F/C: a response using form and color, based primarily on form and with color added artificially.

C/F: a response using form and color, based primarily on artificial use of color.

F(C):   a form response in which variations of shadings are important in defining the outline or important inner details; may also signify the use of the texture of colored areas.

FC':   a response based on form and black, gray, or white color, with these colors subordinate or equal to form as a determinant.

C'F: a response in which black, gray or white color is dominant over form.

C':   a response based on black, gray or white color alone.

FCh: a response based on form and shading, with shading subordinate or equal to form as a determinant.

ChF: a response in which shading outweighs form as a determinant.

Ch: a response based on shading alone.

CONTENT

A:	full animal figure	At:	anatomy
Ad:	animal detail	Pl:	plant
H:	full human figure	Geog:	geography
Hd:	human detail	Arch:	architecture
Obj:	object	Geol:	geology
Bl:	blood	Cl:	cloud

MISCELLANEOUS

P: "popular" response, given by at least one out of every five subjects (P) denotes a minor variation in a popular response.

Orig: "original" response, found no more than once in every hundred records.

Combination: combination response in which two interpretations are meaningfully related.

Fabulized Combination: combination response in which two interpretations are arbitrarily related.

Fabulation: feelings, motives, qualities or events are alluded to with little or no objective support in the blot.

Confabulation: associative elaboration without objective support is extensive and arbitrary.

Contamination: two interpretations fuse into one, or the same area simultaneously stands for two interdependent but logically separate interpretations.

Peculiar: verbalization of response is unsuccessful communication because of illogical, cryptic, or incomplete formulation; also manifestation in the response of irrealistic evaluation of the role of subjective processes or of the objective stimulus.

Queer: the extreme of "peculiar" verbalizations; bizarre formulations or evaluations.

Determination-C: pure C response using bland pink, orange or yellow colors or involving "morbid" content.

Absurd: form aspect of response is extremely arbitrary.

Symbolic: explicit use of form or other determinant to represent an abstract idea.

Confusion: shifting frame-of-reference in the course of verbalizing a response.

Reference Idea: arbitrarily setting up or emphasizing formal relationships between different areas of an inkblot or between different inkblots.

Autistic Logic: illogical, autistic efforts to derive a response or a meaning "logically".

Aggression: content of response includes aggressive actions, feelings or events.

Homoerotic: reversing usual sexual identity of a figure or sexual organ, or seeing mixed sexual characteristics on the same figure.

Oral: content of response includes reference to food, eating, chewing or other oral activities.

Incompleteness: emphasizing incompleteness of figures, especially where figures are usually seen as complete.

SUMMARY SCORES

R: total number of responses.

EB: ratio of $M + FM + Ms$ to $FC + CF + C$ with weights of .5 given to FM and FC, 1 to M, Ms and CF and 1.5 to C.

W%:   percent of W responses in entire record (R).

D%:   percent of D responses in entire record.

DR%:   percent of Dr+De+S+s in entire record.

F%:   first part expresses percent of all pure form responses in entire record; second part expresses percent of responses with strong form (F, M, FM, Ms, FC, F(C), FC′, FCh) in entire record.

F+%:   first part expresses percent of all pure form responses scored F+ or F±; second part expresses percent of all responses with strong form scored + or ±.

A%:   percent of A+Ad responses in entire record.

H%:   percent of H+Hd responses in entire record.

P%:   percent of popular responses in entire record.

Orig%: percent of original responses in entire record

INDEX

In the index, tests will be referred to by initial letters: *B* for Wechsler-Bellevue Scale, *L* for Learning Efficiency, *S* for Sorting Test, *R* for Rorschach Test, *A* for Word Association Test, and *T* for Thematic Apperception Test. Thus, in Rigidity *96, B 112, B 209, A 31,* etc., the *96* indicates a general reference, *112* and *209* are Bellevue Scale references, and *31* is a Word Association Test reference. References will be listed in sequence for each test. Diagnostic terms are not indexed except for especially revealing examples of diagnostic patterns in test results, important differential diagnostic considerations, and diagnostic categories not considered in detail in the text. The Table of Contents indicates the pages on which may be found detailed discussions of diagnostic categories and specific case examples of these.